The Green Snake

The Green Snake

Life Memories

Margarita Woloschin

Floris Books

Translated by Peter Stebbing

First published in German in 1954
under the title *Die grüne Schlange*
Revised eighth edition published in 2009

First published in English in 2010

British Library CIP Data available
ISBN 978-086315-761-5
Printed in Great Britain
by Page Bros. (Norwich) Ltd.

Contents

Translator's Note

Since its first publication in 1954, the present work has gone through eight or nine editions in German, and appeared in a Russian translation. It can be said to have established an important place in the minds of readers for over half a century.

Margarita Sabashnikova, on marrying Max Voloshin, would in Russia be known as Margarita Voloshina. However, she spent most of her life in Germany where she was known as Margarita Woloschin. We have in this book kept the German transliteration of her name as she is best known under this spelling. Max has been transliterated directly into English as Voloshin (like all other Russian names in this book). Minor emendations to the text were made in a few places where this seemed appropriate and necessary.

As many of the personalities referred to by the author are little known outside Russia, this long overdue English translation includes a revised glossary of names to help the reader. A few of the cities mentioned in the book have also undergone a change of name in the course of history. The city known today as St Petersburg (as in the Middle Ages), was referred to simply as Petersburg, during the nineteenth century. It was called Petrograd from 1914 to 1924 and Leningrad from 1924 to 1991.

Peter Stebbing
Arlesheim, Switzerland
September 2009

Preface

When asked by friends to tell the story of my life, I realized in writing it down, that it was symptomatic of the great historical turning point at which we find ourselves. With hindsight, an architectural composition became apparent that I had not been aware of until then, as though secreted into it by some great master. For this reason, it occurred to me that this narrative, not initially intended for the public, might be of general interest.

I have called this book *The Green Snake* after a figure in Goethe's fairy tale in which a path is indicated. Everyone experiencing our time in wakefulness can recognize archetypal pictures in the fairy tale of the forces at work both in and around us.

I concluded the first part of my recollections with a period thirty years before the book's first appearance, not because the following years were less rich in experiences, but because at that time a new segment of my life began.

I would have had to speak of people I had met who were still living and active. For this, perspective was lacking. Since then, many of them have crossed the threshold of death. Their spiritual form appears in a different light. In addition, their work has become a cultural factor. I hope to be able to write about them in a second volume.

Margarita Woloschin
Stuttgart, March 1968

"... the temple is built ... It still rests in the depths of the earth," continued the snake.
"I have seen and spoken to the kings ... I heard these mighty words resound through the temple: The time is at hand!"

From Goethe's fairy tale, *The Green Snake and the Beautiful Lily*

I

Childhood in Old Russia

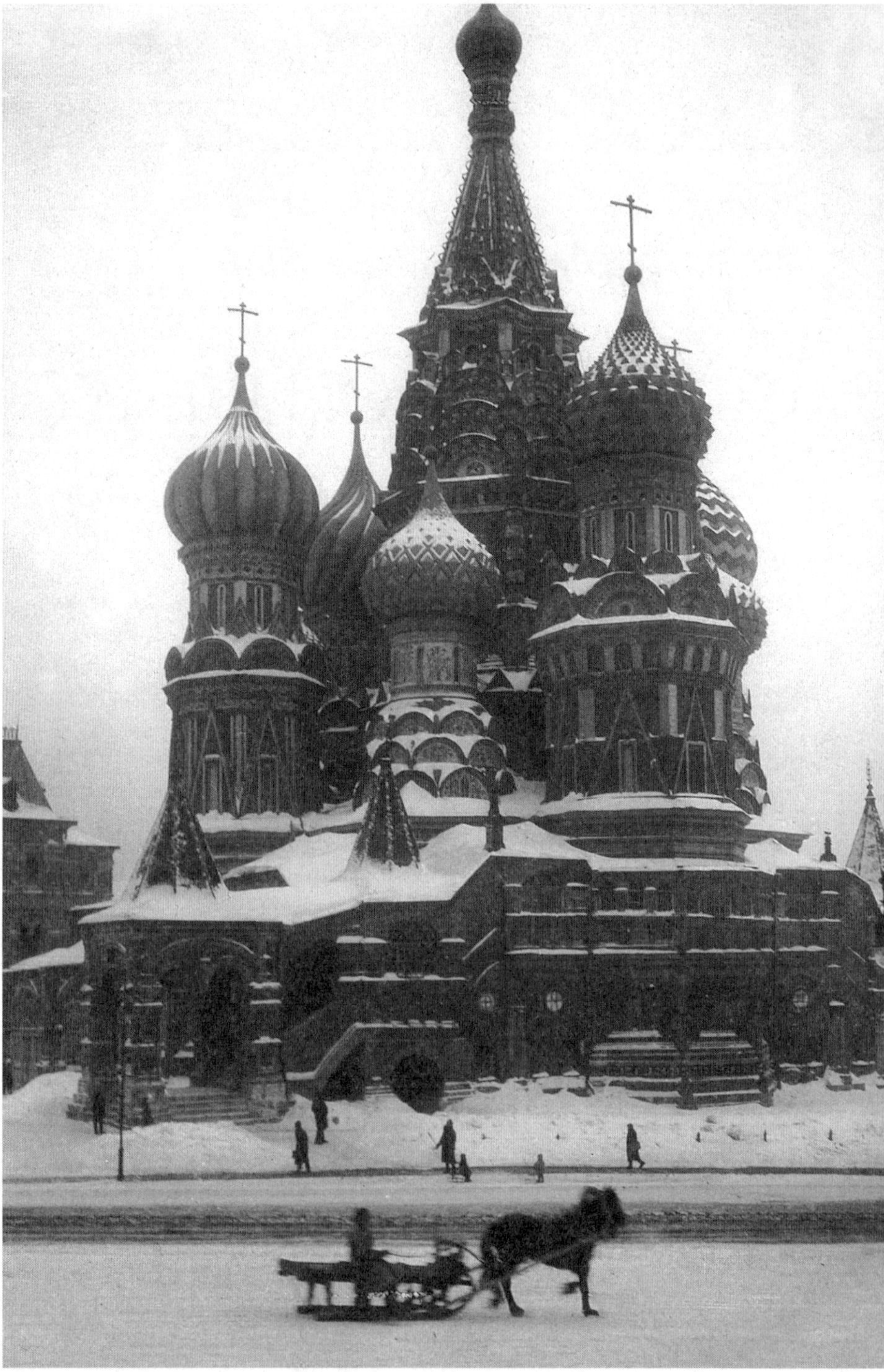

Basilius Cathedral, Moscow

The Wolf in the Egyptian Temple

In Moscow, where the large and small parts of Nikitskaya Street meet in a wedge-shape in front of the entrance to the Church of the Ascension, our house stood, a monumental, two-storey, cube-shaped building painted pale rose, with a garden and a large estate, surrounded by many outbuildings.

I was born on a Sunday at noon, just as the bells of our old clock tower, accompanied by the bells of the forty times forty churches of Moscow, were ringing at the close of mass. It was a cold, sunny day in the year 1882.

On such winter days the snow, as though consisting of nothing but stars, sparkled on the streets and rooftops of Moscow. The sun glittered from the gold, silver and blue cupolas of the churches strewn with gold stars, from their crosses and bright ceramic ornaments. It glittered from the greenish-blue glazed tiles of the old towers, from the shop signs in large gold letters on deep blue backgrounds, and from the gold pretzels over bakery entrances; and it glittered from the straw and horse dung on the streets of Moscow. The frosty, sunny air positively shook from the famed Moscow bell-ringing; from the slow, deep humming sound of the large bells striking, against which background — in manifold rhythms and variations — the smaller bells of the forty times forty bell towers rang out. Bell-ringing counted as a great art in Russia, and on religious holidays, apart from the sacristans, many music lovers and masters from among the simple people and from the pious orthodox class of traders volunteered, so as to gain practice and compete in this art. The sleighs glided easily along, the snow crunching under their runners, and a *"Hau,"* or *"Pravo dershí!"* ("Woah!" or "Stop on the right!") echoed in the frosty haze. Over each chimney stood, immobile, a little cloud of smoke; thus the city appeared as though decorated with white azaleas. So stupendous was the crescendo of the bells that one trembled inwardly from the vibration. The whole city stood as though transfixed under a stream of descending, jubilating angels of proclamation; and the light and the pealing of bells became one in this rejoicing.

Just as the vibrations of tone give a configuration to the sand on a metal plate, so all forms that a person experiences continually have their effect in ordering and shaping their being, particularly in the case of the still malleable child.

Our church could be seen from the two large windows of our upstairs hall. It took up the whole view to the east and loomed, as if out of eternity, large and white in plain Greek forms with its spherical silver cupolas. I regarded it as the continuation of our house into the other world. It seemed uniquely related to the soul, as if it too originated out of that world from which the soul itself came and stood as a guarantee that the earth too could participate in it. From this sight, as a child, I derived peace and confidence, the feeling of being at home here. The clock tower, which bordered directly on our courtyard and was crooked from age, belonged to the oldest monuments of the Yaroslavl building style in Moscow. It expressed inwardness and piety, with its two cubes set one upon the other, a larger and a smaller one, and the eight-sided little tower. Its high roof with eight surfaces interrupted by skylights rested on arches and wood-turned columns. Seeming as if it grew organically out of the ground, and striving toward the heavens, the church itself consisted in its archetypal forms of the spherical shining cupola and the white cube, uniting heaven and earth victoriously.

In the spring, pigeons and sparrows circling the tambour bathed in the water that accumulated on the iron roof in front of our windows (this was the roofing over the entrance driveway), shaking their feathers in the sunshine. One needed only to go past the wooden fence and the brown wooden cabin of the priest, in order to enter the other world. One was then surrounded by choirs, as though the heavenly hierarchies sounded from infinite realms. From the cupola the six-winged red seraphim and blue cherubim looked down with their great eyes; winged animals — lion, eagle and bull — held holy books. Bright, coloured miracles were executed on the walls, with annunciation and resurrection angels, and in the gold of the iconostasis, shimmering in the light of many candles, were the darkened countenances of saints, of the Mother of God and of Christ.

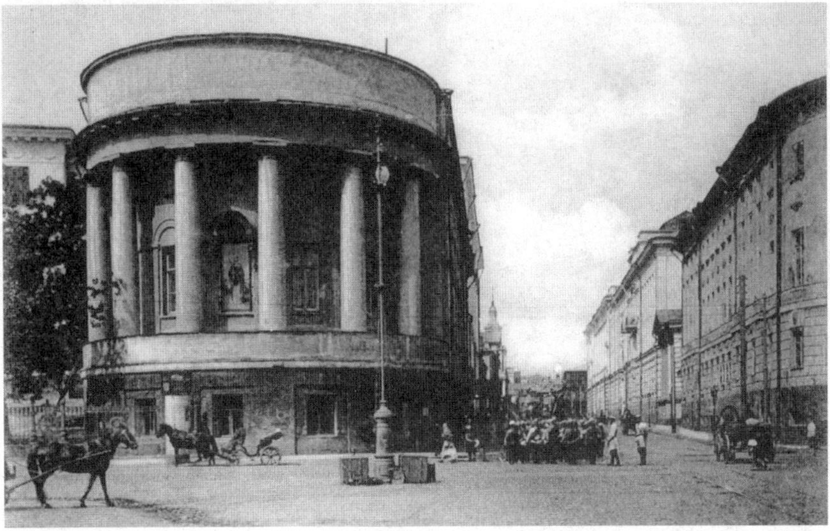

The wide part of Nikitskaya, Moscow in the 1910s (PG Girgenson)

This world projected itself into our house. On great festival days, in the midst of the tumult of receiving many guests, priests and deacons in gold and silver brocade vestments appeared in our hall and, turning to the icons in the corner, began to sing wonderful words. At Christmas, that meant:

> A Virgin gives birth this day to the Eternal One,
> And the earth offers the Unapproachable One a crib.
> Angels and shepherds glorify Him,
> But kings wander after the Star.

They extended the cross to all those present to be kissed, and sprinkled the new, delicate dresses of the ladies, as well as the silk-covered furniture, with consecrated water.

As a small child I experienced Holy Week with such immediacy that I could not understand why we did not all travel to Jerusalem on Palm Sunday, where such miraculous things had occurred. I could not comprehend that it was supposed to have happened only once, a long time ago. When we, my brother and I, were small, we were not yet taken along to the evening services on Maundy Thursday, in which one had to listen to the "twelve gospels" — three Passion chapters from each of the four Gospels — while standing with a lighted candle in one's hand.

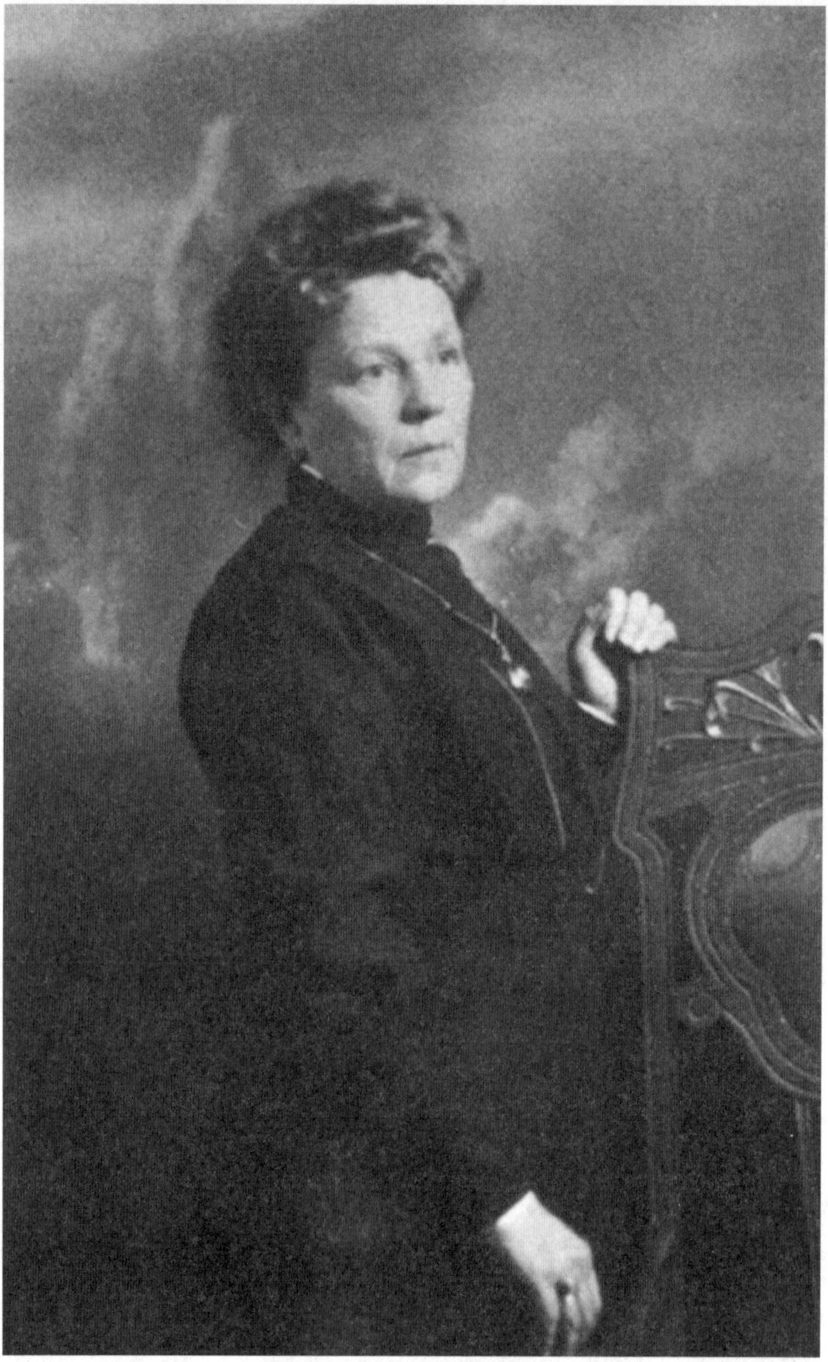

Margarita Alexievna Sabarhnikova, Margarita's mother

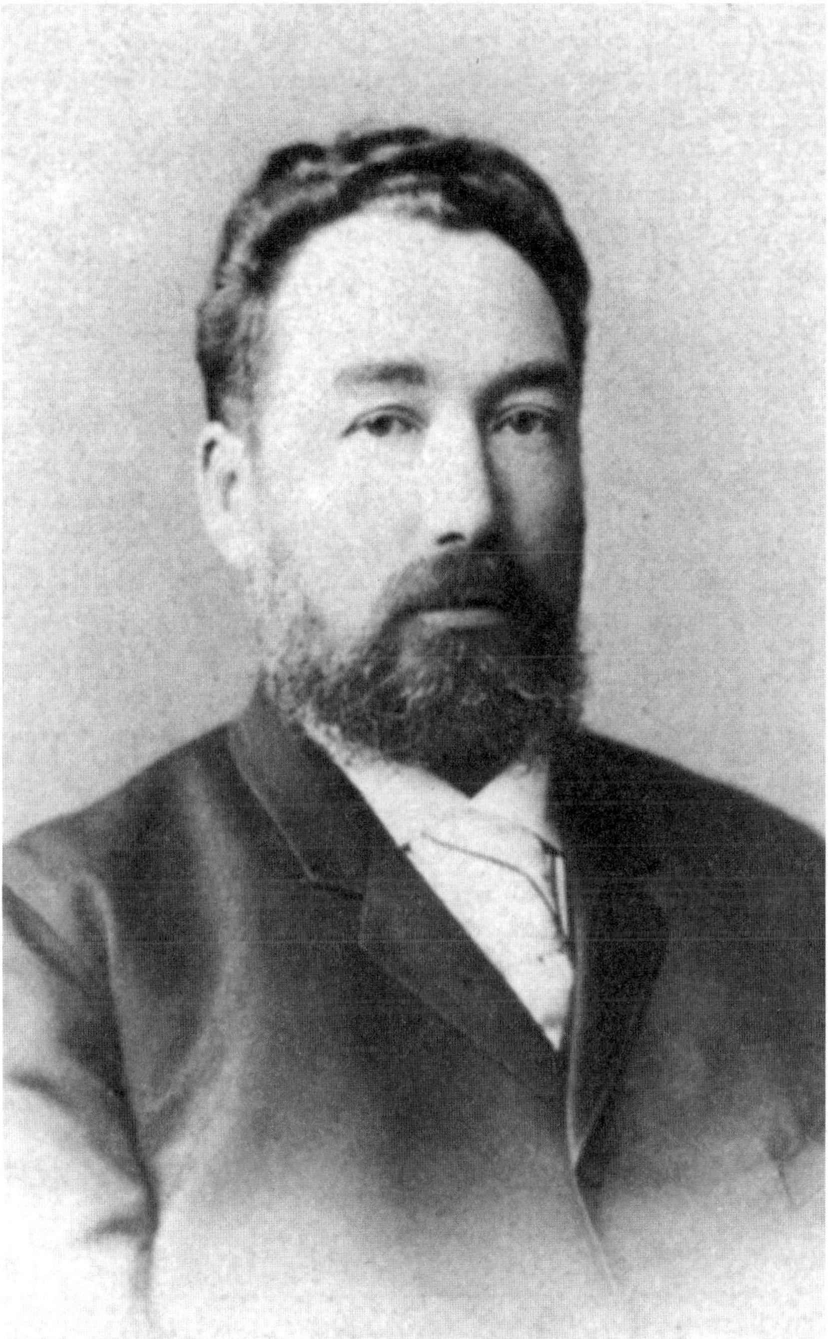

Vassily Michailorich Sabarknikov, Margarita's father

We watched through the hall window as the people, each with a lighted candle, streamed out of the church at the conclusion of the service — the church having now become a source of light. We saw each person protect the flame from the spring air, so as to bring it home still lit and light the holy lamp for the whole year. A protective cover was made around the little flame, with a sheet of paper. People remained standing in order to re-light the candles of others that had gone out. One of the maids brought us a lighted Maundy Thursday candle into the house.

That was what could be seen to the east.

To the south, behind the beautiful lattice of the garden, in which Chinese apple trees, lilac bushes, rowan trees and a large elm grew, lay the elegant, broad part of Nikitskaya Street, from which, through a large gate, the driveway led to the stately main entrance to our house. Grand houses of varying architectural design with gardens and driveways stood on that street. Across from us was the courtyard of the fire brigade with the old tower. I often stood on the upholstery that protected the marble window benches of the nursery, and looked up at two tiny people who strode back and forth around the tower, high up there in the sky — the tower watchmen. If a fire started anywhere in the city during the evening — and they were frequent in Moscow, since many houses were built of wood and then there was still no electric lighting, and often no running water — then fiery-coloured spheres appeared in the sky over the tower. These were signals to other fire department towers. One moment there were three spheres: yellow, red and blue, the next moment there were two red and one green, and so on. "Calling all districts" was the meaning of a combination which the maids noted with horror. But I thought these were miraculous signs, apparitions, heavenly warnings.

In the courtyard of the fire station — from our vantage point everything could be observed that happened behind the yellow walls of the courtyard — a great commotion then took place: wagons were taken out of the sheds, fiery horses harnessed; first, a rider dashed out of the gate with a blazing torch in his hand — the messenger — and galloped in the direction of the fire, in order to investigate the circumstances. Behind him, heavy wagons rolled at breakneck speed, making an incredible noise. On these, men in gold helmets supported themselves while standing between ladders, pumps and vats of water.

The noise was caused mainly by the large round cobblestones with which the streets of Moscow were paved. Such happenings had a ghastly fascination, and I understood why my little brother wanted to become a fireman.

In spring, in the very early morning, a horn sounded on the wide part of Nikitskaya. From the gate of every house one or two cows were let out, and the herdsman drove his herd out of the city to pasture. On the same Nikitskaya our beautiful horses were exercised, and once — it was admittedly in a dream — I saw how an angel in a red gown with a blue cloak waving behind him, flew slowly past along the same broad Nikitskaya. I called the others, so that they too might see him, but when they came, he had already flown away.

To the north, our windows looked onto the narrower part of Nikitskaya, with low white buildings. Across from us stood the famous house of Count Bobrinsky, with his two annexes in a semicircle. No grass and no trees were to be seen there; the huge surface of the courtyard was strewn with yellow sand. Once a month the beggars of Moscow gathered in this courtyard. A lackey in livery stepped out of the main entrance with a large bag and threw money into the crowd. People fell to the ground to gather up the kopecks; confusion and turmoil arose, there were scuffles. The cripples struck each other with their crutches. With horror, I saw scenes that I later came upon again in the paintings of Breughel. The smaller part of Nikitskaya always appeared relentlessly, glaringly blank and sad to me.

Our house had no windows to the west. The grey, blind wall of the big house next door darkened our garden. I knew that a doctor lived in that house. He had a small daughter, the same age as I, and I heard that he "wrapped her in cotton wool." I took this literally, and felt great pity for this girl. I always hoped to meet her on the street, but I never saw her.

The driveway of our house was roofed over and in front of the entrance stood a tall candelabra. The heavy, carved door opened into a large hall. Broad steps led into an Egyptian temple. On the columns, crowned with lotus flower capitals and standing on black bases, colourful hieroglyphs in low relief were scratched into the surface. In the recesses there were two portals, each decorated above with a winged sun: the one on the right was actually the frame of an enormous mirror, which deceptively doubled the size of the room and the number of the columns; the one on the left led via a long corridor to the interior of the house. A dark Egyptian statue stood on a high pedestal between the two portals, the stern guardian of the threshold. A large stuffed wolf that had been shot in our forests later came to stand in this hall.

The lower floor consisted of ornate reception rooms, in which we seldom stayed. Our dining room was decorated in a so-called "Russian" style. The colours were well attuned to each other. Blue-green walls, colourfully painted, carved chairs and corner cupboards, embroidered curtains and upholstery, the tableware in different colours with Russian proverbs painted on them. Especially when illuminated by candlelight from the old Russian silver chandeliers, the delicate, varied colours shimmered as if in a fairy tale. However, this "Russian style" was born from the pure fantasy of the German architect Schmidt, and had nothing to do with the genuine old Russian style, which our art historians rediscovered much later, during my youth. The dark, panelled study which one entered on the right from the Egyptian temple, was decorated fittingly in dark green. On an easel in front of my father's heavy oak writing desk stood an oval picture of my mother in a broad gold frame. Her hair was blonde and slightly wavy, large grey eyes looked out sadly from a slim, lovely face. In this face one would not yet suspect the energetic, socially active woman of later years.

On a lower, open shelf of the carved oak cabinet lay something that was, for me, very mysterious: a large leather sack filled with sand. This was no ordinary sand, but mixed with gold, and originated from the Siberian goldmines of my father.

A wide, bright stairway led to the upper floor, where our living quarters were located.

My parents' bedroom always struck me as festive. A canopy of olive-green silk lined with pink crowned the double bed. But a golden creation placed between the feet of an ebony sewing-table inlaid with mother-of-pearl filled me with particular awe: a vessel with a flame. That is how I imagined the soul in the human breast.

In our children's room the curtains were lined with a thick material. If I wrapped myself in the lower part which was gathered together, it felt like night in the middle of the day. Once, in this darkness, my fingers touched something alien and misshapen. It was no doubt felt or cotton that had come out of a tear in the lining. To me, however, it was as though some horrible entity from an eerie world had intruded into ours. Even so, I put myself into this dark tent again and again, in order to encounter the dreadful, unnameable "thing."

I believe all these impressions of objects, the carved Florentine chests and chairs with animal-plants and human-animal shapes which the child touched, the patterns on the carpets, which its eye followed again and again, had a more profound effect on the soul than the words addressed to it. Later, when I went on long journeys with my little dolls, I discovered mysterious illumined grottos among the loose threads under sofas. The carved legs of the tables and candelabra became unclimbable mountains, the carpets and animal skins turned into peculiar landscapes, and the parquet floors, which reflected all objects like water, became seas.

No parquet floors can now shine as they did, for the guild of floor polishers, the *Polotjory,* has vanished from the world. Every week five or six men appeared in our house, barefoot, in wide black velvet pants and red shirts that reached to the knees and hung loose from a belt at the hips. Everything had to make way for them, the carpets were rolled up, furniture was moved against the wall. Lessons were interrupted when this crowd appeared. Each one tied a sandal onto the right foot, which had waxed brushes underneath; and then they moved in a row through the room, hands crossed behind their backs, with the right foot in front making an arc from right to left, from left to right, while pushing themselves forward with the left foot. Strands of hair hung down into their faces and swung back and forth in time with their movements. From time to time one of them remained standing, and busily rubbed with his foot forwards and backwards. All this took place with elemental force and speed, and in this way they danced through hall after hall, room after room. And when they departed from the house, leaving behind an odour of sweat mixed with the smell of wax and turpentine, our floors shone magnificently. With their visit, the five kopeck coins, on which we had to lay one hand during the music lesson, holding them quite still, disappeared every time from the piano. I loathed these music lessons, because most of the time I had to search the floor for the rolling coins. The guild of floor polishers disappeared from life completely when the houses were "socialized" and the parquet floors made unrecognizable in accordance with the will of the people.

Our People

I was the first child of my parents; my brother arrived one year later. Two of my father's nieces, whose parents had died, were raised together with us, though we had little to do with each other at that time, as the age difference was too great. I visualize my parents during this early period only indistinctly, as though at an imperious distance. The people who actually looked after us were the domestic servants. They were closer to us. When I was born, the liberation of the serfs lay nineteen years away. Our small family was served by four maids, a house servant, a kitchen helper, a "white" cook, who cooked for us, a "black" cook, who cooked for everyone else, a dishwasher, a coachman and a stable hand, two washerwomen, two *dvornicks,* house servants and a stoker. Two maids, who had both come into the house before my birth, stayed with us for forty years. We experienced so much devoted love, so much patience from them that were I not convinced of coming onto the earth again, I would not be able to bear the fact of never being in a position to repay them. It appeared to them perfectly natural to serve us, just as it seemed to us self-evident to take advantage of their care. When my brother, whom they idolized, treated them tyrannically and rudely while at an awkward age, they affectionately called him "our stern little father."

We spent our days with the maids in two sunny nurseries and in the adjoining hall with the view of the church. They sewed and sang monotonous, melancholic folk songs, individually or in chorus, and the words of these songs called forth in me a world of archetypal images, from which, throughout my life, I drew the mood for my artistic work.

My nurse Feklusha, who remained with us for three and a half years, was a peasant from the district of Tula, where the black earth is so fertile. I well remember her beautiful face. Her low forehead was framed by dark, sumptuous, smoothly combed hair parted in the middle. Her almond-shaped, grey-blue eyes, shaded by long black lashes appeared bright in her sunburnt face. Her nose was straight and narrow, her face a pure, regular oval. Her healthy, powerful body exuded vitality. In the expression of her face there was something humble and compassionate. Who knows what she had experienced before she became a nurse. I was perhaps two and a half years old when I saw her cutting grain in the field with a sickle. And to this day I remember her movements, how she stooped and cut along the ground with the sickle, holding the bushels under her left arm and supporting the ears with the sickle in her right hand, she drew a large arc, so as to lay the grain in a heap with the rest. Then she bound the grain together and carried the sheaf over her head, again supporting the rustling ears with the sickle. And she smiled at me out of the golden corn as if from heaven, since I saw her face high up in the sky above me. In the same year, at the train station, I once saw a carriage with barred windows and pale faces behind them. It was a transport of prisoners; shocked, I asked, "Who are they?"

"Unfortunate ones," was Feklusha's answer.

There is a Russian saying, "Nurture as the earth nurtures. Teach as the earth teaches. Love as the earth loves." Later, on hearing the term "Mother Earth," I saw a countenance before me that was similar to my nurse Feklusha.

At the very beginning of my childhood, yet another dear face inclines towards me: Masha, who as a young girl had been trained as a kind of dowry by my grandmother, in sewing, cooking, bottling and hairdressing, in order to follow my mother in her marriage. She was always around us, slept with us and sewed everything for us. If we were sick, it was she who looked after us with loving care. I still see her round face, with eyes set far apart and faint, slightly astonished eyebrows, a small nose and a full, kind mouth. I still see how she warmed glycerine in a spoon over a candle that burned in the silver candelabrum attached to the wall beside my little bed, rubbing it in for me and my brother when we had a head cold, under the nose, on the forehead and behind the ears. How gladly we submitted ourselves to this ritual procedure! She had a "light hand," as the saying went, and did everything well. She told us stories, so that we would stand still while trying on a little dress on the window ledge. Her sensitive soul was easily influenced. If she heard a sad or moving story, a shiver at once ran down her spine. She was infinitely tender toward us. She had a great many relatives, sisters, nephews and nieces, who all visited her, and I am afraid she was too weak in standing up to these relatives, who exploited her somewhat.

She managed all the cupboards with linen, fur coats, silver, porcelain etc., that were in storage. My mother paid no attention to these things. "Where are grandmother Tatyana's carpets? Where is the blue tea set; where is the roll of pink Chinese silk?" our second maid still asked after forty years. After Masha's death, I dreamt that she lamented, as though wanting to ask forgiveness for something. Oh, is the most diligent, most devoted work and effort of forty years in such service not a counterbalance? Work that no one knew of, nor recognized? Was a piece of silk not worth all the clothes she had sewn for my mother? My mother was an elegant woman, who had to entertain and act in a representative capacity. Masha had taken care of the housekeeping by herself for forty years, because my mother had little interest in it. Every summer, when we left Moscow, she remained alone and bottled not only for us, but for all our relations; hundreds of jars of preserves — and what preserves! And her firm fruit jellies cut into rhombuses and frosted, and her *tyanushki*! All this was consumed in great quantities in Russia at that time, as though it were black bread. And for all this trouble — she never had a day off, never any rest — she received nine roubles a month; we took everything as a matter of course, without thanks. She was with us until the Revolution, going hungry just as we did, but continued working until she could no longer stand; then her relatives took her in, who were then better off than us. I do not like hearing Slavophiles call the Russian people a "God-bearing people." It sounds arrogant. But when I think of our servants, then I have to admit, that the love, the humility, the patience that lived in their blood, and radiated from them like a living substance, justified this term. It was a Christian substance. How one was carried by this warmth, given a sense of security, as if in the lap of God!

Later, I shall have more to say about the maid Polya. She had already been with us before I was born, and stayed on for forty years, until her death during the Revolution. She was seventeen when she came to us, a radiant, upright girl with regular features, black, luxuriant hair, which she gathered together in tightly braided pigtails at the back of her neck. She had dark, intelligent eyes, an austere, well-drawn mouth and a striking chin; her neck was like a column. At that time she could neither read nor write, and later she never had the time to learn these things properly, but her good memory made up for this deficiency. She was fanatically assiduous in fulfilling her duties and maintained the living standard of our house at the same level, of her own accord, even when no one required or expected it of her. She was gifted with such organizational talent and with such energy, that she could have filled a ministerial office or become commander-in-chief. A passionate temperament combined itself in her with a sense of justice; she was capable of fighting for the truth. Destiny had assigned her the position of a maid in this life, in which she was not even valued by my mother, since my mother was herself of a monarchical disposition. Polya's relatives were very poor, and all her life she had to make one sacrifice after another for them.

The coachman Terenty was another of "our people," and stayed with us for as long as we owned horses. He was a handsome fellow with dense, black eyebrows, a fine full beard and red cheeks. The blue velvet boyar hat with a beaver brim which he wore in winter suited him excellently. Swathed in his long kaftan (probably, in fact, in several, since he appeared quite fat), he sat immovable as a statue in his box seat. Two grooms helped him dress; they held his colourful, many-layered, narrow silk belt, and he turned around in front of them so that it would sit properly on him. The two grooms held the splendid, snorting team of horses by the bridle for as long as the ladies and gentlemen were boarding the carriage or sleigh; then they let go. And what horses they were, our trotters! Mythical creatures from the stud farm of Count Vorontsov, of astonishing size, beauty and spiritedness. The coachman, in white gloves, had to have considerable strength in his taut hands. Not infrequently, accidents were known to happen on the streets of Moscow with such horses. There was, therefore, always a bit of tension with these rides.

We had eight of these horses, and often visited them in the stable, where, not without a sense of awe, I saw their fiery eyes through the wooden lattice, and heard the trampling of hooves on the floorboards. Terenty later took us to school everyday, and still later to the theatre or to balls, often having to wait for us outside for hours in the frosty night air. He later, unfortunately, became a drunkard.

As small children we were objects of care and attention and, as it seems to me now, rather comfortable "objects." And we gladly put up with everything without protesting. As far as what went on externally, I felt like a little idol, with which all manner of ceremonial actions are performed. Everything took place slowly, festively, reverently, whether we were being fed, dressed or taken for a walk. The procedure for getting ready to go for a walk in winter — and we were taken for a walk twice a day — took a very long time. First, we were dressed in flannel pantaloons, then warm, lined boots reaching above the knee, with a row of buttons to be done up. Then came a silk scarf around the shoulders, a quilted coat was put onto each of us — mine having a cape. This coat was so thick, our arms remained spread apart; mittens kept our hands warm. The fur hat was covered with a *bashlik*, a kind of cowl of fine white or camel-coloured wool, as worn by the Cherkessians in the Caucasus. It was hemmed with silver or gold cords and decorated with a tassel at the top. Its long tails were crossed under the chin and tied together at the back. Wrapped up like that, we could hardly move, and went at a correspondingly slow pace. In the mornings we usually walked along the smaller part of Nikitskaya, dazzlingly bright from the snow and the white houses, and empty of people. In the afternoons we went westwards past our garden, along the wider bit of Nikitskaya as far as Kudrinsky Place. For this stretch, which normally takes at most seven minutes to walk, we needed an endless amount of time. I thought everything on this street, including the church, belonged to us. All the house servants and coachmen sitting in front of the gates greeted us deferentially, even the policeman on the corner, who with his uniform and rectangular beard looked almost like Tsar Alexander III. At the end of the street were the Bavastro dye works, whose sign was painted with a splendid cascade of variously coloured stripes. We never went further than to this corner. That was the boundary of our world. On the other side of the square was "Garden Street" and the large, orange buildings of the Widows' House and the Cadet Corps. Between the blackened ancient lindens of the Widow's Park one saw the golden yellow and red evening sky. This colour chord awakened unutterable feelings in my soul. That was "the beyond." The glowing fields of sunset spread themselves out from there.

When we returned home at dusk, I liked to look into the ground floor window of the otherwise inaccessible house of Dr Sergeievsky. In the large kitchen illumined by petroleum lamps, cooks in white pottered about with copper casseroles amid the steam.

We — My Brother, Alyosha, and I

More rarely, we went past the church to Nikitzky Place, where the shops began. First there was a toy shop. The door was draped with wood-turned wrap-around dolls looking like mummies: the head with painted-on hair and the body with two blue strokes painted in a cross form. On the pavement stood two dapple grey wooden horses and white sheep on green boards. I remember something exquisite which was bought for us there; quite small, colourful, old-fashioned, little wood-turned figurines in wide coats, both ladies and gentlemen. Each of them actually stood on four stiff bristles and their movable feet dangled in-between. If one drummed with one's finger on the table on which they stood, they moved in various directions, turned around, sometimes they took each other by the hand and danced in twos and threes.

On the corner there was a grocery, where one saw large black nuts, pineapples and other unusual things. Later on, the well-known Bartels bakery opened there, where in March the "larks" with little raisin eyes were baked, that tasted so wonderful and ushered in the warm sun. The red-cheeked, yellow-haired little Bartels daughter, a few years older than me, helped her mother with the business during the holidays. She impressed me very much and I would have liked to have spoken with her. However, that was to happen only much later, when she had already become a famous dancer, known as Ella Rabenek.

From Nikitzky Place onwards, we were generally unknown. In this direction we drove by carriage to our grandmother's, through winding, narrow streets, but it was all unfamiliar, whereas up to that point the area was still within our boudaries, including our church. Immediately, the church warden would bring a little carpet and chairs for us at the front, on which we could sit from time to time. The old woman who baked the round loaves of bread with a sacred relief on them brought them to us, whereas others had to buy them at the desk by the door.

The distant, strange, and yet somehow profoundly related world of China, also projected itself into our life. My father, who was born in Kyakhta beyond Lake Baikal, had business connections with China as a tea wholesaler. From there, magnificent gifts were sent to us: rolls of various kinds of Chinese silk; quilted jackets; coats of black satin, lined with red and with round gold buttons; fans with scenes from Chinese life; porcelain figures, vases etc. My brother had a little Chinese costume, silk trousers in an unbelievably beautiful shade of green and a blue embroidered jacket. My mother owned a dressing gown on which miniature landscapes framed with roses and foam-crested waves were embroidered. Chinese guests also came to visit us. They still wore their national costumes and long braids and always seemed a bit mysterious to me. They would approach noiselessly on their unusual soles made of millboard, their eyes looking out as if from an infinite distance, and one could not guess easily what they were thinking. It was uncanny that I was almost non-existent for them. They looked at my brother, inquired about him, while I, as a daughter, did not seem to count for them; I was air. Once they prepared a meal of Chinese dishes for us. I recollect seaweed and rice wine.

In saying "we" in remembering the early years of my life, I refer to my brother Alyosha and myself. I recall how he learnt to walk, how he was escorted and supported with a towel laid under his little arms and around his body. He had a round head with blonde locks, a delicate little neck, large trusting, dreamy, grey-blue eyes, a barely indicated nose and rather full lips that were always slightly open. He was not especially handsome, but so cute and charming that on the street strange ladies, both young and old, enthused over him and our maids often talked about him. I loved him passionately, though he did not, for whatever reasons of destiny, love me. I thought I was perhaps too ugly for him. Early on, my hair was smooth and almost white — later it became curly — and I was teased for having no eyebrows. Touching them with my finger, however, I found them to be actually quite thick. How could I help it, if they were not so visible, because they were nearly white? On the other hand, I was told I had a Greek nose. Even so, I regarded myself as ugly and was unhappy, because I thought my brother disdained me on that account.

I admired him. When his steps were still quite uncertain, he went up to an enraged turkey, which I was afraid of. It happened on our farm, which was sold when I was two and a half. Such early memories are comparable to dream pictures, like the image of two herdsmen leading a bull by the ring in its nose. The animal had dug itself into the ground and bellowed terribly. Then there was a drive into the woods. It was probably the first time I saw a forest, but I do not remember single trees or tree trunks. It simply appeared to me that we drove into a greenish light. We got out and the grown-ups looked for mushrooms. When we got home, my cousin's black knitted jacket was found to be missing and the coachman was sent back to the forest warden. He surprised him at the moment when his daughter was trying on the jacket. From the attitude of the grown-ups I felt that something was not in order; and green combined with black, remained in my mind as an image of something bad.

In the summer when I was four years old, we travelled to the Crimea. The memory of that stay is tinged with foreboding. I did not want to travel, because Masha had to remain alone in Moscow. I decided to cling to my chair at the moment of departure, so that I could not be torn away, but I did not succeed. The mere name "Black Sea" affected me in such a way that the sea really appeared dark to me, in spite of the dazzling sunlight, which hurt my eyes. On the shore I saw cattle being driven along the coast to be slaughtered and a sombre cloud seemed to envelope the herd. My beloved nurse Feklusha took me with her to bathe; I saw her swimming and was anxious. I myself stood on boards between which the water shimmered. Everything was uncertain. It became unbearable, however, when she swam out between the pillars of the bathing facility into the open sea. The expression "open sea" already filled me with terror. I was afraid she would never come back and would drown.

One day my mother said to me, "Do you know that Feklusha is leaving us?"

"Altogether?"

"Yes."

I was unable to speak, to beg for anything. It was as if my heart had been torn out. I saw the sky above me, so far away and as if made of glass, and the sea, boundless and black. I wanted to ask, "Why? What for?" and could not. The next day, when I awoke, she had already gone without having said goodbye to me — my Feklusha!

Once we were standing with Polya near our temporary accommodation on the hillside and saw two cooks getting into a dispute next to the casino kitchen. Suddenly something incredible happened. I could not see what it was about, and did not understand why one of them attacked the other with a knife. They were pulled apart. I only felt that something awful was going on, the air trembled from the horror of what was taking place and I screamed at the top of my voice. Polya carried me into the house, where I cried bitterly. The human being does not only know what a crime is from experience, it is a knowledge we bring with us into this world.

We played "horses" with children from next door and galloped around a little hill, hitting ourselves with little riding whips. I remember the feeling of freedom it gave me. I was my own master and could move of my own accord wherever I wanted. The whips belonged to the neighbours. Then a little demon whispered that I did not need to give the whip back again; I hid it under my bed. But the game was at an end and the joy as well. I avoided the unsuspecting children, who did not ask at all about the whip, was desperately unhappy and yet I did not decide to give it back.

On the morning after our return my two cousins became sick with typhus. My mother looked after them, but my brother and I were sent with Polya to stay with our grandmother.

This grandmother [Natalya Andreyeva], my mother's mother, was someone who inspired respect in me from earliest childhood. For as long as I knew her — she died when I was twenty-eight years old — she hardly changed at all. After the death of her husband, who I had not known, she only wore black clothes in winter and white in summer, made of Chinese silk. The style of her clothes remained the same. She always wore a large shawl and a little bonnet, which left her fine forehead uncovered. Her regular, noble face with its delicate, rosy complexion stayed attractive; her dark eyes were intelligent and lively; though she was not tall, her bearing was regal. At the age of fifteen she had married a nineteen-year-old man. Of the twelve children born from this marriage, ten survived. As a widow, she carried on the business and raised her children. She was the daughter of the Moscow Mayor Korolyov, the first Russian merchant visited by a tsar. This was Tsar Alexander II, the liberator. He wanted to bridge the gulf between the aristocracy, at that time impoverished by the liberation of the serfs, and the merchant class.

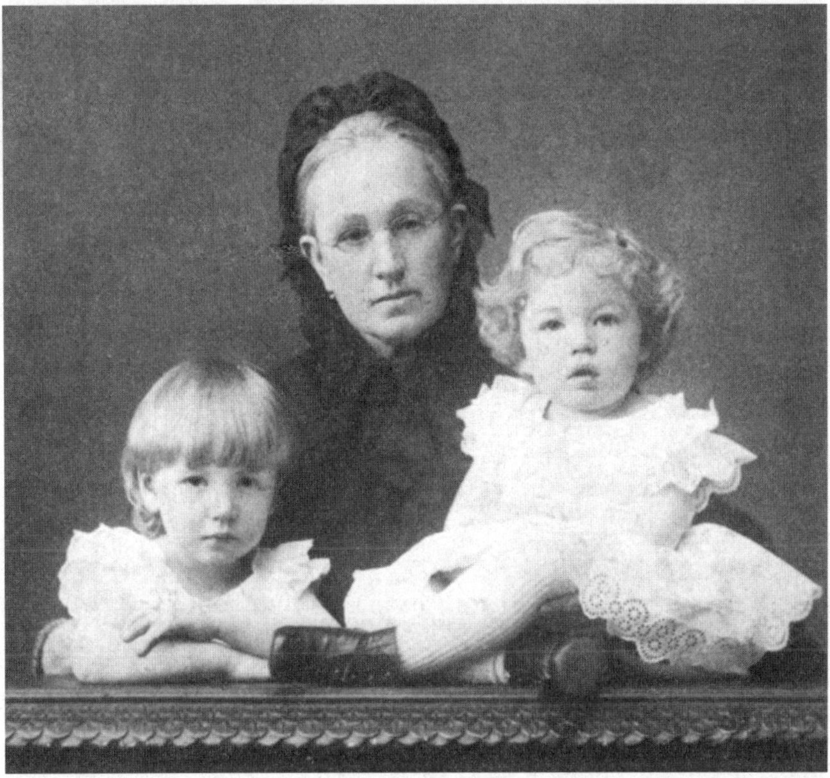

Margarita (left) and Alyosha with their grandmother

This historical moment was immortalized in a picture in which my great-grandfather welcomes the Tsar by offering him bread and salt; behind him stands his young daughter, my grandmother, with two small children; Aunt Alexandra and Uncle Basil. I saw a copy of the picture in my grandmother's house, the original hung in the museum at Grusiny. In this picture the Tsar interested me less than my aunt's peculiar attire. That is to say, the child had on a short, wide little skirt with long trousers underneath. For me trousers were improper, particularly on this festive occasion.

Just as I was convinced that our church and the great Nikitskaya belonged to us, I was also convinced that the paved intersecting street on which my grandmother's house stood, including the neighbourhood church, belonged to her. In fact, not only the intersecting street, but also the whole of Tverskaya Place as well as the Governor General's house, the barracks and the large Dresden

Hotel with the splendid delicatessen underneath it. The latter two did in fact belong to her. Her house stood in a large courtyard strewn with red sand, on which there were some separate houses, which she rented out, as well as some stables.

The class of "noted" merchants living on the other side of the Moskva River at that time was uneducated. Patriarchal Russian customs prevailed; an almost medieval family despotism on the part of the head of household and the omnipotence of money, as depicted in the dramas of Ostrovsky.[1] My grandmother, who came from such a family, could barely read and write. Things were not much better with her husband, the son of a peasant, who had sold charcoal and water from house to house. But their children, my aunts and uncles, received an excellent education. All four sons studied at university, the six daughters received home schooling from university professors and mastered three or four foreign languages fully. As quite a small child, I felt an effervescent cheerfulness in the company of my uncles and aunts. I was the first grandchild and therefore spoiled and made much of. "Adoration of the child" my oldest aunt, Alexandra, called it. It surprised me that they all addressed their own mother with the formal "you" term, whereas I used the informal term. Also, that she, who spoiled me so much, could be quite severe with her children.

Since the house had been intended originally for a much smaller family, and had to be remodelled and added onto again and again as the family grew, it consisted of a labyrinth of smaller and larger rooms, landings and levels. The three storeys were connected by various stairways and back stairs. My grandmother's two rooms were tiny. Oil lamps burned in front of the large iconostasis in the corner, and in this room there was always a scent of olive oil.

Polya had come with us, to look after us, and told us fairy tales. One of them always made a strong impression on me at that time: A little brother and sister collected berries in the forest. The little brother put the berries into the dish, the little sister put them into her mouth. When it was time to go home, the little sister killed the little brother, buried him, took the berries home and said her brother had lost his way. On the grave, however, a willow grew, wanderers came by, cut themselves a flute from the branches and the flute sang:

Quietly sing, O you flute,
Do not break my heart.
My little sister has killed me,
Made her knife red with blood,
Has put out the light of my life.

Pity for the little brother overwhelmed me, and I shared the sister's guilt, because I always saw myself as the sister and my brother in the little brother. As I later learned from him, he too saw the wicked sister in me.

From that stay at my grandmother's house, some strange moods remain in my memory. Even though I did not yet play with dolls, I was given a doll's kitchen stove made of metal. Once, I looked inside this stove, imagined myself being quite small and the inside of the stove as a big room. The walls of this "room" reflected each other, calling forth a bleak infinity. I felt cold and lonely. Repeating the experiment, I experienced the same frightful feeling. Once, while lying on the floor, I saw all things upside down; people hung down from above and, for an instant, I no longer knew which was right. Everything appeared the wrong way round, and I did it again intentionally. It was also a peculiar experience for me when we were driven back and forth along the broad part of Nikitskaya past our house, so that our mother, who did not visit us for fear of infecting us, could at least catch a glimpse of us through the window. We did not see her behind the window glass — the windows were sealed during the winter; only a small ventilator above provided fresh air — but I knew that she saw us. How odd it was, to see our house in this way from outside as if it were a strange house. It appeared huge to me, the windows so dead; was the inside still real if I was outside?

When my cousins had recovered and we went home, everything was organized differently from before. A governess came to us from the French-speaking part of Switzerland, and my education began in washing, dressing, watering flowers and sewing. We now lived together, my cousin Nyusha, who was four years older than I, a quiet and dreamy girl, the governess and I. This Swiss woman, Mlle Schacher, a good-natured, uneducated person, once tried to deceive me in an insignificant matter. I was so terribly offended then at age five that my trust in her was at an end.

In those days we spent every summer at the *dacha*. These villas in the vicinity of Moscow were rented mostly for the summer months by the families of state employees, so that the city dwellers could leave the hot, dusty, noisy city every day after finishing work and spend the evening with their families in fresh natural surroundings. Right behind the train station stood rows of such wooden villas with large balconies, between the pine trees, quite close to each other. Later, I came to loathe these *dachas* on account of the idle, bored clientele that displayed its complete banality — on the open spaces in the park where people danced, and on the railway platform, where young girls in pseudo-Russian, embroidered costumes flirted with high school students. There was nothing rustic in the surroundings of this settlement. I only got to know the true Russian countryside later on, when we went to our estate near Vyazma. But at the time, when we knew no better, we looked forward to the *dacha*.

But we were also glad to go back to the city again in the autumn. At first, one was stunned by the frightful din of the streets, of the carriages rolling over cobblestones. In front of the train station stood the droshkies. Each coachman stood in his carriage, all wore blue suits reaching to the ground with a red belt and peculiar flat hats, and they all shouted, offering their services in wild confusion. But it was Terenty who brought us to our quiet, beautiful house.

Every summer my grandmother rented a country house on one of the titled properties near Moscow, accessible at that time only by horse-drawn carriage. These grand houses with ancient linden parks, terraces decorated with flowers, stairways and gardens, were full of old traditions. The impoverished nobleman had, at that time, to rent out his castles to middle-class citizens.

I remember being shown where Pushkin had lived, on the estate of Prince Vyazemsky. I was also shown a paperweight; a coffin in which a corpse was being eaten by worms, which I was told had belonged to a Freemason. Full of awe, I viewed this room of Pushkin with the paperweight, even though I had no notion then about Pushkin, or about Freemasons.

My grandmother loved flowers. Every day early in the morning before breakfast she went into the garden in her white Chinese silk dressing gown and cut roses, still full of dew, and laid them in a basket that I carried for her. I spent a fair amount of time with her every summer.

My aunts, as different as they were, all had a suggestion of roses about them. Their skin had a lustrous bloom; they had beautiful hands. Though different from each other, the shine in their eyes, the sound of their voices all had a certain lively charm. Was it in their blood? I could not say with what sense I perceived this fragrance, this lustre, as a child. Other people appeared to me as though made of a coarser substance. In fact, where did these aristocratic, wonderfully modelled hands and feet, this posture, come from? From a line of peasants. The youngest, Katharina, who was only sixteen years older than I, was the most beautiful; tall and regal in bearing, with an oval face and large dark eyes that shone like two suns. Her movements were correspondingly graceful. Her voice sounded a deep alto. When she spoke, her temperament entered in, and the words sometimes tripped over each other; she easily lost the thread. She later married the poet Konstantin D. Balmont. She was the closest to me. The older aunt, Alexandra, who helped my grandmother in raising the other children and in running the business, was a writer. In my memory, she is mostly either writing or reading. The youngest aunts would get up late, row on a small river nearby, where I saw yellow and white water lilies for the first time, read novels and flirt with their admirers. In this family, each surpassed the other with witty remarks, wordplay and teasing. It was like a fireworks display.

We grew up, as it sometimes seemed, almost like the king's son Siddhartha, without seeing anything sad or ugly. However, on a Sunday afternoon when we drove by carriage from one of my grandmother's country seats to Moscow, we passed through a suburb of the city. In the small houses I saw broken windowpanes stopped up with boxes. Dirty, ragged children ran after our carriage and begged for coins. I saw sick, embittered women, and drunken men lying in the dust or standing in the middle of the street, cursing, railing or bawling out songs. I was deeply shocked by this. I prayed to God, promising myself solemnly to help these people as soon as I had grown up.

In the winter, in front of our house, an old man sat with two small children and begged. I said to my mother, "Our annex stands empty, we could accommodate them. Please do it, won't you!"

She replied, "We cannot take in all poor people."

"I'm not saying all, I'm saying those out there!" And I did not understand the reasons my mother put forward against it.

The cross streets which led from Nikitzky Place to our grandmother consisted of beautiful houses. But there was one corner where I had a bad feeling every time I passed. From small windows heavy smoke and steam emerged, through which distorted faces could be seen. It was a small laundry, next to a public baths and a wine tavern. Men came towards us who could not stand firmly on the ground, and of whom I had an insuperable fear. Once a drunk sat on the stone steps in front of the entrance to the tavern. Another time I saw a woman in a doorway whose face was purple. She spoke in a hoarse voice to a worker and laughed so cynically and despairingly, that it filled me with horror. Something was not right with the world.

Learning Begins

I was seven, my brother six years old, when our schooling began. Our priest had come to us two years before that, in order to tell us the story of the Bible with the help of pictures. This still falls into the time I should like to call the "mythological" time of my life, since everything that happened then I experienced in another state of consciousness. The priest, known as a kind, fine human being, appeared to me like a divine being, with his long hair and long vestment, and I remember the pictures and stories I listened to as one remembers a dream. These biblical stories, primordial dreams of humanity, mirrorings of higher realities in the picture consciousness of the Hebrew people, whose history had brought them to realization, appeared to the child's soul like her own memories, like a part of her own being. When we played afterwards with our dolls, all these pictures resurfaced again — Noah's ark, the parting of the Red Sea, the Ark of the Covenant. My mother once heard my brother asking me, "How shall we punish them?" (he meant the dolls).

"We shall punish them in their children, and in their children's children," I answered him.

Learning began festively. Our teacher, Katharina Kusminitshna, was still young. She had just lost a dear friend and gone through a severe illness; smallpox. Her regular face with deep-set, large, pale grey eyes under well-formed eyelids and a clearly drawn mouth might have been called beautiful, if her skin had not been eaten away by the frightful pockmarks. During the time of the illness she had forfeited her beautiful golden yellow braids and wore short hair, which at that time appeared strange and unfeminine. I have seldom known such a shy human being. If my father, himself a quiet, shy man, directed even just a few words to her, she turned crimson with embarrassment; she walked fast and with a stoop, her movements were restless. We later called her Kittie and still later Kittiki. But in the lessons she gave us, she was quiet, sure of herself and in complete control. She prepared herself to teach for hours beforehand, and every lesson was a work of art.

I still recall the first lesson quite well. A large, long room had been chosen as a classroom, with two windows facing north. My brother slept in this room; there was a high bar on the door and our toys were in one corner. An oblong table was installed for our lessons in such a way that the light fell onto the side on which we both sat. A green cloth had been pasted onto the varnished wooden table. (So pleasing was it for us to gradually tear this cloth off that, after a time, the table had to be re-covered with a much less congenial black oilcloth). Katharina Kusminitshna sat us at the table, pushed wooden boxes under our feet, so that we could support ourselves on them while our elbows lay lightly on the table. Suddenly, she knocked on the table-top from underneath and asked, "What is that?"

We stared dumbly at each other. Had she gone mad? She wanted us to answer, "That is a sound."

It took a while before she got us to the point of giving this answer. Then she discussed various sounds with us. Next came writing. She first took a goose feather and showed us how it was formerly used in writing. She had also brought some yellow sand, which was strewn onto what had been written, to dry the ink. That was, of course, the best part of the entire lesson. And then we made straight and curved strokes, while she counted, one two ... What she did, certainly all teachers do in the beginning to teach writing, but what was important was the earnestness, the love, with which she carried all this out, awakening in us a mood of devout attention. How I strived to make my straight and curved lines beautiful, and to hold the feather so that it did not make scratches! The reward was the golden sand, which transformed each stroke into gold. After we had been writing and bending over our notebooks in this way for a while, the double doors to the corridor opened suddenly, and there stood a group of people: Our grandmother (whose visits to us were a rarity and signified a festive occasion), my parents, my cousin, all the maids, and who else was there? My dear Feklusha, who had come especially for this day and was moved to the point of tears. With that the first lesson was at an end, and everybody embraced and congratulated us.

The book we made use of in our language lesson was called *The Familiar Word* (*Rodnoye Slovo*). "Familiar" is not quite the right translation, since the Russian word "*rodnoye*" has the same root as "*rodnik*," which means "source"; but it also means "familiar." A mother is called *rodnaya*. *Rodity*means to "give birth." I regret not having found out more about the educator who put this book together, for he managed to do justice in the highest sense to the soul of the child and to the "word," as well a to the homeland, in interweaving short stories, prayers and poems involving the seasons, farm work and the customs of the people. In entering into an experience of the seasons, Kittie knew how to awaken in us admiration for the wisdom of nature. She imparted to us her own reverence for the processes of growth, the workings of nature and the creative activity of the human being. The theme of "bread" occupied us again and again; she brought us all sorts of grains, which we sowed in pots, in order to observe their growth, and since we were big-city dwellers, she brought us pictures showing various kinds of work on the land, models of agricultural implements and actual tools, insofar as they could be brought along; a model of a brick kiln etc. Kittie also acquainted us with the origin of articles in our immediate surroundings, with the work of the cobbler, the joiner. In this way we awakened to our surroundings and felt gratitude for our bond with nature and human beings. Everything was enlivened with pictures, accompanied by poems and fairy tales. A big impression was made on me by picture books of the kind that, when opened, single figures stood up so that what was flat suddenly became three-dimensional. For a long time this appeared like a miracle to me; it seemed to me as though Kittie could perform magic. Right from the beginning we began learning poems, working through them in various ways, phonetically, rhythmically, according to gradations of mood. Then we recited them together expressively and with attention to pitch and accent, at which, oddly, she held a rattler in her hand, so as to underscore the rhythm. Her love of the word aroused this love in us too. Poems struck me as being like prayers. Once, when we gathered in front of the icons, as we did every evening — my cousin, my brother and I with one or another of the grown-ups — I was to recite the Lord's Prayer, but instead recited the poem about the rain that begins, "Gold, gold falls from heaven" (as the sunlit rain was termed), and ended, "this gold we shall gather as fragrant, golden bread in the bread chamber."[2] Everybody laughed, I did not understand why. Why should this poem not be a prayer? Was the sun not the Christ-Sun and the bread not His Body?

Every day I awaited the hours in which we had lessons with anticipation: what would we do today, what was she going to bring? It could be objected that our syllabus began much too early with natural science, appealing too soon to the intellect. That was the tendency at that time. Yet, I have to repeat that whether we observed the crystallization of salt, whether we analysed the ground in letting sand precipitate in water, dissolved clay in water, burnt humus or distilled calcium in water, we observed these phenomena with such awe that the danger of the powers of understanding awakening too soon was overcome by wonder and enthusiasm. Everything became interesting and alive through Kittie's mediation, even the numbers in arithmetic. It is no trifling matter to be able to say that, during the nine years in which we were taught by her, her lessons and even preparing for exams, never became boring for me.

One year later, a Mlle Wilken came from Riga to give us language instruction. She seemed quite outlandish to us; her thin hair, parted in the middle and smoothly combed, was gathered in a small knot at the back. Her grey eyes, under drooping eyelids could have a well-meaning look, but turned steely when she was dissatisfied with us. Her large nose was unusually narrow at the root, with prominent nostrils, her lips thin and pressed together. I do not remember her ever having worn another dress during the four years that she was with us, other than a smooth grey one with a lot of buttons in the front. Around her neck, which resembled the neck of a tortoise, she wore a white neckerchief. She folded her hands and said a prayer while looking to heaven before the first lesson, when we were already sitting at the table with her. This I felt to be so impossible, I didn't know where to look for sheer embarrassment. Prayer was for me either a ritual, quite impersonal matter, like our morning and evening prayers standing before the icons, or something so intimate, a conversation with God, that could only be conducted in deepest seclusion without witnesses. I awaited the second lesson with horror; only she had probably noticed the effect. There was no praying.

Madamoiselle Wilken was an honest, conscientious person, suffused with the Protestant ethic, which she wanted to pass on to us; she was well-read and had travelled far. But she lacked one thing: a Russian *nyanya,* or nanny, would say that she lacked *grace.* Her pedagogical methods were unfortunate. Music was spoiled for me by having, as already mentioned, to search for the greater part of the lesson for the five copper kopek coins on the floor under the furniture, that rolled one moment from one hand, the next moment from the other. The solfeggio was spoiled by having to place black notes of cast metal onto the sheet music, without having sung them beforehand. Every day we had a lesson in the Acts of the Apostles. With this she wanted to kill three birds with one stone: the French language, geography and religion. Meanwhile, we still hadn't the faintest idea what a map signified (we only got a proper introduction to geography two years later from Kittie). For that reason, Asia Minor appeared to me like a rose-coloured woman prancing about that I was not permitted to put up in front of me, but had to view lying on the table. Ephesus, Damascus etc. were little circles distributed quite inorganically on her body. The language of the Bible was much too difficult for us and the whole story incomprehensible, since we knew very little about the Gospel itself. It was exactly the same with the botany lesson, which was also supposed to be an exercise in the French language. We had to describe the shapes of the leaves and blossoms, count the stamens and identify the plants in accordance with Linné, learn their Latin names, without getting to know each plant in its living connection with the surrounding landscape, and the metamorphosis of its shapes. Later, on our journeys with Kittie, it was different thank God, otherwise flowers would quite possibly have been ruined for me as well!

Everything Madamoiselle Wilken wanted to give us, struck no roots. Although we were taught by her for four years, we hardly learned anything from her. She was pedantic and orderly. If a book or anything was missing, or lay crooked on the table, or a speck of dust had not been wiped off, she sat with lips pressed together and stared in front of her. In that lesson, nothing could be done right anymore; we sat for an hour in front of each other in oppressive silence. The result of this education in orderliness was the reverse. I acquired a loathing of the concept of order altogether; order was the same for me as pedantry, and when Madamoiselle Wilken left us, I rejected any kind of order and plunged into chaos. That worked, as long as we had a lot of servants, who brought everything into order after us; in later years, however, I had to re-educate myself out of my disorderliness.

I cannot recall either, that Madamoiselle Wilken ever told me anything that gripped me, in spite of her erudition, and yet I was generally very interested in life. I only remember my enthusiasm being roused once by the description of a grape harvest. That struck home!

The whole life of children at that time was steeped in religious feeling. I was sure that everything I thought, felt and did was visible for God and his angels. When I was quite small I wanted, from the window of our dining room, to look down and see our dog, whose kennel stood next to the cellar beneath an elder tree, and tried hard to climb onto an upholstered bench in front of the window. "Wait till I come and help you!" my mother said to me. She left the room. However, I got onto the bench alone and at once tumbled backwards. In falling, I thought, God is punishing me, because I disobeyed. I fell with my back against a carved candelabra base and had to lie for weeks on an ice bag, since it was feared I might otherwise be left with a curved spine. My brother remembers wanting to suggest a prank to me.

"No one will know about it," he said.

"And God?" I raised my little finger to the sky.

"God is only for grown-ups; we don't need to worry, even if He were to see something, He'll not be so strict with us!"

When I was five or six years old, a wondrous idea occupied me every evening before falling asleep: I wanted to set up an altar in our attic. True, I had never been there till then, because only the stoker possessed the key to the mysterious cloth-covered door at the end of the corridor, and disappeared there from time to time. Every evening I placed this picture before my mind's eye: I am celebrating in front of an altar that I have erected myself in the attic, and all my relatives stand there amazed. During the day I did not know how I was going to carry this out in practice, but in the evening I surrendered myself again and again with enthusiasm to this dream.

I had another peculiar idea: I assumed that objects were not as they appeared to me; being not at all lifeless, they only adjusted themselves, closed their eyes as it were in my presence, so as to then become different behind my back. That's why I attempted to turn around suddenly, so as to "catch" them, but I never succeeded in surprising them, they assumed their usual appearance straightaway.

During a summer in the country, when I was five years old, I modelled a large human figure in clay on a white stone. I moistened the statue with "golden water," as we called the clay diluted with water, that shone like gold in the sun. My work was so beautiful that I was quite taken with it myself. It must have felt like that for the god Yahweh, when he formed the human being, Adam, from the earth. Towards evening, in falling asleep, I began to doubt whether it had all been true and not perhaps a dream that I had made something so splendid, and became impatient to see my work again in the morning. During the night, however, rain fell, and when I hurried to the stone in the morning, only a misshapen lump lay on it. I remember my dismay and that I had no courage to build it up again, since I doubted the possibility of experiencing the same miracle twice.

Once, however, the idea occurred to me, that I could draw a crucifix. I took a sheet of paper, went into a room where I could be alone and carried out my work with a beating heart. When I saw that it had become something, that I really had drawn a cross with the Crucified One, I got quite a fright, hid the sheet of paper in a drawer with trembling hands, not really knowing whether what I had done was a holy deed or a great sin.

My cousins received painting lessons and I took part in them eagerly, although I was only seven years old. The teacher had me draw from nature with coloured pencils, instead of allowing me to create freely with the liquid paint. In that way I was directed too early to a passive imitation of nature, impeding my creative initiative.

At that time natural science interested me more than art. I always wanted in that period to "observe nature," to be a naturalist, and once when a mouse had been caught in our house, I asked to keep it. We bought a very large mousetrap for it to live in; I put newspaper inside, so as to be better able to clean the cage, and placed a little house with cotton wool inside, that I had made from a cardboard box. The whole of the first night I heard the mouse gnawing, and when I went to check on her the next morning, a nest had been built between the house and the thin wall of the cage, made of a substance, a mixture of cotton and chewed-up paper, so that my little house formed an anteroom to the actual living space of the mouse. There was also a little window in this living space through which I could see the little black eye of the mouse. I was delighted, and even more so when on the following day I caught sight of two rosy, transparent little mice suckling on the mother. There one could really "observe nature." In my drawing book, a very exact drawing appeared of this idyll.

"Well, how is your mouse doing?" an officer asked us at my grandmother's Sunday tea reception.

"She gave birth," my brother answered convivially across the long guest table, to the amusement of all those present.

Once I was awoken during the night by squeaking. I lit the candle, hurried to the cage and did not know whether to trust my eyes: a little mouse lay dead, the other one squeaked in the paws of the mother, which bit off its head. I shook with horror. What was wrong? How was something like that possible? After all, she had enough to eat! The cage with the child-murderess vanished from our room. In my heart, however, a frightful riddle remained. Why had she done it? No, something was not right in the scheme of things, and nature itself was not as sacred as I had thought.

From time to time, my parents organized balls for my oldest cousin. The preparations for this were already full of poetry for us. Long beforehand, a mannequin stood in the upstairs hall on which a light tulle dress was tried out that Masha had sewed for Elisabeth. For the petticoat, little silk ribbons with tiny bells were sewn together; golden stars and bows were pinned onto a velvet cushion, and everything was magical and unearthly. We little ones could already dance well — we had dance lessons together with other children from a French ballet master in our hall — and we were allowed to join in at the beginning of the ball. The master of ceremonies, my Uncle Sergei, filled his rôle with great enthusiasm. Once, when he called out, *"Les dames invitent leurs cavaliers!"* I went up to a tall dark gentleman, the brother-in-law of my Aunt Tatyana Bergengrün, who appealed to me because he spoke with an exotic accent (he was a Balt) and bore the name "Otto," unusual for my ears, and challenged him to the next quadrille. He seemed enthusiastic. Bowing deeply to me, he led me on his arm through the halls and presented me proudly as his lady. I was in seventh heaven. Then my mother caught sight of me.

"You're still there? What's this? Straight to bed!"

"But you did allow ..."

"Straight to bed!"

"But I have a cavalier ..."

"March to bed!"

I dragged myself up the stairs to the empty upper floor. What a humiliation! How could I have known? Now he was looking for me, now the dance had begun ... I lay in bed as if in a fever, heard the music and my uncle's voice, which directed *"Et à vos places, s'il vous plaît et balancez vos dames ..."* Had Otto found another lady? What would he think of me? I would never be able to meet him again! With this dance came the mazurka, a Polish folk dance, which I danced particularly well ... What a disgrace! Shame and outrage ... and again, "How could I have known," and, "It wasn't meant to be like that!" I was then seven years old. If I tell this little story, it is because I see in it something that is characteristic of my life's destiny. How often I had to repeat these words later, "How could I have known beforehand; it wasn't meant to be like that!"

My parents once invited guests on a trip by troikas. Before automobiles conquered the world, the rapid drive with horses was a Russian passion. The city dweller hired three-horse carriages and drove to outlying districts. The sleighs were wide, padded with colourful carpets, so that three people could sit comfortably next to each other, the fourth in front on a protruding side-seat. The middle horse of the three-horse carriage ran in a trot; little bells hung under the decorated little arch over its head. The two side horses pulled the harness in a gallop, bending their necks outwards, giving the troika a similar appearance to a bird in flight. "Troika, troika bird!" Gogol calls out, when he refers to the hurtling pace of these Russian outings in his *Dead Souls*. This time we children were allowed to go as well. It was a drive by moonlight! Our good fortune seemed indescribable. In addition, the two Krassovsky brothers, the two nice officers whom I was after all so "terribly in love with," were also coming with us. Never had I been up so late, never had I experienced such a bright moonlit night, such vast snowfields, so many, many stars. It was very cold. In the Petrovskoye-Rasumovskoye Park with the old castle of Count Rasumovsky, later the Agricultural Academy, we dismounted and walked past the castle, whose bull's-eye window panes shone strangely in the moonlight. The huge fir trees were shrouded in snow and Fyodor Krassovsky, whom I after all "loved so terribly," shook the lower branch over me deliberately. Everything sparkled around me, snow and stars, the whole of space was criss-crossed with diamond rays, everything was unreal. Probably as a result of staying up unusually late, the profusion of moonlight, in which

I seemed to swim free of my body in this glittering and sparkling of stars and snow, I perceived things differently than in ordinary everyday life. I was blissfully happy. Behind the fir trees I saw the ice of the lakes which had been swept free of snow. The moon was reflected in them. Two bright lonely pyramids rose up on the ice. They were the artificial icebergs of the skating rink. To me they looked magnificent and mysterious. God knows, what memories from primeval times and primal worlds well up in the soul of the child! Soon after that we drove home. But that brief moment left behind a feeling of eternity in me.

The World Widens

When I was ten years old our house was sold and we were told that we would travel abroad. The elegant widow in fur who acquired our house and came several times to see us with her architect, in order to discuss the planned alterations to the house, appeared to us children like an enemy who wanted to drive us out of our home and change everything irreverently. Out of our apartment, two were to be made, the wall between the living room and the children's room had to be broken through; nothing but wilful, impossible things which affronted us! We had to leave by the beginning of February so that the renovation could begin. However, my brother had not yet recovered from bronchitis, and since the work on the upper floor was not to be postponed, we all moved into the magnificent lower rooms. In the large hall and in the red drawing room our beds and suitcases stood in the middle of the room. It was strange.

Dull thumping could be heard from above as the wall was broken through; we were not permitted on the stairs leading to the floor above and did not see the devastation. The mood was a mixture of melancholy parting and joyful anticipation of everything new and unusual that we experienced and that stood before us.

On the day of our departure, our little white dog howled heartrendingly. The maids went around with eyes red from crying. Towards evening we left. All our relatives came to the train station. My father stayed in Moscow to be near his businesses. We —my mother, the two teachers, Polya, the cousins, Alyosha and I — travelled abroad for three years. The intention was to reduce household costs by this means! That is also why the house was sold.

The sorrow of departure faded into the darkness of dwindling snowfields. The next day, Kittie showed us the great forests in which aurochs still lived. In Warsaw we spent a day in a hotel, because our Uncle Ivan wanted to visit us there with his two daughters. On the drive from the station to the hotel, it struck me that all Polish ladies were dressed in black, which suited them. My mother explained to me that they wanted to display their grief over the suppression of Poland in this way. In the hotel for the first time I saw a room that belonged to nobody. How desolate this opulent room appeared to me!

Uncle Ivan was one of the most engaging personalities I have met in my life. He was the chief of staff of the large, world-famous Tvorki mental asylum near Warsaw. Much was said about the great influence he exercised on his patients through his intuitive understanding. For example, a sick person had imagined he was a mushroom and refused food. My uncle sat next to him in the same squatting position and said he too was a mushroom; after a time, this new mushroom demanded something to eat, and the other mushroom followed his example. During the First World War, when the Russian military authorities required the evacuation of the Tvorki asylum (which later proved to have been completely superfluous), he had to wander for miles with the insane patients — the railway having been destroyed — and explain to each one, in accordance with his madness, where they were going.

Alongside his profession, he wrote poetry and had at that time published a fine translation of a book of poems, *The Light of Asia*by Edwin Arnold. All my Siberian relatives had an artistic vein and were straightforward and natural. Like my father and the two cousins who grew up with us, Uncle Ivan had something touchingly modest and direct in his whole manner. His little daughters, who were roughly my age and whom I was wild about — oh, how pretty they were with their luxuriant long hair! — told us confidentially that their father was in the habit of reading to them from the works of Confucius and other Eastern sages but that, if at all possible, they hid, because it was too boring for them.

Our nearly three-year stay abroad fell just in those years between ten and thirteen which are so important in the development of a child. They had an unusual significance for me.

We spent the early spring months in Lausanne, in a pension surrounded by a park with evergreen trees and fountains. The nature there left me cold. It seemed at first quite cheerless to me, to have to sit with so many strange people at the *table d'hôte.*But the situation was especially awkward for Polya, who felt shy about eating together with others in this manner. At the end of our journey, the poor girl, otherwise as fit as a fiddle, got a stomach complaint. For the first time, I saw people of different nationalities. The Americans were well-built and cheerful. I liked them well enough, but why did the gentlemen sit around in the lobby in such an improper manner, placing their feet as high as possible, higher than their heads? Had they never had governesses? What affronted me with the Germans, who appeared to me very erudite, was that they answered *"Quatsch"* (rubbish) to their wives' remarks, as though they were much more stupid. But these women annoyed me, because they put up with it and waited on their men.

If one does not want to see life as ruled by blind accident, which would rob it of its moral value, but seeks — as in the case of physical phenomena — for the hidden connections, then the destiny of a human being presents many riddles, especially in childhood. At this age nothing happens as a result of conscious decisions; everything is as if determined from outside, and yet belongs somehow inherently to the personality. A sense of this order, incomprehensible to begin with, can fill us with reverence in paying closer attention to life. Such reverence and gratitude take hold of me, when I think about the three-year sojourn abroad of the child I then was. These years involve a crisis. It can be observed with every child, how they awaken between nine and ten to an awareness of their own personality on the one hand, and on the other to a more conscious assimilation of the external world, with which they had felt themselves interwoven until then. The encounter with these polarities expresses itself not only in the child's behaviour — they often become more critical, more difficult — but has its effect on their physical constitution as well. Breathing and pulse beat harmonize themselves at this time. The stream of time in which the continuity of consciousness lives, borne by the blood, meets the "breathing in" of sense impressions, which come from the realm of space. Expressing it in the picture language of the Greeks, Dionysus and Apollo meet each other in these years.

Looking at the child I was before our journey, outwardly withdrawn and seemingly quiet, yet inwardly overwhelmed by shock waves, at four years of age sleepless for half the night on account of some mistrust or perceived injustice. Pity and remorse did not allow this child to settle down. This exaggerated inner life could have taken an unhealthy turn, if a strong influence from outside had not come at the decisive moment, directing it into the wider world.

First of all there were the mighty impressions of the high mountains in Switzerland, where we spent the first six months. We went on long mountain tours, but our lessons with Kittie and Madamoiselle Wilken continued as before, according to the Russian high school programme. It aroused our enthusiasm to go through the geography and history of each country we visited. Under Kittie's guidance both my brother and I started a collection of minerals and alpine flora, which we provided with a text, and were afterwards able to give to a school in Moscow. When my brother wrote to our grandmother during that summer, he merely reported to her at what altitude, longitude and latitude we were located at that moment. For this reason, his letters were extremely short. I recounted stories about waterfalls and gorges, which also did not fit exactly into our grandmother's vision of things. On our mountain hikes, everything I saw became a parable. It was a remarkable process of "symbolizing." Kittie took hold of me, shook me and cried, "Look around you. What formations are these, what strata? What plants did we come across on the path today? Tomorrow I'm going to ask you about everything in the lesson!"

As though I didn't look! I loved the moss with its little grey cups ringed around with vermilion; I loved such things "hopelessly," because I had still not yet discovered the world from which they came, nor where they were "pointing to." The sprigs of alpine roses had a fragrant smell of resin; their hard, brownish leaves were thus quite different from their delicate rose-red blossoms. For this, I knew a corresponding picture from legend. The silvery fields, the snow over the glacier, led directly into the heavens, and the river that sprang from it plunged, foaming, to the valley below through screes, in order to join the Rhone — this language I understood. My brother and I tried to guess in which stones crystals were hidden. When we cracked open a round grey stone with our hammer, and what we had suspected shone out at us, it was a miracle for us each time. Out of what nocturnal ages did it now appear in the light of day, so akin to the stars! And to think that our eyes were the first to behold it!

So great was my love of crystals that, when we arrived in Paris in the autumn, I followed my habit and searched for minerals and crystals in the heaps of stones lying in the streets for road repair work, to the astonishment of passers-by. I did this despite the elegant clothing bought for me the first day in the Magasin du Louvre. And when, on one of the big boulevards, I saw the placard, *Cristaux,* in a store on the other side of the street, I dashed over, despite the considerable droshky traffic, and was very disappointed on seeing vases, carafes and other cut glass in the window. Making up for this, my passion for crystals was to find the greatest possible satisfaction in Paris, when we visited the Natural History Museum in the Jardin des Plantes. The splendour of this collection is such that probably no other can be compared with it. In particular, a huge amethyst will remain unforgettable to me for its size, the sheer perfection of its crystals and the deep violet lustre of its colour, attuning the soul as solemnly and festively as the sight of the starry sky.

That following summer I stood in front of the North Sea. Recently, when I once again beheld from the dunes the surging waves of liquid silver and breathed in the salty air, I was seized by the same enthusiasm as I had felt as an eleven-year-old child, on finding myself for the first time on the threshold of that world of creative elemental forces. A human being who has experienced this majesty will, in later life, not adopt philistine criteria. That summer, when the weather was fine, we had our lessons with Kittie in the dunes. We brought home buckets full of starfish, cuttlefish, crabs and jellyfish and studied their shapes and their life. The following spring I saw the aquarium in Naples, which is incorporated into the sea, and there the cuttlefish and jellyfish gleamed in the blue water in unbelievable colours. I felt as if touched by magic. In this blueness a vast number of cuttlefish of different kinds weaved hither and thither. They opened their delicate stars on reddish tentacles that branched out, closing them again when danger approached. The jellyfish and fish glimmered in unearthly colours and this delicate world with its mysterious appearance, its transparency woven of water and sunlight, contrasted with octopods, snakes and grey armoured crabs, often overgrown with green algae, their eyes looking out eerily from their stony shell. This mute swimming, gliding, weaving and strange gesturing, was subject to the laws of another world and called up hidden, forgotten things from the depths of the soul.

The Times Speak

When we arrived in Paris in the year 1892, the French were commemorating the events that had taken place a century earlier. Special editions were sold on the streets with pictures of the great Revolution. We visited the tomb of Napoleon, the Pantheon with its pictures of old kings. Here for the first time I came in direct touch with history. And in still another way it touched me. We lived a solitary, regulated, but well-to-do life. The only person to visit us was the elderly widow of the German poet Georg Herwegh, who lived as an emigrant in great poverty in an attic room on the Rue du Bac.[3] She was recommended to my mother, who took Italian language lessons with her. From this old woman we often heard stories about Garibaldi and Mazzini, whom she had known personally, as well as Orsini, whom she had helped to escape from prison; also about Alexander Herzen and his wife. And even if I did not understand just what historical battle was involved, and what heroes, I could sense the pathos of a great age through her.

Awakening to the world meant at the same time awakening to personality. For me this began in Paris, when I noticed that I was an object of attention for other people. Opposite our hotel there was a painting school in which I drew plaster heads. The painter to whom the school belonged, admired the colour of my hair, which had become quite curly, and asked my mother whether I might be allowed to sit for her. My mother was afraid I could become vain and did not permit it. However, her concern came too late. I often heard remarks on the street about my complexion and my hair was touched. I became interesting to myself. I still remember looking in a double mirror at my profile for the first time, when I was taken aback by the straight line of forehead and nose. Once, when we stood with Polya in front of a confectioner's on the Avenue de l'Opéra admiring the boxes of chocolates, a tall, elegant gentleman stepped out of the door and gave me a stag made of honey cake. Abashed, I said my thanks, but arrived home quite pleased and after having already bitten off the horns, I told the story to my mother. She was beside herself, reproached me for accepting presents from unknown men, ordered me to throw the cake away and left my room. I sat there dismayed and crying on the bed and continued eating the stag, which was wet from my tears. Suddenly a frightful thought occurred to me: perhaps my mother forbade me to eat the stag, because it could be poisoned. But only the legs were left; I ate these as well, since there was presumably nothing more to lose and waited for death. I did not die, for the cake was not poisoned. But the whole air of Paris was as though pervaded with a refined poison. At that time Lucifer gained entry to my soul.

From earliest childhood I was filled with the yearning to connect with other people. I remember the wonderful experience of carnival, of *mardi gras.* Our family joined the crowds along the boulevards. Colourful paper ribbons flew in the air, hung over the streets and clung to the trees. Each of us held a bag of confetti. It was permitted to throw this over anyone passing by. The whole world was suddenly transformed and separating boundaries between people disappeared. Everybody knew everybody else; all were playmates. We fought passionately and were showered with confetti. People jested and shouted freely, wittily and humorously, as only the French can. It was magical! And the next day, what disappointment! On the streets, nothing but strangers again, indifferent passers-by. Where was the colourful, cheerful companionship of yesterday? Remains of the colourful ribbons on the trees and confetti in the gutters recalled that previous state of mind in which the words *Liberté, Egalité*and *Fraternité,* that I saw every day written in big black letters on the building next to the Place de la Concorde, had seemed actually fulfilled for a moment.

If one were to observe the development of a child impartially, one would find that it repeats the stages of historical development. At first the child regards themself as one with the world: everything is ensouled, just as they are ensouled. They live in dreams, in which they are not separate from the universe. Humanity has likewise "dreamed" these dreams in its myths. Later, in their play, in their feuding, the child recapitulates previous ages, which they had lived through as an individuality in earlier times. Various talents may also make their appearance as "reminiscences" that are later on completely lost.

It seems to me that there was some such reminiscence, in a brief encounter at the beginning of our journey in Lausanne. This happened when an American girl, Cecile, whom I liked very much, suddenly and without reason showed antagonism toward me and, along with two boys, began to "wage war" against me. I resisted courageously being taken captive when they tied me up. With the strength of desperation, I defended myself against the three stronger children and freed myself successfully. Yet I felt a certain wistfulness over this victory. Cecile's summer hat was left floating in the fountain. No petty antipathy, only knightly honour resided in such feelings, belonging to another age.

My mother, who had been inactive in Moscow and frequently sick, developed a lively interest in child welfare abroad and visited children's homes and schools in Paris. She also wanted to get to know such homes in Brussels, so we travelled from the North Sea to this city. There a young Russian moved in with us who, despite her aristocratic descent, was an anarchist. On her recommendation I attended the Free School in Brussels for several months, so called in contrast to the Catholic schools. Two older daughters of our neighbour, the well-known socialist, Professor DeGreef, also went to this school. They put a few revolutionary ideas into my head. But a revolution was already taking place in me. My mother wanted to raise me and Alyosha in the Orthodox religion. Every Sunday we had a lesson with her, in which she taught us Russian prayers. I felt the need to protect myself from her vehement approach. I was religious, but doubted the necessity of a church. Alone in the sleepless hours of the night, I drew up a kind of confession, and wrote my "theses" on a sheet of paper:

> One does not need a church. (By "church" I meant a building.) The whole of nature is God's temple and natural science is divine service. Priests are not needed, since all are equal before God. One does not need prayers, since everyone has to speak with God in his language. Either there are no miracles, or every flower, every crystal is a miracle.

I carried this piece of paper, folded together, in the pocket of my black smock, which all schoolgirls wore over their dresses in Belgium. I believed that this declaration, which I wanted to communicate to my mother, would be a terrible blow to her. I therefore postponed the step of giving it to her until her return from her planned trip to Moscow. On the first evening after she came back she told us, full of enthusiasm, of her meeting with an idealistic elementary school teacher, described her self-sacrificing life and gave a thorough account of a religion lesson, at which she had been present, and in which this teacher had taught the village children the Lord's Prayer. Now the truth began to dawn on me regarding the nature of this prayer and of prayer altogether, as well as with regard to the essential nature of the Church, which is not only a physical building, but an invisible edifice made up of souls in heaven as well as on the earth. I went up to my room and ceremoniously burnt my "theses" in the stove.

Until then, nature and natural science had occupied me most of all. When my father, on a visit to Paris, gave us a microscope — a very good one, a Chevalier — and we went home after making this purchase, I was in a festive mood and said, "Now nature can have no secrets from us anymore!"

I liked to paint, but the pictures in the Louvre that I saw at that time, interested me only according to their content. When Madamoiselle Wilken was able to name the school to which a picture belonged on first sight, and I had checked the Baedeker and found that she was right, she appeared to me gifted with magical powers. That spring, however, a greater understanding for art awoke in me. It began in Bruges where I admired Memling, and attempted to make a drawing of the spiritualized figure of St Catherine. And in Holland it was the art of Rembrandt that made a deep impression on me, particularly his picture *The Night Watch.* How unrecognizable it became after the restoration! In experiencing the weaving of light and darkness on and around objects, the lighting up of colour, I felt I began to approach the realm of art.

And now came the trip to Italy. In Milan, where we met up with my father, we looked at Leonardo's *Last Supper,* not yet restored. It was no more than a bare trace, like the dusting of colour on a butterfly's wing, and yet what incredible life, what motion went through the group of apostles! Subsequently, after it was restored, I did not find this life anymore. In Florence, where we occupied a villa entwined with white and yellow roses not far from the Cassino Park, I had the feeling of having found my home again. The colour of the Florentine sky, the bridge over the Arno, the Piazza della Signoria, the names I heard, pictures and statues I saw, everything spoke a familiar language. Our lessons continued as before, except that Kittie dictated a biography of Raphael to us, and historical novels were read to us in the evenings, in which Savonarola and other Florentine figures were described. The main experience of Florence, in fact of Italy altogether, was for me at that time, Raphael. I could immerse myself for hours in his pictures, follow the gestures of his figures that shone as though in the golden light of sunset. The inner soul-sun that revealed itself in these pictures, entered into me like a renewing life-stream, as though right into my blood. And what feelings, experienced almost as thoughts, rose up in the child's soul in Rome in contemplating his *Disputa.* I attempted to get to the bottom of this picture with its mutual interpenetration of different worlds.

Later, in the subjective moods of youth, I could not make much of Raphael. He was too impersonal for me, too general, and his "perfection" no longer spoke to me. Still later, however, as a mature individual, I rediscovered him and comprehended my earlier childish delight. I understood Herman Grimm, in saying that in Raphael we have one of the four streams that flow directly out of Paradise.

Rome, where we lived in a series of rooms in a hotel on the Piazza d'Espagna, was then still similar to what it was in the time of Goethe, the time of Gogol and the painter Alexander Ivanov. The Forum and the other ruins were not fenced off from the streets. Grass grew around them and they were partly covered in ivy. There was much that one had to look for on one's own. The general population still went about in national costume. The primitive vegetable stands and markets were wonderfully lush and colourful. In my album I drew ruins, Roman types, the heads of Roman emperors and tribunes in the Capitol Museum. An old friend of Alexandra, the old-fashioned miniaturist Rizzoni, took us around the city to picturesque trattoria, and to the studios of then well-known modern painters, as well as into the ghetto. That was my strongest impression. Suddenly we found ourselves in a world, which so startled me at first that I did not want to go on; a street with shabby laundry hanging all askew, through which dirty water ran as in a sewer. Feet slipped on peelings, garlic, the remains of fish and all kinds of rubbish. From the dark doorways old people looked out, with hair that hung out from under a headscarf. Beautiful, half-naked children with frizzy hair played there. In the eyes of the old men I encountered a primal astuteness.

The faces of the people allowed me to forget the dirt and shouting of this nether world. I saw girls with luxuriant, completely red or blue-black curls and skin that shone like moonlight. How finely formed their hooked noses were, how well-shaped the lids around their dark eyes! I had never yet seen such beauty in my life. Through the depravity of the surroundings one had a presentiment, in these colourful rags, of a royal, indeed a god-like race, from which these human beings were directly descended and that had impressed its form on them.

And another unforgettable image: Spanish pilgrims came to Rome, bringing relics of a saint from Spain, who was to be canonized by the Pope. Leo XIII, who otherwise rarely showed himself in public, celebrated a mass in St Peter's. The brother of the doorman in our hotel belonged to the Swiss Guard, thus we were allowed to stand in St Peter's near the place where the pope was carried past. The crowd was so dense that my little brother would have been crushed if a clergyman had not taken him on his arm. While the Pope was being carried from the Vatican to St Peter's, the cheers of the populace in the church were like an ever-increasing surge. The distant chorus gradually drew nearer and filled the whole space. *"Viva il Papa, il Re, viva il Prigionero!"* I saw above me the intelligent, fine, translucent face of the Pope, as though carved of ivory, and his hand with an amethyst ring raised in blessing. His appearance was almost like that of a mummy. The fanaticism, the frenetic ecstasy of the people appalled me, that of the Spanish women in particular.

When we all stepped out of the church and looked out from the steps onto the magnificent square, it seemed enlivened by a colourful mass of people, much bigger and more majestic than before. The Spanish pilgrims pursued us in visiting the churches and catacombs. I was quite apprehensive about them when they scratched out stones from the mosaics in the columns with their nails, or rubbed their clothes on the holy monuments. Many years afterwards I met Russian pilgrims, simple peasants, who had come from Jerusalem to Rome, and whom I was able to accompany on their pilgrimage to the holy shrines of Rome. Theirs was another spirit.

In art it was now mainly the Sistine Chapel that signified a stupendous experience for me. In all his works, Michelangelo transported one into a remarkable state, as though a storm were taking hold of one; it was as though something germinal still lived around these works, seeking embodiment. I felt this especially during our stay in Florence on the return journey, in his unfinished works, and in the sketches in his house.

In the meadows around Lake Lucerne the large pale yellow primroses were in bloom when we returned from Italy. At that time, I occupied myself exclusively with painting. I wanted to paint a large picture: the vision of Isaiah. My youngest cousin had to pose as a model for the prophets, for the angel, for the god Sabaoth. Again, later on, she had to stand, sit, lie, crawl, ideally fly — in a word, serve me as a model in every possible and impossible position, which she patiently did. The angel held a pair of fireplace tongs with a piece of coal, which was to come into contact with the mouth of the prophet and my picture came to grief because of these tongs; in such an ugly manner did they disrupt the composition.

After all these great things, one might think, any kind of further enhancement would be impossible. And yet the summer in the Engadine was in a sense the crowning experience of our journey. In this region the air is permeated by the sound of innumerable ice-cold streams, above which one directly senses the black abyss of space beyond the illumined atmosphere. The larches had turned yellow when we rode on horseback over the Bergell to Chiavenna and through the gorge of the Via Mala on the way back.

Our final stop abroad was the Weisse Hirsch near Dresden. There we spent several weeks in a branch of the sanatorium of Dr Lahmann, from whom we learned modern hygienic viewpoints and brought home with us guidelines for a rational way of life, for example, an almost meatless diet. Before our departure for Moscow, the news arrived of the death of Alexander III. On this evening we went to the Dresden opera, in order to hear Richard Wagner's *Tannhäuser*for the first time. But I felt obligated to be very sad and to think the whole time of the Tsar. Thus the revolutionary ideas I had acquired in Belgium were not so far along. As regards Berlin, I only know that in the evening we looked at harshly lit faux diamonds in a shopping arcade, and that we could not fall asleep on account of the music from a variety show in our hotel.

Then came Warsaw with Uncle Vanya and his daughters, and then Moscow.

The Strange Homeland

It can be imagined in what an expectant mood we children pulled into the Moscow railway station after three such eventful years. No less curious about the "foreign" children were our relatives, awaiting us on the platform. I had already noticed on a visit to Brussels by one of the aunts, that our foreign education was not altogether approved of in Moscow. I at once recognized our grandmother from a distance, the two uncles, Sergei and Alexei, and the aunts Alexandra, Marya, Katharina and the recently widowed Tatyana, whom I had not seen since my earliest childhood. I was struck by her great beauty. In the vestibule of the one-family house in which we were now going to live, Masha and other domestic servants awaited us. I believe Polya was the happiest of all to be returning at last to familiar surroundings; she immediately displayed her energetic activity.

Our lodgings consisted of ten beautiful, sunny rooms. We recognized the carpets, the furniture and other objects from our old house — everything was like home. To my surprise there appeared to be a black pot of buckwheat porridge on the covered tea table, such as peasants bake in the oven. On closer examination it turned out to be a layer cake, a patriotic symbol, which our aunts had brought for our reception. The mood was cheerful and high-spirited.

"We shall take a look at everything here and judge!" I said brazenly.

"With us there is no criticism, only positive achievement!" was the answer, spoken by the tall, slim, regally beautiful Aunt Katharina. I felt her to be the most loving. Aunt Alexandra, the writer, was particularly sarcastic.

The street in which we now lived belonged to the old, exclusive quarter of Moscow. Most of the houses were from the beginning of the nineteenth century and in the empire style, which had undergone a unique development in Russia, fitting itself harmoniously into the Russian landscape. These houses, painted grey, white or yellowish, with a series of columns, were usually surrounded, like country manors, with wings, non-residential outbuildings, gardens and parks. Because of that, this long and wide street, along with other parallel streets and a labyrinth of cross streets and small squares, had a patriarchal character. Old trees, for which openings were sawn out of the fences, overshadowed these little streets with their mighty crowns. In spring there was an intoxicating smell of grass, birches, poplars and lilac blossom. The numerous churches and chapels with silver or gold, or star-studded blue onion cupolas and ancient bell towers were surrounded by bushes. Between snow-covered branches, in the blue winter twilight, the candlelight could be seen shining through the low arched windows. Each house and each street had its "face"; every dog, every crow. Every sparrow appeared to me different than in the West. Everything was somehow more alive. And all the more did this extend to the people, as it seemed to me then.

Our street, the Pretshistenka, ascended on an incline from east to west, and there stood the house of the general staff, brown with white columns, and the antiquated, orange-red fire brigade building with its look-out tower. Next door to our house there was a boarding school for aristocratic girls founded by Catherine the Great. I saw these poor young girls being led in twos in a long line down our street, in old-fashioned hats and clothes worn a hundred years before; these now looked quite odd and rather ugly. Such institutes pursued the aim of shielding the girls for as long as possible from the world; here Rousseau's ideas still had their peculiar effect. In my window stood an anatomical plaster figure for the purpose of studying the muscles; the principal of the institute sent someone to tell us that they would like this figure removed from the window — young girls should not see such things.

On this street one frequently came upon students in uniform with bright buttons and blue collars, on their way from the university to the teaching hospital. Behind each one I imagined an Alexander Herzen, a Michail Bakunin, or a hero from the novels of Ivan Turgeniev. Often one also came across an old man with a flowing beard, in a peasant's smock, with a round woollen hat; small, penetrating grey eyes looked out from under bushy eyebrows. It was Leo Tolstoy, whose house was situated on a side street. Later I got to know him personally.

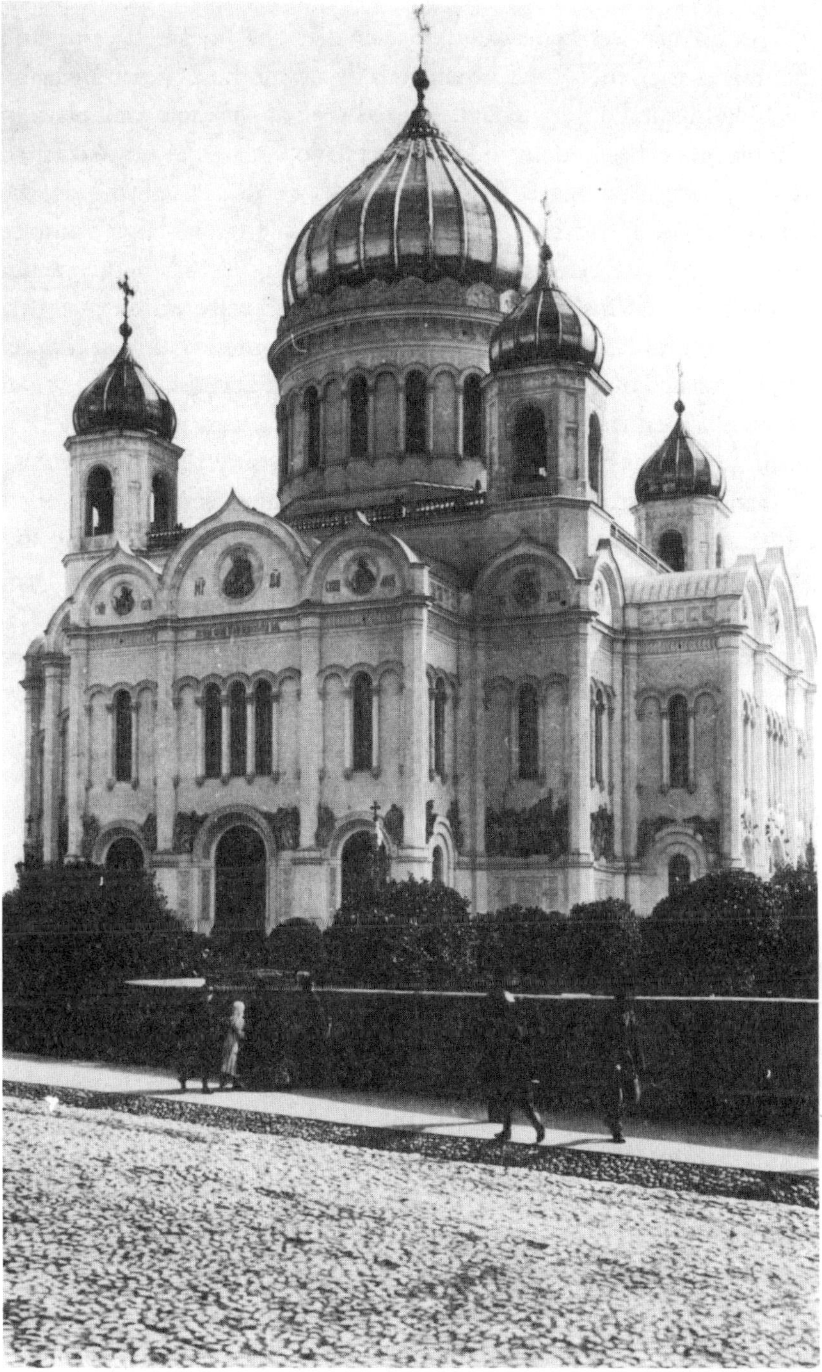

The Church of Christ the Redeemer, Moscow

The further west one went, the smaller the houses became and the longer the fences; then the grounds of the huge new university teaching hospital began, which counted then as the most exemplary in Europe. Since it served an educational purpose, patients were accepted free of charge. Compared with the weak, warm gas lighting on the streets, the dead, cold and glaring electric light from its large windows had an oppressive effect. I again felt something of that nether realm I had discovered inside my tin doll's stove at the age of four; vaguely sinister and fascinating at the same time. The grounds of the teaching hospital passed over into a broad meadow. And beyond, at the edge of a slope, loomed the white walls of the venerable and historic Cloister of the Virgin, with its massive, notched corner towers capped with red tiles, and there stood the Paradise Gate and the majestic cupola of its cathedral. If one took a footpath to the right around the high cloister wall, along the edge of a pond planted with willows, a large level area opened up: the vegetable gardens of Moscow, reaching as far as the Sperling Mountains. This cloister and these "mountains" — not proper mountains, only sandy hills formed by the Moskva River — were part of the life of many Russians.

Can it not be said that the regions we see and experience, the paths we go on, belong to us as part of our destiny, prepared by the spirit for the spirit? Are they not for that reason sacred and familiar, being so intimately bound up with our existence?

Our street began to the east, at a large compound on which stood the Church of Christ the Redeemer on the high bank of the Moskva River. This church was later blown up by the Bolsheviks. Altogether a magnificent building of enormous size, with the gold of its large cupola and its white marble reliefs! From here a splendid view opened up to the indented walls of the Kremlin, the green, pointed roofs of its old towers and its many golden cupolas, which blazed like burning candles in the setting sun. Equally colourful and picturesque was the view onto the opposite side of the river and the part of the city lying beyond.

Our first visit the next day was to our grandmother. Her astute, lively glance was directed searchingly at me. I was unusually tall for my thirteen years, and wore my curly blonde hair loose, which may well have appeared out of keeping with what was normal to her. She herself had not changed at all. The house too was the same, only it seemed smaller to me than before. There was a different smell to every room and every corridor, just as before, and all the old-fashioned, accustomed objects stood in the same places. However, in the corner of the large, low-ceilinged dining room, I saw a splendid new cast of the *Hermes* of Praxiteles, and on the wall a large reproduction of the Velázquez portrait of Pope Julius II. Aunt Alexandra occupied two rooms on the lower storey, which had very low ceilings. Beautiful original landscapes and genre pictures hung in her study. The cabinets in this room, as well as in the adjoining corridor, were full of very fine, superbly bound books. She arranged to have these bindings made herself, with considerable love and good taste. Her library of art history and literary works was both rich and extensive. Later, at the beginning of the Revolution, before everything could be taken from her, she still had time to donate her entire collection of books to the Union of Writers. In this way it was saved. Alexandra had received the same thorough education as the other daughters, but had extended and advanced it by systematic study, the only one of the ten siblings to do so. Without need of guidance or direction, she went her own independent way. Thus she was able to help her mother and take the place of her deceased father. She remained with her, sacrificing her personal life, and mediated between my grandmother and the demands of modern life. (Even though intelligent, my grandmother was still uneducated and very emotional). My aunt had helped in the education of her younger siblings and in running the businesses. The lack of physical forces, which made my grandmother nervous and irritable, she ameliorated by establishing an ordered life. In their style and emphasis on the thought content, her literary, critical essays and books had a masculine character. She belonged to a generation which, in spite of its positivism and scepticism, possessed high moral standards and was quite particularly selfless. She had fine facial features, but was not as attractive as her siblings; her arched forehead suggested a predominance of intellect, her lips were rather thin and sometimes distorted by nervousness. In her grey eyes there was both earnestness and humour. She could be sharp-tongued. I owe her a great deal. But at that time her sarcasm, her strict demand for thoroughness was irksome to my rather fantastic, pretentious nature. I had a faint suspicion that she disagreed with my mother with regard to our education, and hence harboured a small, unconscious sense of protest against her.

Our lessons with Kittie resumed the day after our return. I went with my brother to see her in the mornings. It was dark, but not cheerless in the lodgings of our old tutors. How interesting for us was the walk through the many crooked alleyways and across Arbatsky Place with its market! The little church with a mural on an outer wall, depicting St Eustace kneeling in front of a stag with a cross between its antlers, was like no other in the world. The tall elms overshadowing the little street from both sides, the antique medallions made of stucco on small wooden huts, the coloured glass of their covered porches; all this was unexpected in a large city and stirred one's imagination. In the market place, I saw the simple people — my people! Peasants in sheepskins sold hay and heads of cabbage from creaky carriages; hats with ear-flaps tied above on their heads, coloured mittens on their hands. The women wore large, colourful headscarves. I heard scolding there such as I had never heard before. I looked with interest into the faces of each of the passers-by and encountered the same astonished, questioning look. This was not the matter-of-fact, indifferent look of western people; it was as though each one asked, "Who are you?" My glance could not merely pass over them, but was caught firmly by each person. Many things appeared unusual to us in Moscow, but we too obviously attracted attention as well, due to certain foreign characteristics we had acquired.

A Motley Society

Of the sons of my grandmother, Uncle Seryosha visited us every evening, a tall individual of virtually classic good looks, with black hair and blue eyes, bordered by dark lashes. His good-naturedness amounted almost to simple-mindedness. But he possessed a wonderful talent for reading aloud; at church services he read the Epistles and the Psalms in a strong, pleasant voice. He read rhythmically, with that unsentimental, impersonal fervour which characterizes ritual speaking in Russia. My mother wanted to turn this ability of his to our advantage; perhaps she also wanted to provide him with cosy family evenings to divert him from card-playing and restaurants with gypsy women. He read us old classical works every evening, such as *Rostam and Sohrab*, *Nal and Damayanti*.[4]

His brother Alexei, equally tall and handsome, only blonde, later came to grief over wine and gypsy women. I was curious about the oldest brother, Vassily, who was seldom seen, as he lived on his estate. I was told that he lived according to certain "principles." But what principles were they? He did not handle money, for example, and had his employees pay for everything. He had his thick hair cut only once a year, very short, and then waited until it had grown again to a "Zeus mane." He wore sandals on bare feet, and a peculiar round cap on his head, worn by no one else. He was devout and interested himself in translations of Psalms, without an underlying guiding thought. Limited in the same way as the two other brothers, he only had less humour. He also had less of their easy-going, unassuming nature, in telling the same anecdotes and being the first to laugh, so that in the end one had to laugh as well.

At that time my Uncle Michail, the youngest, had chosen a diplomatic career in St Petersburg. He was more delicate in health than the others, almost feminine, and blushed easily, betraying a certain nervousness. To me he was a riddle. Did a deeper, more serious soul-life perhaps conceal itself after all behind his easy manner and well-nigh cynical opportunism? I could not make him out. Confronted by my direct, probing questions, such as only young people put, he hid behind ironic answers. Quick off the mark and very funny, he had complete command of many languages. Even when speaking Russian, he trifled with a slight English accent. Perhaps he was looking to find the perfect social form in diplomatic circles. Later he became an attaché of the Russian legation in Stockholm, Tokyo and Munich and was just about to be transferred to Rome, when overtaken by the Revolution in Moscow. Being a diplomat of the old regime, he was put in prison, from where, however, he was able to escape abroad. Needing a secure livelihood, he was happy to find it in Innsbruck with the Jesuits. There, at the age of fifty, he sat in school, together with young theology students. He eventually died in Innsbruck as a Jesuit father.

I have to mention another figure who haunted the house of my grandmother, Aunt Shilova, a distant relative of my grandfather. She had been taken in because she was a bit abnormal and wore a peculiar, high hood, which rose above her low forehead making her spindly figure appear still more so. Her face, with little red cheeks and protruding eyes was mask-like. She went through the rooms as though borne by the wind, rustling her silk skirts. When she received visits from her poor relatives, she treated them haughtily, whereas my grandmother showed them respect.

Every Sunday, acquaintances and relatives gathered in my grandmother's large, lower dining hall for tea; there were magnificent gateaux and tartlets. At the end of the long table, at the samovar, sat my graceful, cheerful Aunt Marya, who that same year married Prince Dimitri Volkonski. During our time abroad, we had had almost no acquaintances — I was starved for people — and the guests who frequented this house were no ordinary ones. There was the famous lawyer, Prince Alexander Ivanovitch Urusov, a representative of the old, aristocratic order; a tall figure, whose rather too fashionable clothing did not quite go together with his grey hair. Later, I often visited his house and he showed me his large library, in which he had added annotations, newspaper clippings and critical articles to every book. Relics of his friendships with famous actresses were also preserved in cabinets; collections of their pictures and letters, programmes, newspaper reviews, dried flowers, gloves, little ribbons etc. His intimate friendship with the great Eleonora Duse had also found a memorial here. I was permitted to look at photographs of this great artist, from her youth until the last years. He knew how to embellish his life with a certain style. He was known as a connoisseur of French literature, and promoted Flaubert and Baudelaire, reciting masterfully from their works. He once wanted *Lisez Flaubert* (Read Flaubert) inscribed on his tombstone. My grandmother, who did not understand French, remained sitting at the table during these readings, as did Aunt Shilova, who at once nodded off, and then awoke with a start, repeatedly crossing herself and murmuring a prayer, thinking she had fallen asleep in church during the reading of the Epistles.

The young, gifted architect Modest Durnov with his fiery, sombre, somewhat Mongolian eyes, the lopsided smile of his dark lips, his biting sarcasm, appeared to me "demonic." I felt him to be in some way split in the depths of his soul. Coming from a modest background, he made a career as an architect. His considerable ambition and his passions stood in contradiction to his otherwise distinguished and original thoughts. He visited us, becoming interested in my painting. Sometimes he held talks on modern painting in the Artists' Club, and invited us to attend. Whenever Prince Urusov and Durnov met with my aunts, a dazzling tournament of clever thoughts arose. But at these Sunday teas a few boring academics, colleagues of my Aunt Alexandra, professors of literature and art historians accompanied by their wives, and a few writers, also appeared. They seemed filled with a sense of their own importance, and from time to time one sensed a kind of envy of my aunt, since, as a well-to-do member of the middle class, she had ascended to the hierarchy of intellectuals. Yet she was no dilettante: she became a member of the Society of Literary Arts by virtue of her serious literary achievements. And this amounted to acceptance into the Academy. She endured her colleagues with humour.

Among our earlier acquaintances, the young officer Vladimir Krassovsky was the only one to visit us. He spent every evening with us and was very devoted to our family. We soon noticed that he was in love with my younger cousin.

Nyusha (i.e., Anna or Annusha) was then seventeen years old. With her large, brownish-grey, shining eyes she looked out confidently into the world. Both sisters had fine, dense eyebrows; called "marten brows" in Russia, these belong to the Russian conception of beauty. Her older sister, Elisabeth, was tall, had an aristocratic nose and a small mouth. Nyusha was of medium height, with supple limbs and slow movements. Her speech was even slower. She had a petite snub nose and a well-formed mouth. She could not quite deal with her abundant, splendid chestnut-brown hair and, therefore, twisted it into a smooth, spiral form. She had begun taking singing lessons. I have never since heard such a lovely, warm voice. A friend once said, "If someone can sing so beautifully, why should they speak?" Nyusha almost never spoke in front of strangers. There were people who had gone in and out of our house for years and yet had hardly heard a word from her. She sat silently behind the samovar and poured tea. When we were alone among ourselves, she could be quite humorous and tell stories. At a masked ball, on the stage, in playing charades, when made up, she was suddenly transformed and revealed herself as a brilliant comedienne. Her calmness sometimes irked me. We lived together in one room, and before going to sleep, I would talk about all manner of things, impressions of intense interest to me, wanting to know her opinion, since she was extraordinarily impartial. "What do you say to that, Nyusha, what's your opinion?" Silence followed. The silence lasted a long time. I waited. Probably she is already asleep, I thought, and then, after ten minutes she would say, "I really don't know." But when she did know something, then she knew it with certainty, and one had to reckon with her words, for they carried weight.

To further our education, my mother hired a teacher of the history of literature, Lebedyev, a professor in a cadet corps. He wore a uniform with a red collar and gold buttons and appeared quite good-looking with his full beard. What he said was altogether nebulous, however. He stuttered, repeated himself and one did not know what he was aiming at. He brought us reading matter from his library, very thick books: Xenophon, Caesar, Tacitus and other antique works in translation. These lay on my table for months without my studying them thoroughly. He did not introduce us to this reading matter and never asked us about it. I read only a few things with any real enthusiasm: old Indian dramas, Greek tragedies and Dante. I could not see any underlying plan in his teaching. Having briefly touched on Dante, he remained a whole winter on the subject of Giovanni Boccaccio. I still recall the coughing fits, with which I was seized at one moment and Nyusha the next, when we had to read the *Decameron*during the lesson. Without batting an eyelid the professor took up the book and read the novella to its conclusion. I believe he was not quite in his right mind. How could my mother have talked with him for hours about our education without noticing anything? Probably, it was because he agreed with everything she said.

At that time Mrs Avenarius played a large role in my life. She was an old friend of my mother's, a Russian of German descent. She had married a widower, who after his death left her his little daughter from his first marriage, a sickly child of my own age. The stepmother raised the child with the greatest love. So that her Nadya would not grow up alone, she adopted a second girl of the same age, also called Nadya. To distinguish them, she then called her Nadya, Nadyusha. All of us together were now to have history lessons with Mr Lebedyev. More order prevailed in these lessons than in the literature lessons, because Mrs Avenarius was always present herself, and because we had a good history book to prepare us and had to write essays one after the other. Since our friends lived on the other side of Moscow, the lessons took place alternately at their house and at ours. At the time I did not feel I had much in common with the two girls, but I loved their tasteful house. I admired Mrs Avenarius with her selfless, down-to-earth qualities, her single-mindedness, her clear, thoughtful decisions, even though these often appeared to me rather conventional. I recall this mature, kind-hearted woman with the deepest gratitude. Despite my fantastic nature, which must have been alien to her, she tried to help me. I came to regard her irregular, equine face with bucked teeth and small, dark, kind eyes, as beautiful. She alone I forgave a lack of understanding in visual art and literature! After the history lesson we would stay for supper, and Mrs Avenarius gathered us at the piano for choral singing of Russian folk songs with their slow wistfulness, suddenly interrupted by amazingly high-spirited refrains. These left me deeply touched by the spirit that lived in my people. This folk spirit was also something I encountered in the character of the city of Moscow.

The Coach Trip through Moscow

To reach Mrs Avenarius' house, one had to drive through the entire city. From our patriarchal, aristocratic Pretshistenka Street, the route went past the Church of the Redeemer, past old, architecturally valuable private houses to the magnificent Rumyanzev Museum, a sanctum that shone like an acropolis on a hill overgrown with bushes. It was not only a sacred place by virtue of the wonderful harmony of its architecture, effective every time one saw it, but also on account of what it contained and what emanated from it spiritually. The rich, lovingly collected and managed State Library was located there. In the large reading room with two rows of windows I always felt a religious mood. Later, the portrait of a deceased librarian, Nikolai Fyodorov, hung in the entrance hall. As a quite humble employee of the library, he had enriched its treasures immeasurably by means of his comprehensive learning. If he noticed someone studying earnestly, he approached them, endeavouring to be helpful in every way. He found the right books for them, guided them in their studies and gradually became their spiritual adviser. If he inferred that his charge was in financial need — many students at that time in Russia had to survive on very little — he helped them out by means of his small salary. He had written a book, *Common Deed*. His idea was that all the thoughts of humanity that strove for truth, in complementing one another, wove *Christi Corpus Mysticum*, i.e., built an invisible Church. He was the soul of this house. Tolstoy once visited the State Library. (This occurred in my youth, when Tolstoy was already quite old.) Fyodorov was fetched, since he had the most extensive knowledge. Having been given a guided tour, the great author said, "But all this is after all only useless junk."

Wounded in his most sacred convictions, Fyodorov retorted, "Old fool!" and left the hall.

Tolstoy, who was very sorry to have hurt the man, went to his lodgings to ask his forgiveness, but was not received by Fyodorov.

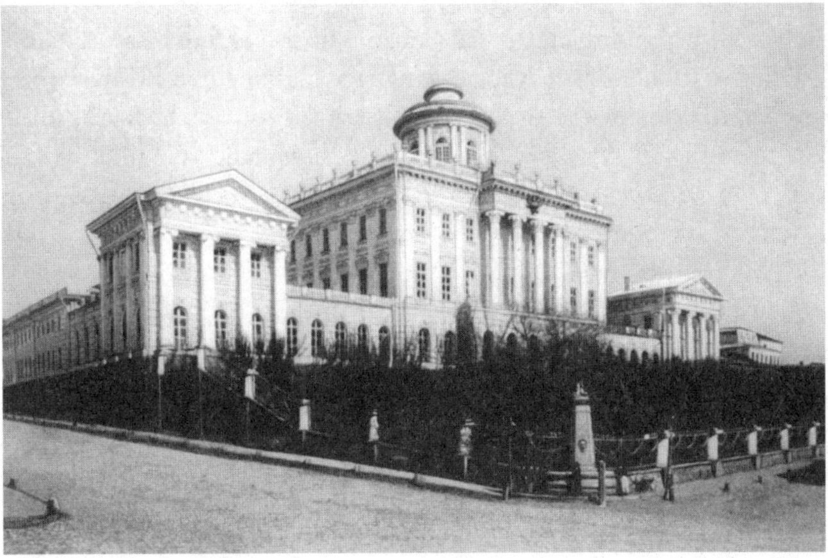

The Rumyanzev Museum, Moscow, around 1910

In the beautiful, sunlit halls, along with ethnographic collections, there was also a small, select range of pictures by Russian painters. The grand picture by Alexander Ivanov, *Christ Appearing to the People,* took up a whole wall of the first hall. I always welcomed the sight of this building from outside, from the carriage. But I salute it today as well, for it sheds its light into my life up to the present moment. And were a bomb to destroy this building tomorrow, with its architecture that might be called, in Plato's words, "a geometrized deity," the spiritual building would still continue to exist. So many selfless will-impulses and eternal thoughts have given substance to it. No power will be able to destroy what once arose through selfless love. It will be taken up and incorporated into the spiritual building-substance of our Earth.

Continuing, we passed by the National Archives, shimmering through the trees, white, built in the Gothic style, and therefore making a somewhat romantic and unreal impression in Russia. On the right, the "golden-headed" Kremlin appeared, on the left we drove past the old and new University buildings, painted orange, in the courtyard of which stood the memorial to its founder, the poet Mikhail Lomonosov, that son of a peasant who came to the capital on foot all the way from the White Sea without a penny in his pocket, in order to learn there. Later, he not only founded Moscow University, the Academy of Visual

Arts in St Petersburg and other scholarly institutes, but also produced the first grammar of the Russian language. Driving past this building, one had to think instinctively of all the leading spirits who had studied and taught here. They were for the most part intellectual fighters in a time of fear and general paralysis. Vassily Klyutshevsky, the outstanding historian, the now world-famous geologist, Vladimir Vernadsky, and the philosopher Vladimir Soloviev all lectured here in my youth.

Universities were also attended by the poorest, who gave lessons in order to exist, and could seldom permit themselves a warm midday meal. The university was the soul of Moscow, and the young people studying there, its conscience. In my time there was a split between the idealistic, social impulses brought by young people to the life of the university, that really lived as a genuine force in their hearts, and the content they received from the materialistic sciences and in the form of social theories. Between the deadening, antiquated tendencies of tsarist absolutism and the Orthodox Church serving it, and the no less deadening materialistic tendencies of academia, this youth had to struggle to find its path.

On the other side of the street, opposite the university, there was an unusually long building, the *manège* (riding school), built for exercise routines on horseback and public festivals. Into this riding school, students who took part in illegal gatherings at the university (any gathering was prohibited) were chased by Cossacks, and held prisoner there until they were transported to various prisons. It was very "convenient," and emblematic of Russian life, that this building stood directly in front of the university!

We drove on further, over a long, extensive plaza, the so-called Hunters' Market, at which game, fish, butter and vegetables were sold from small stalls. From among the owners of these stalls — rich, uneducated people — the political party was constituted that supported the absolutism of the tsar, the so-called Black Hundred. These "truly Russian people," as they called themselves, felt instinctively that the Russian folk soul was endangered by political Freemasonry, materialistic science and western social theories. Prompted by dull urgings they did not know what else to do, other than rant against education, persecute and organize pogroms against the Jews, while propping up the politicizing Orthodox Church. I still see these thick-set men with pot bellies, dense beards, red faces dripping with perspiration, staggering under the weight of heavy church banners. At the Hunter's Market there was a chapel, and I remember the strange mood I experienced when I once drove home from the theatre and saw these people assembled in front of the chapel for a nocturnal service. That signified a political demonstration. The next day a pogrom broke out somewhere in the provinces.

At the far end of this Hunters' Market, on the corner of the broad Tverskaya Street, stood the fine empire-style Assembly Building. Symphony concerts also took place there. I know no more beautiful concert hall than that white-columned hall. I remember particularly the ambience of the general rehearsals in the mornings, at which the faint daylight penetrating from the chancel windows appeared quite blue, compared with the candlelight of the chandeliers. The white of the hall and the columns shimmered mysteriously in this dim light. Wherever I came upon such whiteness in twilight, in the snow or on the blossoms of the white rhododendron, it conveyed for me a feeling of the presence of spiritual beings. Are angels not called "Spirits of Twilight"?

I often experienced Arthur Nikisch as a conductor in this hall. I loved these general rehearsals more than the actual concerts, to which people did not go only for the sake of the music, but also in order to glitter and sparkle themselves. The famous Moscow beauties came rustling into the front rows, accompanied by their very rich men and a squad of admirers. These beauties were indeed bewitching and marvellous to look at in their diamonds and pearls. While the ladies and gentlemen surrendered themselves to the music, their servants waited below in the vestibule, guarding the expensive fur coats wrapped in canvas bags, and often falling asleep on them. But the coachmen, if the winter cold became too much for them, danced outside around one of the big braziers burning on the corner of large squares, while clapping their hands.

To the right, between two red brick buildings in the Russian style — the Historical Museum and the City Hall — the little chapel was located with the miracle-working icon of the Mother of God of Hybernia, in front of which praying people crowded all day long. At night the sacred image was driven from house to house in a four-horse, closed carriage accompanied by priests. A rider with a torch rode ahead of the carriage. The two coachmen in the box seat were not permitted to wear hats and tied a cloth around their heads instead when there was a severe frost. Once a year, the sacred relic was also brought in this manner to my grandmother during the night.

Our route went further, beyond Theatre Square with its imposing large Opera House and the Little Theatre, where classical dramas were performed. Here the so-called Chinese Wall began as well as the original lively and colourful shopping area of Moscow. This is where the famous Sandunovsky Baths were situated, which surpassed the Baths of Caracalla in size and splendour. In an enormous marble hall, through clouds of steam, one saw naked figures washing themselves with zealous speed, or being rubbed dry by naked women bath attendants who wore nothing but small aprons. In the public baths people beat themselves with bundles of birch branches, prepared in the summer; the leaves of which swell up in the steam. My mother believed one could not get as clean in the bath at home and required us to drive there; it was a horror for me. Until then I did not know that the human body could be so ugly; there were skinny and fat witch figures! One could really only compare this scene with hell. Will a time not come for us after death, when people appear in front of each other undisguised? Only then shall we recognize ourselves in our ugliness and have to bear it, in order to arrive at purification! In Russian life we often see pictures that are like precursors of the future. Does one not find these soul-realms in the novels of Dostoyevsky, where one person stands naked before another?

We still continued driving, now through the bustle and chaos of the actual commercial centre, where the old Chinese Wall, small chapels, American sky-scrapers, "empire" houses disfigured by posters, merged into a peculiar motley world. In summer there was an indescribable din from wheels fitted with iron, rolling over cobblestone streets. There was confusion in the completely disorderly traffic, in which collisions and a lot of cursing arose. One saw endless columns of heavy wagons pulled by immense horses and accompanied by wildly yelling Scythians. There were simple droshkies with scraggly ponies, single farmer's carts, light elegant carriages of members of the upper class. In addition, there was the same stark contrast among different types of people: fat complacent traders, refined and elegant ladies and gentlemen, people tattered and embittered in their poverty. All too often one saw ugly scenes on the

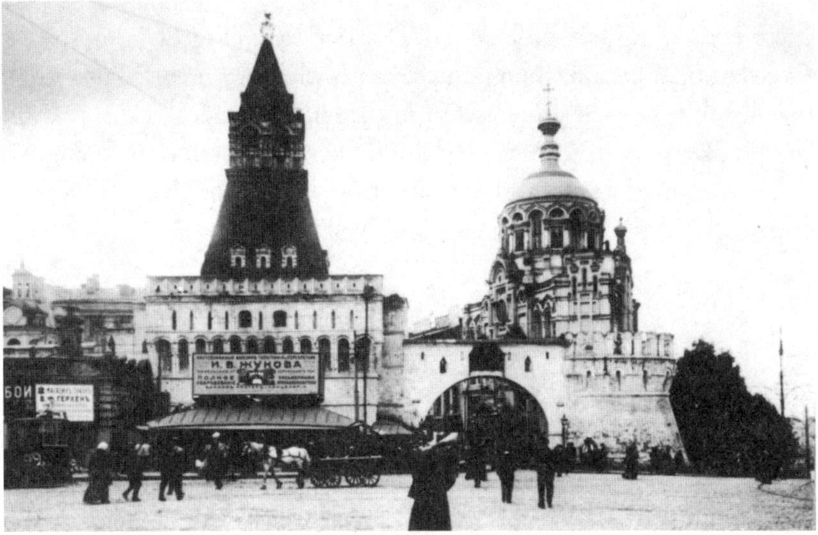

The Chinese wall and the Epiphany Church

street, a drunk would fall to the pavement. If a policeman whistled, calling a droshky coachman to take this helpless person to the police station, the droshky coachmen in their long blue kaftans only hit their ponies, disappearing into the side streets, wanting to evade this unpaid duty. Suddenly the street would be free of droshkies.

Often the strange feeling overcame me, as though this whole mad world would have to plunge into the abyss.

The broad street certainly became more orderly where the post office building stood, next to the large painting school, and opposite it, the little old Church of Prolus and Laurus, patron saints of horses. On the feast days of these saints many horses were brought there to be blessed, decked out in their finery. Next to this little church there was a tea house, where peasants of the most diverse orientation gathered on Sunday mornings — those belonging to various sects, traditional believers, atheists, followers of Tolstoy, as well as the Orthodox — all wanting to discuss spiritual questions. Later on, I attended these interesting meetings with my brother, until they were prohibited by the police. This exceedingly long street led into the Red Gate Plaza and, at the historically famous little Church of the Three Saints, our carriage turned into a small cul-de-sac, in which the quiet house of Mrs Avenarius was situated, surrounded by a garden.

Here everything was ordered, with a friendly, bourgeois atmosphere. Conventional pictures hung on the walls, the brown coffee pot stood on the table; one felt protected from the chaos outside. At this point, I should like to say in advance that this domesticity retained its bourgeois order the longest when the Revolution broke out, but the Terror eventually struck these dear people as well.

Auspicious Signs

At Christmas, together with the Avenarius family, we undertook a little journey to the historical monastery of St Sabbas[5] near Zvenigorod in order to go skiing there for a few days. When we saw the monastery and the large, ancient cathedral in the evening after a long sleigh ride, the monumental building gleamed a soft white in the moonlight amid dense pine trees, which loomed into the starry sky as if cast in silver. We entered the cathedral and were received by festive choral music. The murals and the gold of the iconostasis glimmered in the warm, dim candlelight.

The monastery hostel was situated right in front of the monastery. These hostels were known in Russia, in contrast to other guest houses, for their cleanliness, but especially for their good, sumptuous catering. Monks were usually good cooks. Fish from the White, the Black and the Caspian Sea, from the Volga and other rivers and lakes were expertly prepared. During the long fasting period it was not permitted to eat meat. What fish soups and fish pies could be had there! We had not chosen this stay for ascetic reasons.

The next day my brother became sick with scarlet fever; my mother remained with him in the monastery and the rest of us travelled home.

On the upper floor of our house there was a low, spacious room; suitcases stood along the walls. A large mirror hung opposite the windows. I fled to this room if I was in an elevated or sad mood. There I performed fantastic dances, recited poems or sang. Once I saw a face in the mirror against the light, surrounded by an aureole of gold, two very earnest eyes bored themselves into me with the question, "Who are you?"

"I am I, and all the possibilities in me and the whole inevitableness."

These were the exact words I told myself at that time. This thought went through me like lightning and it shook me. One still unknown to me, that had already determined my path, looked through these eyes. I knew ... I bore my destiny in me; I had brought it with me. But at the same time I could choose, and could also miss opportunities and go wrong. Necessity and freedom, both were in me.

Following this experience, I saw through other human faces into their being, revealing themselves in their destiny and in their freedom. I experienced this polarity, at first unconsciously, later more and more consciously; first in terms of feeling, then in actively coming to terms with life.

My birthday was in January. I was thirteen years old. My mother was still looking after my brother in the monastery and my father asked me what I would like as a present. "Baudelaire, *Les fleurs du mal,*" was the answer. "The Flowers of Evil." The good man went to the bookstore and asked for the book. This work, however, was forbidden in Russia by the censor, and instead he brought me two other volumes by Baudelaire: *Petits Poèmes en Prose* and *Les Paradis artificiels*.[6] I did not find a connection with the second volume, whereas I soon knew the little *Poèmes* by heart. I particularly loved one called "The Gifts of the Moon." I myself wrote at this time my own little prose poems, created out of a world that had neither to do with my surroundings nor with my reading matter. On certain evenings I would feel now something is there that wants to take on form; I attempted to become conscious of it, just as one tries to do with a dream that has slipped away. Rhythms and images emerged in this way that had been surmised, joining together to complete each other. It was a hard task and it was often three o'clock in the morning before I had it and knew the piece by heart; then I quietly went to sleep and wrote it down only the next day. This period of time, from my twelfth to my fifteenth year, was filled with such pictures, the significance of which I only now begin to understand. In painting it was like that too. At first, painting from fantasy appeared to me an impermissible venture. Then I risked it all the same. I remember how I was once so astonished by a large picture that seemed to have come off successfully, inasmuch as it corresponded to the inner picture, that I got up several times during the night and went into the next room where it was, to convince myself that I had not merely dreamed it. Aunt Katharina and her artist friends found my creations very interesting, without necessarily having considered the pedagogical effect of praise.

For the first time, I experienced spring in Russia consciously; even in the city of Moscow it was tremendous in its magic. The damp earth breathed, the sap-filled grass shot up everywhere between the cobblestones and on the courtyards. With the fresh foliage of the birches, it was as though green angels swung censers in their branches. And this fragrance mingled with the incense coming from the doors of all the churches and chapels, for it was the great season of Lent.

During Holy Week we went to every service in a small neighbourhood church, full of simple folk. It was as if one was embedded in the substance of piety, which probably lived in this form only in Russia. For confession, however, which has to precede communion, we drove to the church at the Red Gates, which the Avenarius' attended; the old priest there was said to be very wise. Quiet reigned in the church while those confessing stood in a line in front of the folding screen behind which the priest received the confession of each person. From time to time, deep sighs were to be heard under the vault, followed by the soft parting prayer of the priest. I remember that it was as if an abyss opened up before me, when the last person in front of me disappeared behind the folding screen. I no longer know much about the confession itself, only how the priest covered me with the stole in saying the prayer. We drove homeward through the city. In the spring twilight the gas lanterns appear golden, the silhouettes of the houses stood out black against the pale green sky. The celestial spaces opened up alarmingly and at the same time auspiciously. Something vibrated in space filled with budding forces. The cool air streamed into the eyes, moist with emotion. It was as though One who is invisible and infinitely beloved was quite near. I repeated to myself the words of the priest, "The Holy Spirit weaves in nature. By means of the creation, the Creator can be recognized."

For the first time, I experienced the night service from Easter Saturday to Easter Sunday. Dressed completely in white, we went to our church after eleven o'clock at night. In the semi-darkness, one heard the choir singing in a minor key — these are the words of the women and the disciples who seek Christ, lamenting. Then there is silence. The first stroke of the bell in the large tower in the Kremlin is awaited. Then all the bells of the forty times forty churches in Moscow reply, as well as those of the surroundings. A procession goes around every church with the sacred banners leading the way; everyone holds a lighted candle. The chiming of bells is so strong, it drowns out the choir. Chinese lanterns flicker along the streets and on the bell towers, making the night quite bright. Arriving once again at the church entrance, the priest finds it locked. The church now represents "Christ's sepulchre." He knocks. From inside the words ring out, "Christ is arisen." At this, the choir starts jubilantly singing, "Christ is arisen. In death He has conquered death and granted life to those who are in coffins." The people enter the church, in which all candles now burn brightly. Each one kisses the other three times with the greeting, "Christ is arisen," and receives the answer, "Truly, He is arisen." Meanwhile, the priest goes from one chancel to another and opens all altar doors as a sign that the spiritual world is now accessible and, turning from time to time to the congregation, he proclaims, "Christ is arisen," and like the roar of the sea, there rolls back to him, "Truly, He is arisen!" I believe there were no atheists on that night who did not become devout in their hearts.

In the year 1918, during the Revolution, we experienced the following. At the end of a large anti-religious rally a village priest indicated that he wanted to speak. There was no wish to grant him this. "Only three words!" he requested. "Well then, say your three words, but no more," the chairman sneered. The priest climbed up to the podium, turned to the assembled people and called out in a loud voice, "Christ is arisen!" And as if with one voice came the response, "Truly, He is arisen!" The old man was immediately arrested and led away. His fate can be imagined.

To come back to my first Russian Easter celebration ...

After this church service the Easter Mass began in which the beginning of St John's Gospel was read, "In the beginning was the Word." In the cathedrals it is read in twelve languages, in ordinary churches in three; Greek, Slavic and Russian. First one hears it from the depths of the chancel, then it comes to the gallery, then it resounds in the church itself. At this mass, during the transubstantiation, the priest prays for suicides. In my youth, intercession on behalf of their souls was forbidden in the Orthodox Church, probably because the demons of suicide were dangerous for the living. On that night, however, the forces of good were victorious. In a white tent pitched against an outside wall of the church, the cylindrical yeast cakes (*kulitsh*) with red roses made of paper were set out, as well as a sugar lamb ornamented with gilded horns, and the *paska*, a pyramid made of pressed, sweet curd cheese. On the plate next to it there were eggs in variegated colours and a lighted candle, so that the whole display was quite picturesque. From every household these things were brought to be blessed. The priest, who on this night wore a golden robe, sprinkled everything with holy water and each person took their things home with them in a bundle. At the door of the church there was a large table, on which everyone laid money, eggs, a piece of *kulitsh* or *paska*; this was immediately distributed among the poor by the priest.

When we arrived home for the sumptuous and colourful Easter meal, I received my Easter present: the book *The Light of Asia* by Edwin Arnold, translated from English by my Uncle Ivan. It is the Buddha legend. I began to read it at once and was so enthralled by it that I could not do otherwise than dance through the whole suite of rooms. Dance was my refuge both in joy and in pain.

In that year my mother joined an association for the welfare of the poor. Each member voluntarily assumed responsibility for the welfare of the poor in several houses. My mother displayed a lot of energy for this; she also set up a private, free, job placement office. This office was at first located in a small, forgotten cross street leading to the Moskva River. Later on, this undertaking grew to the point where it was taken over by the city of Moscow. Old people's homes and children's homes were also established. At that time the meetings of this Welfare Association were often in our house. We children were able to observe everything through a chink in the door and mimicked the phrases of the elegant, sentimental ladies. The misery in Russia was wretched. From time to time my mother sent me on various assignments to dark cellars and night shelters, so that I could see how things were in that no-man's land. Once, toward evening, I went to the job placement office on an assignment from her. A storm was approaching, the wind churned up the dust and the smell of the poplars, which stood out brightly against a black cloud, was intense. My pink, striped blouse swelled out in the wind, my hair fluttered. Suddenly, as I was about to cross the narrow street, a pilgrim stood in front of me, an old man in a long white shirt. I thought he wanted to ask me for alms, but he only said, "You seek good fortune in faraway places, but your good fortune is right beside you, and suffers." And went on.

We were to spend the summer on our estate, Bogdanovshina, located between Vyasma and Smolensk. We had not yet been there and waited with impatience till the house, then being renovated, was finished.

I remember the mood in Moscow at that time quite well. It suddenly became very hot and dusty. Large bunches of lilacs stood on our tables. We drank iced coffee. Through the large, open windows the noise of the droshky wheels on the cobblestones could be heard, the songs and shouts of workers repairing the houses, and towards evening accordion music. In front of the wine shop on the corner across from our house a red-haired defrocked priest carried on, drunk, cynical, forgetting any sense of decency, he danced and sang popular tunes, and was scolded and mocked by passers-by.

In the Country

Since we were on holiday, we went every day as far as the Cloister of the Virgin, in order to paint landscapes. The prospect that the student who gave Alyosha Latin lessons might come with his brother, a painter, to stay with us in the country, corresponded to my most fervent wishes.

At last things were far enough along that it was possible for us to move into the house in Bogdanovshina. Polya was sent ahead with a team of cooks and laundresses, and the servant Michailo, to organize the household. Then we travelled there too, my father, Kittie, the cousins and I. For the time being my mother remained in the city with my brother, who was recovering from measles. We travelled all night. The train stopped at every small station and during these stops, half asleep, I heard the nightingales competing with a chorus of frogs. When we stepped out at our station at six in the morning, the solemnity and purity of nature awaiting us there was so great, we had almost to expand inwardly so as to be able to take this magnificence, this purity into ourselves. The morning sun shone through the winter crops and the fresh birch leaves.

A *tarantas* (a carriage, open or covered according to the weather, in which six people can sit) waited for us. The coachman wore a blue shirt, a sleeveless Kazak made of black velvet, with a carmine sash. His little round hat had peacock feathers pinned onto it. The troika, with a large bell over the middle horse and smaller sleighbells on the harness of the other two, carried us on winding roads over a hilly plateau. Strips of emerald green alternated with dark ploughed fields. The blue of the distance unfolded on all sides in the morning light. We drove through only a few villages. They consisted of two rows of thatched log cabins, a small duck pond, and a "stork well" with a bucket hanging from a beam. The little bells of our troika lured fair-haired, barefoot children out, in torn white or pale rose shirts. Some of the children stood out with their almost angelic looks.

They ran in front of our horses to the village boundary, lined up in a row at the gate and opened it for us. Women appeared in blue, handwoven bodice-skirts (*sarafans*) with red and silver stripes at the hem, tied with a sash. They wore white embroidered blouses and carried water in two buckets hanging from a wooden yoke over their shoulders. I was struck by their easy, rhythmic gait, their heads remaining quite still as they moved. Imparting a regal quality to their greeting, they first inclined their heads a little backwards and then forwards. Bearded men ploughed the fields.

In the vast surrounding landscape there were isolated clumps of maple and linden trees.

After a two-hour drive we caught sight of the old lindens and birches of our estate. The horses first took us around a pond, through a carved entrance gate onto a broad meadow surrounded by outbuildings. The cries of the starlings and crows in the old lindens, the sunlit, shimmering splendour of their foliage, the scent of the earth and of the grass, were all intoxicating to the senses. A pine-log superstructure had just been erected over the stone lower storey of the house, still surrounded by scaffolding. I went through the lower rooms, over the terrace and into the gardens. A pathway led past a row of tall, old hazelnut trees and around the garden compound, which was not fenced in. There were no flower beds bordering the lawn. Old apple trees, which looked almost like dancing figures, because of their twisted, hollowed-out trunks, stood amid tall grass. Beyond the tall hemlock and campanula one saw swaying cornfields and distant blue forests, with meandering roads. In a corner of the garden stood an ancient linden, its mighty trunk held together by an iron ring. Its branches hung down to the ground, forming a domed roof, under which many people could stand. Within this shimmering green hall stood a table of blackened wood, built as though for giants.

I had never before seen such enormous trees as those in our garden.

I sat on a half-rotten bench at the end of an avenue where the hemlock grew as tall as a man between birch trees, and was thrilled. Then I became dizzy. I went inside, into the large sunny room on the second floor that had been designated for Nyusha and me, into my bed behind a white net curtain. My limbs hurt and I was overcome by a fit of shivering. It was measles. Between fever fantasies I heard the carpenters hammering on the scaffold and the screeching of the starlings. A workman with black hair and a fine, very distinct profile brought an icon, a countenance on dark blue enamel, and hung it up in the corner on the pine wall. I lost consciousness.

When I was permitted to get up after my illness, I went to the window and looked out at the large meadow below, through which a path led from one gate to another. Beyond a cowshed and the small estate manager's house, I looked out onto a hillside with cabins and a white church with its bell tower. The church and the tower seemed too close to each other, and Polya told me the architect had built the church one metre too narrow, with the aim of enriching himself, and when he was finished, he hanged himself in the church out of remorse. It seemed to stand under a dark sign. The old priest who had served the community before we came had gone mad. His three daughters, likewise mentally ill, still lived in the village, in the parish cabin. His successor was a drinker and suffered from a persecution complex. When the people gathered around him at the conclusion of the mass in order to kiss the cross he was holding, he struck out with it, as if defending himself against enemies. Later, having become a complete alcoholic, he threatened to burn the village. I saw him, finally tied to a farmer's cart, being driven to the Vyasma asylum.

The same year we came, the church was desecrated one night. Yet in spite of all these things, I have hardly experienced the ritual anywhere as strongly as in this church. The piety of the people, the sanctity of the earth, kept the service pure regardless of the priest.

At the point where the village began, stood the tavern. Each Sunday evening, on the green bank of the pond next to it, a colourful round-dance took place with singing, if this curious recitative shouting can be called singing. Much as frogs croak, birds sing and insects emit sounds in order to unite themselves with universal space, so these people held forth. From a distance, I could only make out the words, "I have lost my little golden ring ..." Young women and men could be seen dancing in the middle of the ring, the women moving "as a swan swims," whereas the men hopped up and down like a flame. Behind the pond and beyond the cornfields and hedgerows stood the ancient little church at the edge of the forest, in which a service for the dead was performed once a year.

In our room there was a door which was supposed to lead onto a terrace. It opened, however, into thin air, or better said, into a splendid old linden tree, since the terrace was still missing. It was also never built, because we did not want to chop down the old linden. Thus a green world of weaving shapes loomed directly toward us. A greenish-golden light, a sweet fragrance during the blossoming period and a deep humming sound like chimes filled the room; then the bundles of starry blossoms with their silver wings trembled under the burden of the hard-working bees. What a give-and-take, what a sun-imbued life!

From our third window one looked down onto the round tops of the trees of our garden, the avenue, the fields and the infinite expanse of the forests beyond. The sunsets could be awesome, such that the pine wall over my bed glowed carmine red.

Now I was able to go outside once more, and my light, eagerly hurrying feet bore me on unknown paths. The air wafting over the meadows was full of scents: thyme, clover, wormwood, daisies, fresh foliage. I felt this to be a living language of the earth. What entity received me here, spoke to me so tenderly and at the same time so mightily?

Our property lay on a high plateau that formed a watershed. Perhaps for that reason, the view on all sides reached so far, the air was so alive, the cloud formations so grand. The soil was fertile but sandy, so that the many paths which wound between fields and forests, became neither dusty, nor marshy. Something different could be experienced on each one. Each part of the countryside had its own particular "countenance" that asked to be recognized and named. I can quite well empathize with the words of Gogol when he says, "Russia, why does everything in you direct eyes so full of expectation at me?"[7] I seemed to encounter these eyes continually. A feeling of obligation to redeem the silent earth by a single word could grow to the point of anguish.

Three trails led out of the western gate. All three first went over fields, then one disappeared into an old forest, where grey birches, pines and maple trees grew in dense proximity to each other. This trail, which my father built to the peat bog, was very wide, lined with deep ditches and overgrown with grass. Juniper bushes and huge ferns grew there between tree stumps. There was a solemn feeling to this shady avenue, surrounded on both sides by an impenetrable thicket. It was as though at any moment one could meet the straggly, wrinkled *Lyeshy*, the Russian woodland sprite. Suddenly the path and the forest broke off, and across a trench one stepped onto soft, marshy ground, overgrown with white, flowering peat moss which yielded at every step. An unending forest of dwarf pines grew here and it seemed as though the sun warmed the resin-filled air more powerfully. Here and there on the peat moss, similar to edelweiss flowers, one saw shining red berries.

The mood along the second trail was quite different. It led into a bright birch grove with a meadow and a long pond. In the autumn the gold of the birches shone in magnificent colours against the deep blue of the sky and pond. Here in the copse, on a carpet of heather, one might imagine meeting the Greek god Pan with his flute.

The third forest pathway led to a remote village, which we never reached even on our outings by horse-drawn carriage. The deep ruts always remained full of water. On the forest glades, the trees stood in picturesque groups as in a park; birches, aspens and glorious pines, dense and regular to their very tops.

Our favourite walk took us on the varied path through the village, between fields and woods beyond the deserted Sikeyevo estate with its old linden park. A wall of high pines protected the orchard from the north wind and formed a circle at the end, in which we discovered a round marble pool, surrounded by a partly ruined circular marble bench. Several clumps of blossoming bushes and a half-overgrown pond remained of the former garden. Nothing was left of any buildings other than a huge shed which had caved in, the shingle-covered roof broken in the middle. It loomed amid the fields like an ichthyosaurus. We used it as a slide. In such a place, once looked after by human beings and then left again to the workings of nature, there is a peculiar atmosphere. It is as though a particular kind of elemental being ensouled it. Nowhere were the meadows and wooded areas more magnificent than around this park. Nowhere was the blue of the distance more luminous. And yet, every time I walked or rode past this estate, I came home with a feeling of sadness.

Whenever I was here in the summer holidays, I felt the need to pay attention to what the earth had to say to me. I did not want to read books, because I was concerned it might divert me from what was most important. Often I moved my bed onto the balcony over the courtyard, so as to be there at night as well, fearing I might otherwise sleep through something. Toward morning, when the stars grew paler and finally only one star flickered large and feverish over the birches, everything took on a peculiar appearance; the sheds had a severe look in the dusk, the old birches and the forests loomed like islands out of the mist. Then a slight shiver went through the tree tops and the little pond rippled with flakes of mother-of-pearl. And all at once our horses came galloping home through the gate from their night pasture, their manes aflame in the morning light. They rolled themselves in the dew, panted and whinnied. In the village the gates creaked, whips cracked, shawms sounded. The day announced itself in a thousand different tones and drove the mystery of the night away.

When it rained — and it could rain for days — how it roared, giving off a damp odour from the broad green meadow seen from this balcony. Everything green then became still greener, the wooden sheds darker, the old lindens brighter, and the pond beyond the carved gate lay like a heavy, crinkled coat of chain mail. The forests appeared farther away through the curtain of rain; for immediate experience, however, they came closer, integrating themselves into the magnificent spectacle, now immersed in the all-pervading element of water. It was as if countless beings wove sky and earth into a unity. Later, when the mechanistic theories banished such feelings, one experienced oneself separated from the world by the rain, lost in empty space. The lonely individual soul felt its existence to be still more meaningless, its isolation more profound.

My brother's nice teacher, Maxim Kontshalovsky, who had come with us onto the estate and who had interested me in Moscow, turned out, in living with us, to be somewhat superficial. He remained stuck, like so many Russian intellectuals, at the stage of scepticism and nihilism, as befits a final-year grammar school pupil. Passive, easy-going people often remain at this point all their lives. We awaited the arrival of his brother Petya Kontshalovsky, the painter, with all the more impatience.

Mother Earth

The setting sun shone through the cornfields when we drove home from the station with Petya. He won all hearts already on the first evening, including those of the grown-ups. His manner was masculine and tender at the same time, and he treated people indulgently and humorously like children. He turned with loving interest to the unassuming Kittic and our earlier governesses, who were staying with us, and to whom no one else paid any attention to. But still more tenderly did he speak with horses and dogs. The very next morning he asked my mother for permission to paint me. This time she allowed it, but for reasons of propriety she always remained present at the sittings.

For the previous weeks in Moscow Petya had worked with the famous painter Vrubel as a pupil and helped him on large decorative murals and wood carvings for a house. I knew Vrubel from his illustrations for *Evil Spirit* by the poet and novelist Mikhail Lermontov. The non-naturalistic character of his work, his way of working in crystalline surfaces, was something quite new at that time. His pupil Petya worked in the same manner. My figure arose, mosaic-like, on a variegated, geometric background. He also painted very large poppy and cornflower pictures in watercolours that looked almost like crystals, and modelled a group in clay "Andrey and the Polish Woman" based on *Taras Bulba* by Gogol, in flat surfaces.

In the evening he read us Gogol's *Dead Souls*, which I then heard for the first time. He read masterfully and, when he related something of his own, it had Gogol's colourfulness and humour. With his fine baritone voice, he sang duets with Nyusha, whom he particularly liked. But the most splendid thing was that he could drive a three-horse carriage so well. And now our trips of discovery began into the more distant countryside. I usually sat next to him on the box seat. From the side I could see from time to time how the eye of the left chestnut horse filled with dark fire. Next to me, under his beret, Petya's pale profile stood out against the sky, with his short, straight nose and a cigarette between his curved lips. He spoke quietly to the horses, one moment cheering them on at a lively pace, reining them back the next. The fast drive, the undulating fields and forests, running parallel one moment, crossing over the next like the themes of a fugue, transformed the space into music and motion. Strips of blue-green oats, emerald flax, golden corn and rosy, blossoming buckwheat, both near and far, fanned out and closed in again. For inner experience this countryside was like a remembrance; like a memory become visible, time that had become space. It was as though everything making its appearance had lived earlier within and now returned. How could we be aware of the world, without recognizing it? Individual birch trees flew towards us with branches hanging down, the blue distance beyond, with isolated, impoverished villages here and there. Occasionally a manor emerged out of the undulating fields like a dark island, a house with strange architecture hidden mysteriously behind lindens. Perhaps it was built, as often happened earlier, by a nameless serf sent to study in Italy by his master, and coming home a great artist, to serve as a slave once more. Later, art historians found many important anonymous works of art in forgotten corners of Russia. It is peculiar how harmoniously the Greek style united itself with the Russian landscape!

On one of our distant rides we came to a large field full of daisies, an endless sea of undulating white blossoms, over which silver waves shimmered in the afternoon heat. In the centre, a rectangle of ancient pines rose up like a dark island. No path led there. We got out and went through the high grass to the strange "forest cathedral." The pines grew very close together, forming a nearly impenetrable mass. In the middle we found our way into the cool, dark interior, smelling of pines. There, amid rampant dog rose bushes, raspberries, jasmine and campanula, we discovered crumbling crosses and gravestones with unreadable names. For miles around there was no village, no estate, not a trace of anything pointing to this solemn place. The beauty of this "Island of the Dead" in the silvery sea of blossoms left a strange feeling in me, and the question: Was it significant for this forgotten plot of ground, that we had discovered it, that human eyes had taken it in?

Once, on one of our outings, we came quite unexpectedly to a grandiose white baroque castle with two wings and a garden laid out in the style of Versailles. The place appeared uninhabited. The gardener, with whom we drank tea from Sèvres porcelain, took us into the castle. Passing through a hall, we stepped out onto the other side, from where the castle dropped off in terraces to the Dnieper, which was not yet very wide in this region. On the opposite bank a tiny, impoverished village could be seen, as well as endless fields and woodland. I learned later that this castle and the church belonging to it, a rotunda, were built by the famous Italian architect, Rastrelli. The estate had not been inhabited for years, since the last resident, a chief councillor, had become insane. His mother donated the castle to the district administration as a home for mental patients. Other relatives protested and the judicial proceedings lasted for decades. We visited the castle quite often. Once, when we returned there, lunatics in grey nightdresses thronged around us. Everywhere, in the park, in the church, even at large, we came across these strange figures.

When the harvest began, the surrounding fields became animated by the setting out of sheaves, and the rows of colourfully dressed woman reaping. Each cultivated strip stood out more starkly from the rest; the countryside became immeasurable. I saw Egypt here. In the Russian countryside, cutting grain is women's work, they wield the sickle. But the man sows.

Once, when it had already grown dark, I stepped out of the woods and saw a group of men and boys kneeling at the edge of a broad ploughed field. In the distance a priest in silver robes strode over this native soil as if on the waves of the sea. In his left arm he held a small basket of wheat seeds, with a lighted wax candle stuck onto the rim. He sowed while saying a prayer; in front of him a child carried a large dark icon of the Mother of God on a linen cloth. The forests stretched far away, the stars already shone in the sky, the wheat appeared golden in the candlelight. Only men were permitted to be present at this prayer service preceding the winter sowing, and I stood still behind a tree.

At the end of August, the Kontshalovsky brothers had to leave, in order to take up their studies again; one of them to the university, and our hero, Petya, who had had to repeat a year of high school the year before, to school. Thus we stayed on alone in the now "deserted" house. To our sorrow we heard that there had been strife between Petya and my mother over some trifling matter, in which we all had to admit that he was absolutely in the right. He never came to see us again.

The ponds beyond the carved gates became deep blue, the stubble fields shone, as though the earth were evolving to become a sun. The stars were large and vivid on dark frosty nights.

At this time Kittie introduced us to Greek mythology. From our stay in Italy, I knew the figures of the Greek gods, experienced there in sun-imbued marble. They seemed familiar, as though part of my being, but I am grateful to have first got to know the myths on our estate, where they became interwoven with the elemental power of the countryside. The light-filled figures of Olympus appeared in the shapes of the evening clouds. On clear autumn nights, when we lay on the high stacks of straw, higher than the roof of our large threshing floor, I recognized the names of the Greek gods in the starry script. In later years, deep, serious conversations were held on these stacks of straw with our friends who, in accordance with the Russian custom, often lingered with us for months. Each one sat in inward contemplation, without looking at each other, and questions and answers were spun as though from star to star, while the mice rustled about beneath us.

One heard the hunting bugles and the flute of the shepherd sounding across the countryside. Greece was present.

Nyusha became engaged to Vladimir Krassovsky, but she was still too young and frightened of marriage. "He looks upon me as his property," she said, and dissolved the engagement. I believe it was the only time in her life that she hurt someone and she suffered all her life because of it. Even up to her death she sought him in her dreams, in order to ask his forgiveness.

The last event of our sojourn in the country was a wolf hunt. The farmers of all the surrounding villages formed a chain that encompassed a large region in which the wolf was presumed to be. They strode in there yelling wildly; the whole forest screamed. A lot of foxes and hares ran past us, but the wolf was killed well away from the hunt in a fen by a peasant. He brought it to our house, when all the neighbouring estate owners — mostly rather odd characters — came to us after the ineffective hunt. I still see the childlike, pockmarked face of the happy hunter, with his big nose and goatee beard; he had felled the huge animal with a primitive weapon held together with string. He received three roubles for it from us.

Lucifer and the Secondary School Pupil

On our arrival back in Moscow, preparations were underway at my grandmother's house for the marriage of Aunt Marya with Prince Dimitri Volkonski. At the banquet after the wedding I sat next to the poet Konstantin Balmont, who married Aunt Katharina one year after that. On later occasions as well, I always had to sit next to him at the large family festivities in my grandmother's house. He did not fit in at all in a bourgeois, patriarchal house and gave undisguised expression to his contempt and boredom with the people there, pointing his little red beard in the air and screwing up his eyes, so that two light green slits were all that could be seen. I had to converse with him about poetic matters. On the other side of me sat my paternal uncle, Sergei Sabashnikov, still a student, who later founded a famous publishing house in Moscow with his brother, Michail.[8] A third brother, Fyodor, who lived in Paris, was known for his edition of the manuscripts of Leonardo da Vinci. Sergei surprised me with his sharp power of discernment and a scepticism which, as I observed later, concealed a sensitive, despairing soul. Most of the guests were relatives of the bride, since Prince Volkonski was not a resident of Moscow. I saw these blood relatives in some cases for the first time in my life. In almost every face I found common features, recognizing something of myself in these strange people, from whom I actually felt alien by nature. This was unsettling and the question arose for me, "What do I have to do with these people to whom I belong by blood? How does the bloodline I am immersed in relate to my being?"

That winter I received instruction from the painter Abram Archipov, who was a very good colourist. But how did he have me work? I had to draw all the curtains in his bare drawing room and draw plaster casts in charcoal by lamplight. I did that every day for two years! Only in the holidays did I paint as I wanted, on my own.

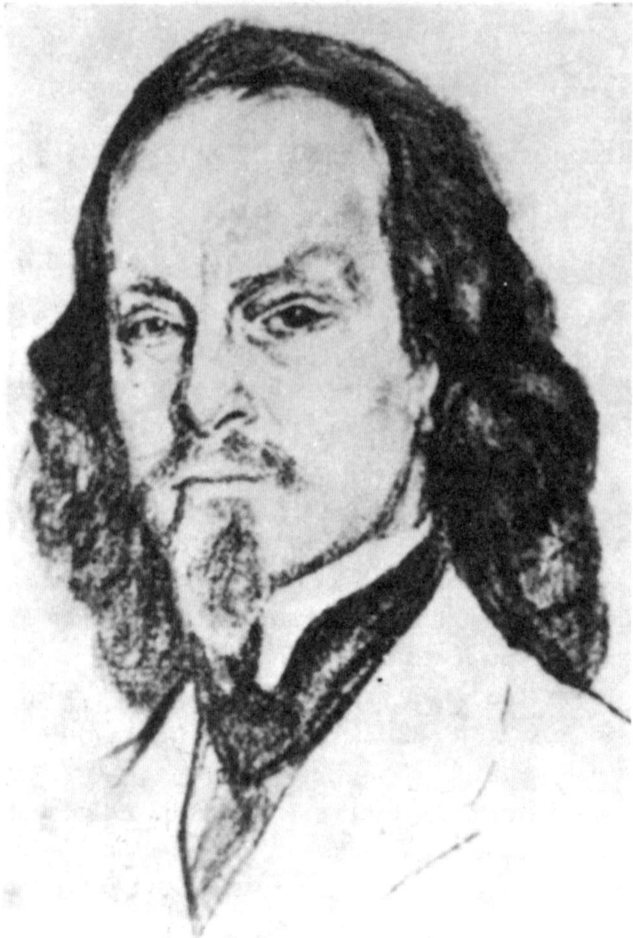

Konstantin Balmont. Drawing by Woloschin, 1909

In the spring of 1896, preparations were made in Moscow for the coronation of Tsar Nicholas II. As with all Russian intellectuals, not much was made of this occasion in our family. However, we were naturally interested in the many exotic guests to be seen in the city on these warm days in May. I particularly remember the Koreans with their remarkable, translucent black hats; but colourful skirts from Buchara, turbans from Persia, Chinese and Japanese *kurmas* also enlivened the city.

We were able to observe the arrival of the Tsar and Tsarina from the hotel at the Plaza of the Governor General, which belonged to my grandmother. We sat in a porter's lodge and were able to see the

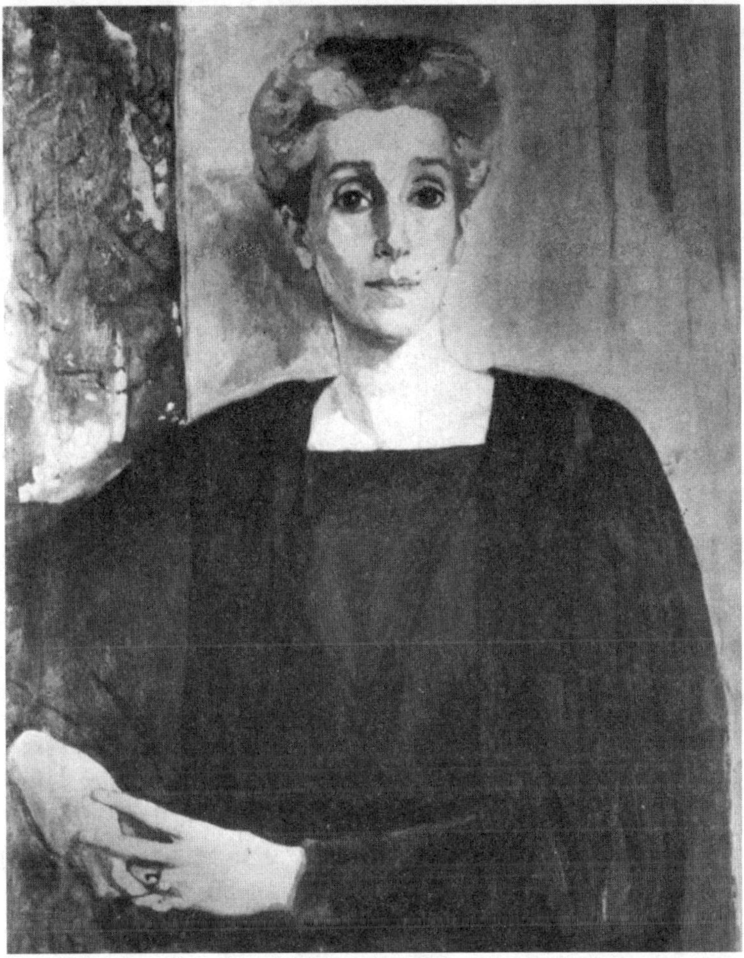

Katharina Balmont. Portrait by Woloschin, 1912

Tsar from quite close, over the heads of the guard, as he approached gradually on his horse and rode past us. He sat casually, in fact almost slumped in the saddle, his colonel's uniform appearing creased. I could discover nothing in his face other than what I had already seen on cheap oleographs of him in every kiosk. The Tsarina, in splendid national costume, drove past in a golden carriage embellished with jewels, harnessed to eight white horses. She bowed to right and left with the whole upper part of the body, in accordance with the old Russian custom. This profound greeting can be stirring in its humility, but in her case it seemed stiff and unnatural. Her regular facial features appeared rigid. Reddish spots on her face caught my eye that seemed to betray her agitation. The Tsarina-widow followed her in an equally opulent carriage. Then came three hundred horsemen: Don-Cossacks in scarlet red; Ural-Cossacks in sky-blue kilts; followed by the Pavlovian grenadier regiment, whose members were all required to have obtuse noses like Tsar Paul; then came twenty-four gold carriages with red velvet upholstery. And so it went on. The German envoy Helmuth von Moltke was pointed out to me in one of the carriages. From Petrovsky-Razumovsky to the Kremlin, for almost eight kilometres, the road was strewn with red sand, and soldiers formed an honour guard. People crowded in all the windows and along all the walls. Women in white sat on the reviewing stands. The clergy stood in front of the churches in their gold and silver brocade vestments, with gold banners. The Tsar was received in the Kremlin by representatives of every Russian municipality; one saw Russian peasants, Kirghizes, Tatars, Georgians, Armenians and people from the most diverse tribes and regions.

In the evening, Moscow was magnificently illuminated. In our landau, decorated with flowers, we drove in a long line of other carriages through the city. We all wore white dresses and light-coloured hats, which resembled little flower baskets after the fashion of the day. In the carriage in front of us sat Koreans, behind us Japanese. Moscow, a fantastic city in itself, appeared that evening like a fairy-tale vision. The towers and churches, the indented walls of the Kremlin, all architectural lines on the houses were ablaze with lights. From the Kremlin quay one saw a sea of light on the other bank of the river. Factories on the other side of Moscow were likewise illuminated.

All I know is that I soon looked at nothing anymore. This whole *fata morgana*, which did not seem to end, began to have the effect on me of a nightmare. Was it a premonition, or did I simply sense the untruth of this whole deception? This was the eve of the coronation. The next day, it had been announced that a great public celebration would take place on the military training ground of Hadynka. Everyone was to receive a mug with the image of the two-headed eagle on it, as a memento. This was the customary practice. But it had been forgotten that newspapers and railways had meanwhile come about, and that everyone who felt so inclined could now travel to the celebration.

The following morning, I went to the dentist. "Have you heard," the old man asked me, "that there is a frightful crush on the Hadynka field?

At our police station there are already six dead!" When I went home I saw closed carriages on the street with the dead and wounded. People said the crowd could not be contained. The field was like a kettle and the police were unable to prevent masses of people streaming there from all sides. The news concerning the number of victims continued to rise throughout the day. More than two thousand people were crushed to death on that day. In the evening a ball was to take place in the French embassy. The Tsar was advised to call off his appearance there on account of the catastrophe. But he did not want to allow himself to be influenced on the first day of his reign; he went to the ball and danced. That is how his reign began. Our friend Vladimir Dzhunkovsky, who was at that time aide-de-camp of the Grand Duke Sergei, the Governor General of Moscow, told us about events at court. Thus we learned things that were otherwise not known.

To me it was an indescribable disappointment that we did not go to our estate that summer. My mother travelled to England, in order to get to know welfare organizations in London, and my cousins accompanied her. My brother was sent to Mrs Avenarius in the country, while I spent the summer at my grandmother's villa near Moscow. I could not comprehend why the peasants, even the trees and the earth, were so different here than on our estate. I could not derive anything from this part of the country. I knew nothing as yet of the fact that every region has its own elemental world, its own spirituality. A dreadful homesickness almost made me ill.

When I visited my brother at the Avenarius' I hardly recognized him. I had not thought it possible that someone could change so much in such a short time, physically and emotionally. From a delicate child, he had transformed himself into a big lout. I was quite shaken by it and found him unapproachable. I myself began to feel different, as though incarcerated in my body and subject to its weight. On awakening I often had a feeling of anxiety, "Just as I now dive down into my body without willing it, I shall someday — in death — be catapulted out of it against my will." Life frightened me. *"Alright, let's go!" the parrot shrieked, when the cat got him.* This little tale typified life, as it seemed to me. Everything became ghostly. Earlier I had been given over to pity, feeling responsible for all the suffering in the world. Now I said to myself, "Why do you need to suffer so much? What does all that have to do with you? You can find a world in your own soul, to which you can flee." The beautiful cosmic images which had earlier prompted me to write, deserted me. Instead I wrote lyrical poems:

> Be not afraid of the weaving of dreams!
> Alone in dreaming, yet free of the world,
> Look into your soul's non-spatial realms,
> Dwell, O king, in your own tent.

I had no one to confide in, who might have helped me out of this unhealthy mood.

Aunt Katharina, to whom I was close, married the poet Balmont at this point, against the wishes of my grandmother, who even cursed her on parting for marrying a divorced man. They went to live in Paris. Balmont's poems, however, only reinforced my feeling about life.

That year I was to attend a secondary (high) school with the aim of graduating in two years. There were many good private schools for girls in Moscow, including a classical one, where I could have received a solid education. However, my mother had a peculiar fear of the future, and convinced herself that a state school diploma would have greater validity. Thus I went to the fourth Moscow state secondary school. It was housed in one of the orange-coloured buildings which had signified the boundary of the world for me in my childhood. Now I looked out of the large windows of my classroom onto the old linden park of the Widow's House. This large park, in which I could experience the moods of the seasons, was the only good thing about this school, apart from the mathematics teacher. The other teachers were so indifferent and uninterested, that hardly anything was to be learned from them. Among my many classmates I did not find any with whom I could become friends, though I yearned for friendship. The clever ones despised me because of my silly behaviour. To enliven the boring lessons, I fooled around, causing others to idolize me. Thus I sank ever deeper into my dreams. I hated this school, in which my time was stolen from me. But what did I do with my own time? I read Byron and enthused about Napoleon. I even wrote a novel about the latter, which had very little to do with the facts of history. A few sentences of Nietzsche that I did not understand justified my attitude to life, so far as I was concerned.

The year 1898, in which I reached the age of sixteen, stands out in my memory as having a certain radiance, a certain poetic gleam. It was not only that the winter was sunny and frosty and the snow sparkled and crunched under the horses' hooves, or that the spring was sudden and filled with the rushing of streams, the scent of birch, popular and lilac. A change took place within me, affecting all experiences after that. The dates have remained in my memory. Thus I know that on December 19, the last school day of the year 1897, three students came to us: Max Kontshalovsky, his younger brother, Mitya, a philologist and exceptionally handsome youth, who resembled Petya, and a third, David Ilovaysky, who was studying natural science. He was stocky and his broad Egyptian face with a small beard had something withdrawn and sardonic about it. He was a friend of Petya's and hence already suffused with a certain charm for me. We had heard nothing of Petya in the years since the Kontshalovskys had stayed with us. It remained unfathomable, that among the hundreds of faces one encountered, with greater or less interest, one of them impressed itself on the soul like a seal, transforming it, so that the world became a greater reality. Thus it was with the impression I had of Petya's friend at that time. This face dominated my thoughts and dreams for years, emerging with elemental force as though from a forgotten world. He belonged to a famous line of Don-Cossacks; twelve of his forebears had fought against Napoleon. Petya spent every summer on his estate on the Don. These young people had come to offer us tickets to a benefit ball for their grammar school. They visited us again the next day. At that ball I danced a quadrille with David.

After a long silence, he said, "Petya told me a lot about you, a young lady who is afraid of nothing."

"Oh," I responded, deeply pleased, "he probably had in mind that drive in which he was guiding the troika and I disappeared from the box seat next to him when we took a curve at full speed. He got quite a fright, but I had not fallen; I jumped intentionally into the ditch and was able to climb back quickly onto the box seat, even before he brought the horses to a halt."

Then there was another long silence. But before the dance ended, I decided to ask, "Do you love chemistry?" Chemistry was for me full of wonders and riddles.

He answered, "Yes, it is a nice science."

I believe it was our longest and most significant conversation, nourishment for my love for many years. Petya's brother brought me books of poems and notebooks from history lectures, but my mother did not make things easy for our guests. She was critical and disapproving, and since she represented an ideal for me then, I imitated her attitude outwardly. That was contrary to my nature, but I thought it belonged to an appearance of dignity. Apart from anything else, I was very inhibited in David's presence. My cousins were quiet; thus the admirers gradually stayed away, but the dreams remained and the yearning persisted.

In later years, whenever a meeting might have come about, it was thwarted by chance occurrences.

A few weeks afterwards, another event took pace in my life. On a January morning, Terenty drove me as usual to the school, which, however, I found closed on account of a "snow day." The sun shone like a crimson ball through the frosty haze; the snow crunched and sparkled. In my room at home, the beech wood crackled in the white tiled stove. I opened a book that had lain unread for some time on my writing table, the famous *Diary of the Painter Marya Bashkirzeva*, a Russian noblewoman who had lived in Paris and wrote in French. She began it at age fifteen and kept it up until her death at the age of twenty-four. Strictly speaking, this girl, full of admiration for herself, was a personification of egoism and ambition, but this egocentricity, which would have been silly and repulsive in any other person, was fascinating in her case, by virtue of the intensity and honesty with which she regarded her own existence, and the wonderful style in which she wrote. In such a soul, which burned up the body so early, Lucifer, the lord of wishes, can be recognized. After reading several chapters, it was as if a spark had gone over from her spirit into mine. I ran to the mirror: It was not as it had been three years before, when I encountered a "presence" in the mirror that met me from out of eternity, the glance of my immortal being that fulfilled its destiny by means of this mortal "persona," this mask, at the same time reshaping it. Now a rose-golden glow appeared before me demanding to be granted existence through mirroring it in other souls. The passing moment, the transitory, wanted to attain permanence by forceful means. In spite of the terrible frost, I went out of the house and, for the first time, went into a fashion store to order myself a black velvet hat as Marya Bashkirzeva had done, and described so well — only with the difference that I was inexperienced in matters of fashion and the little milliner who lived on our street was no *Parisienne.* The hat turned out accordingly! Then I bought myself a thick black notebook for a diary and began to write in order that no experience would be lost to the world having to do with my person, which had suddenly become so interesting to me. It was a tentative attempt to express the inexpressible: the weaving of light and darkness around things, the moods of nature through times of day and times of year. In the process, a lot of vague feelings emerged, and there were a great number of interjections! "One buries every moment," I wrote, or "Is there a consciousness that knows of me and bears me within it? Am I lost in the world?" Everything was experienced mainly with regard to myself — the "enchanted weaving of one's own being." This exclusive, dreamy life led to a painful awakening.

In the spring of 1899, I had to work very hard to catch up on everything I had day-dreamed away for two years, so as to prepare for my final exams.

That spring, Russia celebrated the one-hundredth birthday of Alexander Pushkin. Many festive events took place in May; the graduation celebration of my class stood under this sign. I was to recite the monologue of the old monk Pimen from *Boris Godunov.* Love poems were frowned upon in the school, being considered detrimental for young people. I learned prior to the concluding celebration that I had done well in the exams and would receive a medal; thus I had nothing to lose. So instead of the monologue of the old chronicler — in the large overcrowded hall, in the presence of government ministry representatives, senators and decorated generals — I hurled Pushkin's *Invocation* from the podium, in which the poet calls upon the spirit of his deceased beloved. I began quietly and mysteriously, "Oh, if it is true that at night, when the living rest asleep, the moon alone keeps watch in the heavens ..." Then to my own astonishment, my voice rose to urgent entreaty. The principal, the ladies, school inspectors, everybody froze; but there was nothing to be done. I spoke to the end, and the audience applauded wildly. The singing teacher (Anastasya Verbizkaya, authoress of the much read trashy novel *The Key to Good Fortune*) embraced me and advised me to go onto the stage. Then there were the embraces of my classmates; I came home intoxicated with my successes, my medal and my dramatic renown. But all this met with no response at home. Katharina Balmont, who had just returned from Paris, even laughed at me, "All pretty young girls are told they have to go onto the stage." Perhaps she realized that her earlier educational methods had not borne any good fruit. And suddenly I was overcome by a frightful depression: this was not only the consequence of over-exertion leading up to the exams, the many sleepless nights, it was the consciousness of a terrible emptiness and loneliness. Now my schooling had finished, I had gained no friends, acquired no appreciable knowledge, life was actually starting and I stood facing nothingness.

II

Going to the Sources

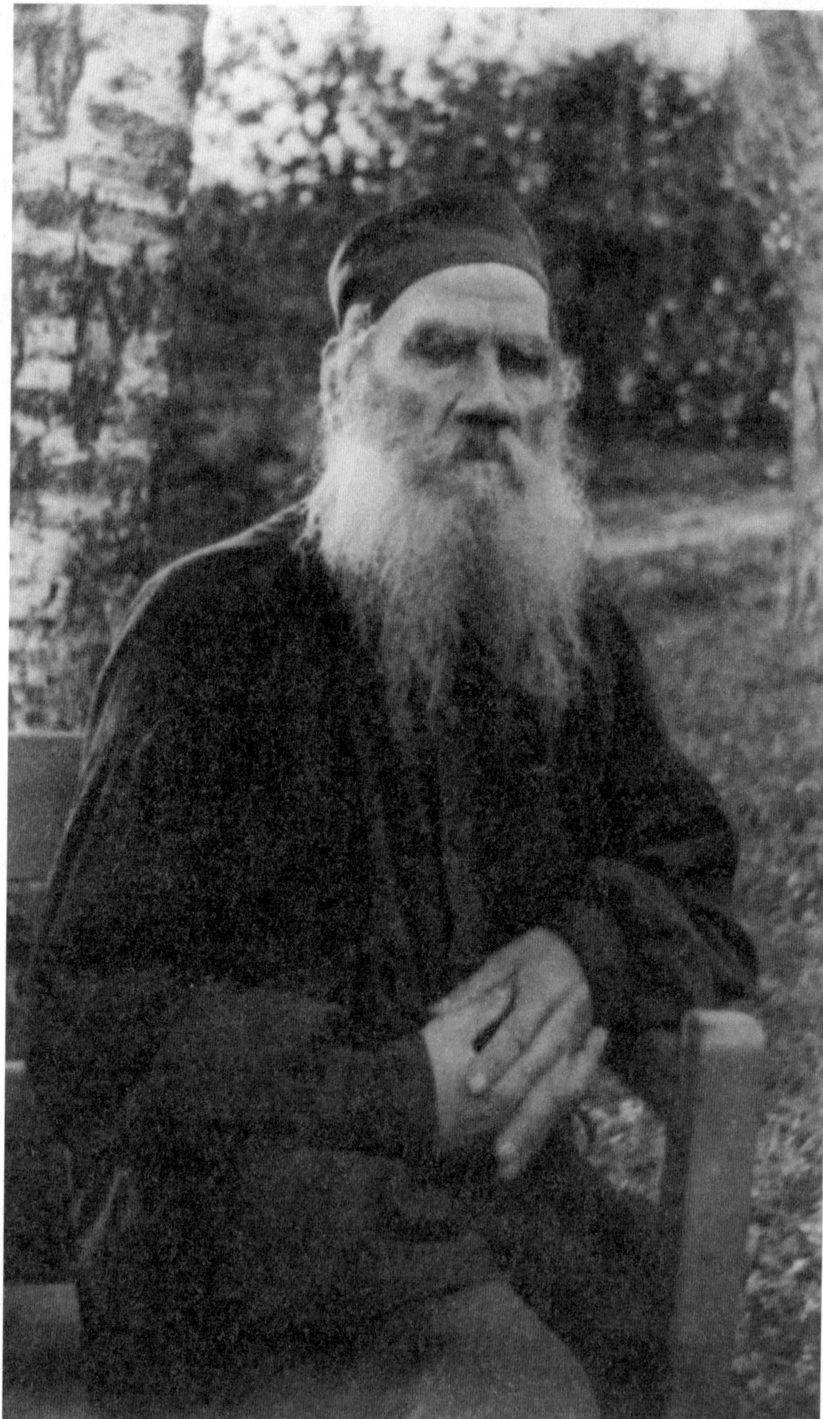

Leo Tolstoy around 1897

A Conversation with Leo Tolstoy

It had already counted as a settled matter since my childhood that I was to study painting. More from the law of inertia than from my state of mind at that time, I went to St Petersburg, in order to work in a studio that was considered a preliminary stage to the academy, and in which the then famous painter Ilya Repin taught. Up to then, in the summer holidays which lasted four months in Russia, we had always had one teacher, either for painting or for natural science. Once I said to this painter, who guided us in a completely naturalistic way of painting, "Does it really make sense, to repeat what is already there? A quite different art has to arise, revealing a world that has never existed before, and that's what I want to search for." He answered that it was a presumption on my part, to want something different from what the best artists had already achieved.

I experienced the same disappointment with the natural science teacher. He was a nervous young man with bushy blonde hair, watery, short-sighted eyes and an unusually fast tempo in speaking. His words fell like so many peas. And the facts he communicated fell in the same way; next to each other without inner connection and meaning. The world fell apart.

The literature of that time also brought me no satisfaction. The two most famous writers apart from Tolstoy, whose works we read and who were then usually forbidden by the censor, were Anton Chekhov and the poet Balmont. The lyrical poems of Balmont were rich in rhythms and sounds, and flushed with erotic passion and infatuation. The novels of Chekhov reproduced, in their ingenuous language and fine painterliness, the bleak conditions in Russia, without redeeming them or raising them to their archetypes, as Gogol, for example, did. By this means Gogol's art brought about a catharsis, whereas Chekhov, with his agnosticism, only led to resignation and scepticism. All I could experience around me in society was a morbid flight from the self and from the fundamental questions of life — a flight into personal passions, into social activity, into academia. Morality was a matter of convention, meant only to save us from chaos; religion at most a poetic tradition, an aesthetic experience that accompanied the experience of the seasons. Artists argued whether art existed "for its own sake" or whether it had to be the illustration of ideas. In my childhood I had experienced the great masters so intensely, that neither of these two directions appealed to me, but intellectually I was not able to deal with this problem.

I now arrived in St Petersburg in the family of my Aunt Nina Evreinova, the older sister of the two brothers, the publishers, Michail and Sergei Sabashnikov. Aunt Nina, a rather delicate mother of four children, was a quiet, refined woman and a brilliant musician. Musicality expressed itself in the movements of her tall figure, in the "listening" mode of her violet-tinged eyes, in the expression of her mouth. She was close friends with Mrs Balmont. Both were tall, of exceptional beauty and complemented each other in their being. Katharina Balmont stood by her friend in the tragic circumstances of her marriage. Severe difficulties that she had endured brought on states in which she had second sight, and frequently experienced fearful visions. Later, I became very close to her; at that time I was too young to understand her life. In her house I got to know the life of very wealthy and aristocratic circles. In the painting studio, on the other hand, I was together with young people who lived in the greatest need. The social problem presented itself to me for the first time in such a crass form.

Very soon, my studies, pursued with eagerness and reverence, also became a problem for me. We painted during the day, and in the evening drew from the nude. Repin, who was very taciturn, praised my studies from nature a few times. But when we sketched compositions based on a set theme, several times I got the worst grades. These tasks were not discussed, and I did not understand what it was about my sketches, which were not naturalistic, that he didn't like. The next time around, I had painted a group of farm workers from a photograph and got the best grade. That made me think. Now I really did not understand why I painted, what significance my painting was supposed to have for the world. At exhibitions one saw, besides the naturalistic genre and biased, narrative pictures, those that showed the suppression of the masses, as well as paintings in a sophisticated, decadent style, inspired by the eighteenth century, which could flatter a blasé taste. Suddenly my studies seemed quite pointless to me. I felt like a parasite. How could I justify the privilege of a freelance profession before the masses? In the Christmas holidays I came home in a troubled mood. No one could help me in my misery. I then thought of Tolstoy.

For every Russian, Tolstoy was an integral part of life. We knew his novels before we knew life, especially *War and Peace*, which I first read during the time of our return home to Russia. In our quarter of the city lived the people described by Tolstoy in this book. I saw patriarchal Moscow through this prism. The mood of the various seasons was as he described, and I even rediscovered the people from the upper social classes and the peasants who had lived a hundred years before, in the people I met. In particular, I wove a picture in my mind, as did so many Russian girls of that time, of the poetic soul-world of a Natasha Rostova. From my childhood on I knew Tolstoy's stories of the people, his novels and essays, insofar as the censors had allowed them to be published. I often saw him walking along our street, the Pretshistenka. Then, with a beating heart, I would follow him and wonder: How is it possible that the human being out of whose soul that world arose, that lives in me as my very own, now goes in front of me, an old man of medium height, in a sheepskin coat? I see his slightly bent back and his grey beard wafting in the wind, see him from outside. He, however, neither sees me, nor knows me at all. At that time I had such a strong inner relationship with him, that following a dream in which he visited me, I felt his presence as immediate, continuous and palpable.

In my soul deprivation, in which I had been given either conventional or merely resigned answers, I recalled Tolstoy as being the only one who did not want to accept life passively, just as it had taken shape for centuries, but who was convinced that something lived in every human being that could distinguish between evil and good, and that everyone was co-responsible for what happened in the world. With elemental power he justified his conviction, that one can and should live the truth one recognizes. He appeared to me the conscience of the world, and I decided to go to him with my question.

My mother was acquainted with Countess Tolstoy. She had also once met Tolstoy himself through the Committee for Helping the Hungry. She now took me along on a Sunday evening (it was January 1900), on which the Tolstoys received visitors. A footman led us into a small drawing room where the countess sat with a prince, a relative of Tolstoy. The conversation was at first trivial. Then I heard footsteps in the hall. My heart beat faster. However, at that moment I was not thinking of the great teacher, but of the man who was able to understand Natasha so well. In the brown doorway, Tolstoy appeared in a Russian smock, his aged hand on his belt-strap. Deep light-grey, sharp eyes looked out from under bushy eyebrows. I knew this face so well from pictures: this fine forehead, this broad, not-at-all beautiful, typical nose of the Tolstoys, the flowing beard.

He gave each of us his hand and began at once to speak with indignation about what he had just learned concerning the inadequate wage of the coal shovellers on the railroad of the Kazan line. "Can one exist with a family on that? Isn't it white slavery? And we put up with it?"

Then the conversation turned to the Boer War. "Isn't it disgraceful that a war is possible in our time? One simply cannot grasp it. Every human being knows that war is a horror. If one were to question each person about it, they would oppose it. But no one has the courage to resist it. No one has the courage to act according to his conscience and refuse to do what is inhuman. If everyone were to act according to his conscience, war would become an impossibility. But since only very few summon up this courage, they have to languish in prisons and are finally shot, and the monstrousness continues."

Suddenly Tolstoy turned to me and said very earnestly, "Please, promise me that you will do everything so that in your time a war is no longer possible."

I blushed, but said resolutely, "I shall do it."

How often I had to think of this moment later, when I experienced, and now experience again (I write in the year 1942), what has become possible in my time. Tolstoy, who died in 1910, did not experience the World War.

On arriving home, I wrote him a letter, in which I requested an audience with him.

The next day I told my Aunt Alexandra, the writer, about it. How she rebuked me, "An arrogant, pretentious young teenager, who hadn't even taken the time or made the effort first to study his writings, who had experienced nothing, achieved nothing, mastered nothing and who had the brazenness to rob the great man of his time. Look," she continued, "all my life I have occupied myself with Tolstoy. And I have not had the immodesty to make claims on his time." (After a time she published her book on Tolstoy's novel *Resurrection*, and on Ibsen's drama, *When We Dead Awake).*

I believed she was right. I felt crushed, but what was to be done? The deed had been accomplished. There was no way back for me.

Smitten with remorse and trembling I went the same day to Tolstoy, to fetch the answer to my letter myself. The footman opened the door for me. The Countess came towards me down the stairs.

"Come into the drawing room. I'll tell Lev Nikolayevich right away that you are here. He wants to speak with you."

He came, had me take a seat, and spoke to me so earnestly and warmly, that I felt reassured. "Now, you want to ask me something?"

Looking into his eyes, I had the feeling that these eyes saw through me completely. He knew how serious I was about it, and would not take my request amiss. Perhaps I didn't even need to tell him anything, for he would know himself, why I had come to him. Meanwhile he said, "I have heard that you are a pupil of Repin; this Sunday I admired his pictures in the Tretyakov Gallery. What a captivating brush he has!" (On that Sunday I too was in the Gallery, walked behind Tolstoy and attempted to guess what his thoughts were.)

"Yes, I paint, but I would like to serve the people with my art. That is my question: How can I serve humanity with my painting?"

Tolstoy answered, "I do not now usually give advice, because I am misunderstood. But I believe you are asking me quite seriously and I would like to answer you. You must relinquish your way of life, the way of life of a well-to-do girl. Art is the fruit of love, it is born of love, as a human being is born of love and brings something new into life and transforms it. You must do without your money, live with the people and work just as every peasant woman does. If you were to live in the untruth in which all rich people live, could you then understand the masses? It is as though you sat in a high tower and let things down with a cord, which are not needed down below at all. It is wrong to live differently than the majority of the human race lives, and nothing good can come of it. You can paint only on the side for relaxation, in the same way one plays chess."

I asked, "But if one is to be effective by means of art, one has after all to perfect oneself in art. Does genuine art not have its effect on a simple mind? This Sunday I saw two peasants standing in front of the picture by Vrubel, *Christ Walking on the Sea,* and listened to their conversation."

I wanted to report on the beautiful conversation, but Tolstoy interrupted me angrily, "That is just what is so outrageous, that our trained painters serve this stuff up to our people. They represent God as an old man, paint all kinds of miracles and superstition that ruin the Gospel, just as a spoonful of tar ruins a tub of honey. Have you read my Gospel, the Gospel in my version that I have cleansed of all mystical rubbish?"

I had to admit that I did not know it.

"Then read it."

I didn't want to believe my ears, on hearing these words. How the miracles in the Gospel were to be understood I didn't know. But I felt that the essential nature of Christianity lay precisely in what was mystical and mysterious in that document, not in the moral teaching. How could one simply eliminate that? Even if I would not then have been able to express it in concepts, it was still self-evident to me that a temporal earthly phenomenon had an eternal archetype in the spiritual realm, and for that reason, an old, bearded man could be a true and effective image, as a symbol for the creative Father-principle, that worked through him.

I looked into Tolstoy's eyes, which shone through his eyebrows like the eyes of Pan through a forest thicket, wiser than nature herself. I felt the greatness of his personality, the power of truth which worked in him. But the words I heard at this moment I perceived as naïve, even foolish. For an eighteen-year-old girl, this contradiction was incomprehensible and unbearable. It went through my soul like a fissure. At this moment the Countess entered the room,

"Lev Nikolayevich," she said, "is certainly giving you the advice to give up art. Do not listen to him. He is also against music, but I'm not letting it be taken from me. If I have not completed my piano piece every day, something is lacking for me."

Tolstoy stood up and said goodbye. The Countess accompanied me down the stairs and asked, "How did you find him? He is becoming so weak. I'm very worried about him; I try to feed him well, and have everything cooked with chicken bouillon; but he is not to know that ... He thinks he's a vegetarian."

I arrived home shattered. The shock expressed itself in strong physical pains throughout my body, so that I had to lie in bed.

After a few days I went away to St Petersburg, where I occupied myself inwardly, exclusively, with Tolstoy. In the studio I was interested in pursuing conversations with one of his followers more than painting. From my aunt's maid I received copies of his writings banned by the censors (there were such maids at that time in tsarist Russia!). When I travelled in the spring with my father and Nyusha to the Crimea, I at first saw nothing of the enchanting, magnificent natural surroundings of the south, so obsessed was I with my brooding. Only in Bakhchysaray, the former residence of the Tartar Khan with its fountains and minarets, with the old castle and the ancient, unchanged eastern way of life, did I awaken to the world that can be so rich and varied. On this journey I had the opportunity of getting to know Maxim Gorky who was then a rising star. I also met Sergei Bulgakov. From a convinced Marxist, he changed at that time into an idealist. Later he became a priest of the Orthodox Church and played a significant role, particularly among Russian emigrants in Paris.

The questions that had been stirred up did not let go of me. Problems of art and the social order led me to deeper questions concerning the meaning of life altogether. During the same period in which I went into the religious teaching of Tolstoy, Vladimir Soloviev wrote his *Three Conversations,* in which he fought against the spiritual tendencies of Tolstoy. I only obtained his writings a year after his death (he died in 1900). And it was a good thing that I had to get through these problems on my own. I was glad to find confirmation of my own thoughts later on in Soloviev.

Tolstoy inquired after me of an acquaintance. "I believe I embarrassed the girl," he said.

Two Bucketfuls of Cold Water in Answer to Existential Questions

As a result of the time I spent in St Petersburg, I acquired some distance from our domestic life. While I had previously beheld an ideal in my mother, and had admired her unconditionally, I now observed everything critically. At that time she was very active. Our friend Dzhunkovsky presided over an association for combatting alcoholism, which had been instituted by the Government. In Russia that actually signified a contradiction in itself. On the one hand, the trade in spirits was a monopoly of the state and one of its main sources of revenue; on the other hand, it was fought against. In every district of Moscow good, cheap, non-alcoholic dining places were opened, next to which my mother established lending libraries with reading rooms for the people. How I loved the sight of peasants and factory workers absorbed in their books! Later my mother also started adult education courses. From this a publishing house arose, which brought out literature appropriate for self-education, with important scholars participating. In this way much was undertaken out of idealism, and with enthusiasm. Critical as I then was, I saw less of the sincere wish to serve the people, whom she actually loved — for that was, in fact, what spurred her on — but more her ambition to play a role. She loved "the word," as she was in the habit of saying, and put on plays with her course participants, which she wrote herself especially for the occasion. Even at a mature age she continued lessons with a well-known reciter, and one could hear her practising modern poems between her many business phone calls. She always worked free of charge, but otherwise seldom showed generosity, much to my indignation. I did not express my opinion in words, but she sensed my criticism from my silence. In this way a certain tension arose between us.

We all spent the summer in Loviisa in Finland. There I had to sleep in the same room as my mother and the tension was aggravated. She demanded feelings from me which I did not have. From what sources could I have drawn love, since I despaired of the meaning of life? And so she reproached me and made scenes. Poor mother! By the passionate, despotic nature of her love she managed gradually to spoil life at home, even for my meek cousins. She herself suffered most from putting up this wall between herself and us, with her lack of forbearance. It would probably have been a release for her if we had opposed her with equal intensity. But we avoided her silently, and so she became more and more isolated.

Once, when I had to bring food for my sick cousin from the nearby canteen into our villa, a youth offered to help me. He brought the dishes to us and seemed not to want to leave. That was our first meeting with the later well-known Egyptologist Vikentyev, who became a fellow traveller with us for many years. At that time he was a graduating senior. On our sailing trips in the Gulf of Finland, conversations developed among him, my brother and me concerning the mysterious analogy of the spectrum and the tone-scale. We asked ourselves, whether secret spiritual laws did not after all reveal themselves in nature. The colour theory of Goethe preoccupied us, and the following winter our friend showed us some of Goethe's colour experiments. How this was to be reconciled with Newton's theories, the soundness of which we did not at that time doubt, was a big problem for us. At this time I also read an Englishman's biography of Goethe, from which one could not, unfortunately, make out Goethe's essential personality. Goethe had it easy, I thought; a belief in God was the prerequisite for him. In his time, natural science did not as yet force materialism upon one as an inevitable consequence, and the social question appears not to have been a problem for the Olympian.

On the return journey from Loviisa we visited the Imatra waterfall. The sheer force of the water plummeting from the rocks and following, in falling, its own nature free of constraint — the waves surging up, being driven back, raging to and fro from above and below and crashing into each other — conjured up armies of white knights arising continuously anew; foaming horses, shaggy witches, all springing skyward and filling the air with fine mist. This thousand-voiced, thousandfold element racing into the abyss, in which every part seemed to drown out the whole, that itself remained the same in its diversity, awakened inexpressible things in the soul. I stood on the wooden bridge, which trembled from the shockwaves of air, drenched from the spray and deafened by the uproar of this furiously jubilating element. A mechanical occurrence only? Why then did the soul respond so powerfully, as though in this plunge into the depths it were experiencing something of kindred origin?

In St Petersburg, since the Hermitage painting galleries were closed that day, I spent a few hours in the collection of jewellery and other objects found in excavating the Kurgan burial mound in the steppes. Mythological animals and ornaments of ivory, copper and gold appeared to me of great beauty. They seemed related in a certain way to the elemental impressions I had had a few hours earlier in front of the waterfall. Why was it no longer possible in our time to produce something like that? What was the source of this creativity? I did not know the answer to this question.

In October we travelled to the World Exhibition in Paris, where I had not been since my childhood. The features of the beloved city appeared to me distorted by this Exhibition, which I experienced as a monstrosity. In my state of mind at that time, with no basis for living or direction, I felt lost amid these goings-on. The Bengal illumination of the Trocadero waterfalls, the phantasmagorical whirl of skirts of Louise Fuller, the artificial exotic dances of the renowned beauty, Cléo de Mérode, but especially the fascinated audience itself, left only emptiness and desolateness behind as far as I was concerned. Amid all the artifice, the question haunted me as to the meaning of this culture, the meaning of life altogether. Either there was a real spiritual world that I could recognize as clearly as the truth of mathematics, or everything was pointless, and words like "good" and "evil," "beautiful" and "ugly" were conventional phrases. Once I fled alone to the old part of Paris, where the bustle of the Exhibition did not penetrate. I went into Notre Dame Cathedral and looked for a long time into the violet, red, deep blue glow of the rosette, climbed the tower and observed the enigmatic grimaces of the gargoyles and the chimera over the city. Then I visited the morgue, a low, eerie building on the Seine, where all those who had met with some misfortune during the night and all suicides lay, to be identified by their next of kin. Today I still see those corpses in front of me, in particular, that of an old woman with dishevelled hair and bloated face, one eye closed, the other turned defiantly to the sky. I thought: If there were no spiritual world, neither the dreadful nor the beautiful could move the soul so deeply. From these solitary wanderings I took along experiences that became signposts for me. At the World Exhibition itself only one event roused my enthusiasm: the Japanese theatre with the famous actress Sadayakko, the first woman to appear on the Japanese stage.[9] Every gesture of her performance is still alive in me; it was no naturalistic realism. Everything proceeded rapidly, one had to be very attentive and observe keenly, to follow all the nuances of the play. One was surprised and released inwardly, when at the high point of emotion everything suddenly passed over into stylized movement, a fight, for example, became a rhythmic rod dance. This art has its roots in an ancient culture. I thought why is it not permitted for us to cultivate such art in our time? These old cultures stood artistically higher than ours!

For me there came a time of earnest confrontation with materialism. I read Darwin and Haeckel and drew conclusions from them that signified something devastating for me. However, I wanted to be opposed inexorably to myself and my subjective inclinations. I learned later from Haeckel's biography, that just in these years in which I was brought to despair by his teaching, he had a happy experience in love. I said to myself: If this materialistic world picture were to correspond to the truth, then human beings ought not to talk of morality. If the human being is to be regarded as a higher animal, then he is dependent on the struggle for existence. Egoism would then not only be justified, it would be the highest ideal. Human destiny would be a complex of meaningless chance occurrences. If nature was nothing but a dead mechanism, then everything the human being was able to experience of the moods of nature was only subjective feeling and illusion. One ought not to even speak of colours and tones, for in reality they were only vibrations. Landscape, which I had experienced so strongly before, became for me the corpse of a once-loved friend. It went so far that I could not look up at the starry sky without a shudder; at this soulless, infinite space, in which dead bodies supposedly circled mechanically. During a ball, as we ran in a line through the halls, I imagined the house without a roof, and right above us the abyss of space in which our earth raced along into nothingness among other bodies, just as we raced through the rooms.

I recollect conversations that winter with student friends. By twilight we went to the Cloister of the Virgin and skied from there over the snowfields to the Sperling Mountains. In a hut we drank tea to warm us up and returned home in the bright moonlit night. What a despairing struggle for insight there was in the conversations we had on the way, particularly with Alexeiev, later a well-known professor of chemistry at the University of Tomsk.[10] At that time the famous speech of Dubois-Reymond of August 14, 1872, concerning the limits of knowledge occupied people's minds.[11] What was matter, how did consciousness arise out of material processes? In answer to these questions natural scientists could only say: We shall never know! If that's how matters stand, I thought, then human life is an unworthy affair, and one is actually obligated to have done with it. Not only did I think this. I felt it to be so. I saw every day as a pointless procedure, a comedy unworthy of the human being. Then again, the question arose for me: From where do I have the concept of "human dignity," where do I get it from? If the human being is only a part of mechanical nature, why does he want what is not in her? Where do these questions come from?

Once I asked my father, "What do we live for?"

"For each other, because we love each other."

This answer did not satisfy me. In that case, I said to myself, he only continues living with us out of pity. My mother noticed that I was in a state of inner crisis, and spoke with an older doctor with whom we were friends. Everyday I had to go to him in a water sanatorium, where buckets of cold water were poured over me. The dear, sensible man took the time everyday for conversations with me about the progress of humanity.

"I see none," I replied, "on the contrary, everything is gradually becoming shallower and uglier."

"Just wait," he consoled me, "a revolution is coming, and then we'll both sit on the radical left."

The good man died, thank God, before the Revolution. Even if he did not understand my problems, I was grateful to him for these conversations. He told me about his work and the suffering in his life, and that bound me closer to existence.

Once, when he had gone away, his young assistant opened the book of medical records, read the report about me and asked, "How is it with your gloomy thoughts?" My innermost thoughts were thus revealed to a stranger! When the doctor returned and asked how I was feeling, I said everything was fine and he discharged me as healthy. However, I must note here that I now have to see the two buckets of cold water I was given everyday as something positive. Even if they did not in themselves solve the existential problems I had, they did after all strengthen my body, and the unsolved existential problems could no longer have such a destructive effect on me.

At that time my brother began to awaken from his apathy and I discovered that he struggled with the same questions as I did. Once he took a pistol and went into the country. Nyusha and I had the greatest fears for him. She followed him. Now it was up to me to prove to him that life had a higher meaning. I recall many evenings in which we paced up and down the room searching, like two drowning persons, for a secure hold. This hold appeared to us to be mathematics. Insofar as we were able to assimilate mathematics, I thought, which was after all something objective and absolute, this absoluteness lay both in us and in the world. In addition experiences such as the following convinced me that there was a spiritual conformity to law.

In a light, floral-patterned summer dress, I once rode in a barouche fitted with springs and rubber wheels, through the most populated street of the city. In front of us a vehicle drove slowly, which our coachman, Terenty, could not overtake on account of the traffic. In the rear wall of the black, closed vehicle there was a small grated window. In such vehicles criminals were transported. And just as I looked, a pale face appeared behind the grating. A man looked at me and smiled. Even now, if I recall this cynical smile, this desperate gaze, I still feel the same horror. At the time, it was as if my blood congealed, and I could not evade the gaze. I said to myself afterwards: There are deeper worlds than those our understanding can grasp. If there were no higher worlds, there would also not be these abysses.

That same summer, while on our estate, we once rode by moonlight to the station in order to send a telegram. I waited outside while my brother saw to his assignment at the post office. From a lighted window of the station building a child's voice could be heard, singing. It might have been a four-year-old child that sang to their toy. The purity of this solitary little voice in the nocturnal landscape was so stirring that I could have wept. On the ride home, everything seemed to come to life; out of every bush and every tree a being arose. I asked what is it that you perceive in the purity of the child's voice, in nature, if the world is only a mechanism? Is it not evidence that there is another reality? Yet when I woke up the next morning, the old doubts were there again.

In order to further extend our education, my mother arranged courses in art history in our house, to which friends and acquaintances were invited. The lectures were held by the old Professor Alexander Kirpitshnikov, who was actually more of an archaeologist than an art historian. His presentations were rather dry and boring. Only on the first evening did he relate, with a certain emotion, why he had dedicated his life to research. As a young person, he had seen a copperplate engraving of a man reading, completely absorbed in his book. A lamp threw a small circle of light onto the open page; while on all sides it was dark. "And I thought," said Kirpitshnikov, "how fine it would be, if in the impenetrable darkness of the world that surrounds us, at least a small, limited subject were illumined by our science." Something in me rebelled against this mood of resignation. That would certainly not be enough for me, I thought.

The professor began with Byzantine art, which he called naïve and awkward. He went into archaeological disputes in detail. And so our guests came to these courses mainly for the more interesting second part of our evenings. After the customary tea, we played charades with long improvised dramatic presentations. Nyusha, who was otherwise so quiet and uncommunicative, transformed herself completely when she had dressed herself up, and developed both imagination and humour in these games. In spite of my "negative attitude to life" I joined in enthusiastically as well. The whole house, cupboards and chests, were rummaged through, and our maidservant had a lot to put away afterwards. For a few hours I forgot myself in this frenzy. But when the guests were gone, the emptiness that stared back at me was all the greater.

When we were to give talks ourselves, I chose the theme, unusual at that time, of the monster in medieval art. (The grotesque was then not yet fashionable.) The good professor could tell me little about it. He recommended a few books. I sat in the sunny hall of the State Library in the Rumyanzev Castle and read Eugène Viollet-Le-Duc,[12] and the medieval *Bestiarium*. "The blood of the elephant cools the fire of the dragon's blood" or "The unicorn kneels before the Virgin, under his horn there is a little mirror ..." These images fascinated me on account of their mysteriousness, without my being able to make anything of them. Later I got to know them as being pictures of a real soul-world.

At Christmas, the charitable association (called Welfare for the Poor) of the city of Moscow arranged Christmas festivities for poor children. My mother organized these in our district and we helped her, along with our friends. In a gloomy restaurant rented for the purpose on the notorious Market Place, the children of the poor were assembled. After a traditional Punch and Judy show, which enthralled me every time, no less than the children, the lights were lit on the great Christmas tree. In the adjoining room presents were distributed; each child received calico for a dress or Russian smock, a toy and a large bag containing a gingerbread man (*spekulatius)*. A friend of my brother, who took on the distribution, had a charming way of responding to each child, in having them choose among the various things and recommending this or that material as being particularly suitable; a way of treating them that was entirely new for such children. In the meantime, I play-acted with the other children around the tree. *The Golden Door* was especially popular; the enigmatic verses of this play, deriving from ancient mysteries, united us in their special rhythm, arousing enthusiasm. Oh, those little children with their mostly either too long or too short, shabby little dresses, with such different faces, still so malleable and unformed and for that reason so rich in possibilities! Out of these eyes, the Angelos of each child looked into our appalling world. Their shy, trusting look, their thin, delicate, sticky little hands — cold ones and hot, quiet and nervous —one after the other they took hold of my hand! A few happy hours in the year was all I could give them. I myself was perhaps the happiest in these hours. But then, when we were finally left alone in the empty, desolate hall, the same monster gawked at me again: What was the meaning of life, when out of such dear children, such disagreeable grown-ups so often emerged? I saw only a retrograde step, a decline, in the whole of civilization, and also in the life of single human beings. In a few years, the Angelos that today looked out through these children, would be obscured and buried by the brutality, the vileness and injustice of everyday Russian life!

Going to the Sources

Every year on Palm Sunday a fair was held on Red Square along the Kremlin wall. All over the great square bundles of balloons surged like clouds, and were let go from time to time, disappearing into the blue. There were all kinds of things to buy: twittering birds in little cages, flowers in pots, bouquets, folk pottery, carved and amusingly decorated toys. There were also valuable old icons, crosses of copper inlaid with enamel, church implements, precious brocades and other antiques. Bundles of palm candles with paper roses and little angels of wax were sold. Every Muscovite — of no matter what position — felt obligated to roam around this market; book lovers in particular came upon their treasures here. Poor students bought their textbooks second-hand at the market. Since I could not go that year on account of having the flu, a student friend of mine, who I knew actually went hungry, had a gift presented to me through Polya, a book he had bought at the market. I was deeply moved. The book was Plato's *Phaido*, the dialogue concerning the immortality of the soul. I read it immediately. It was the first light on my path. After a few weeks another book of destiny came into my hands: the *Bhagavadgita*. Certainly, at that time I understood this work only partially, but the materialistic world conception was shaken. From now on I regarded the whole external world as appearance.

Soon after, we went with Mrs Avenarius and the two Nadyas to our estate. It was spring, the apple trees were still in blossom in our magnificent garden; the lindens stood bare of leaves. Our garden seemed to me like a vision in white. I read my *Bhagavadgita:* the world was no longer a mechanical creation, but a dream, a maya.

In these weeks my brother came from Moscow with his three friends; they had passed their high school exams and wore new student uniforms. They suddenly counted as adults; since for young people in Russia the transition from high school to university signified an important step. One went on walks at night until sunrise, on long trips by troika and made music a great deal. Nyusha and Nadya were good singers, Lyubimov accompanied them outstandingly on the piano, and among all these gifted and attractive young people there lived unspoken the first love. I joined in all this and appeared to be the life and soul of whatever was happening, but remained inwardly uninvolved. I was as though dead and saw myself as being like that deceased ancestor of an old Slavic clan, whose body was taken from one tribal family to another to preside at the banquet for the departed.

One day Mrs Avenarius stopped me and gave me a good talking to. She had observed how I was becoming more and more otherworldly; how I floated over life and took for granted everything done for me by others. "This attitude is unhealthy, in fact immoral." Such sermons are seldom effective; this one, however, struck home. I attempted to connect myself to life in a conscious manner. What I did at first as an exercise gradually became second nature.

We spent the autumn in Saraysk, a small provincial town in the administrative district of Ryazan, where Mrs Avenarius owned a house and garden at the edge of town. In Saraysk I met the ingenious sculptress Anna Golubkina, a pupil of Rodin. Her relatives — simple gardeners — had a cucumber business. She did not have the money to live in Moscow or Paris, and had at that time to give up her artistic work, so as to help at home. She was a large, impressive figure, stern and abrupt, but when she smiled, which happened rarely, her face sparkled with a childlike quality. Later, I visited her frequently in Moscow as well, where she was able to devote herself to her art with the help of friends. Her life of endurance, her uncompromising, original manner of expressing herself, never abstractly, but vividly and descriptively, exerted a great influence on me. In her presence I sensed all the errors of the conventional, sentimental upbringing and attitude to life of the nobility, and yearned to escape my milieu.

During the winter semester I worked diligently in the studio. Konstantin Korovin came often at that time to give advice or make corrections, which usually consisted in his standing next to me and whispering into my ear something concerning the beauty of the colour revealed on the model and in the background. He whispered, "In seeing your way of painting, I can imagine that you could paint a picture ..." And then he would describe something like the following:

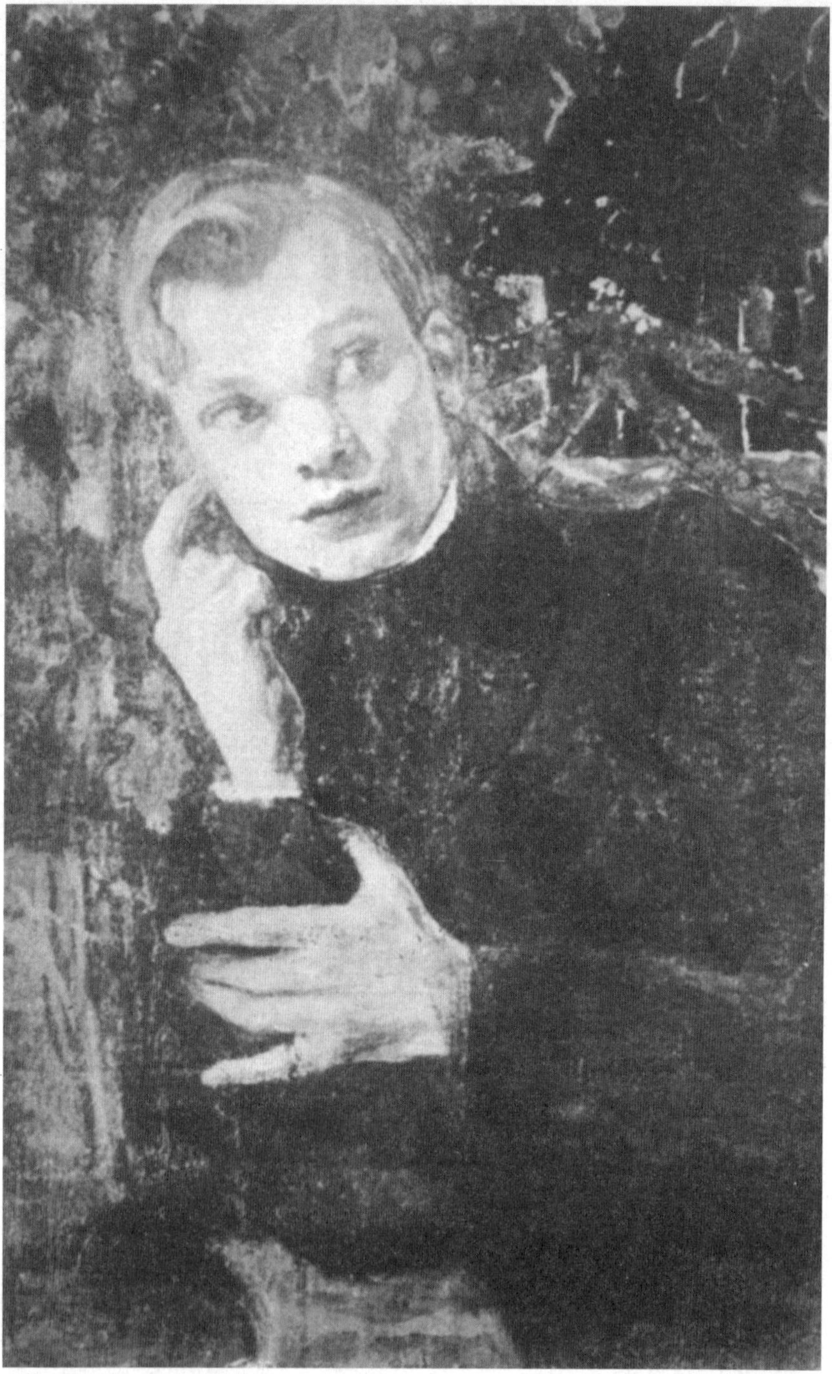

The painter, Michail Tchuyko. Portrait by Woloschin, 1905/6.

"Snow outside the window with blue shadows ... and in front someone in a white, light dress with little violet flowers, etc. ..." His whispering actually did have an inspiring effect and I made considerable progress at that time.

My ideal in painting then was Michail Vrubel, already mentioned above. He had the tragic destiny to go blind, and on that account became mad. One of my fellow students, Tchuyko, a small person, similar to a silenus (satyr), who at first appeared to me repulsively ugly, turned out to be an admirer of Vrubel. That established the beginning of our friendship, which continued for decades.[13] We transferred our admiration for Vrubel at the time to his wife, a very fine soprano, who typified Vrubel's fairy-tale figures, when she appeared in the poetic operas of Rimsky-Korsakov in the private opera house of Mamontov. In those days we also heard the young Fyodor Shalyapin there.

Shalyapin, the singer, had a voice which filled the room as if soaring from an inexhaustible fountainhead, with no boundaries, since it sounded forth from his throat as though from the unfathomable reaches of the cosmos. Through his art he bore witness for me, that the human being is of divine origin, that the human kingdom is a divine hierarchy. Every word, as it was formed by him with its vowels and consonants and carried by his voice, was like a new act of creation: infinitely rich in modulation and completely true, truer than any external reality. The gestures too of his powerful figure — he was a head taller than everyone else on the stage — were more real than everyday reality; his hands, which changed with every role, spoke an equally decisive language. Life disclosed itself in its great mystery through him. I did not ask any more about the meaning of life: I experienced it. Shalyapin became for me the measure of authenticity and greatness in art. Only later did I learn from his autobiography, how consciously he worked. At that time he seemed to me almost overshadowed by a daemon, of greater than human stature. When I was told that he had questioned the historian Klyutshevsky about Ivan the Terrible before taking on that role, I was astonished; it seemed to me that, conversely, Klyutshevsky would have had to question Shalyapin about the nature of this tsar.

Now I no longer attempted to comprehend life by means of reason, but groped my way to its sources by means of actual experience. I trusted feeling. Art showed me that feeling does not have to be subjective and, in painting, I gave myself over to the life of colour.

In Moscow at that time there was much of beauty to be experienced in the realm of art. In the Little Theatre, in which classical direction and a fine tradition prevailed, we had outstanding actors. The Stanislavski Theatre with its performances of Alexei Tolstoy, Chekhov, Ibsen and Maeterlinck among others wrestled with new forms of expression in dramatic art and production.[14] The visual arts also received new impulses by means of both the exhibition and the periodical called *Mir Iskustva* (the World of Art). At that time the Impressionists were having their say. The critical literary magazine *Vesy* (the Scales) helped us to appreciate the French moderns.[15]

In the Rumyanzev Museum I copied the watercolour sketches of Alexander Ivanov for the Bible. I wanted to reproduce them on the walls of our village church. For twenty years of his life (from 1837 to 1857) this painter had worked on a huge painting in Rome, *Christ Appearing to the People.* In the foreground one sees groups of people on the Jordan. They are listening to the sermon of the Baptist. In the distance Jesus strides over the hill towards them. Although his figure is relatively small due to the distance, and dressed in a blue cloak that partly merges with the blue background, it has the effect of being large and central to the composition. Arising out of the context of the period, the work is painted in the classical style. It exerts a strong effect. In the same room, hung with studies for this picture, there were two revolving stands with watercolours illustrating Old and New Testament scenes. I consider these among the most beautiful to have arisen from the art of recent times. In these sketches the artist showed himself completely free in his creating. Even if he derived much from the traditions of ancient Assyrian, Egyptian and archaic Greek art, and especially from Christian mosaics and icons, this was transformed by experience that was all his own. The concurrence of physical reality with the spiritual and archetypal, the essence of the biblical events, was arrived at unpretentiously and in a masterly fashion. A pitcher, a robe, a gesture; everything was earthly and at the same time spiritually transfigured. His triple auras were unique and convincing, painted in a glazing technique one over the other, interpenetrating each other, conjuring up an unearthly space. The reason his sketches were so little heeded lies, I believe, in the fact that at the time he brought them to Russia, naturalism was prevalent, which was then superseded by Impressionism and Expressionism. That they are now [at the time of writing] not

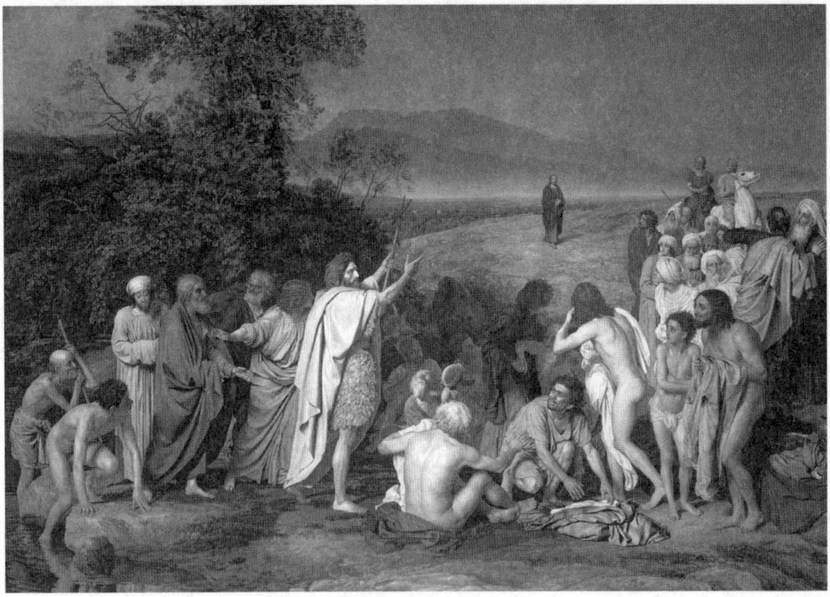

Alexander Ivanov, Christ Appearing to the People, *1857.*
Tretyakov Galerg, Moscow.

acknowledged in communist Russia, is self-evident by their content. If they have not faded altogether in the meantime, they will be discovered at some point. A marvellous small picture by Rembrandt, that hung in the same sunlit hall, where it yielded an agreeable odour of oil of turpentine and paint, did not detract from the artist so misjudged by his contemporaries.

Meanwhile, something occurred in Moscow that also hit our family hard. As a protest against the rigid tsarist regime that spread its crippling influence over all areas of life in Russia, a revolutionary mood prevailed among academic young people, becoming more and more noticeable in those years. The rumour circulated that the students planned a meeting in which to demand academic freedom. All gatherings not sanctioned by the police counted, however, as a political crime. One morning my brother declared that he was going to the university to just such a gathering. He had put on high boots, which he otherwise only wore in the country, took a sausage with him, and what proved most fateful, a Finnish knife. These knives counted as weapons and were strictly forbidden. It seemed to me that Alyosha, then not yet eighteen years old, was playing "robbers." He told me later, he had wanted to give up his life, in which he still saw no meaning, but that he had wanted to do this at least in the cause of freedom. As I drove past the university buildings and the large *manège* at midday on the way to my grandmother, a regiment of Cossacks stood there, whose scarlet kilts shone in the February sun. I knew well enough what the presence of the Cossacks meant here.

I found my grandmother in her bedroom in front of the icons.

"Is your brother at home?" she asked me in a threatening tone.

"No."

At that she shrieked, scolding him, so that I got quite a fright.

The mood in our house was extremely dejected. Towards evening a few of the students who had taken part in the meeting came and told us that everyone who had only demanded academic freedom had been allowed to go home. My brother, however, had declared himself for political reform, and that implied rioting ... and consequently the death penalty. My mother was beside herself: one moment she raged against him, the next moment against the others who were so cowardly as to go away or had even stayed at home altogether. One moment her son was a hero, the next a criminal. Then our friend Vladimir Dzhunkovsky appeared, at that time the Governor General of Moscow, to inquire after my brother, and promised my parents to bring him home. The students entrenched themselves in the tower hall and barricaded the spiral staircase leading up to them. The Cossacks could not reach them by this route, so they broke through the wall of the adjacent building and forced their way in. The students were then escorted at bayonet-point out of the university and into the riding school. My brother left the hall last. Dzhunkovsky waited for him at the gateway to the university courtyard. "Alyosha, your mother is waiting for you, come with me!" but the young fellow walked proudly past him, without saying a word. After a night spent in the riding school, the young people were taken to the Butyrki Prison, located in an outlying area of Moscow. Our whole family rode every so often in a large sleigh through the melting snow to this prison, to visit our convict. Two armed soldiers escorted him to us. Once, when we came to visit him, we were told the students had declared a hunger strike, and my brother was too weak to appear. This hunger strike was a protest against soldiers having been posted to keep watch in the cell of the female students. One can imagine our fears. The sentence awaiting the "politicals" was known to be the harshest ... death by hanging. By means of a petition to the tsar, however, it was commuted to life imprisonment. My brother was transferred with two of his friends to the Kursk Prison, under the jurisdiction of Dzhunkovsky's brother. In August of that year Alyosha was personally pardoned and released. He could not, however, complete his studies in Russia. Thus he went to Germany, to study engineering, beginning with a practical year in a factory in Altona.

Earth Shone Through

While these events were taking place I continued working in the studio. Absorbing myself in the pure world of colours and tones, I became receptive to another reality. At first this world came in strange dreams. Whole novellas took shape that later on in my life were as though realized in metamorphosed form. From sleep I also brought along images and guidelines for art. At that time I read *The Brothers Karamazov* by Dostoyevsky for the first time. The figure and words of the monk Sossima made a deep impression on me. Questions concerning the problem of Christianity presented themselves to me. For several days in early spring I stayed at my Aunt Anna's country house to recuperate.[16] Her husband [Yakov Polyakov], who managed a factory, lived alone there at the time. I often fled to this house from the tumult of the city. To my astonishment, I became aware that this otherwise solidly grounded man occupied himself with spiritual problems. He gave me *The Justification of the Good* by Soloviev to read. It was my first encounter with the philosopher. A golden light imbued my soul, and the whole of nature around me became a revelation of this light, this love. The mother-of-pearl of the tree trunks and the violet of the leafless treetops of the birch forests, interspersed with dark green pines, the fragrant violets among the brown leaves of the previous year, the emerald flaring-up of the new green, the breathing of the damp earth and the delicate blue-greenish sky — everything had arisen from the creative Word, from the same love that, active within the soul, traced creation back to its origins. I saw the world around me as my very own once again. The divine world manifested itself in world processes, revealing itself in me, in my love, in my thoughts. Colours became more real for me as well and disclosed their living soul quality.

In these days my young Uncle Sergei Sabashnikov, the publisher, also came to the house to restore himself. I attempted to describe my experiences to him, but his one-sided materialistic education did not allow him such perceptions. "How," I said to him, as we walked through the forest, "can you believe that these violets, this joyous chorus of birds, this golden light, are only the result of mechanical processes, things that have come about meaninglessly and by chance?"

Yet that was his conviction. Though so clever and musically gifted, he remained rigid and tense in his scepticism. I would gladly have helped him out of his tenseness which was actually despair, but was unable to do so. It was not enough for me that this new world I had discovered in me and around me was to remain only my subjective affair. Yet without coming to terms with natural science, I could not justify the objective validity of these thoughts to others. So as to stand on firm ground, I wanted to get to know the boundaries of science and decided to study natural sciences at the Women's University in Moscow. (At that time women were not yet admitted to the state colleges). My mother approved of this, for quite different reasons: an inexplicable anxiety about the future, the fear that we could become poor at some point. She wanted me to take up a secure profession, for instance, that of laboratory assistant, since with painting, she thought, one would not be able to earn one's daily bread. So I had myself enrolled. The new semester began in the autumn, but between spring and autumn a lot can happen.

In May we were invited with many other young people to the estate of Mrs Avenarius. As the large new house was not yet finished, we were all crammed into the little estate manager's house. I slept in the living room, a transit room for everyone during the day. There I was overcome by an odd sleep; I slept for eight days, day and night, appearing only at meals as a dreaming figure. This peculiar sleep involved a submersion in a living sea of extraordinarily refreshing pictures. In a dream someone gave me instruction in painting. Today I still remember a few of the words. When this condition had passed, I began to paint assiduously and made unexpected progress that summer.

I also spent several weeks that summer at my grandmother's on the Sokolovo estate. It was the house where Alexander Herzen had once lived with his friends and described in his recollections. In my large round room under the roof I painted a self-portrait. This picture became important for me in that it brought me my first public success.

At this time fate put Pascal's *Pensées* into my hands. Pascal and Soloviev became two pillars of a gateway that led me to a new

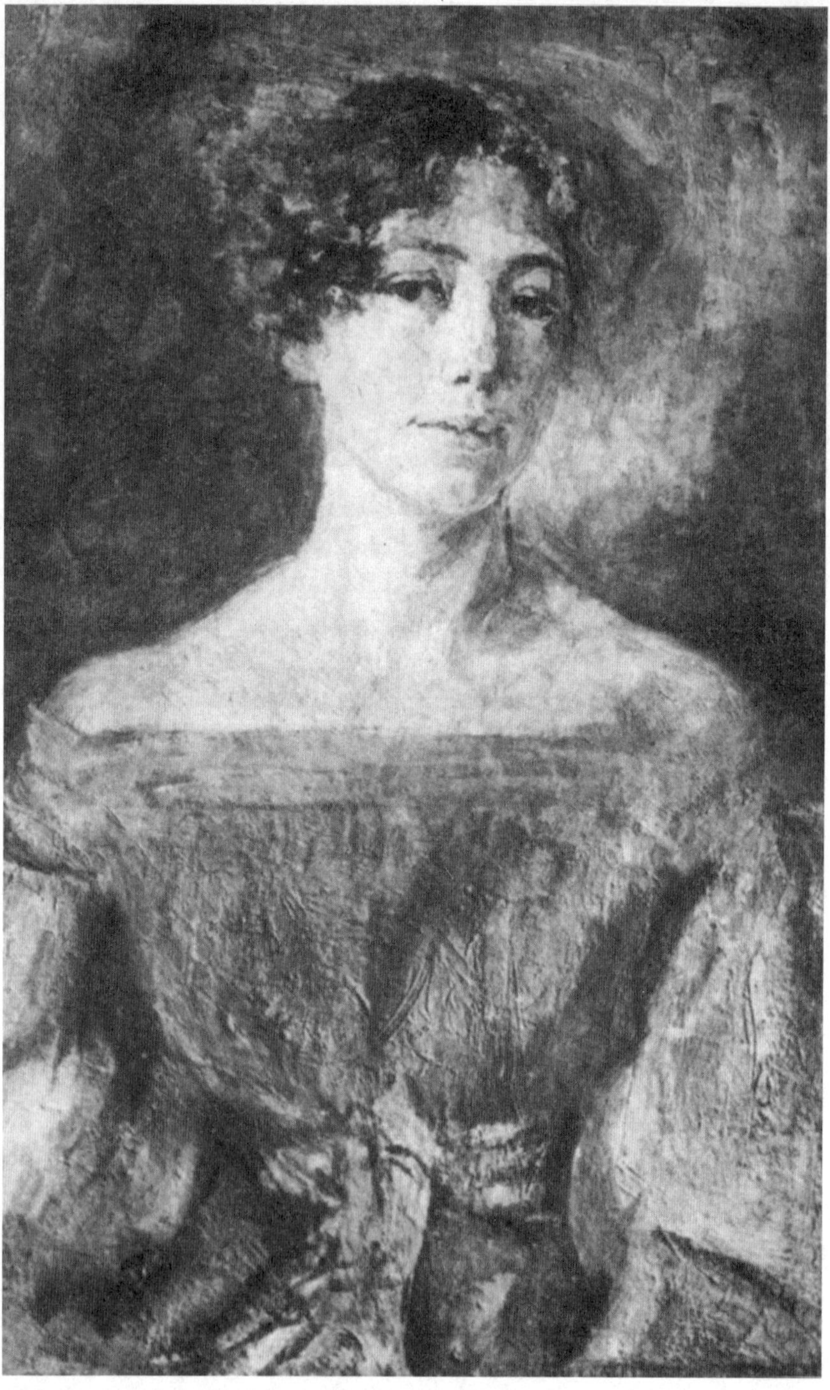

Margarita Woloschin, self-portrait aged 21, 1903.

Christianity, and I experienced a profound feeling of happiness at that time. Thinking no longer contradicted belief. Half a century earlier, here in this house, Alexander Herzen had given up, once and for all, on the belief in a spiritual world. For him that also meant breaking with those of his closest friends who did not take this step. Herzen took satisfaction at every young person who had the courage to deny the reality of the spiritual world. What to Alexander Herzen and the best minds of his time had appeared as a deliverance for human beings, amounted in our time to the denial of one's humanity. In that same Sokolovo house, a young person now celebrated the discovery of a new, unrestricted path to Christianity, compatible with thinking!

I read Nikolai Leskov's *The Clericals* aloud to my grandmother. It was about a Russian priest's life of suffering. What Christian substance lived in that artist, through whom the Russian folk-soul revealed itself as through no other! I sought to experience this Christian substance wherever it showed itself in Russia. I was happy to have found a world that united me with the people. It was also the world of my grandmother, whom I loved very much.

And on our estate, where we spent the rest of the summer, this Christian substance came to meet me; I breathed it in deeply from the landscape, from the faces of the people, from the books that I read by Gleb Uspensky and by Pavel Melnikov, who described the history of the piece of earth on which we lived. Every Sunday I went with my cousin Elisabeth to our village church. The ritual act had a different effect in the country, in the atmosphere of this people bound to the land, than in the city. I experienced the chalice, raised over the fields, seen through the arched windows of the church and over the kneeling peasants, as the sunlit heart of the earth itself. It has been said that, in the Russian Church, one feels oneself as though in the archetypal cell of the earth.

In the autumn, nature was transfigured by mildness. Warmed by the sun, the straw of the stubble fields shone like gold under an improbably blue sky. As the foot glided over the hot stubble, the shiny straw itself seemed to be of heavenly origin. It was as though the summer sun, having sacrificed itself to the earth now radiated from the earth into space in the shimmering pure red of the foliage. I had to think of the words of Fyodor Tyutchev:

These straw covered huts,
This barren, mute landscape,
Land of suffering, land of forbearance,
You, land of my poor people,
Neither note, nor comprehend
Will the eye of a stranger,
What there appears and secretly shines
In the humility of your beauty.
Under His cross' heavy burden
In the guise of a serf
Has wandered all across you, native soil,
Christ, blessing your fields.

From this time on a deep friendship united me with Elisabeth. She seemed to me like the embodiment of Russia. Only now did I notice how beautiful she was. Humility and dignity expressed themselves in the bearing of her tall figure. Humility and dignity also in the high arc of her eyebrows; almond-shaped eyes, a slightly hooked nose and a very small mouth gave her a similarity to the Russian icons of the Mother of God. Not distracted by the free-thinking movements that prevailed at that time in our circles, she went her own religious way from childhood on. She was considered uninteresting and had earlier appeared to me old-maidish. My mother was of the opinion that Elisabeth was so limited that she would never be up to the demands of life. She always wanted to tell her what to do and did not allow her special character to unfold as long as she lived with us. Only my father repeated often, "Elisabeth has a wise heart." The maturity this woman possessed and what character, showed itself only later in the terrible years of the Revolution, when she became not only the support of her own family, but of many other people besides, whom she helped with truly boundless selflessness.

In that summer so rich in experiences, which we three sisters spent on our estate, my picture of Nyusha emerged that was later to become very successful and was acquired by a museum.[17] In a raw silk dress of our grandmother's, with shimmering rose-coloured stripes — found in an old chest — she sits on the balcony railing, a grey lace shawl around her shoulders, a small bunch of cornflowers in her hand. In the background, golden birches, through which a pale blue sky shimmers. Perhaps the effect this picture exerted on people and, as I hear, still exerts today, can be explained by the fact that these colours really did live in me.

In the autumn my Aunt Alexandra, the writer, took me with her on a trip to Italy. We visited Vienna, Venice, Bologna, Padua, Ravenna, Florence and Rome. My aunt smiled at my outbursts of enthusiasm, but demanded thorough study from me as a counterweight. I had to explain to her the architecture of the churches, the characteristics of a particular style or master, having prepared myself on the preceding evening. She did not share my admiration for Byzantine mosaics, Egyptian sculpture and archaic art, which were solely of academic interest to her. On the other hand I did not then understand her admiration for Raphael, whom I had certainly loved as a child, but, only much later, recognized as supremely great again. This dissimilarity of our inclinations did not derive only from our age difference, but from my orientation towards sacred, hieratic art, which in those years was not yet fashionable and came entirely from me. It may be seen as connected with the dawning of a new age. We have now to reach further back into the past, where the sources are to be found which the future is to reveal to us once again on another level of consciousness. My aunt, with her old, closed world-view, had no relationship to this. In the Arena Chapel in Padua, however, in front of the frescos of Giotto, we were in complete agreement with each other in our enthusiasm.

Following these experiences, I arrived late in Moscow for my courses in natural science. The dreariness and boredom of the lecturing professors appalled me. Every day spent in those grey auditoriums seemed to me lost. I now only loved painting. My scientific resolutions evaporated. But my mother did not agree with my wanting to give up these courses so quickly, and so I put up with them for several months. An incident came to my aid. The fine, well-known painter Viktor Mussatov visited us. He was hunchbacked, but despite his deformed figure exercised great charm as a human being. His monumental and romantic pictures of human beings in landscape settings were festive. He had gone through the French School, but his pictures were full of the Russian poetry of Turgeniev. On seeing my pictures, he wanted me to send Nyusha's portrait and my self-portrait to an exhibition of Moscow Painters.[18] He was on the jury. The opening was the next day. The morning after that, my delighted father showed me several different, very favourable reviews. Nyusha's portrait became the focus of the exhibition. It was reproduced in the largest newspaper, and later exhibited by Diaghilev in St Petersburg in the World of Art exhibition. Then it was taken by him to Paris to be included in a retrospective exhibition of Russian art, where it appeared in the catalogue. This first success gave me the courage to give up studying natural sciences, though my mother still took this very much amiss.

An acquaintance, wanting to do something to promote Russian culture, had various artists paint historical pictures, which peasants could then buy in inexpensive reproductions at the market, to decorate their walls, as was the common practice among the Russian people. It was an enthralling task. I too was awarded such an assignment, and chose the theme of "The Murder of Tsarevitch Demetrius at Uglich." After the first few rather stiff sketches, I decided to let the picture arise entirely out of colour movement. There was the flight of steps leading up to the castle in Uglich, in the background towering storm clouds, in the foreground a mother kneeling, dressed all in white, supporting herself with outstretched arms astride her dead child, protecting it like an eagle. The crowd of horrified, multicoloured bystanders. In the distance tumult and pursuit, like red flames. In the way I painted then, I was nearer to my present ideal than in the intervening period.

Only now do I comprehend just how symbolic of the destiny of the Russian people this tragic murder of childlike innocence is.

Old Marvels

I had always sought the special substance, not to be grasped in words, that I perceived in the Russian people, in the Russian landscape and also in old Russian history. Through all its barbarity there shone, like a sacred aura, Christian spirituality. So this work on the historical picture that was requested of me came as a welcome task. To connect myself still more intensively with old Russia, I undertook a journey to Rostov and Yaroslavl in February. It was bitterly cold, with a lot of snow. An elderly Siberian relative was assigned to accompany me; a nice but talkative provincial woman. We arrived in Rostov in the evening. In the stuffy hotel room — the bed stood in a wooden enclosure, as was frequently the custom — I read an essay by Vladimir Soloviev by candlelight. It dealt with the spiritual reality that manifests itself in history, and this idea filled me with a feeling of blessedness, and was a beautiful prelude to the impressions which followed, which I took in with this other reality as a background.

From the kremlin (citadel) one looked down on the city as though onto a sea of cupolas. The singular kremlin churches, each built over a gate of the kremlin wall and connected with each other through a corridor in this wall, rose with their cupolas, tall and slender, into the sky. The interior spaces of these churches were also distinctive: the chancel took up two thirds of the church and was separated from the congregation area not only by a thin gilded iconostasis (picture-wall), but by a high stone wall. Three doors led into three vaulted spaces, connected with each other by arched openings. The paintings in these vaulted spaces were very lively and appeared to dissolve the wall; it was as though what took place over the chalice during the Eucharist was to reveal itself in these pictures. One looked into three worlds: the world of the Father in pictures of the Creation story; the world of the Son in pictures of the Gospels; the world of the Holy Spirit in the visions of the Apocalypse of the future of humanity.

The churches were disproportionately high in relation to their width and length. Six-winged hierarchical beings were painted on the domes of the cupolas, on the pilasters, and when I entered the Church of John the Evangelist, the wind whistled in the cupolas and my footsteps startled pigeons nesting there. It was then as though I heard the wing-beat of the Cherubim.

I wanted to paint one of these churches; pale rose with dark blue starry cupolas, towering into the frosty sky. However, in the intense cold the oil paint froze on the brush. At a barracks opposite, we ventured to ask whether I might paint the church from one of their windows. The officer, probably bored beyond words in that backwater, was keen to oblige us and sent soldiers into all the rooms to check from which window the church could be seen. One after the other, they reported back on the view from the various windows. One of them was silenced in mid-sentence with a sweep of the hand, which amused us, and I was able to paint in the comfort of a heated room.

The Museum of Antiquities in the kremlin afforded me unforgettable impressions. Persian, Byzantian and Norman elements blended themselves in Russian applied arts into a marvellous distinctiveness. We admired the folk pottery in which the prototypes of eagle, lion and other animal forms appeared; the carved, and in some cases colourfully painted, wooden implements, sunlike breadboards, moon-shaped ladles, crystalline salt bowls, chests, tables, sleds, carved and brightly coloured window frames — everywhere a mythological world in colour. Still more impressive were the brocaded garments and diverse folk costumes, headgear in which the face of the woman appeared as though surrounded by a large halo; a net of pearls covered the forehead, strings of pearls hung from the temples, framing the neck and cheeks. A large diadem, often in the form of a triangle, completely embroidered with gold, genuine pearls and precious stones encircled the head at the hairline, inclining somewhat toward the front; from its peak a broad veil flowed down at the back. Thus decorated, the woman's countenance appeared as if looking through a window out of the heavens.

We undertook a sleigh ride to the ancient stave church on the Ishna creek near Rostov. This church was a monument of Nordic architecture in wood; it was covered with shingles in the form of oak leaves. Slender and unassuming, blackened from age, it stood in the broad snowy landscape under the opalescent sky. Inside, the dark pine wood had a warm and intimate effect. The broad trunks appeared as though, over time, they had grown together into a single surface. The altar wall consisted of wood carvings; only the middle one, the royal doorway, was gilded. The old icons were decorated with large, real gemstones. By candlelight the gemstones in the dark wood had a mysterious, warm effect.

The churches of Yaroslavl belonged to a folkloric art; they seemed to grow organically out of the ground. Their fresco paintings were quite new to me, especially the rich ceramic decorations outside.

The Nikolo Mokry Church was remarkable. I caught sight of its smooth white walls over on the opposite high bank of the Volga, under a white frosty sky.

In my youth the first snow fell at the beginning of November and stayed on the ground until mid March. Since then the climate has changed. With the first snow falling during the night, one woke up with the feeling of a wonderful stillness. Going out of the house, the air and the white ground were pure as on the first day of creation. Every sound, a dog barking, the cawing of a crow, the pealing of a bell rang out with a strange clarity and stood alone, superimposed on this stillness. On the white, virginal ground, the first footsteps, animal tracks and sled tracks were like a new script of destiny. A floral headscarf, the red feet of geese, a sprig of fir, everything coloured appeared in the white as though from another world. On wintry paths I experienced my own thoughts as being a world of moving coloured figures, which I watched. As small children we dug passages into the mountains of snow in our courtyard; how starry and warm this snow appeared to me! At twilight everything was submerged in blueness. Later, while skiing or on sleigh rides, no transition could be discovered between earth and sky; one's consciousness widened. At night the little "snow stars" under one's feet often glistened like the heavenly stars above. One was surrounded by a shining sphere and looked upon by billions of angel eyes.

To return to my story ... when we arrived at six in the morning at the railway station in Moscow, it was still nighttime. The frosty air in the entrance hall was filled with a dense haze: the breath of a crowd of peasants in sheepskins. In this crush, I bumped into an acquaintance in a tailcoat. It was Polyakov, the publisher of the periodical *Vesy* (the Scales).

He asked astonished, "What are you doing here at this hour?"

"And you, if I may ask?"

He replied, "We are going to my sister Netty's wedding."

And he asked me to come with him to the waiting room. I said goodbye to my companion and found the bride, the daughter of wealthy parents, in a circle of writers whom I knew. I learned that the marriage ceremony was to be performed secretly in the country by a priest who had been bribed, since the bridegroom, a writer, had not yet settled his divorce papers. The bride, whom I had known since my childhood, struck me in her white dress like a sacrificial offering. Her subsequent destiny vindicated this premonition.

Meetings

Full of these impressions I hurried to Katharina Balmont, to tell her everything just as I ordinarily would. She happily informed me, however, that the poet and painter Max Voloshin, with whom she had become friends in Paris, had just come to Moscow. She was pleased that I would get to know him the same day, since we were all invited that evening to the famous art collector Sergei Shtshukin.

In a house that was an architectural pearl of the eighteenth century, Shtshukin had a collection of the best Monets, portraits by Renoir, Degas, Toulouse-Lautrec and an entire hall of pictures by Paul Gauguin, whose art I had not known until then. This French painting took me by surprise and filled me with enthusiasm. I would have liked best of all to have gone to Paris immediately, in order to come to terms with it more intensively.

I had already seen a portrait of Max Voloshin. It was hanging at the time next to my pictures in the exhibition and portrayed him as a "character from the Latin Quarter", a corpulent man with a lion's mane, in a long cape, a pointed hat on his head with an immensely wide rim. In reality, however, he was not so bad. His hair was admittedly outrageous. His sweater and short trousers could be deemed inappropriate in that elegant company, but his kind-hearted, childlike eyes and his genuine enthusiasm allowed such flamboyance to be forgotten. On the way home he told me more about the French painters, who were part of his world.

Soon he became the subject of many of the conversations in our circle. That was in fact a peculiarity of Russian society at that time: this passionate interest with which every new person was received. It had nothing to do with the curiosity of a provincial city; the newcomer was accepted as destiny. It was recognized that because of him the constellation of the community would be a different one; a new impetus would come through him. Max was original, not only on account of his dress, which shocked some people, but also on account of his odd paradoxes and his unprejudiced attitude regarding every thought and every person. He was a cheerful person; for Russia unusually cheerful. His joy in all the phenomena of life had something childlike about it, even though he was already twenty-nine years old. He gave the assurance that he had never suffered and didn't know what suffering was; a wanderer, "close to all and strange to all," as it said in one of his poems. His poems had an impressionistic character. He also made beautiful translations of poems by Emile Verhaeren and painted unusual landscapes. After his departure he sometimes wrote to me about his impressions of Paris in a very stylized upright handwriting; his letters seemed to me a little laboured, a kind of playing with paradoxical ideas. I did not occupy myself further with him. Life brought me too much else that was interesting.

At a costume ball the famous patron of the arts, Savva Mamontov, stepped up to me and praised my costume; I wore a white tulle dress with little roses and had curls at the temples. Mamontov was a generous human being and gifted with genius. Through his private initiative, and with his money, the railway was built from Moscow to the White Sea. In the North Station, which he had built, hung the large decorative panels of my teacher, Konstantin Korovin, which depict northern landscapes, the northern lights and reindeer. The private opera house of Mamontov was in many respects artistically superior to the imperial one. In Shalyapin's biography one can read how Mamontov discovered him, helped him get his training and onto the stage. After his bankruptcy Mamontov was put in prison. I got to know him only after this terrible blow of fate — he must have been about sixty years old at the time.

He spoke appreciatively of the picture I had exhibited and invited me, along with several painters and poets, to his house the following evening. He lived outside Moscow, and since it was Mardi Gras, we went by peasant's sleigh with a troika. The house, a wooden hut, consisted of one large room with a fireplace, on which oxen could have been roasted. A bench ran along the wooden partition, which was covered with a precious rug. In the corner stood a table, on which a modest, but exquisite dinner was prepared. An eighteen-year-old girl, Tatyana, who had a splendid voice, lived with him. She was lithe and acrobatic and dressed that evening as Hansel, which made it possible for her to perform her tricks. Since she was very light, she could stand on Mamontov's shoulders while singing, without his feeling her to be a burden. He appeared very proud of her and her singing. She showed me some small sculptures he had modelled in prison and spoke of him with the greatest awe. Some said she was his illegitimate daughter, others considered her to be his mistress. At dinner, Mamontov sat down next to me and began to question me on what I had already seen of art, my favourite painter, etc. He was apparently satisfied with my answers. The picture of Moscow would have remained incomplete, had I not mentioned this fleeting encounter with the man who exercised such a great influence on Russian culture.

Two years had gone by since the death of Vladimir Soloviev, but his spirit-figure overshadowed Moscow, and not only the small circles of his friends and followers who lived close by in the district between the Pretshistenka and Arbat, and viewed life from an apocalyptic-mythologizing perspective. I did not then know these circles. But in the whole atmosphere of the city, in the sky — particularly in the glow of sunset, which sometimes flared up like red wings behind the fire department tower at the end of our street — amid the turquoise blue and gold of infinity, his proximity could be felt. Something rose up as though from the other world into our daily routine. I felt it in what took place between the trees and the setting sun, in the light, in the meeting of human beings. I asked myself, whether others also experienced this mystery.

Once in the Library for Foreign Literature a student was pointed out to me, the young poet who had already published his first books under the pseudonym Andrei Belyi. He was the son of the mathematics professor Bugayev and may have been a few years older than I. When I caught sight of those blue cherubic tiger-like eyes under his dark eyelashes, I thought: he too experiences, as I do, the riddle of human existence and the transparency of things. Later, I read the exchange of letters that arose in those years between him and Alexander Blok, who was then also a student. At that time they did not know each other personally, only through their poems. These betrayed a common experience. "How do you see her?" (meaning the being called Sophia in mysticism) one asked of the other, and they spoke about "her" quite philosophically and matter-of-factly, as two scholastics might speak of the supersensible. The first cycle of poems by Alexander Blok is called

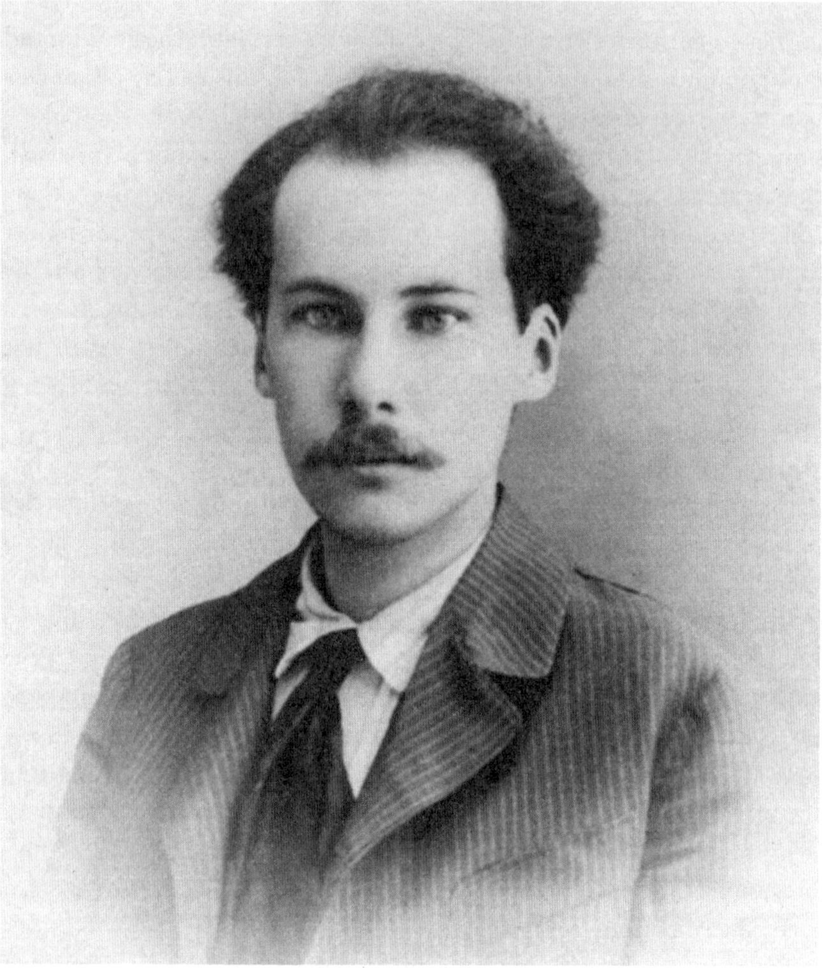

Andrei Belyi, 1904

"Poems to the Beautiful Lady." They are full of the longing to meet with that spirit figure, which the poet feels to be in the Russian forests, behind stars and snow. Vladimir Soloviev, who experienced and saw this spiritual reality — the first to do so in modern times after Dante, the last to do so in the Middle Ages — wrote:

> Here it was permitted me to see death's impotence.
> The power of time was overcome through love.
> Eternal friend, I shall not name you,
> In shy solitude my song rises up.

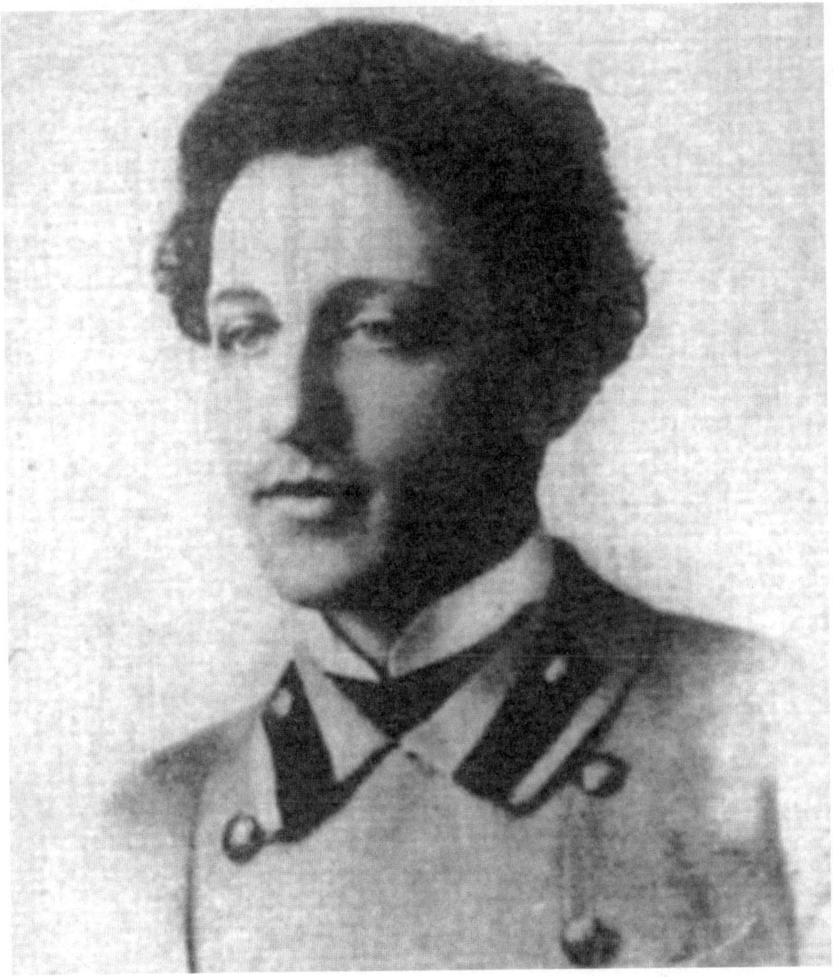

Alexander Blok, 1903

He does not name her. Alexander Blok, on the other hand, designating her "beautiful lady," sought her later in the erotic-earthly, and her features became distorted. For that reason, in his passionate poems, always so rich in rhythms and tones — blown by snowstorms and carried by the vastness of the Russian expanses — there is later despair, desolation and even cynicism. I did not get to know Blok personally in the first period, only in that second phase.

How Andrei Belyi found his direction I shall report on later, since we met each other on that same path. At that time I had the opportunity of exchanging a few words with him only once. It was at a dinner following a lecture by Balmont, when I sat next to him. From his first glance, I knew once again I was not alone in my peculiar feelings with regard to life. Valeri Bryusov was also present that evening. He and Balmont, then already middle-aged, were founders of the Symbolist School. Balmont lived in words as in a fiery, sparkling stream, elementary but thoughtless. In his narcissism and eroticism there was something naïve and therefore innocent. I can understand why his wife, Katharina, an independent, strong personality, not given to blind idolizing, still loved him unconditionally and saw something positive in him, in spite of the sacrifices she had perpetually to make for him. In Bryusov I sensed a lot of posturing. With his thick black eyebrows and square jaw he appeared to me like a Moscow small trader modelled on Klingsor. His poems, chased in form, aspiring to be monumental, did not interest me. I sensed in them an aim expressed in the words of Alexander Ostrovsky, "By my horrible deeds I astounded the world, and the dead will be thankful that they are dead!" For some young people, Bryusov was both a master and a black magician. A kind of spiritual battle took place between him and the young Belyi. Bryusov was later to describe the relationship between the two of them in his novel *The Fiery Angel.*

The Evening Glow of a Culture

In spite of the many stimulating impressions in Moscow, I longed for a larger world in which to learn and work. However, my parents thought I could quite well stay at home. Thus I turned the room that had become free through the marriage of my older cousin into a studio and tried to paint. But it was not easy to establish an artistic atmosphere in a bourgeois house.

For the picture "The Murder of Zarevitch Demetrius" I received two hundred roubles. Since I had meanwhile come of age, I declared that I wanted to go to Paris. This declaration was not easy for me to make. In the end, I travelled to Paris in the care of my Aunt Tatyana. Since she was very withdrawn and loved independence, she allowed me my freedom. We spent the night at an old hotel opposite the Odeon on the Jardin du Luxembourg. Every morning Max Voloshin fetched me, in order to take me to the museums, churches, artists' studios and to the surroundings of Paris — Versailles, St Cloud, Sèvres, St Denis.

Full of joyful expectation I stepped out every day in the silvery morning light and breathed the air of Paris, filled with the smell of violets, mimosas and coal. With this air one drew in at the same time an atmosphere woven over centuries, and was taken up and carried by it. One experienced the dynamic of a history oscillating between contrasts. In its tensions and excesses France's spirit remained ever true to itself, retained its measure and its rhythm, as though this dynamic only fulfilled a perfected and predetermined form after all. This measure lived everywhere, in the thin veils of mist, in the white arcs of the bridges over the silvery Seine, in the expanse of the avenues and public spaces, the seclusion of the churches and gardens. One was not overwhelmed by the magnificence of this city, in which everything was at the same time friendly and intimate, made by human beings for human beings. Time became intimate as well, since tradition projected into the present. The crack of the whips, the little bells of the horses, their hooves striking the asphalt, the shrill and yet harmonious shouts of the women selling vegetables, the harassing call of the newspaper vendors, the melodic honking of the cars, still rare at that time; all these sounds were different than in other cities and disclosed France's particular way of living.

But Paris was not only France — through its museums and libraries it opened gateways to all points of the compass, into all countries and times. One felt united in one's mind's eye with humanity and with all cultures. What good fortune it was to decipher the secret script of time, to be taken up into its stream, lifted out of one's isolation, inserted into a whole and thereby confirmed in one's own existence!

I was often overwhelmed by the strength and enigmatic nature of these impressions. The transition from one hall in the Louvre to another, for instance from the Egyptian to the Greek, could affect me like a shock. However, Max deflected untoward impressions with suitable aphorisms found quickly — perhaps too quickly. With him it was almost a literary game, to find such formulations, but in his childlike, playful manner I found protection from the abysses of the past and present. He was a good comrade on these wanderings and drew tirelessly from the abundance of his knowledge; from memoirs, chronicles and historical works.

Modern Paris enthralled me as well with its flowers seen against the grey background of the city, its ladies' dresses and millinery. That year the ladies' hats were extraordinarily attractive and varied. My aunt bought me a large hat with two bunches of cornflowers on each side and a cornflower blue velvet band. It entered the annals of poetry through a verse that Max wrote.

In the Molière performances of the Comédie Française, serene and well-balanced, I believed I had come upon the spirit of France. I sensed this spirit on hearing the music of Rameau and Grétry played on old instruments, and also in recent music, at the première of Debussy's *Pelleas and Melisande*.

In the months of May and June, I worked in the atelier of Lucien Simon, the serious Breton painter, and made sketches at the Académie Collarossi. In the evenings we were often in the atelier of the engraver Yelisaveta Kruglikova, visited by many artists from different countries. There one could experience Spanish and Georgian dances or hear modern poets of various nations recite their poetry.

One of the most powerful impressions of my life was the first appearance of the young dancer Isadora Duncan, who really resurrected Greece in her art. The whole space around her seemed to me filled with blossoming forms, and my love of dance, which I had had from childhood, awoke in me with renewed vigour. We siblings danced almost every evening together in our schooldays, and I performed the Russian national dance with a certain "inspiration." With Duncan I believed I saw the path to a new art of dance which had something god-like about it. The art of Sarah Bernhardt with her peculiar stylizing spoke to me more than the naturalistic manner of the great Eleonora Duse. And the brilliant cabaret singer Yvette Gilbert enthralled me so much that I would have liked best of all to become a variety singer myself. On later reading this artist's memoirs, I understood how she could evoke such enthusiasm. She was a great individuality, who pursued her new performance art with iron determination and absolute conviction. Yet, in spite of their originality, such single geniuses were but the evening glow of a culture.

A call to return to Moscow tore me out of this world. It was 1904. In the midst of the exhilarating impressions which Paris brought me, I had not been sufficiently aware of what was happening in the Far East. When the news came of the defeat of the Russian fleet [by the Japanese], I was startled out of my dreams. My Moscow friends, who lingered with me in Paris, were shaken. Travelling through Russia on the way home, the reality came to meet me in shocking pictures. En route, the front carriages of our train frequently picked up conscripted soldiers; women could be heard weeping. Driving past the station, I saw groups of people that reminded me of the Calvary scenes of the old masters: peasants holding women who had collapsed in a faint, faces rigid or distorted by pain. It was as when the plough throws up new land, tearing up the roots. I looked into a gaping wound. Oh, this people was not made for war; like a hostile power, violently it struck, horribly and perversely. How defenceless these human beings were, old and young, given over to pain, mute and hopeless. From the front of the train one heard the bawling of drunken soldiers, the sound of which mixed with the whistling of the locomotive and drowned out the despair, while it carried us into the eastern distance.

At home the mood weighed heavily. Nyusha, who worked as a nurse in a military hospital, told me, in her objective and at the same time artistic manner, of heartrending incidents. She herself had become gloomy. Throughout my long absence, she, who otherwise shared my life and my work, had felt her existence to be bleak. She was unable to come to grips with the new experiences.

My father was oppressed by major financial worries, and my mother devoted herself, as always, to her many-sided social activities, with which she sought, as it seemed to me, to mask her uneasiness. She suffered on account of my estrangement, only worsening it, however, with her attitude of rejecting everything that interested me. In our house there was the same mood as in Russian life in general: hopelessness and stagnation! Whenever I came home full of enthusiasm, I had the feeling of being extinguished, like a candle that lacked oxygen. Everything in this bourgeois life followed well-trodden paths. Unable to change it, I aspired to get away from home.

Questions of the Times

Thus in the autumn we travelled to Paris; Nyusha, in order to take singing lessons, I, in order to paint. I had various pictures in me that I wanted to carry out. But I lacked all practical initiative, a definite plan of work. In accordance with my mother's wishes, we lived in a boarding house. I had only a tiny attic room with a view onto the Boulevard Montparnasse. There was no longer enough money for a studio of my own.

Max, whose life and work as a journalist consisted everywhere in finding out what was interesting and describing it interestingly, conducted me to the studios of individual painters and sculptors, to exhibitions and to all manner of other events.

We went to a Russian dance evening. Most of the guests there were descendants of well-known Russian emigrants, of early freedom fighters, of comrades of Garibaldi, Cavour, Herwegh. However, I only encountered an elegantly got-up Parisian society and was very disappointed at the superficiality of the individual people I conversed with.

We also attended a revolutionary Russian gathering. In a hall behind a café a very primitive audience had come together, mainly of unkempt students in slovenly dress. Fresh, red-cheeked faces, among which one could recognize newcomers from the Russian provinces, were present, along with quite pale ones betraying hunger. The spirit of political propaganda in the uneducated, fanatical speech shocked me. Was the salvation of Russia to come from these people? I looked at the clean-shaven, finely modelled faces of the French waiters observing these Scythian nomads wryly, and felt ashamed.

That autumn I no longer experienced Paris only as a traveller enjoying its beauties, but stood horrified before this self-enclosed world, rushing toward the precipice in its madness.

Unmoulded as I then was and almost completely adrift, I took in all these impressions unprotected, and they became a nightmare for me. Even just the fact of an exhibition oppressed me; I felt it to be a cultural absurdity. I saw that painting had no direct place in life, that it signified a demarcated world for itself and that it only concerned the artists, a few dealers, a few patrons and a few connoisseurs. The painters Alexander Benois and Konstantin Somov were then staying for a few months in Paris. I was with them quite a lot. Through them I was introduced in an outstanding manner to the art and culture of the eighteenth century. The gifted painter Somov drew his inspiration from this period. The unreal aspect of this epoch, a mixture of the poetic and grotesque, as well as a refined perversity, came to expression in his peculiar, aesthetically perfect pictures. How far removed was this world from what my soul was actually unconsciously seeking! And yet I was also taken by the beauty of that age.

On a visit to a motherly friend of Max, Madame de Holstein, I met Odilon Redon whom Max and I were then able to visit in his apartment. How unusual was the world to which his soul attuned itself and which he portrayed, without concerning himself about success, pursuing neither naturalism nor impressionism. He showed us portfolios with pastels in wonderful colour harmonies, which in their mood were reminiscent of old Gothic glass windows; colourful, imaginary flowers painted in watercolours and unassuming drawings in charcoal that sometimes intended only to render a gesture, a mysterious impression. He himself, already an older man, was at first admired and understood by only a very few people. He smiled quietly, looking straight ahead, as only someone can smile lovingly and objectively, who regards the things that want to come about through him. Later he became more generally recognized. I particularly remember a charcoal drawing by him showing the head of Satan, the gaze full of superhuman sadness, directed into infinite empty space.

Madame de Holstein, one of Odilon Redon's few admirers, was a Russian living permanently in Paris. At that time she had lost her second husband; her children were married. She provided for her existence with literary work and gathered an elite of French and Russian intellectuals around her. Of small build, she carried her head high. A crooked chin, possibly the result of an unfortunate operation, gave her lively, intelligent face a combative character. One sometimes had the feeling as though she were riding away on a little horse. For her the whole world divided itself into what she supported and promoted, and what she negated and fought against. One could not really reproach her with being lukewarm. When I asked her about her impression of van Gogh, after the first exhibition of his complete works in Paris, she briefly answered (quoting Baudelaire's *De la Beauté*): "*Je hais le mouvement qui déplace les lignes* (I detest the movement that displaces lines)." At that time I was her protégée; later, as a result of my friendship with the poet Vyatsheslav Ivanov, whom she rejected, I ended up in the category of the damned. At her residence I got to know a circle of French poets; René Ghil, Sadia Levy and others. I understood then, how hard it is for the French to derive something new from their overly formed language; to what artifices they have to resort to create something that does not sound banal.

Together with Max I also went to different *variétés* in fashionable, as well as in poorer, parts of the city. Max felt in his element everywhere in the world so long as he could make a few paradoxical remarks about it. His imperturbability and cheerfulness had a reassuring effect on me in all this chaos. I admired his tolerance and saw profound maturity in it. When he had an original idea or something interesting to report, he resembled, in his ponderous, graceful motions, a young St Bernard dog playing with a rag between its teeth.

Great, unsolved questions lived in my soul, but I no longer doubted the reality of the spiritual world. Concerts of the musician Blanche Selva, who played a series of Bach preludes and fugues in the Scola Cantorum with terrific energy and objectivity, also enabled me to experience this world as a direct fact. Through Soloviev I had found the conscious path to Christianity, but I did not see in his ascetic ideal the means of transforming our civilization. In the Collège de France I listened with interest to lectures by Henri Bergson on the Neoplatonists, though his approach to questions of the spirit did not satisfy me. He claimed the human being could come to knowledge of spiritual truths by means of intuition, and seemed very satisfied with this assertion and with himself. Over and over again I asked myself: Where are those who know, who can lead humanity out of the impasse it is in?

Max, who occupied himself with various occult movements from the time of the French Revolution, described to me the deeply moving scene where, at a banquet right before the French Revolution, a member of the nobility predicted the impending tragic downfall in all detail to those present and to himself. The prophecy, documented in memoirs, very soon came true. I asked myself: If the future can be foretold, how can this be reconciled with human freedom? The question of the freedom of the human being seemed decisive, since it was clear to me that without this freedom, every question concerning morality, concerning good and evil, was futile.

These questions occupied me more than my painting, and apart from a few landscapes and the portrait of Tchuyko, I painted nothing during that time. Next to a fountain covered in vines with blue grapes against the green background of a park, with ivy garlands between vases, I painted his pale face, rather like a young, eaves-dropping silenus. His suit is blue; a garnet on his ring shines amid the blue and green shadow of foliage. The Municipal Gallery of Moscow later bought this picture. Tchuyko had come to Paris, prompted by my enthusiastic descriptions. He was touchingly devoted to both Nyusha and me, and protected us like a nanny, for instance at the evenings at Kruglikova's, where things sometimes got a bit risqué. If he foresaw that the boundaries would soon be overstepped, he whispered to me that my cousin was tired and wanted to go home, told her the same about me and accompanied us home. He admitted this to us much later. Paris was disastrous for him personally. He could not do without this city, and his delicate, sensitive soul succumbed to it as to a poison, to which the French themselves are immune.

During those days I already had the first meeting with Trifon Georgievich Trapesnikov, the art historian, who accompanied me and my cousin to Chantilly. I felt that the same questions lived in him as in me, and was sad that our meeting was only brief. I met him again in later years, and there was much that we experienced and collaborated on together. At that time in Paris, he was a seeker just as I was.

Suddenly, that spring Max did not visit me anymore. I was taken aback and very disappointed. I did not know that my relationship to him purely as a friend pained him. Nyusha returned to Russia, so I was truly alone. Then a friend of Mrs Balmont, Miss Anna Minslova came from St Petersburg and took a room in my boarding house. I had already come to know her in passing at the time of my attempt to deal with materialism. At a concert she had said, "The violin has a soul." I envied her in being able to believe something like that, and yet was annoyed at her for not wanting to explain this remark, so as to enable others to accept it. She was now forty-five years old. Her figure was shapeless, her forehead excessively large, as with the angels in old German paintings. Her protruding blue eyes were very nearsighted, but looked as though into immense distances. Her reddish-blonde parted hair, with permanent waves, was in disarray. The bun threatened to loosen, and a rain of hairpins kept falling around her. Her nose was coarsely shaped and the whole face a bit puffed-up. Most peculiar of all were her hands; whitish, soft and with long slim fingers. She held one's hand longer than was normal, trembling slightly. That was what struck me as especially unpleasant at our first meeting in Moscow. Likewise her way of speaking: she lowered her voice almost to a whisper to conceal strong emotion, and had accelerated breathing. Her sentences were cut short, and she often emitted only single disconnected words. Most of the time she had on a worn, black silk dress and an amethyst on her finger. She lived in St Petersburg with her father, a well-known lawyer. Miss Minslova derived her wide knowledge, she told me, mainly from the chronicles of different epochs and countries, which she read in the original. She felt herself unappreciated and not understood by people in her circle; her mystical inclination was regarded as madness. Her father, said to have been a clever and astute man, belonged among the materialists and sceptics. However, everyone recognized her extensive knowledge and abilities in the field of chiromancy and graphology. She said that Katharina Balmont had been the first person with whom she had found a deeper understanding. One of Miss Minslova's forebears had been a Frenchman, which is perhaps where her French humour came from. I have never come across anyone who took in the other person with such intensity. She gave herself up completely to the other person, saw the highest in them that they might perhaps one day become, so that in her presence everyone felt raised above their ordinary affairs. Later on, some of her earlier friends were inclined to consider her a flatterer, and accused her of charlatanism, since in her letters she addressed each of them personally as being the closest, dearest and most precious. She saw the intimate wishes each harboured as being what destiny had predetermined them for, and supported them in this, fettering them to her to an extraordinary extent. In fact, she promoted the mutually contradictory endeavours of different people, while each one thought she had only their aims in mind. Whenever she appeared, there was always a whirl of people and events around her. She would

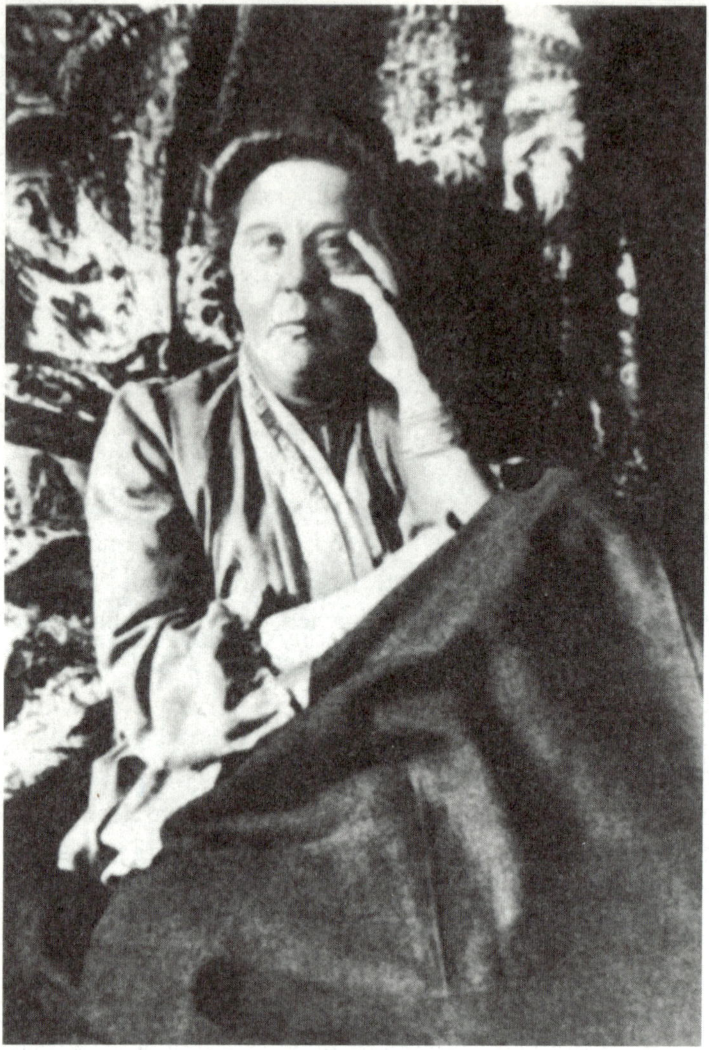

Anna Minslova in Paris, 1905

arrive sporadically for a few weeks. After the death of her father she no longer had a home. Amid this whirl, she was not the point of rest, but was herself passionately swept along. My friends later told me quite grotesque things in this regard. While considerable, her spiritual forces were not schooled by objectivity or self-control, but worked chaotically, unpurged. Even if by her means, many were able to look as though through a window into another world, she wreaked havoc all around her and lost her own bearings.

But I am hurrying ahead. During that period in Paris she appeared like a fay to me, able to answer the questions that lived in me. I accepted her instructions trustingly. Her sympathy heartened me; in her orbit it was as if everything that only glimmered in me began to blaze more brightly. She looked at my palm and discovered great things. She had come to Paris for a theosophical gathering at which Annie Besant was expected from India. Passing through Berlin, she had visited the German branch of the Theosophical Society and spoke of its director in mysterious allusions, though without naming him.

I introduced her to Tchuyko and met Max at her place once again. Both also ended up under her spell. In their palms as well, she read great destinies, and in this way we all felt lifted in our self-esteem.

We wandered again through Paris, but how Paris was transformed by her presence. She described pictures from the past that emerged in front of her. Once, in the Palais Royal, she characterized groups of people from the time before the Revolution so vividly that I asked her from where she knew all this. She named a few authors, Goncourt among them; I read these books, but found nothing of the kind in them. Once — it was evening, and the waning moon stood in the sky — we went past the place where the Knights Templar had been put to death. At that point she was gripped by such horror that I became fearful for her, but she did not articulate what she experienced.

Apart from that, she told us a lot about occult movements at the time of the French Revolution and about the witch trials. While she spoke I felt the entire air around her to be full of horrors; she was herself afraid of the states in which she experienced the past so strongly. Thus we spent the time with her in a peculiar atmosphere. We went with her to a lecture by Mrs Besant. What she said seemed to me quite primitive and fatuous, and her manner of speaking more that of a political agitator. I sensed no mystical deepening. Only her loose white gown was "mystical."

Paris once again acquired its summer charm, with its shady avenues of chestnut trees, its wagonloads of red roses or cornflowers. A visit to an exhibition of old English painters in the Bagatelle Castle was the last experience of this stay in Paris. The breeze blew rose petals through the large windows and doorways in front of the paintings of Gainsborough and Reynolds.

In this blessed time I received a letter from my mother in Zurich. Alyosha had to prepare himself there for his technical exams and she wanted me to "watch over him!" How reluctantly I left Paris and my friends there! Switzerland seemed to me sober and oppressive, and at first I felt quite unhappy there.

In his first letter Max wrote:

> The dead heart allotted me by destiny,
> That felt neither blessedness nor deep sorrow
> A grey little bird, warmed to life through you,
> Humbly I take it from your hand.

And in the second: "There is a law in China, that a person who has saved another from death, is responsible for their destiny. Thus I may also not desert him, but must share his destiny with him." I was touched by these lines and at the same time startled. Our friendship in that case meant more than I had foreseen. I accepted this simply as an obligation, without taking account of whether my response would suffice for a lifetime connection.

The Meeting

In Zurich, as I could find no model, I began to paint a self-portrait. My face was reflected in the second glass of a three-sided mirror so that, as a result of the double mirroring, the two sides should not be exchanged. I painted myself with flowing hair so that it formed a sculptural, rose-gold mass on both sides of the face. Each of these surfaces, composed mosaic-like in colour and form, were reminiscent of a pearl oyster. The face I painted in bluish, cold-rose and warm-rose tones. Behind the head, the surfaces were set forth in the same manner, forming an architecture. The eyes looked out with great intensity, as though gazing out from eternity itself. Later this picture was bought by the directors of a museum in Moscow; to which city it was finally sent, I could not find out in the chaos of the Revolution. What amazes me today is the fact that the architecture in the background and the treatment of its surfaces reminds one, in every respect, of the sculptural forms of the Goetheanum that was built twenty years later.

Hardly had my mother left than the "guardian" undertook a trip to southern Germany with a friend, Lyubimov, who often spent time with us. On a hot afternoon hour between two trains, we made a quick visit to the museum in Stuttgart. I remember the "Salome" by Lukas Cranach. Nuremberg was at that time still a quiet, well-preserved old city. Lyubimov knew how to organize a trip in style. Visits to churches and museums alternated with evening outings into the countryside. Everything appealed to me enormously: the architecture, the scenery, the air. I had not until then experienced the essential character of Germany. In the Germanisches Museum I sensed the dynamism of spirit that broke out of classical norms. It is as though a "soul storm" swept through sculpture and painting. The youthful, future-oriented, Christian element in this spirit took hold. It shook my previous conceptions of beauty. The altarpiece by Riemenschneider in Rothenburg, where we lingered, appeared to me like a song of the

Cherubim. In Würzburg as well, Riemenschneider captivated me. For the first time, in his "Adam," I encountered a non-naturalistic, transfigured human body in sculpture, such as I had only had a presentiment of in some of the sketches of Vrubel.

In Zurich we occupied ourselves with Richard Wagner. In the auditorium of the Institute of Technology I heard lectures by Professor Saitschik on the *Ring of the Nibelung*. His ideas concerning the myth interested me, even though I rejected the speaker himself in some respects, since he evinced no awe of the depth of what he was enunciating and appeared rather to play with the underlying thoughts. Without clarity or certainty, there was something in me like a sense of anticipation. The world was so enigmatic and strange. I had not yet found my path. Even having made a decision in my personal life, I was basically still dissatisfied. At that time my brother lived in a state of quiet desperation, despite a happy flirtation with a petite American. His studies did not interest him; for him, life had no goal. Like many young people then he was enthusiastic about Oscar Wilde for a time. When *De Profundis*, which the poet had written in prison, came into his hands, he went along with this transformation and began reading the Gospel. It is indicative of that time that my mother viewed this as something abnormal. She wanted him to go to a well-known psychiatrist, Monakov, then staying in Zurich. This man warned him against the Gospel as against an unwholesome book. It is incidentally, characteristically Russian, that the same Dr Monakov who espoused atheism so radically at that time, found wonderful words for the being of Christ in a book he wrote later on.

At this time, my brother and Max got the idea that one had to "step out of oneself," out of one's limited personality, in order to become aware of the spirituality of the world. In hopes of thus coming out of themselves, they decided to hike from Zurich to the St Gotthard Pass. They reappeared afterwards in a wretched state: tired and bedraggled. I do not know whether they succeeded in "getting out of themselves." In any case, they did not find the spirituality of the world. In the meantime, I immersed myself in old writings (translations of the *Vedas*, the *Genesis* of Fabre d'Olivet; of Sohar and Porphyrios). Quite frankly, I did not understand a word. But one thing became clear to me: there were other states of consciousness in which the world was seen differently. Have we, today, lost them forever?

I then read, toward the end of summer, the announcement of a lecture to be given in the Theosophical Society. The title referred to a path leading to knowledge of the spiritual world. The speaker's name, Rudolf Steiner, was unknown to me. We decided to hear it, although I rejected theosophy disdainfully out of hand as a dilettantish compromise between oriental wisdom and western materialism. The same day I received a muddled letter from Miss Minslova. She informed me that Dr Steiner, the Chairman of the German Section of the Theosophical Society would be speaking in Zurich. She didn't want to influence me in my decision to hear him, gave me no advice, but if it interested me ... That seemed odd, since she was otherwise not so reticent with her "influencing."

Two ladies, in lively conversation, sat in front of me in the hall. One of them, whose profile I glimpsed from time to time, had golden hair and such a blooming and delicate complexion as one otherwise only sees in children. As she turned toward the door, I saw unbelievable eyes, fiery blue, like sapphires; a mouth, delicate but firm, with a distinctively formed chin. I also noticed her beautiful small hands. At one moment she laughed heartily, at another she appeared indignant, whereby the blood rose quickly to her cheeks. I observed her with interest because she was so unlike the other ladies in the hall. An older gentleman with a white beard — a venerable apparition — stood beside the rostrum. That must be Steiner, I thought; but then, following the lady's glance, I saw a slight figure enter in a black frock coat. Very black hair fell slantwise across his beautifully arched forehead; his eyes were deep-set. What was it about this figure which gripped me so? It was the power of uprightness by which the whole human being was carried. There was a spring in his step as he crossed the auditorium, but his head remained quietly poised as he moved. His neck was held back like an eagle's. How can anyone look so astonishingly like an eagle, I wondered. "Look," I said to my brother, "that must be a yogi." It was Rudolf Steiner. As he began his lecture, I was glad to find that I could follow quite well, since I had been doubtful beforehand whether my German would prove adequate. He spoke in detail about the education of Helen Keller, blind as well as deaf and dumb, and about the efforts of her gifted teacher, and he pointed out that most human beings are deaf, dumb and blind in the spiritual world but may develop organs of perception for this objective world by means of a deliberate schooling. It was not so much the content of this first lecture which impressed me as the personality of the speaker himself. At the end, the old gentleman announced that Dr Steiner would answer questions the next day in the meeting room next door to a restaurant.

I pondered my question. I had, at this time, discovered that the most tormenting riddles are those which live only in feeling. A question, I thought, is like a vessel: if it is rightly formed, the answer cannot help but fill it. And there was something definite that I wanted to know. I could conceive a condition of soul in which one is "out of oneself" and, as a result, knows more than one ordinarily knows; one is in a kind of ecstasy. I had experienced something of this kind in an autumn landscape and in an Egyptian museum. But afterwards, only a vague recollection of the experience remained with me. How can one, I wondered, come to a knowledge of the spiritual world in full possession of one's waking consciousness and without losing the ground beneath one's feet? I wrote this question on a slip of paper in order to submit it, as I feared that, in my embarrassment, I would be unable to formulate it rightly. I was afraid to go out alone the next evening and asked my brother to accompany me to the meeting. But he only replied, jokingly; "You go, I'll stay here at home on the sofa and pray for you; then nothing will happen!" How my guardian angel must have smiled at my concern that, just on this occasion, I should look my best. I put on a pale grey linen suit from Paris and wore a hat ornamented with tiny roses!

Along the walls of the meeting room sat, for the most part, heavy-set, conservatively dressed men. In a corner, I saw the ladies of the previous evening, who appeared to belong to Steiner's party. In the centre of the room stood a long table. Rudolf Steiner stepped up to it and gave a short address, then he waited for questions. Everyone was silent. I made up my mind, stood up, went up to him with my slip of paper, but did not hand it to him, putting my question orally instead, blushing deeply and with beating heart. He looked at the paper I was holding, looked at me and said, "That is indeed an important question!" In my embarrassment, I did not return to my place, but sat down next to him at the table. Despite my twenty-three years, I was easily embarrassed. Dr Steiner answered my question somewhat as follows.

There are thoughts and sensations which are dependent upon the place where we find ourselves at that moment. We have one set of thoughts and feelings in Moscow, another in Paris. But there are also thoughts and feelings which are independent of space and time. When we cultivate a soul content of this kind, we nourish what is eternal in us, we strengthen it, make it independent of our physical body. He spoke at length about meditation, by means of which supersensible organs are moulded in our soul, capable of perceiving the objective spiritual world. He spoke about the schooling of thinking, that should become more active, more living; about the schooling of feeling, which, in becoming objective becomes an organ of perception; about the schooling of will, which must be consciously taken hold of and guided by the I or ego. He spoke of the fact that, in our time, the human being can attain spiritual reality, not by dampening down consciousness, but by strengthening it, and by schooling ourselves in this way we will stand more wakefully and capably in everyday life. He briefly described the three stages the spiritual pupil has to attain: of imagination, inspiration, and intuition. For the first time I heard of a path to knowledge of the higher worlds corresponding to our age. I studied Rudolf Steiner's profile close at hand, heard his warm, enthusiastic voice and received each of his words as a joyful message. Is it really possible that there is, in our time, a man who knows; a genuine herald of the spirit? He then closed his discourse, turned to me and asked, "Have I answered your question; is that what you wanted to know?"

The next question concerned animals. It was put by one of the two ladies, who spoke with a Dutch accent, which had something childlike and fresh for my ear. She sat next to the "golden one" and appeared also to accompany Dr Steiner. She was tall, had soft brown hair; she radiated warmth and vitality. In response to her question, Rudolf Steiner sketched a magnificent picture of world evolution. He showed that the evolutionary theory of Haeckel is a great conception, valid for the sense world, but that the human being was originally a spirit being and gradually prepared a body over a long period of time, forming it from outside until able to enter it, in order then to spiritualize it from within. Those bodies, however, which were already too hardened to be able to undergo further development, could not accommodate a spiritual individuality. These are the animals, beings who remained behind along the way, our stunted brothers. The single animals could not take the ego into themselves. In the spiritual world, however, each animal species has its group ego; the single creatures are like the component parts of this group soul. He also spoke of animals as being, like the

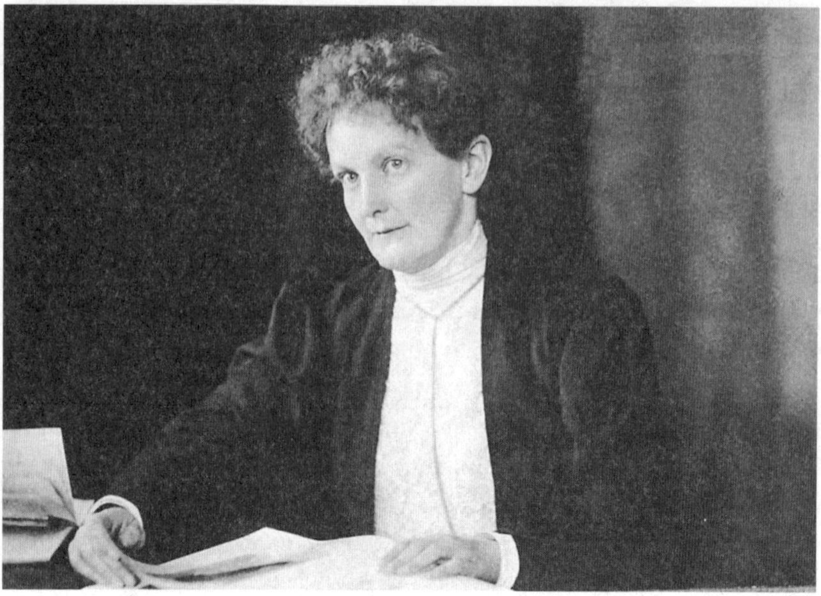

Marie von Sivers, 1906

other kingdoms of nature, stages left behind on the path to becoming human. They sacrificed themselves for the sake of human beings, who will, when a certain stage of evolution has been achieved, redeem them.

At the end, a hale and hearty old man stood up and said in Swiss German, "I have studied the Bible and have studied your Indian books and eleven thick volumes of world history and am convinced that everything the Bible prophesied actually happened, and everything that Indian wisdom says is false."

To this, Rudolf Steiner answered, "What spiritual science has to say is not drawn from oriental wisdom. There has always been a Christian esoteric wisdom which affirms the great truths which were taught in the East, but it has more to say." And then he spoke of the event on Golgatha as the central world event, which by its very nature, could never be repeated. It is just through spiritual science that one can come to understand the Bible rightly and weigh every word.

As I heard these words, I knew I had found what I was looking for, the new, conscious way, in freedom, to the living Christ.

Rudolf Steiner concluded the evening with a few words. He shook hands and said, "You did not ask me in vain, isn't that so? If you have further questions to put to me, write to me!"

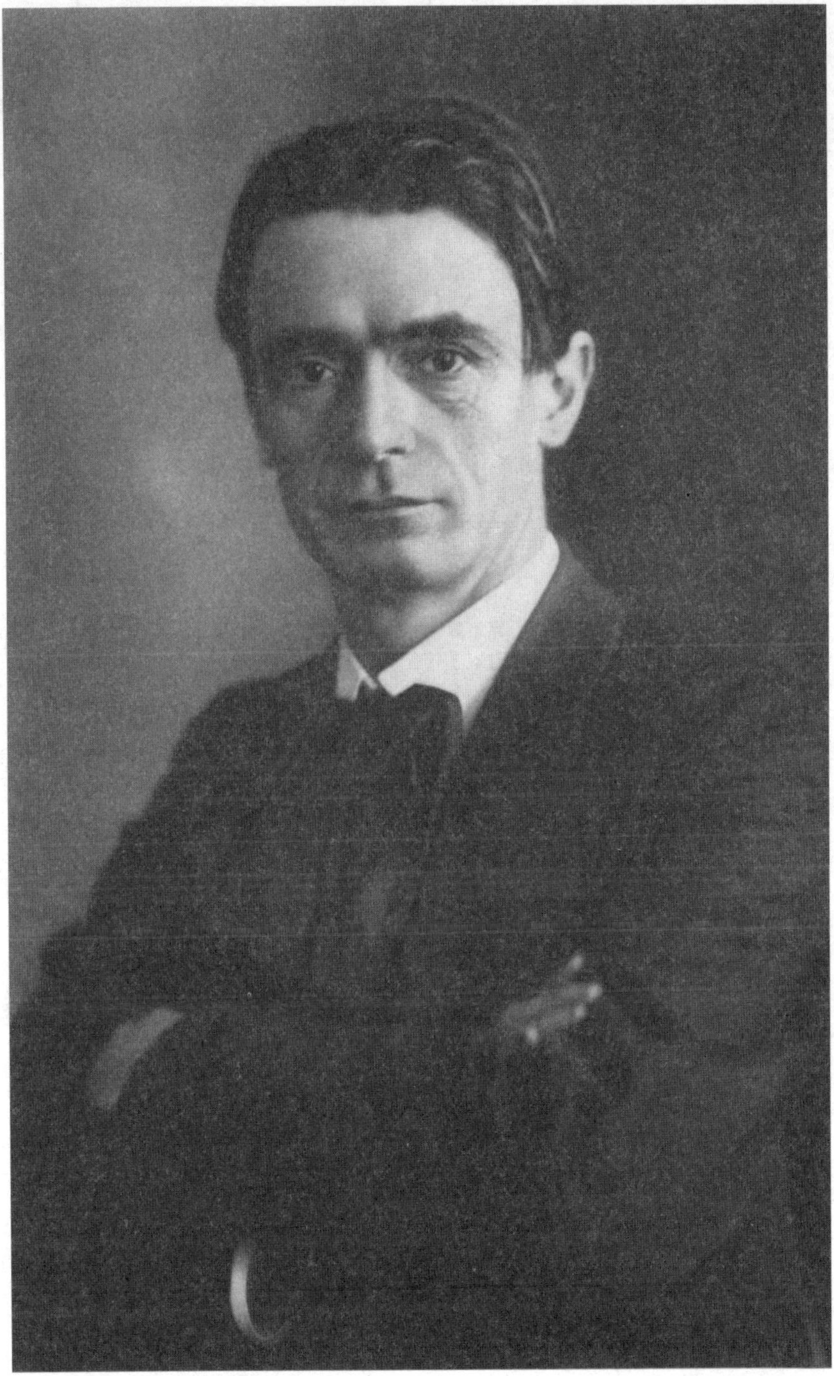

Rudolf Steiner, 1905

I met his glance for the first time; his eyes, surrounded by black eyebrows and lashes, were golden with the warmth that shone through them. It seemed to me that I had always known them; I was torn out of the stream of time. But he continued, "I want to introduce you to Fräulein von Sivers; she is also Russian," and he led me to the lady with the golden hair.

"I know Miss Minslova," I told her.

"Do you also have psychic tendencies?" she asked me ironically, with a strong Baltic accent. I only later understood the irony.

"No, none at all."

"Tomorrow we are travelling to Basle; Dr Steiner is holding a lecture there," she said looking at me expectantly. But the thought did not occur to me that I could go with them, even though I was otherwise inclined to travel.

The next day I wrote to Miss Minslova in Berlin, in order to learn further details about Rudolf Steiner, asking her to send me a photo of him, as well as a few of his published writings. The photo I then received from her corresponded to the impression I had on meeting him. From Miss Minslova's disconnected talk I then gathered some personal references concerning Rudolf Steiner and his collaborator, Marie von Sivers, the daughter of a Baltic general in the Russian service.

My brother and I then occupied ourselves exclusively with publications which Miss Minslova sent us. As was foreseeable, he did not pass his exams. Actually, we were not at all sad about it, but felt relieved, since he no longer had any interest in technology. My parents were less pleased. Until letters had been exchanged with Moscow and decisions had been reached, we wandered through the autumn countryside around Zurich.

The Hour has Arrived, the Human Being not Yet

It had been decided that Alyosha was to study agriculture in Leipzig; whereas I was expected in Moscow, and so we journeyed together to Berlin, at the end of October. There Miss Minslova fetched us from the train station. In the car on the way to the boarding house I already heard broken-off sentences: "The old mysteries live ... they are here ... you will also experience all this in time ... be there yourself ..." I listened with the greatest interest; but that I could "be there" myself eventually ... I considered myself too worldly for that. Our lodging house was close to the house on the Motzstrasse where Fräulein von Sivers and Rudolf Steiner lived. Also located there was the branch of the German Section of the Theosophical Society, which had just had its general meeting. So, right away, we met Fräulein Scholl and Frau von Bredow. Fräulein Scholl, the leader of the branch in Cologne, was a broad figure with a round face, plain straight hair, earnest grey eyes, which — like her voice — conveyed a feeling of serenity and confidence. Behind her quiet mien, one suspected, lay a choleric temperament: for me she was a knight who stood up for the truth with her whole being, once she had recognized it. She could be filled with righteous anger against untruth. When I think about Frau von Bredow, who died young, I see her surrounded by a gentle radiance, like the pearls she wore around her neck, a "beautiful soul" shone in her calm, distinguished manner.

A message from my parents awaited me at the pension: because of the revolution which had just broken out, I was not to return to Moscow. From Miss Minslova, we learned that we were permitted to attend Dr Steiner's lectures, held daily for a small circle. During the first weeks, nine people took part in addition to ourselves. Later there were twelve. So we found ourselves directly part of the "zodiac," as the circle jestingly came to be called, that first came together around Rudolf Steiner. Among its members was Frau von Moltke, wife of the general, later Chief of Staff, Helmuth von Moltke. Frau von Moltke was a regal figure. Two white strands of hair, which fell away on either side of her parting in the middle, formed a diadem around her falcon head. Her manner was resolute, unconventional, almost brusque; one felt a strength, as of inner iron, radiating from her personality.

Sophie Stinde, as well as her friend Countess Kalckreuth, also belonged to the "zodiac." They guided the branch in Munich, where the leading role fell to Sophie Stinde. She was the sister of Julius Stinde, the author of the well-known novel, *The Buchholz Family*, and possessed the same dry humour as her brother. Her art — she was a serious landscape painter — she sacrificed for the spiritual scientific work. Her light blue eyes looked out from under eyelids curved like those of Frederick the Great. Through her northern aloofness, one could sense great warmth. I have, personally, much to be grateful to Sophie Stinde for. Her friend, Countess Kalckreuth, daughter of a well-known landscape painter, had earlier been lady-in-waiting at court. Her unnaturally tall build caused her, when she spoke with people, to bend down toward them, and this motherly, humble attitude corresponded fully with her friendly nature which shone through her beautiful eyes.

Apart from Rudolf Steiner, Marie von Sivers, later the wife of Dr Steiner, also stood in the centre of this circle. I have already described her appearance. Every time I saw her, I was moved again by her beauty. Her eyes were like sapphires and kept their radiance until her death at an advanced age. Only in the high mountains can one experience such a blue. Alpine air surrounded her. The cold and purity of a crystal united in her with the fire of enthusiasm. She was royal and unapproachable, although she in no way placed herself above others. She possessed a childlike immediacy and sparkling humour. Above all, she was an artist. After completing her education in Germany and in Paris, she had wanted to become an actress. At first, she sacrificed her art to the theosophical work, finding her way after a time, under Rudolf Steiner's guidance, to a new art of speech formation that seeks to give back to the spoken word its original creative life.

No one was more aware of Steiner's greatness than she. And yet she stood at his side, independent in judgment and ready to act on her own initiative. For that reason, she probably remained till the end the one person to whose judgment he ascribed an inner validity.

Rudolf Steiner stood in front of a blackboard; we sat in a semicircle around him. It gradually grew dark while he spoke, and the lamps were lit. He spoke about the preliminary stages in the spiritual development of the earth and of the human being. I often asked myself what capacity in us enabled us to follow these descriptions at all, since those states of the earth, those stages of human consciousness, were so little like anything we know today. I had to marvel that there are still words in our language to describe them. Did these descriptions speak so strongly to us, because something of these past worlds has still remained in us and around us, and is now raised into the light of consciousness through the spoken word, as something related to us from the beginning, primordially our own? The human being, united with the universe from the very beginning and only gradually becoming loosened from it, is perhaps to be thought of as a hieroglyph to be deciphered, in which the whole world lies concealed — a fruit of the past, in which, at the same time, the seed of the future lies. It was borne in on me that I was no accidental guest on this earth, but co-responsible, able to become a collaborator in the act of redemption.

The myths in which I had lived since childhood, now proved themselves to have been substantial reality. An earlier stage of consciousness had dreamed reality in true pictures. It was a liberating thought to me, that the human being's entanglement in matter, right down to our intellectual concepts which I so detested, felt to be pernicious, and wanted to flee, that this descent was a necessary stage in human development, without which we would never attain freedom.

Every Russian has the social question very much at heart. The basis of western social theories is class war, the continuation of the Darwinian struggle for existence, in which the human being is seen only as a natural being and not also as a moral being. The ideas of the Russian socialists, however, are founded on the principle of brotherhood, of mutual assistance. Prince Kropotkin even saw this principle at work in nature and described it in his valuable natural scientific work *Mutual Assistance in the Animal Kingdom*. The search for the solution to the social question in this direction, Steiner characterized as the future mission of the Slavic peoples. What a caricature of this — what a changeling — Russia got instead after only twelve years! Yet when Steiner already spoke at that time about coming catastrophes, about the war of all against all, about the splitting of the atom and the consequent destruction, I listened to him uncomprehendingly — what catastrophes could possibly occur in our so stable and humane civilization?

The small handful of listeners, of which most did not distinguish themselves at all by having particular talents, were unassuming people, but they recognized the significance of the hour. They practised a path of meditation which Steiner indicated for each one according to their individual disposition. The "important people," the rhetoricians and those with doctorates, came later. The only person endangered by their soul constitution on account of an ecstatic nature and visionary tendencies, but having considerable élan on the other hand, was Miss Minslova. And I stood at that time under her influence, unfortunately. Max was able to free himself for a short time and came to Berlin to attend the lectures.

The fact that Rudolf Steiner, this scientific spirit, led a section of the Theosophical Society, I at first found disconcerting. Now I understood that he did so, because in this circle he found people who were concerned about a concrete spiritual path. He wanted to indicate to them the path corresponding to our time, one developed consistently from the natural scientific method. On assuming the leadership of the German Theosophical Society, Steiner made it a condition that he be able to conduct his work quite independently, and be free to teach a spiritual science originating from his own research. It was from this source and not out of tradition, that he developed his Christology. What Steiner brought forward was something entirely new for our age. In the meantime, much of what he wrote and spoke about has influenced the general culture, whether people are aware of it or not. Even those who feel obliged to oppose Rudolf Steiner's teaching owe him, in many cases, the more living comprehension of the very dogmas they advocate.

After the lectures, Steiner remained in the room and answered questions. He inquired of me each time, whether I had been able to follow what he had said. What was most striking about him, apart from his earnestness, was the warmth which radiated from him. Through friendliness and humour he sought always to bridge the chasm we felt between ourselves and him. Besides gathering in this small circle every afternoon, we heard Rudolf Steiner speak in the context of the Theosophical Society, to which we did not belong. We also attended his public lectures in the *Architekten-haus* and the history course he gave for the workers in the Karl Liebknecht School.

At the beginning of the academic year, my brother had to leave for Leipzig. But he remained connected from then on with spiritual science. One day Marie von Sivers said to me, "There will be an apartment available on our floor. Wouldn't you like to rent it and work under the guidance of Dr Steiner?"

"No, I have to go to Paris."

How right the pilgrim was, who, in my childhood said to me, "You seek your good fortune in faraway places, but your good fortune is right beside you, and suffers."

III

Paths and Detours

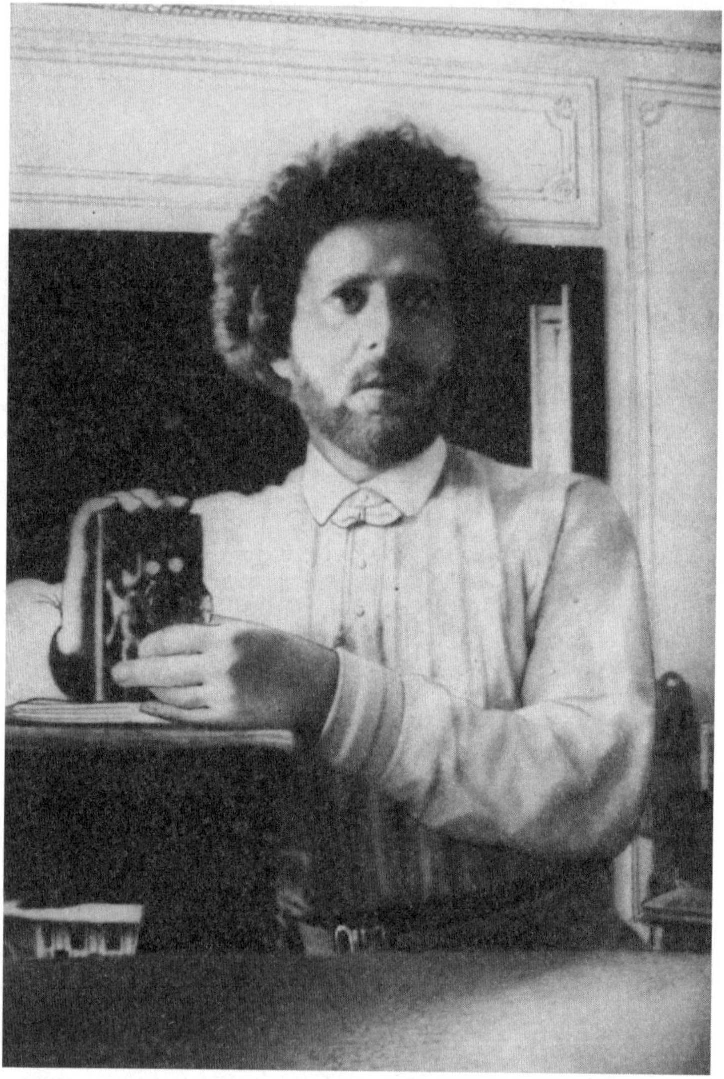

Maximilian Voloshin. Self-portrait photograph, Paris 1905.

Paths and Detours

The winter months of 1905, which I spent with my cousin Nyusha in Paris, stood under the sign of the Russian Revolution. Grand Duke Sergei, the Governor General of Moscow, was murdered by a young social revolutionary. An old emigrant by the name of Mark Natanson lived in our pension. Illumined by this fanatical revolutionary, I saw the Russian events from a different perspective. I had learned from Moscow that the Grand Duchess Elisabeth, the widow of the one who had been murdered, visited the young murderer in prison to ask his permission to secure a pardon from the Tsar. But he declined her offer. I told Natanson of the Christian attitude of this woman. He retorted scornfully that this criminal — he meant the grand duchess — did not deserve any sympathy. The radical logic of this otherwise venerable and well-meaning gentleman had a perplexing effect on me. I could not ignore the fact that the conditions in tsarist Russia were untenable. The revolutionaries waged a justified battle on behalf of the people. Terrorist actions performed by individuals cost them their lives. It was a sacrifice, and yet the revolutionary "tactic" contradicted my ethical feeling.

I still continued to dream. I could not yet unite spiritual science with life. The magnificent perspectives of world evolution and the ghastly present remained disconnected in my consciousness.

I was also oppressed by having to tell my parents of my decision to marry Max, since I was afraid of my mother's wrath. Inwardly, I was very dependent on her and perhaps did a lot for that reason to spite her, in order to assert myself. I stood under the influence of Miss Minslova, who persuaded me that Max and I were meant for each other. It was only strange that I was not at all happy. However, my announcement to my parents was so resolute that my mother did not protest, with some help from Mrs Balmont, who appreciated and valued Max to an extraordinary degree. My father wrote me full of love and trust.

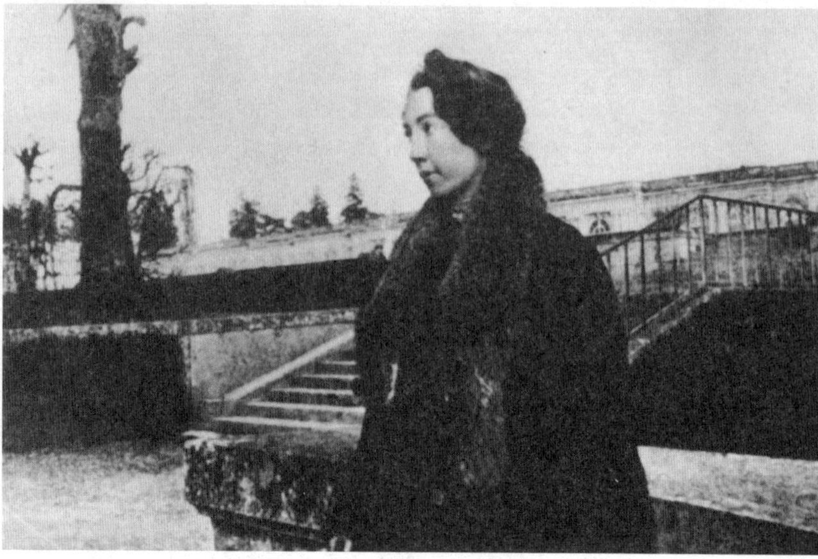

Margarita in Versailles, 1905. (Photograph, Max Voloshin.)

Only our three maids, Masha, Polya and Akulina, on hearing of my engagement, sat together at the table and cried loudly in chorus. They had imagined a different bridegroom for me. Only a prince was to take me home. Max did not correspond to their ideals.

In April I went to Moscow and Max followed me soon after. In these weeks I was in a peculiar state of mind. Everything around me was alien to me. I was inwardly absent and the church marriage celebration, so beautiful in the Orthodox Church, felt like a dream that had nothing to do with me.

After the wedding celebration, we travelled at once to Paris, where Rudolf Steiner was expected within a few days. My Aunt Alexandra was disconcerted by the fact that Miss Minslova also took a seat in our compartment, as she could not stand her, and referred to her as "Anna, the prophetess."

In Paris we stayed a few days longer in Max's studio, until we had furnished a small sunny apartment in Passy, with a few sofas, carpets and a lot of shelves for Max's library. Our most beautiful possession was a cast of the enormous head of the Egyptian Queen Tiye, portrayed as a sphinx. We had not yet moved, when a telegram notified us of the arrival of Rudolf Steiner together with friends. As he did not want to live in a hotel, we found a furnished apartment for him nearby. The ladies who came with him looked after the household themselves, and Miss Minslova dried the dishes reverentially.

He had come to Paris at that time to hold a lecture at the Theosophical Congress. Colonel Olcott was also present. We heard that Rudolf Steiner was not understood in this circle. He trod a new path of exact clairvoyance, as a continuation of the natural scientific method. The others lived on atavistic, partly mediumistic capacities and from the traditions of an often falsified eastern wisdom. It was held against him that he viewed Golgotha as the central event of human evolution. This was seen as one-sidedness, as a kind of fondness on the part of the western human being for Christianity.

For a small circle of hearers Rudolf Steiner held a cycle of lectures in his apartment on the Rue Renoir, originally intended for Russians.[19] But Edouard Schuré also took part, the author of *The Great Initiates*, who then met Rudolf Steiner for the first time and "recognized in him his Master," as he said. The respect which Schuré, older and more famous, accorded Rudolf Steiner, gave evidence of magnanimity. Schuré belonged to the circle around Richard Wagner, to those with a presentiment of the mysteries, giving artistic expression to this presentiment. I personally found his works somewhat journalistic, yet they did signify for many people the first contact with the essence of the mysteries.

Apart from Schuré, other Congress participants gradually came to these private lectures, and the listeners sat crowded together in the drawing room and in the bedroom.

Dimitri Mereshkovsky and his wife, the poet Zinaida Hippius, and their friend Dimitri Filosofov were also staying in Paris. When Max and I told them of the presence of Rudolf Steiner, they expressed the wish to get to know him, and so we invited them over, along with other Russians. Even today, I think back to that evening, which was to have been a festive one for us, with utter dismay. Mereshkovsky came loaded with prejudices against Rudolf Steiner. Zinaida Hippius cowered on the couch and observed Rudolf Steiner in an arrogant manner through her lorgnon as a curious object. Mereshkovsky himself, very agitated, started to cross-examine him like an inquisitor.

"We are naked and poor and parched," he cried out, "and thirst for truth!" But one had the feeling that they did not feel themselves to be so poor at all, but were actually convinced they already possessed the truth.

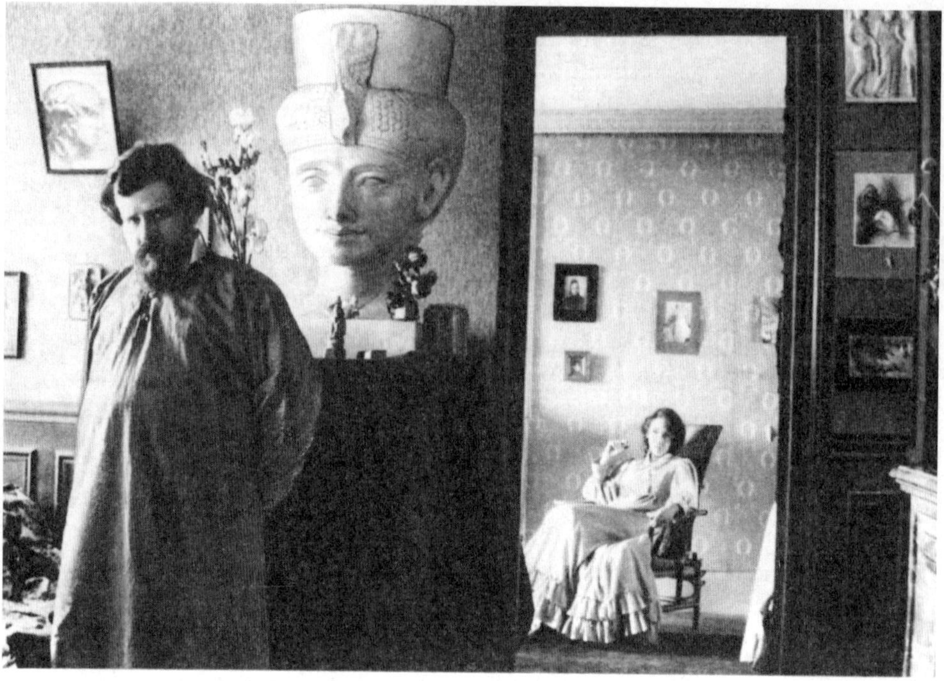

Max and Margarita in their Paris apartment

"Tell us the ultimate truth!" Mereshkovsky shouted, to which Rudolf Steiner answered, "If you tell me the penultimate one."

"And without the Church, one can save oneself?" I heard Mereshkovsky call out, beside himself. Thereupon Rudolf Steiner cited a well-known mystic of the Middle Ages, condemned by the Church as an example of a human being who found the path to Christ without the Church. I am unable to relate further details of this conversation; I only know that the mood remained polemical to the end in consequence of the indignation Fräulein von Sivers directed at Mereshkovsky. Rudolf Steiner held polemics to be fruitless and came up to me, who had not participated in the dispute. He looked at a fine reproduction of the *Centaur* of Rodin and explained to me that in the image of a centaur, an evolutionary stage of the human being is imaginatively portrayed. Here the human being was still united with the forces of the earth and possessed an instinctive wisdom. For that reason, knowledge of the art of healing was ascribed to centaurs. Then I put a question, which had always occupied me. What did it mean to speak of the spirit of a landscape, the spirit of a tree? He explained this to me lovingly and in depth.

Rudolf Steiner never tired of sharing his insight and knowledge wherever he got a hearing. The poet Minsky came over to us, pointed to the head of Queen Tiye and asked, "What significance does the smile of the sphinx have?"

To this Rudolf Steiner answered, "The sphinx looks into a far future, where what is tragic has been overcome."

I only understood later what he meant by that. Rudolf Steiner finally left, in the company of his indignant ladies.

From the eighteen lectures in Paris, in which Rudolf Steiner described the evolution of the world, I should like to single out one fact only, which can serve as proof of the correctness of spiritual scientific research. He told us that in comets, the order of earlier cosmic periods intrudes into our time, modified by present conditions. The beings of those periods required nitrogen compounds, just as the beings of the earth today require oxygen compounds.

In the year 1910, one could read in the newspapers about the latest scientific findings, to the effect that in the spectrum of comets prussic acid compounds could be identified, so that spiritual scientific research was confirmed by natural science four years later.

Under the impression of Rudolf Steiner's personality, we decided to move near to where he then lived. Max was able to get an assignment as a correspondent for his magazine in Munich, so we gave our apartment to the Balmonts and Nyusha, so as to move to Munich during the winter. Prior to that, however, we travelled to the Crimea, where my mother-in-law, Yelena Kirienko-Voloshina, awaited us. At that time my health was poor, and Max thought it would be less tiring for me if we made the journey by ship. Thus we went down the Danube from Linz to Constanta.

On the journey, we suddenly decided to make a detour to the large exhibition in Bucharest. The main interest of the exhibition consisted in the splendid Romanian embroideries and the portrait of Queen Carmen Silva. The relatively small city appeared to us a mixture of the Orient and Paris, with its many cafés. The gentlemen wore top hats and white trousers. The food was excellent in this city; one ladled it for oneself from many simmering goulash pots.

When we arrived, late in the evening, in Constanta, we learned that the Russian Black Sea fleet was on strike and the journey by ship came to a standstill. We waited in vain half the night in a gloomy sailor's dive, in which the mutinous crew of the Russian ship boozed. There were some strange faces, but the strangest was a crazy gypsy woman, who loitered among them. When it turned out that the voyage from Constanta to Yalta would be impossible, we took the ship to Constantinople, in order to await the course of events there.

In consequence of the detour to Bucharest, we had spent more money than we should have and found ourselves in a difficult situation. Fortunately, however, as Russians we were permitted to stay at no cost in a monastery hostel, where we spent several days in expectation of a transfer of money from Paris. It was during the hottest part of the summer. The monastery was located in the unpleasant district called Galata. Max suffered from asthma attacks. We spent many hours of the night on the roof, since we could not sleep. On the first night, from Friday to Saturday, the Muslims sang on the street. On the second night, from Saturday to Sunday, the Jews made an indescribable noise. But worst of all was the caterwauling of the Levantine Christians during the third night, from Sunday to Monday. On the fourth night, we at last slept in a splendid hotel for European diplomats, where we felt we had to conceal ourselves from the elegant clientele. At that time I wore a lot of valuable rings, a scarf of black lace and a liberty cap with a green silk band tied under the chin. Apparently, that made a strange impression on the hotel receptionist, since in taking down our particulars, he asked, *"Monsieur est de Paris et Mademoiselle de Constantinople?"*

I am grateful to destiny for bringing us to Constantinople against our will. The opulence of the Byzantium that once ruled the world, the beauty of the Orient that lulled one to sleep, the murmuring fountains, the mosques humming with prayers like beehives, the imperious attitude of the Turkish people, as compared with the unbridled greed and deceitfulness of the Levantine Christians, all this imprinted itself on my view of life. We viewed the princely city in all its splendour with its mosques and minarets when we departed at dawn, having spent the night on the deck of the ship. The following night, however, we had to sleep between decks, since we were travelling third class for reasons of economy. The sea was stormy; Tatars, Turks and Jews with large families, among whom we had to lie on the floor, became seasick. When I wanted to climb onto the deck, the captain turned me back. I saw the elegant clientele above and understood for the first time the feelings of those who always have to remain on the lower deck of the ship of life.

At sunrise I saw a Turk kneeling on a prayer mat with raised arms and a rabbi with a Torah scroll tied to his forehead praying in a white coat.

Koktebel

The Gulf of Koktebel is known for its shimmering, translucent pebbles of volcanic origin in subtle shades of rose and violet, polished by the sea. They shine like genuine precious stones on the sun-drenched beaches. At the end of the cove stands the silhouette of the extinct Karadag volcano, with its rocks rising pillar-like out of the sea, somewhat like a Gothic cathedral. Up on this mountain, twenty-eight years later, Max was laid to rest, in accordance with his last wishes. He felt himself profoundly connected with this piece of earth. He loved the strange mountains which rose up like single mythological animals cast in bronze. There was no vegetation other than isolated thorn bushes and thistles. He loved this bare, arid and cracked ground, the peculiar cloud formations and the endless expanse of the blue sea, fringed with white. His poems, particularly the beautiful cycle, *Cimmerian Twilight,* bear witness to this.

The coast was almost unpopulated. Our two houses stood alone, surrounded by stunted acacia trees. Not far from them, Polyxena still lived, the sister of the philosopher Vladimir Soloviev, with her friend. The old mother of the now deceased Soloviev lived with us. I often saw the old woman absorbed in deep prayer, sitting on her little balcony. Polyxena, a poet, had the large blue eyes, black lashes and eyebrows of her brother and could laugh loudly and heartily, just as he had. This laugh of Soloviev was in fact famous. Apart from that, with her hair cut short, she resembled an African boy. On account of the thistles and thorn bushes in this region, she wore trousers like my mother-in-law.

My mother-in-law was a character. She looked like *Goethe in Italy*, as painted by Tischbein, and wore high boots and wide trousers not only in the country but also in the city, to strengthen, as it seemed, her self-awareness with this show of originality. She was very beautiful and rather shy at the same time. She was the first to settle here on the cove of Koktebel, on the north coast of the Crimea. She first of all built a house for herself and, later, one for Max. In her own house she took in boarders in the high season, so that her son could live the life of an artist. The relationship between them was peculiar. On the one hand, she loved him passionately, on the other hand she felt irritated by something in his nature, which made his life with her very difficult. She had a genuine sympathy for me, which withstood all trials.

In Koktebel, Max was like an Assyrian priest: he wore a long shirt and kept his Zeus mane under control with a garland of wormwood. The crowd that came from Theodosia to Koktebel to collect transparent coloured pebbles could not always excuse such eccentricities in the two of them.

Theodosia was a beautiful old town with cultural and artistic traditions. Among Max's friends I should especially like to mention the painter Konstantin Bogayevsky, a quiet, earnest person of great sincerity. His tireless search for the soul of the landscape around Theodosia became a long ordeal for him. His pictures were cosmic and religious in mood. His colours resonated like various metals, reflecting out toward the viewer. One might assume their creator awoke with every sunrise to the sound of trumpets. He combined a deep respect for every individual with dry humour. In writing these recollections, I learned from Crimean refugees that all his works had been destroyed in wartime bombing raids, and that he himself met his death in a frightful manner.

Everyone coming from the two main cities to Theodosia, whether poet, painter, musician or philosopher, was glad to visit our friend Alexandra Michailovna Petrova.[20] To reach her, one had first to go through a courtyard, on which a huge white acacia grew. An outside stair led directly into her single, meagrely furnished room, in which there stood only a piano, a narrow sofa, a table and a few chairs, and which was nonetheless exceedingly cosy. When she prepared her unrivalled coffee, it was almost like a ritual act, the secret of which she let me in on. But it was not the coffee that brought people to her. I have seldom met a person who followed everything of importance in cultural life with such warm-hearted interest. Her black, fiery eyes, her voice, somewhat hoarse from smoking, her nervous little laugh, are unforgettable. She experienced and entered into every idea, every phenomenon with her whole being. She wrestled to come to an understanding of every human being and every cultural development.

She could only putter around, as she suffered from a heart condition, but she shared in many destinies and took a profound interest in current events. At first she protested against our new "crazy teaching." She believed one ought not to approach these things with thinking. She was particularly worried that it could inhibit me in my art. Once she said to me, "I struggle to come to terms with Rudolf Steiner the whole time. I have to admit to you that I cannot do anything more than read his works; everything else appears to me too rarefied." Later she joined the movement. The destiny of the Jewish people in its tragic aspect was a painful problem for her up until her death.

In the autumn we travelled to Moscow to my parents, from where we had wanted to move to Munich. But things were to turn out quite differently. Max, who had to hold consultations with his publisher in St Petersburg, got to know a circle of poets, philosophers and painters there, whose spiritual level he compared to the Alexandrian epoch. The centre of this circle was Vyatsheslav Ivanov. In the corner tower of a large house, high above the Taurus Park, in a semicircular converted loft, the most significant conversations were supposedly conducted. Max also wrote to me that, on the floor below, two small rooms were available to us; a larger room next to them would soon be free. He now asked me whether we should not spend that winter in St Petersburg, where he could write articles about the artistic life there on assignment from his publisher.

Vyatsheslav Ivanov in St Petersburg! The poet who had signified for me a world in which, for years already, I had found my spiritual home! I knew most of his poems by heart. A lot of people were put off by them, because of their unusual Greek rhythms and their archaic, religious and at the same time intellectual character. Just a few months before that I had read his treatise *The Religion of the Suffering God* with enthusiasm, in which he spoke as a researcher, religious philosopher and poet about various Dionysian cults of Greece. In the worldview of Vyatsheslav Ivanov the Greek experience of the spirituality of nature united itself with Christianity. In this connection, he stood higher for me than Nietzsche, whose *Birth of Tragedy out of the Spirit of Music* had exercised a decisive effect on me.

It was a breathtaking prospect for me that Vyatsheslav Ivanov, who had spent a number of years with his family in Geneva, was now in St Petersburg, that I would soon get to know him, and even live in the same house with him. Self-evidently, I wanted to spend some time in St Petersburg and I telegraphed wholeheartedly, "Yes."

And Munich? And spiritual science? It was enough for me at that time that it existed. It was so beautiful to live in the tremendous pictures of world evolution, to know that everything has a meaning and that there is a path to knowledge of spiritual worlds, on which I would certainly one day embark. It is, admittedly, odd that I, who almost from childhood had intensively and consistently sought this path, suddenly felt relieved on learning that this path existed, and now allowed myself time. Max and I went about the world like two children playing!

Although reluctant to talk about purely personal matters, I should like to relate something of the following period of my life, because I believe this to be symptomatic of pre-revolutionary Russia and of that "Luciferic" culture which, in my opinion, flowered especially in Russia then. It took place in the framework of the rigid tsarist bureaucracy, which no one was capable of shaking who did not want to become a revolutionary. This detachment from life while floating in one's own world of ideas and feelings independent of reality, the fondness for such independence from the real world, the overestimation of oneself, eccentricities of all kinds — these things could only develop to this extent and in this manner in the intellectual circles of Russia.

I was completely wrapped up in just such a subjective world. I fancied myself too good for practical matters, in which I was absurdly helpless, even if I did not admit it to myself. The preponderance of a world of feeling, not limited and mastered through purposeful willing, gave rise to oversensitivity, to a hypertrophy of the soul, which consumed my body. In his selflessness, Max was far from castigating me for my otherworldliness, finding my weakness touching and lovable. He treated me with indulgence. I suffered under my own tendencies, and often appeared to myself as no more than a shadow.

The Tower

It was a cold November morning, and a strong wind blew from the sea over the firmly frozen Neva when we arrived in St Petersburg. We moved into two tiny rooms; we never got the large one that had been promised to us! Through my corridor-like little room, in which I slept on a narrow chaise longue and in which there was space for only a small table on which we ate, one entered Max's still smaller room. It was really nothing more than a ship's cabin with a couch. The wide windowsill served as his writing table. Our windows, through which the grey sky of St Petersburg could be seen, were enormous. But these quarters did not disappoint me. What did their crampedness matter when the gods celebrated their festivals directly above us!

The first visitors to come right after our arrival were the young poet B. Dyks, whose real name was Boris Leman, and his blonde, boyish and bird-like cousin Olga von Annenkova. Boris had a peculiar appearance — dark, with an unusually narrow face and an olive-green tinged complexion — and a guttural voice. Something ancient Egyptian united itself in him with a hyper-modern bearing. There was a mysterious air about him that could perhaps be explained on the basis of his "second face": he was a civil servant in some ministry or other, where there was nothing to do. He and Olga were effusive admirers of Max. They began at once, with one voice, to recite his *Stella Maria*. It sounded like a litany; I struggled in vain to suppress a violent fit of laughter.

The next day we were invited to the theatre studio of Mrs Kommissarshevskaya. The artists had rehearsed choruses from the Greek drama *Tantalos* by Vyatsheslav Ivanov and wanted to surprise him with it that evening. It was the first time I had heard a choral recitation, and I was profoundly moved by the powerful and objective effect of this art form, by means of which this work of the great poet acquired tremendous power. I saw Ivanov for the first time during the interval. He thanked the artists and Mrs Kommissarshevskaya and

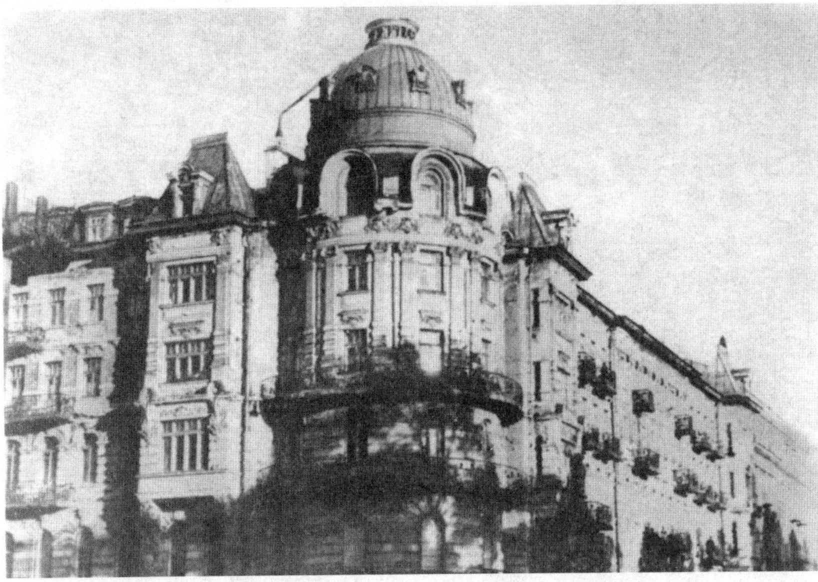

The Tower above the Taurus Park, St. Petersburg

appeared quite moved. But I got a fright. Didn't he look like the evil priest from one of my dreams who came towards me, stooped, through a small doorway in a low, vaulted room and whom I had never been able to forget? I did not want to believe that the human being standing before me really was the poet, in whose world I lived as though it were my own.

Vyatsheslav Ivanov was about forty-two years old at that time. He was tall and slim; light reddish-blonde hair fell in small single locks on both sides of his high forehead forming a kind of *oriflamme* banner. His face, with its little pointed beard, had a warm colouring and seemed transparent. His small grey eyes had the expression of a beast of prey. His delicate, in fact all-too-delicate smile, as well as his high nasal voice, I perceived as being effeminate. When he spoke, he accompanied each syllable with an out-breath, which lent something festive and sacral to his way of speaking.

Oh, I thought, dismayed, if only I could wake up from this dream and get to know the *real* Vyatsheslav Ivanov in reality! But it was no dream. His wife, Lydia Sinovyeva-Annibal, was described to me once as "that powerful woman with the loud voice, who hurls Dionysus at everyone's feet." She resembled the sibylline figures of Michelangelo. The posture of her head had something leonine about it: a strong, upright neck, a

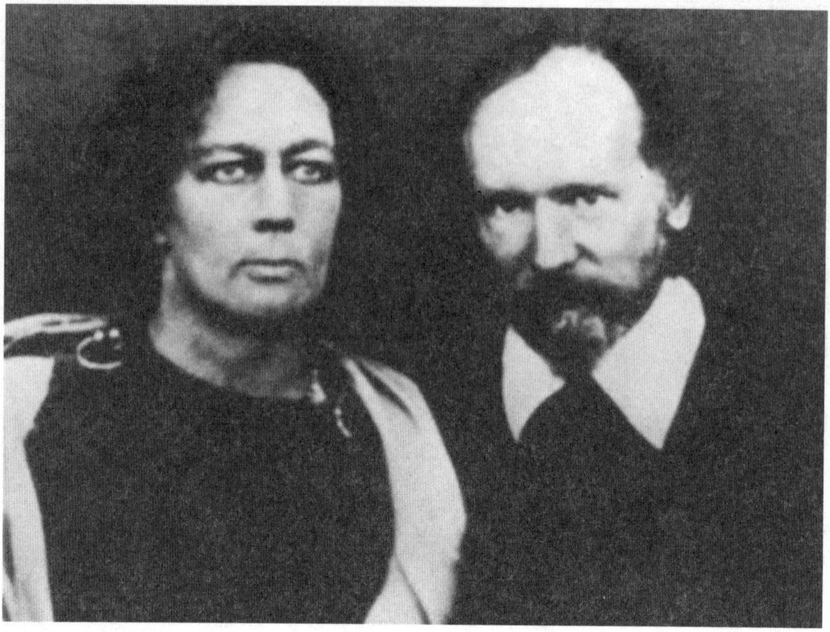

Vyatsheslav Ivanov and Lydia Sinovyeva-Annibal

keen glance, her small adjacent ears, all reinforced this resemblance to a lion. But the most peculiar thing about her had to do with her colour: her hair was blonde, with a pinkish hue, whereas her skin was dark, which made the white of her grey eyes very bright. She was a descendant of the Abyssinian "Annibal", the famous Arab of Peter the Great, from whom Alexander Pushkin was also descended. As her everyday attire, Lydia wore a tunic and draped her powerful, beautiful arms with a toga. The combination of colours was quite audacious. On that evening she wore white with orange, which had a festive effect. Max, who was already completely under Ivanov's spell, was disappointed that I was not immediately enthusiastic about him.

Right away, in the first days after our arrival, we visited Alexei Remizov and his wife. At that time he had begun to write poetry in the style he inaugurated, in which he made use of the Russian language in all its range of colour, in its own melody and rhythm. For the first time in modern poetry, in his legends and apocrypha, which had a half-pagan, half-Christian character, diverse elemental beings and the whole realm of the heavenly legions appeared, with which Russia is so richly endowed. In seeking the Russian style, his early poems in prose were a revelation to me.

He now came to meet us. Shivering, he had wrapped himself in a knitted cloth with holes in it. Between hunched shoulders his head peered out like a chick from its nest. Short-sighted, he opened his eyes wide as though shocked. At the same time, he smiled humorously and kindly. He had a nose like Socrates, a brow such as one sees in representations of Chinese philosophers, and mountains of hair which stood in tufts.

The cloth with holes and the crouching posture "belonged" to him as did his exaggerated Moscow patois, in which the words were pronounced slowly and with emphasis. I once asked Remizov what the *kikimora*, a female elemental being of which children were frightened, looked like, for he was knowledgeable in these things. He answered me didactically, "Just like me; that's what the *kikimora* looks like."

Although he was then only twenty-six years old, he appeared to me much older, like a sage. Remizov was from Moscow, from the semi-educated class of strictly Orthodox merchants who lived on the other bank of the Moskva. Patriarchal customs still prevailed there and the head of the family exercised a despotism at the expense of other family members, particularly poor relatives, who were dependent on the wealthy, just as Alexander Ostrovsky has portrayed in his classical dramas. Remizov came from just such a burdened and demeaned family that lived by the grace of their rich relatives. When the catastrophe took place on the Hadynka military training ground at the coronation of the tsar, he was there amid the crush of people as a grammar school pupil. In the mayhem, he was somehow pushed upwards. Stepping over the heads of those in the crowd, he came to a mounted gendarme, to whom he clung. This gendarme booked him for improper conduct toward a policeman. He was arrested, expelled from grammar school and banished to a small provincial town in the north. As he did not belong to any revolutionary party and was quite unknown to the other political exiles there, they took him for a police spy and demeaned him in every possible way. Finally, he was suspected by his landlady on account of a silver spoon that had disappeared. It was related that his present wife, the young, proud Serafima Dovgelo, had likewise been banished as a revolutionary. Relations between the two of them were somewhat peculiar. They did not converse as though on familiar terms, but addressed each other with their full names "Serafima Pavlovna" and "Alexei Michailovich," which was not customary in intellectual circles.

Next to this beautiful woman of renowned Lithuanian lineage, "whose daughters were wooed by Polish kings" — as she remarked in passing — Remizov appeared unprepossessing. He spoke her name only with the greatest deference.

Serafima Pavlovna was tall. She later became excessively corpulent. Her round, open face, framed by blonde locks, was radiant; her voice deep and loud. She did not mince her words where the truth was concerned. I liked her very much on account of her honesty and openness. She knew what was good and what was bad. The Remizovs were poor, impractical and perpetually plagued by financial difficulties, to the point of disaster. For that reason, their little daughter was raised in Dovgelo Palace. Because of the incident on the Hadynka, he had not been able to finish grammar school and could not, therefore, attend a college of higher education. Thus, advancing his position was closed to him. When we got to know the two of them, Remizov earned a living carrying out a census of the dogs in St Petersburg. He went from one courtyard to another collecting statistical data. But that was somehow part of his particular way of doing things. By 1906, Remizov had become a rising star in the literary world. He often recited his works in the Tower at Vyatsheslav Ivanov's. He read with emotion and with an unusual, musical cadence. Not hearing him in person, but only reading his poems, they lost much of their charm.

On our visit we were very warmly received, and after tea they showed us their "treasures": root formations, little blocks of wood, artificially or naturally created elementals and imps, which hung over his writing table; a colourful, eerie, lively world that he apparently needed as inspiration for his work. Remizov showed them to us with great seriousness, naming them and telling us about their characteristics and deeds. His wife's treasures consisted of various antique objects embroidered with pearls from the Dovgelo Palace. They seemed no less important to her than the little monsters were to her husband.

I could understand Remizov wanting to hide his wounded and over-sensitive soul behind his peculiar conduct — to which his stylized, squiggly handwriting belonged — as though behind a protective covering. Spiritual realities revealed themselves to him by penetrating into the nature of folk traditions, which he knew as no one else did, and in this regard he had a presentiment of many things. Above all, Remizov loved and cultivated what was traditional, emotive and original in language, whereas he detested the classical-academic terminology as being bloodless and impoverished. He trained younger writers in this living language, such as Michail Prishvin, who was later to become well known.

Remizov knew both the hell within and outside in the world, and undoubtedly had a certain leaning towards the bizarre and adversarial, as well as to the inscrutable. In his art he gradually lapsed into mannerism and, when I last saw him in Paris in 1937, this mannerism had degenerated to the point of grotesqueness. I was unable to bring him to engage in normal conversation and we had after all been very good friends. He lived at that time on a pension provided by the King of Serbia to six of the most well-known Russian expatriate writers in Paris. But Remizov wrote nothing, since as an emigrant it was not possible to get anything printed. He spent a lot of time gluing fantastic boxes together, putting them one inside the other. In these he kept "honorary diplomas" written in calligraphy for the members of the Monkey Club he had founded earlier in St Petersburg. This is how I found him thirty years on from our first acquaintance, after he had experienced the martyrdom of the Bolshevik Revolution and emigration.

Max and I were invited one evening to visit the painter Somov, whom we knew from Paris. The room in which he received us and in which he painted his pictures was simply and tastefully furnished. The wallpaper was cornflower-blue. There were several old pieces of mahogany furniture, a crystal chandelier in the Biedermeier style and, as the only decoration in the room, a valuable porcelain stood on the chest of drawers: a white Dionysus with blue grapes amid foliage in an unnatural green. The artist was as modest and understated as ever. There was something resigned about him. He loved antiquity and only looked back, without hope of a future, genuine culture. At a late hour of the evening the poet Michail Kusmin appeared. They seemed happy to see each other. Out of what epoch did this strange human being come to us, so unusual in appearance? Of slight build, his face, with its large, dark, almond-shaped eyes brought to mind those portraits of Fayum painted on coffins, as seen in museums. His ascetic face with its little black beard also recalled the countenances on Russian icons. However, his manner was extremely unassuming. With an unprecedented openness and innocence he read his unabridged diary to his friends from time to time— to whose circle I later belonged —

without wanting to present his life other than as it was. He submitted himself to his friends as if to a higher power, and suffered indescribably over every break in a relationship. In this he was sincerely devout, and this devoutness bore a strict Orthodox character. He composed the music to his fine poems himself and sang them for us at the piano. I was thrilled by his Alexandrian Songs. There was no posing with him, everything was childlike. The frivolity of the eighteenth century (on which he was as much an authority as Somov), Russian Orthodoxy and Hellenism combined in him to form a peculiar mixture.

When Max and I drove home by sleigh on that cold night, we talked about how, among these over-refined people, we appeared to ourselves rather like barbarians. They looked back, while we sought the future.

While I was sitting alone the next day in Max's "cabin," Ivanov came to see me. We spoke of the evening in Kommissarshevskaya's studio, and I took the opportunity to tell him what his poems meant to me. I knew the collection, *Pilot Stars,* almost by heart, but I particularly loved the *Dryads,* which depicted in such an essential way the dreamlike, cosmic weaving of trees, their tentative probing of space. Vyatsheslav opened his small eyes wide; I felt his gaze bore into me. For several minutes he remained mute. At last he said, moved, "My poems are serious, they are very difficult, and when I am celebrated, I actually find little understanding; I am astounded ..."

He had come to invite us to an event the following Wednesday, when the philosopher Nikolai Berdyayev was to speak about Eros, as an opening to a general discussion on this theme. During the second part of the evening the poets were to read their new works as usual. But just then he wanted to take me upstairs to see Lydia.

The Ivanovs had lived in St Petersburg for one year. They had left their children behind in Geneva with a female friend, where they attended school. As already mentioned, they occupied a tower; all the rooms had walls that were either round or at an angle. Lydia's room into which he at once escorted me, was wallpapered a glaring orange. There were only two low couches and a peculiar, tall wooden container, colourfully painted, in which she kept her manuscripts rolled up. Vyatsheslav's room was narrow, with fiery red walls, so that it was like stepping into a glowing oven. The way she ordered her life was quite unusual in Russia at that time. All the women in our circles retained at least one cook, but Lydia did everything herself alongside her literary work and their many receptions, as she could not bear having anyone in her apartment who did not share their life completely.

Joining them, I felt like a small rabbit trapped in a cave with two lions. I sensed that Lydia was equal to her husband in intensity and originality. She met me with unusual interest. This intense interest in people was characteristic of both of them. "Vyatsheslav and I," said Lydia, "love to look at the dreams on people's faces." They seemed at that moment to experience a dream on my face which stirred them both, and my only fear was that when they awoke one day, they would be very disappointed.

Vyatsheslav Ivanov was the centre of the cultural life of St Petersburg at that time. With his enthusiasm and his gift of empathy, he possessed the ability to augment the creativity of others. He would assign certain themes, encourage, praise or rebuke, often in an exaggerated manner. In this way he awakened in each person a world still unknown to them, which slumbered within and conducted, like Dionysus (whose priest he appeared to me), a chorus of his followers.

In addition, he was a kind of inspirer in the personal lives of many of the people around him. In his fiery cave one made one's confession and received his counsel. His daily rhythm was uncommon. He did not get up until around two o'clock in the afternoon. Then he received visitors and worked through the night. But at that time, he frankly did not work all that much.

On this first visit I only sensed the extraordinarily intense, and for me still mysterious, life of the two of them. Out of their alliance they brought forth something new. They wanted to set an example, and to stand for an idea passionately held. "What is it?" I asked myself.

The Magic Garden

Wednesday evening arrived. In the large semicircular room of the Tower, illumined by no more than a tiny window during the day, candles now blazed in a golden candelabra, by the light of which the little golden lilies on the grey wallpaper and the golden hair of our host gleamed softly. There were more men than women in this company and, apart from Lydia, no woman who signified anything special. Among those present, I recognized Somov, Kusmin, the painter Bakst (the pseudonym of Leo Rosenberg), and the young poet Sergei Gorodetzky. Apart from them, the Remizovs came, as well as Boris Leman with his cousin, the writer Georgy Tchulkov, who had just written his *Mystical Anarchism*, the student Modest Hoffmann, author of the book *Community-Building Individualism*, and various publishers and theatre directors. I met the philosopher Berdyayev for the first time that evening. Later on I was to associate with him quite a lot in Moscow. He was tall, broad-shouldered and of imposing appearance, with black hair and a goatee. His Romance origins — his mother was French — were at once noticeable. But at first I was rather disconcerted — in fact even alarmed — by a nervous trait which affected him repeatedly, in which he would open his mouth from time to time and stick out his tongue. However, that seemed neither to bother him, nor his listeners.

Today, I remember nothing of his introductory talk and just as little of the speeches of the others. I only know that the thoughts expressed about Eros seemed to me quite new and profound, and that my enthusiasm knew no bounds.

Lydia, Somov and Gorodetzky sat on the large table, pushed back near the door to make room for the many guests; they represented the gallery. If a speaker spoke too abstractly, he was pelted with oranges. Gorodetzky may have been twenty-four years old at the time. Unusually tall and slim, with his bird-like face he resembled the Egyptian god Anubis. There was something attractive in his youthful freshness and unspoiled nature, as well as his humour. He was then just beginning his poetic career, under the wing of Vyatsheslav Ivanov. In the second part of the evening the poets recited their latest works. From his new book of poems, *Eros*, Ivanov read the incantation of Dionysus, who appears as half-youth, half-bird, and other poems which had an almost magical effect on me. But they were different from the earlier verses I had known. It was a cycle of experiences which spoke of passion, anguish, in fact resignation. Filled with sympathy, I pondered the reason for this grief. After all, I experienced only the most beautiful harmony between him and Lydia. Then Gorodetzky recited his traditional poems, so original in their rhythm. It seemed to me that Ivanov criticized him too harshly; a certain tension was apparent between master and pupil, which I interpreted to mean that Ivanov was deeply disappointed with his pupil in not being able to keep pace with him, and in distancing himself. Only much later did I comprehend the very personal nature of this disappointment! Remizov read the *Slumber Song of the Bears*, Kusmin his graceful *Summer Experiences*. The poems of Max seemed to me, as compared with those of the others, too "engraved," not lyrical enough, perhaps even rather rhetorical. The French influence was noticeable. When the guests dispersed in groups to other rooms, Vyatsheslav Ivanov came up to me and we exchanged our impressions. I noticed that my harmless words again affected him peculiarly. He remained silent for a while, and then said, "Through you, I feel compensated for so much." I did not understand that.

At this time, Lydia was working on her book *The Tragic Zoological Garden*. It was a collection of interconnected stories, each one describing an experience from her childhood and the encounter with an animal. During these weeks I had also written a children's story for a periodical edited by the poetess Polyxena Solovieva.[21] Lydia found my style more artistic, formed and nuanced than her own, while to me hers was more dynamic, though somewhat gnarled and severe on account of sentences piled one upon the other. In this book her strong, truth-seeking nature revealed itself, as well as her wild, impetuous temperament and independent, rebellious character. "Only brought to a state of peace through solitude, and by the deepest blue," as a verse of Vyatsheslav says of her. *The Tragic Zoological Garden* recounts the path from paradise into the earthly world and the new covenant with the divine which every child goes through, in recapitulating the development of humanity as a whole. The story was filled with a strong sense of brooding: one breathed earthly air, the scent of sun-imbued herbs touched things, sensed the gestures in one's own limbs and perceived earth existence in all its abundance. I still see Lydia sitting with her feet on her couch, filling small, loose pieces of paper with her large, oblique, slightly shaky and yet bold handwriting. How different these two people were could be seen just from their handwriting. Every letter of Vyatsheslav was gem-like and winged, the lines animated, light, like all his movements. When he was talking to you, he raised himself from time to time on tiptoe, taking a step now forward, now backward, so that his figure danced like a flame in front of his listener. His hands, first held closed, then opened like a flower, or raised, had the same kind of buoyancy. Lydia on the other hand, as already mentioned, had all the force of a Michelangelo. Her voice was strong and she had originally wanted to become a singer. In speaking, she was at first tentative, then unexpectedly blunt. In comparison, Vyatsheslav's speech was accomplished in its form, the thoughts chiselled; his almost byzantine, intricate sentences were infused with enthusiasm one moment, with indignation the next. I always sensed a creative tension between these two allied human beings, as in a duel. Today, I am of the opinion that it was Lydia who provided the actual spiritual substance, whereas he only shaped it artistically and intellectually. Whenever she let herself be persuaded by his muddled speculations, which stood as often as not in the service of his passion, she found herself on the wrong track. Not only weaker spirits, she too, though concerned about truth, could be dazzled by his shimmering, multicoloured "light." I can still hear her say, "In the end Vyatsheslav is always right after all," and she would say that at moments when this required considerable sacrifice of her.

Both attested to an unusual interest in me. With her this expressed itself in passionate warmth. His manner of treating me was flamboyant, alternately teasing, provocative and inquisitive, and — as already described — full of emotion, which alarmed me. Sometimes he reminded me of a golden bee, when it cautiously and yet tenaciously sucks the nectar from the blossoms.

On account of his work as a journalist, Max was preoccupied continuously: he abandoned himself completely to the new impressions of St Petersburg. Thus the three of us were often together, the Ivanovs and I. They wanted to initiate me into their way of living. I learned much about their life, full of inner storms, when they related how earlier poems had arisen. They had spent time in England, Paris and above all in Italy. For both of them, this marriage was the second. He had deserted a loving young wife and a little daughter in joining forces with Lydia. They also told me about the people they had met and the experiences they had had the previous year in St Petersburg. It took a very long time, however, before I understood, in its full reality, the interest which the male members of our circle above all showed for each other and which so impressed me. The fact that we were together with people here whose emotional life followed abnormal paths was something of which Max and I, in our naivety, had no idea. With the Ivanovs, I sensed above all the search for new, living relationships between people. Out of new harmonies between human beings, so they hoped, a new spirituality would arise, becoming flesh and blood; a future community for which they sought like-minded individuals. Thus, Vyatsheslav Ivanov organized evenings where only men came together. For her part, Lydia wanted to try forming a closed circle of women, a constellation capable of releasing from each soul something uniquely its own. She invited me to participate in this. At these meetings we were to have other names, wear other gowns, so as to create an atmosphere that raised us out of everyday life. Lydia was called Diotima; I was given the name Primavera, due to my supposed resemblance to Botticelli's figures. Apart from the conventional, innocent wife of the poet Tchulkov, and a primary school teacher who misunderstood the whole thing and conducted herself in a rather bacchanalian manner, no women turned up wanting to take part. The evening came off as dull, and no new spirituality was born from it. After that, the attempt was dropped.

At that time I began to paint a portrait of Lydia: in her orange room she lay like a sphinx in front of me on the couch, supporting herself on her elbows. I chose to paint her *en face*. But in the December darkness of St Petersburg it was difficult to make any progress, and she was then taken seriously ill with pneumonia and had to be taken to a hospital. During her illness, Miss Minslova appeared. We introduced her to all our new friends, and with the sibyl present, a life that was already fantastic became still more so. As always, a commotion arose around her; in particular, her meeting with Vyatsheslav Ivanov turned into a spiritual thunderstorm. Through her, he learned for the first time of the path into the spiritual world, and was seized with the urge for knowledge, with a yearning for it — and with protest at the same time. I observed these spiritual tournaments and explosions with rapt attention. The sibyl herself was enthusiastic about the poet, and this word is in fact rather too weak to characterize the level of her feeling.

At this time I suffered a state of exhaustion which doctors could not explain, and so Max took me for a few weeks to Finland. My guest house was situated amid snow-covered forests and lakes, two hours from St Petersburg. Max had to go back after a few days. Making up for that, our friend Lyubimov visited me. In the midst of sparkling, crunching snow with blue shadows, we breathed an air which, I don't know why, smelled of violets, and skied or went by sleigh through the countryside. At this time of year the sunsets take over from and merge with the sunrises, the sky reflecting the colours of amethyst, emerald and amber. The frozen lakes lay like copper shields between the pine forests, which shimmered like old silver. When Lyubimov left, I began to paint. Max had given me a splendid shell: within its emerald green there shimmered rose, violet and blue lights. The colours were truly remarkable. I could imagine landscapes there populated by mythological beings. I wanted to recreate this, but my colours remained too pale as compared to their magnificent luminosity and I gave up. Every day I received letters from Max; he told me the Ivanovs wanted to travel to Geneva, so that Lydia could recover from her pneumonia. They offered us their apartment in the Tower for this period. For the time being, however, Lydia had phlebitis and had to lie down.

Though I yearned for Max, nothing could stop me anymore when I heard that the Ivanovs were to go away soon. Without announcing myself beforehand, I fled to St Petersburg. I wanted to surprise Max at dinner, but when I arrived jubilantly at our quarters, I found everything dark and empty. I left him a note and went upstairs. The Ivanovs were just then sitting at their table and I was welcomed warmly. Lydia sat in an armchair with her legs stretched out, on the high armrest of which sat a splendid calico cat, quite decoratively, just over her head. What a welcome feeling it was to be once again in the fiery element of these two! They informed me that a Miss Svanseva needed our room and that we could move into an almost empty attic room in the Tower.[22] Vyatsheslav was as jocular, challenging and provocative toward me as ever. Lydia, who in her severe illness had been on the verge of death, was affectionate, but serious. We spent several hours in the most intense conversation, and yet I kept listening for a ring at the door and Max's arrival. When it finally sounded and Vyatsheslav went to open the front door, I ran behind him. It was indeed Max; I rushed towards him, but Vyatsheslav turned around and stood in my way. I veered to the right, he did the same, I shifted to the left, but he continued standing between us. We laughed at the joke which, however, as I realized later, was not quite as harmless as it seemed.

The Somnambulist

The mutual existence — we now lived together — became so animated for all of us, that the Ivanovs did not want to go away at all anymore. Max's mother joined us from Koktebel, and lived on a lower floor of the house, becoming the fifth member of the group. She went into raptures over Ivanov, like a teenager. As the Wednesday evenings had been cancelled, most acquaintances thought the Ivanovs had gone away. Only their most intimate friends visited the Tower, so we were now fairly isolated.

On one occasion, Alexander Blok read us his new book of poems, *Snow-Mask*. The poet's appearance made a significant impression, his face as though chiselled in marble, his profile resembling a knight of the Middle Ages. His large bright eyes looked into the distance. His voice was compressed and his monotone yet musical way of reciting conveyed a sense of restrained passion. One had the feeling that this knight had got lost in our age, where he was unable to find what he was looking for: the image of the divine feminine which he extolled in his manifold rhythms. These verses spoke of yearning and despair, to the point of cynicism. In those years the situation was altogether such that people bore a longing in their souls which could not find satisfaction in the bourgeois stagnation of the general culture. They sought escape in dreams, while Lucifer led them to believe in an illusory form of experience called Eros. In the life of almost every artist I met at that time, there was dramatic tension of some kind. A faithful marriage would have been hard to find, and those who adhered to one were in some degree despised by the others.

An art magazine commissioned me to make portraits of Remizov and Kusmin. I drew them in charcoal, Remizov wrapped in his cloth with his wall imps in the background, naturalistically grotesque. Kusmin appeared stylized in the manner of a mummy portrait. The two drawings, life-size, turned out well, but Vyatsheslav Ivanov made too much of them, showing them to visitors before they were finished, and saying exaggerated things about them. It became too much for me, so that I wrested a picture from him almost violently.

In half-pretended anger, I ran with it to my attic room, in order to hide it. He followed me, took hold of my arm and begged me, deeply moved, "Please, stay with me, do not abandon me!" What could that mean? I told Max about it, who was no less astonished at this scene than I was. Vyatsheslav Ivanov devoted a lot of time to my education. He read the *Fioretti* by St Francis of Assisi with me in the original Italian. The story tells how St Francis met St Clara in the St Angelos Church for a shared meal, at which "more was spoken about holy matters than eaten." It relates how a light spread out over the whole countryside, such that the peasants of Perugia took it for the flames of a raging forest fire and hurried toward it, till they became aware that it was a spiritual fire. This story made a deep impression on me. It corresponded to my most cherished ideal of love. That appeared to me to be the only right kind of love, from which something spiritual arises, having objective meaning for the world.

In reading the Gospel of St John, Ivanov acquainted me with the Greek language. The second part of *Faust* I also experienced for the first time through his reading it to me. I still remember how, in speaking the words of the woman of Samaria in the final scene,

"By the well, where once before / Abraham's flocks were driven, / By the jar, that cooled the Saviour, / That to sacred lips was given," he was overcome with emotion. He covered his face with his hands and wept. "And Goethe is considered to be a cool Olympian! Here every word is imbued, transfigured by Christian love; even a small jar is transfigured!"

The approval Ivanov showed of my poetic attempts, which I had until then never properly come out with, gave me courage to write new poems. At various poetic gatherings at that time, he had me read a sonnet on autumn I had written; this took a great deal of conscious effort, considering my shyness.[23] But his glance compelled me; I was under his spell. He wanted to introduce me to the art of poetry, and from his instruction a systematic course came about in which only Max, Lydia and I took part. These lessons later provided the basis for a public seminar. This work was enthralling since he spoke as a poet and at the same time as a researcher. From his knowledge of Greek mysteries and rituals, he elucidated the nature of metres and rhythms, giving examples from both ancient and more recent classics in the original language. He had mastered ancient and modern languages with consummate ease. Max's poetry was also stimulated and enriched by this work.

At that time I was visited by a young student, Strauch, the son of an acquaintance of Fräulein von Sivers who had passed away. He brought me a little book of his mother's: Goethe's *Fairy Tale of the Green Snake and the Beautiful Lily.* Every page was covered in the margins with Rudolf Steiner's comments, in which the nature of that little *mysterium* was revealed. We read the *Fairy Tale* and the commentary with enthusiasm. The events and characters of the story became a kind of secret language in our circles.

With the *Fairy Tale* it became apparent to me for the first time that the characters and occurrences are true, inspired fairy-tale images of spiritual realities, which can be recognized on various levels as forces: in one's own soul, in the history of humanity, in the evolution of the world. They are no mere allegories.

A king's son loves the beautiful Lily. However, her touch has a deadly effect on every living thing. There are two possibilities by which to reach her across the great river. In the morning and in the evening the giant casts his shadow across the water, while at midday the Snake arches herself to form a bridge between the two banks. (The snake has always stood as an image of the earthly ego, enclosed within itself). We see in the will-o'-the-wisps, who describe themselves as upright gentlemen, the abstract intellect, which licks up the gold of wisdom wherever it can be found, in order to strew it about as minted coins; as abstract concepts. The coins are consumed by the Snake and the gold is transformed in her into an inner light with which, patiently and inquiringly, she illumines the objects on her path, loyal to the earth, probing her way from experience to experience. In this way she also lights up the subterranean temple where the three kings sit, the gold, the silver and the bronze: three soul-forces, which the soul perceives unconsciously (as subterranean) within itself: thinking, feeling and willing. The fourth, the mixed king, who rules in our time, in whom these three elements are chaotically mingled, stands leaning against a pillar.

The old man with the lamp whose light transforms the objects on which it falls, enters the temple. Moving and mysterious words are now exchanged there.

"How many secrets are known to you?" the golden king asks the old man.

"Three," replies the latter.

"Which one is the most important?" asked the silver king.

"The manifest one," replied the old man.

"Will you disclose it to us?" asked the brazen king.

"As soon as I have learned the fourth one," said the old man.

"Why should it concern me?" mumbled the composite king to himself. (How familiar this voice is to us!)

"I know the fourth one," said the Snake, approaching the old man and hissing something into his ear.

"The time is at hand!" exclaimed the latter with a powerful voice.

The fourth secret, the secret of the Snake, is not pronounced, but in what she hisses lies the solution of the *Fairy Tale.* The old man knows the secret of the three stages of the world's past development. *The fourth secret, the secret of the Snake, of the earthly "I," that passes through earthly experiences, is the secret concerning the free decision to sacrifice oneself, not gathering these experiences for oneself, but in order to build, by means of them, a bridge between the sensible and super-sensible worlds.* The Snake disintegrates into single precious stones, out of which a lasting bridge arises, which unites the two shores of existence, now not only for a few, but for the general populace. The temple now rises up from the depths on the other shore and becomes manifest. Here the marriage takes place of the youth, who has gone through death and resurrection, with the Lily, the most exalted bride. Even if at that time these pictures affected me more as moods, they still never left me. It is the nature of what has been born from reality that it leads over years or perhaps decades to truth. "What is fruitful alone is true."

Later, I performed this *Fairy Tale* as a puppet show. The luminous Green Snake, the will-o'-the-wisps, the lamp and the stars, the morning and evening glow had a magical effect in this miniature Mystery Play. It met with considerable approval, performed during the Third Reich in Germany, when everything else was forbidden that went in this direction. It seems to me now to have been the best thing I have done in my life.

At the end of February my dear father came for a few days to St Petersburg on business, and my good fortune seemed complete. I spent a lot of time with him in his hotel. He was invited several times to have meals with us in the Tower and was received in a hearty manner by the Ivanovs. There was a fine accord among us all. "Your father radiates a quiet magic around him," said Vyatsheslav. Lydia was also impressed by his modest, kind nature. The good man beamed in his quiet way, pleased to see me so happy and appreciated by everyone ... Thinking back to that time, I remember, on going to sleep, being as if submerged in a sea of light and waking up permeated by this light. I was grateful that each day brought a renewal of my association with these friends. And the best is yet to come, I thought.

My parents had agreed that we could spend the summer with the Ivanovs on our estate, Bogdanovchina. It meant much to me that Vyatsheslav would experience this countryside and bestow words upon its mute soul with his gift for poetry! It was as if everything I longed for most in life were being fulfilled.

Once, when my father was occupied with business and I waited for him in his hotel, an ardent longing for my friends took hold of me. I took a sleigh and drove quickly home. In the Tower everything was quiet and empty. I sat alone in the large dining hall, dim by day, and listened to the silence, which was filled with mysterious life. I believed I heard the pulse-beat of existence itself. I took fright at what I sensed approaching there. Good fortune gave way to an inevitable destiny. Shuddering, I went back to my father, without having seen anyone.

One evening Vyatsheslav said to me, "Today I asked " for his opinion about the growing closeness between you and me, and he expressed himself as deeply gladdened by it." To me this answer was quite natural. After all, I knew how much Max admired and was fond of Vyatsheslav. He had merely told the truth, since that was how he actually felt. But I gradually began to notice that it was Vyatsheslav who could not bear my closeness with Max. He took a more and more critical view of his writings and his thoughts. Objectively, I often had to concur with Vyatsheslav. Max was too fond of paradoxes. He played with thoughts. But in human terms it was painful for me. Vyatsheslav often intimated to me that Max and I were two people of divergent mental configuration, of different "confessions," as he put it, and that a marriage between two people of different faiths could not last. Deep down, I knew it myself; Vyatsheslav only put it into words.

Following a lecture on Eros which Max held with scandalous success, "*pour épater les bourgeois,*" and with which I was fundamentally unable to agree, I discovered that I could no longer say "we" in regard to Max and me. It was no easy matter for me to come to such a realization. Perhaps I was only able to bear it because I felt so fulfilled and supported by the friendship with Lydia and Vyatsheslav, believing myself in complete unison with them. Soon it became clear to me that Vyatsheslav was in love with me. I said as much to Lydia, adding, "I must go."

However, she — for whom this fact had long been a matter of course — replied, "You have entered our lives and now belong with us. If you were to go, something dead would remain between us ever afterwards. The two of us can no longer do without you." Then the three of us spoke together. They had a peculiar idea: if two people, such as they, were united with each other, they could love a third. It was as when a mask which fitted two could also correspond to a third. Such a love is the beginning of a new human community, indeed of a new church, in which Eros is incorporated, to the point of becoming flesh and blood. *So that was their new doctrine!*

"And Max?" I asked.

"No, he does not belong in this."

"But I cannot simply leave him!"

"You must choose," said Lydia. "You love Vyatsheslav and not him."

Yes, I loved Vyatsheslav, but in a manner such that I did not understand why Max should be excluded as a result. I felt childlike and awkward compared to these two great individuals. I was afraid of being inadequate, and could no longer be as happy as before. Max was also unable to feel the same as before.

In speaking to Miss Minslova about my conflict, she laughed at me, "You expect a pure source to bubble forth from the crater of a volcano!" In her sibylline fashion, she referred to the earthly fire through which I would have to go. For my part, however, I thought of the *"fuoco spirituale,"* the spiritual fire over the forests of Perugia. Did I have to renounce this ideal?

As spring approached, Max's mother, who shared our life with enthusiasm, grew melancholy. She had such states of depression from time to time. Did she have a premonition of disaster? She wanted to go home, the more so as her presence there was necessary because of the onset of the season. Max, not wanting to let her go alone in this state, travelled with her. Perhaps he also thought — fanatic of freedom that he was — that it was necessary to leave me completely free in my decisions. But *was* I free?

Vyatsheslav demanded obedience of me. I was not to doubt the correctness of his ideas. In a sonnet he wrote for me at that time, he warns Psyche, who approaches the beloved with a lamp:

Wherefore trust the lamp's weak light,
And not the heart's sure tidings?
A god am I, and no monster.
On foreign soil you shall wander,
Tormented by love's longing,
Protecting with delicate hand the flame,
Calling your close friend in separation.[24]

And Lydia? Did she really believe in the possibility of a third member of the union, or did she see this as the only way to maintain the partnership with her husband? She seemed to suffer as well, for she once said to me, "If I do not see you, a protest rises up in me against you. When we are together everything is alright again, and my mind is at peace."

After Max had decided to go to Koktebel, not wanting to remain alone in the Tower, I went to Zarskoye-Selo, the summer residence of the tsars, for distraction. The windows of my room looked out onto the old park in which Alexander Pushkin had spent his childhood and youth. The general arrangement of things, even in minor details, was still reminiscent of him. I went walking a lot by myself in the old Linden Park. The poems that arose there appeared that spring in the almanac *Flower-basket of the Horae*. It was early spring, the time when the snow thawed, when the sky is a delicate greenish-blue, with yellow-green, shining moss on the old tree trunks and an enlivening breeze. In the north this affects one inspiringly with its promise. The one unpleasant thing during this stay in Zarskoye was the presence of the agents of the secret police, who stood on every corner, and were in the habit of following unfamiliar persons. These gentlemen had old-fashioned moustaches, domed hats and pea-coloured coats. This attire had been assigned them quite some time ago, so they would not be distinguishable from the citizenry. Meanwhile fashion had long since altered, their uniform remained the same, and so they in fact stood out.

They were referred to as "pea-coats." However, they did not especially bother me, as I was completely absorbed in my work, and looked forward to showing the results both to Max and to the Ivanovs. I was naïve enough at that time, to be by no means fully aware of the conflict that had arisen in my life. I thought, everything would be resolved, once we were all four living and working together on our estate.

At one point Lydia visited me, at another Vyatsheslav. We wandered through the Park; he told me about the plan for a periodical an admirer wanted to make possible for him, so that, as she had expressed it, his genius would be presented to a wider circle. His idea was to create a unified whole from a close collaboration among individual writers.

In this way, a single spirit was to speak through a diverse circle of individualities. He spoke of the cathedrals of the Middle Ages as having arisen in this way. Today, his ideas appear to me rather illusory, but at that time I was enthusiastic about them. As always in his presence, a lot of ideas came to me, so that he said with emotion, "And you will be the winged Nike on the bow of our ship!" Poor Nike! How soon her little wings were plucked from her ... as always happens with the wings of illusion!

Before travelling to Moscow at Easter to see my parents, I spent some time in the Tower. These days were suffused with a peculiar mood. The spring nights were bright, and in the Tower everyone remained awake till sunrise. Stormy arguments took place between the married couple. They wanted me present. Both emerged refreshed from these thunderstorms, but I was exhausted afterwards, not properly understanding the cause. What I could comprehend well enough were the reproaches Lydia made to her husband concerning his idle life. "I don't want to have to contemplate your leisurely life anymore. What have you accomplished this winter? The book of poems called *Eros*, and the twelve sonnets to Margarita you spat out.[25] I yearn for a rigorous working life ...!"

It was Holy Week. To gain strength and enlightenment, I wanted to attend every service and go to communion. Remizov read us his new poem *The Sufferings of the Lord*. In this work, the demonic element in the world was portrayed with extraordinary force. It was as though the poet identified himself gloatingly with evil. The conclusion, "However, at the Cross stood the Mother, Star of Stars," was no adequate counterweight. Hell triumphed.

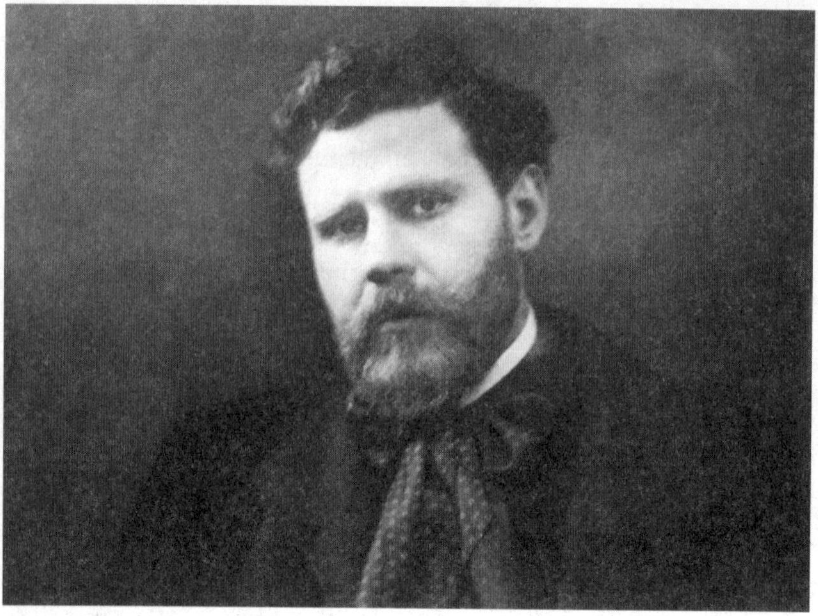

Maximilian Voloshin, 1906

When Remizov had finished reading, Vyatsheslav stood up, full of indignation, and said, "That is blasphemy. I declare my opposition to it."

Remizov, already wounded by life, cringed and left with his wife in silence.

Max sent Vyatsheslav a cycle of very beautiful new poems: *Cimmerian Twilight*. They were written in a strange, antique metre borrowed from Vyatsheslav. But they were harshly criticized. I was surprised that Max did not write to me, but assumed he wanted to leave me free. We were all supposedly going to meet up with each other soon in any case. Later I learned that all his letters sent to me in St Petersburg had been redirected to an unknown address in Berlin. In these touching letters, he begged me to come and join him; he suffered dreadfully. He received all these letters back again several weeks later. Was it some incomprehensible mistake, or did a conscious will lie behind it, trying to separate us? I only much later reached the point of asking the second question. However, I am unable to answer this even today. I would certainly have travelled to see him. Instead, I drove to Moscow to my parents, after which we were all presumably going to meet at our estate.

When the "somnambulist" arrived in the worthy house of her

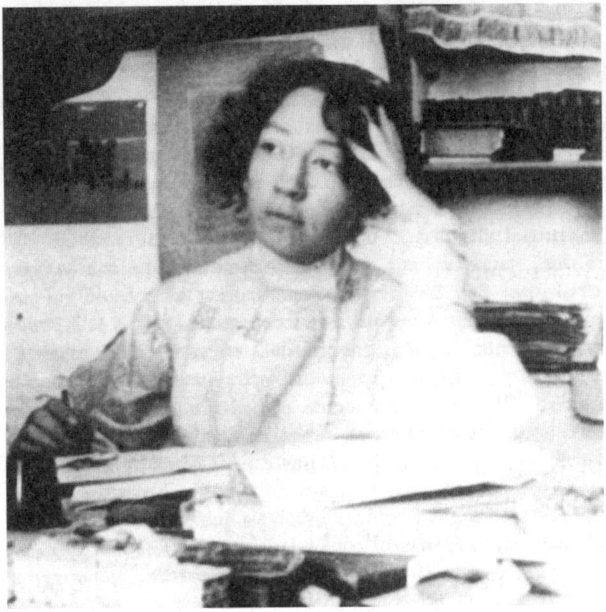

Margarita at Koktebel. 1906

parents, she felt obligated to explain honestly to her mother how matters now stood in her life. She would never separate herself from the Ivanovs: Vyatsheslav would not be able to live without her; and both Max and Lydia had given their assent to this. My mother was horror-struck; she told me that I could go to the Ivanovs only over her dead body. And she was in such a state that I had to believe in this "dead body." When I reported this in a letter to the Ivanovs, the prompt reply was that under these circumstances they would, of course, not be coming to Bogdanovchina. They would instead rent a manor house in a western province. I would be welcome there at any time. Their children had meanwhile returned to St Petersburg with the family friend who had looked after them in Geneva.

The time I spent in Moscow was frightful for me. I felt like a criminal. Every possibility seemed ruled out, for with every step taken, or not taken, I would incur distress to one of those nearest and dearest to me. A decision being imperative, I lost sleep. My grandmother's house, the old patriarchal family morality, my mother's despair; everything conspired to exercise enormous pressure on me. At times, I felt physically sick from indecisiveness. Hardly had I decided in favour of one thing, than another course appeared more appropriate.

To put an end to this dreadful state, I made up my mind to travel to Max in Koktebel; but to make a digression to the Ivanovs without my mother's knowledge. The detour involved about two days travel.

In the large, sunny rooms of their country house, permeated with the scent of fields, I met my friends. I found them more youthful and fresher than in the Tower: Strict and serious, surrounded by her children, Lydia seemed to emanate a quiet strength. She was in a creative mood and working on an extended dramatic work. Vyatsheslav read me his latest poems; I communicated to him my discoveries concerning mathematical laws to be found in the Lord's Prayer; a task which had helped me keep my head above water during the last few weeks. He was full of fatherly affection, which suited me just then. Never was he in fact closer to me; it felt like a home-coming. I can say that this day with the Ivanovs was something of a blessed dream, though I sensed that their friend, as well as Lydia's eldest daughter Vera, were not favourably inclined towards me. This eighteen-year-old, blonde, beautiful girl seemed to me to have become the third member of the union. The Ivanovs perceived deep wisdom in Vera's rationality, seeing in her "the measure of all things." Lydia was more reserved toward me than before. She could not comprehend my helplessness.

"Genuine love does not deliberate, it is a categorical imperative!" But her last words were, "Let us just continue and trust life!" They promised they would come to Koktebel soon.

But they did not come and all my letters remained unanswered.

Max, whom I had informed of my detour beforehand, received me touchingly. The whitewashed walls of his house were decorated with garlands of wormwood on my arrival. There were no flowers in this region. We went through the countryside he loved so much. Only now did I comprehend its austere beauty. Yet this time spent together was unspeakably sad; between us stood a phantom which held me spellbound. Along with my cousins, who soon arrived, Miss Minslova also came to see us.

At the end of the summer a telegram arrived for Miss Minslova from Vyatsheslav: "Have joined Lydia in marriage through her death." She had died of scarlet fever in the space of three days. My first impulse was to travel to see him at once! But Miss Minslova, whom I trusted unquestioningly, resisted this idea and travelled to see him alone, promising to telegraph me immediately if my coming there seemed appropriate. But I received no news. Only later did I learn she had promised my mother to prevent my seeing the Ivanovs again. Apart from that, she wanted to be the one providing consolation herself.

From her pneumonia, Nyusha had been left with injury to her lungs and needed to spend time in the south. I accompanied her to Rome, where we stayed for the winter. Meanwhile, Max was alone in St Petersburg. His letters were full of concern for me. He did not see Vyatsheslav anymore. The letters of the sibyl, who was in the Tower, left me in uncertainty.

In Rome, I painted a portrait of Lydia in the attitude of the *Moses* by Michelangelo. I began it in red, her colour in life. The solemn earnestness of the picture, however, called for dark violet.

My brother, still studying agriculture in Leipzig, visited us that spring in Rome. He had become a keen student of anthroposophy, but as often happens at the beginning, it remained rather abstract in him. When I mentioned my mental anguish, he said scornfully, "That's a lot of nonsense; we have to develop *buddhi* within us, only in *buddhi* is love real." He preached that to me in the Colosseum. The recesses of the huge ruin seemed to stare at me from all sides, like eye sockets.

During the fasting period preceding Easter, I went to the Russian Church and, to my surprise, found it overcrowded with peasants in traditional costume from every region of Russia. I spoke to some of them in the courtyard following the mass. They surrounded me, full of the urge to tell me about their experiences. They had come from Palestine, had been in Bari to worship the relics of St Nicholas, and were now making a pilgrimage to Rome to the grave of St Peter and other saints. For the Feast of the Resurrection they expected to be in Jerusalem again. In answer to my question concerning the various regions they came from, a tall old man in a huge fur hat stepped forward and said, "We are not from Siberia or the Urals, not from the White and not from the Black Sea, not from the Volga and not from the Dnieper — we all come from Christ's Grave; *that* is the spiritual home of all of us." I wandered through Rome with them. They strode about the streets as if it were the most natural thing in the world, as if in their own home village, speaking with the Italians, from whom they bought picture postcards, as if they understood Russian. And things actually went quite well. "What cleanliness there is everywhere here! God grant our Imperator Tsar good health for that!" an old woman pilgrim said while crossing herself, never having seen a big city, and not being clear about the fact that she was now in a foreign country. "And hot water is provided free of charge!"

The old man was indignant about the fact that in church paintings here "the sinful flesh is shown exposed." And a young nun from the Urals, with large black eyes and black eyebrows framed by a black cloth, told me that she had wanted to see Augustus Tiberius, who ruled at the time of Christ, and had forced her way into the Museum of the Vatican. "But, oh my dear!" she said, full of horror, drawing in air while she spoke, "Can you believe it. He stands there completely naked!"

The Novice

In the spring Nyusha, who had meanwhile recovered her health, went to her beloved Paris, to Balmont. Now I could go at last to St Petersburg. On the way, I visited the two ladies in Munich who guided the anthroposophical work there. Fräulein Stinde asked me whether I intended to visit Dr Steiner in Berlin.

"No," I said, "I first have to go to Russia, in order to clarify my life. In my present state of mind I cannot make claims on his time at all."

She thought about it for a moment. "I shall ask you even so," she replied, "to go to the Motzstrasse and personally hand over a letter from me to Dr Steiner."

I was at once received the next morning by Rudolf Steiner. After glancing at the lines of the message, he enquired how things were going with me. I had to admit, things were not going at all well for me.

"I don't want to press you," he answered, "but would like to help you as an older brother, if you want it."

I attempted to describe the uncertainty in which I found myself and that so tore me apart. He put various questions to me. It particularly interested him what cultural mission Ivanov had, in my view. I said that he was able to connect the nature-spirituality of the ancient world with Christianity. I also told him about his poetic works and about his capacity to awaken the creative element in the people he came in touch with.

To this he replied, "When I last saw you, you were more creative and richer than now." For that reason, he thought I was not yet strong enough to be together with Ivanov. I would first have to find myself, and for the time being not think about him at all. I doubted whether I would succeed in that. He wrote on a piece of paper, "The human being can do what he should do, and if he says, 'I can't,' then he does not want to." He gave me two further meditations and explained to me how I should apply them. Then he enquired after my present interests.

I stammered something about Greece, how it was revived in different cultures, and also about the peculiar relationship between Russia and Greece. He wrote down the titles of books I should read: *Michelangelo* by Herman Grimm, Goethe on Winckelmann, *Psyche* by Erwin Rohde, *Renaissance Culture in Italy* by Jakob Burckhardt ... "Though he is a philistine, it does not matter." Steiner also recommended to me his own brochure *Goethe as the Father of a New Aesthetics.* The great warmth that radiated from him had the effect on me of an enlivening force. After this conversation, he told my brother, who was in Berlin at the time, "It was just possible to seize destiny by the coat-tails."

I stayed on in Berlin and occupied myself with the recommended books. But to stop thinking of a particular topic was not such a simple matter. Leo Tolstoy relates a game that he made up with his brothers and sisters during his childhood: one had to sit in a corner and not think of a white bear.

I decided for the time being to remain in Germany.

In May of that year, 1908, my brother and I travelled to Hamburg, where Rudolf Steiner intended to speak about St John's Gospel. Just before the departure from Berlin, we saw him at the railway station from the window of our compartment, as he went past us with his rapid, purposeful way of walking. He returned with two railway officials and dictated something into the complaint book in Marie von Siver's presence. As I was told later, one of the employees had given her an impertinent reply. A Christian initiate and a complaint book? From my eastern point of view, I was surprised by this.

At that time I had to wonder at many things, including the people who made up the circle around Rudolf Steiner. The men appeared to me pedantic and philistine and the women prosaic and at the same time sentimental. The kinds of people who had followed a spiritual messenger in previous ages would certainly have been different, I thought. It did not occur to me that they might be the same ones, only transformed by our unspiritual age. I also did not consider the fact that the cultural elite of our time still drew from sources belonging to a past world, and for that reason were not yet "beggars of the spirit." At that time I had no sympathy, as can easily be imagined, for the excellent qualities of the people around me: for their competence, their diligence, reliability, their good will and dedication to the cause — qualities on which Rudolf Steiner was able to build his work.

The lectures took place in the white room of a bourgeois house. Rudolf Steiner stood before a yellow silk curtain next to a little table. On this first evening he spoke about the prologue to the Gospel of St John, "In the beginning was the Word." In doing so, he took a lily of the valley from the little bunch of flowers in front of him: Just as the lily of the valley arose from the seed and the seed is hidden in the blossom, so the whole world and the human being arose from the Word. It was at first a silent world, for the human being was mute to begin with; yet the Word was concealed within him, as the seed is concealed in the blossom. And the Word began to sound forth from the human being: *"I am."*

After the lecture he came up to me and asked, "Could you dance that?"

I was not surprised at this question, since I had felt the need from childhood to dance every deeper experience, and I was convinced that Rudolf Steiner "knew everything." I answered him, "I believe one could dance everything one feels."

"But the essential thing today was feeling after all!" He repeated this sentence and remained standing in front of me for a while, looking at me, as though waiting for something. But I did not ask him anything. In the autumn of the same year, after a lecture concerning the correspondence between rhythms in the cosmos and in the human being, he came up to me and said, "Dance is an independent rhythm, a movement, whose centre is outside the human being. The rhythm of dance leads back to primal times. The dances of our time are a degeneration of the ancient temple dances, through which the deepest world secrets were revealed."

And again he stood waiting in front of me, and again I asked him nothing. I did not then know that the words of a teacher are always meant as an indication, without encroaching on the freedom of the pupil. What he had waited for, I only understood four years later, when in answer to a pupil's question, he elaborated the basis of a new art of movement. The question had to be asked by someone, only then did he answer.

Through Vladimir Soloviev, what lived in me as Christian substance found a basis in thought. Rudolf Steiner's Christology placed this central mystery in specific relation to the stages of world evolution, to the phenomena of history. Thus illumined, what was most distant in time and space united itself intimately with one's own being.

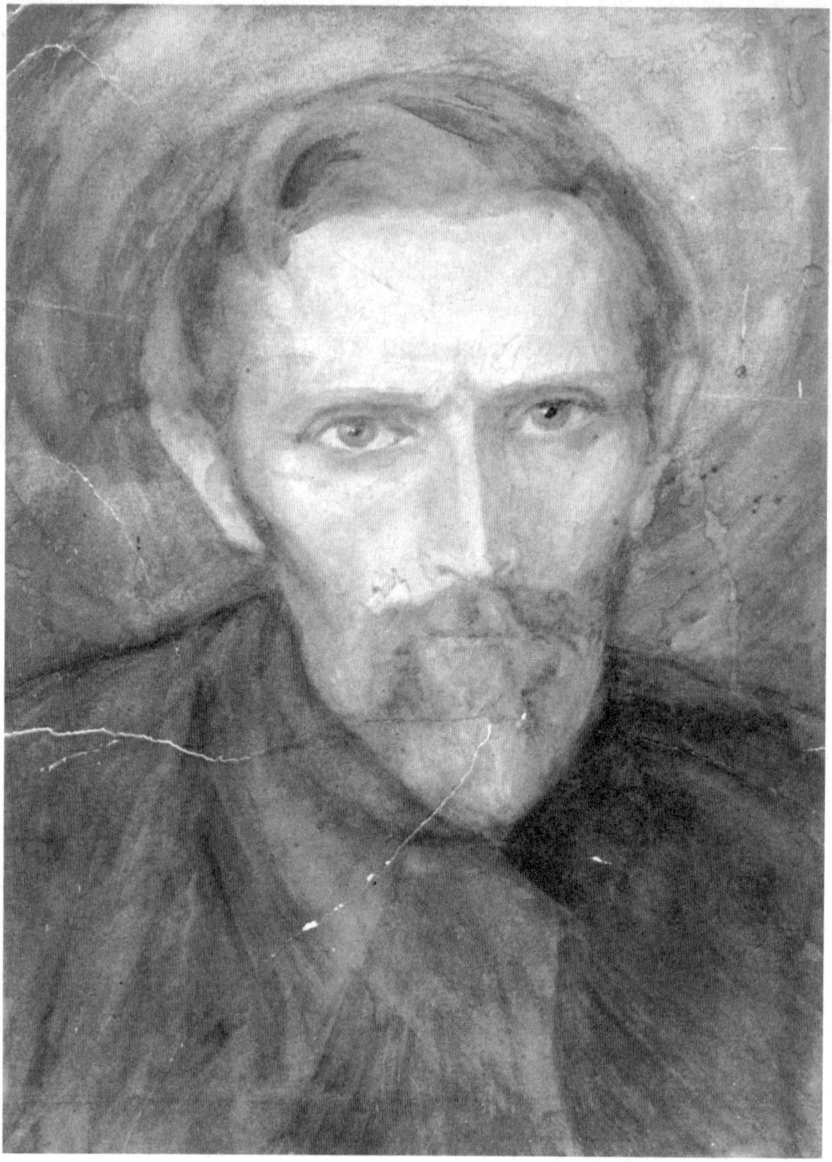

Michael Bauer. Portrait by Woloschin around 1920

In the state of mind in which I found myself, conscious of guilt and torn out of every connection with my previous life, I experienced all that I took in at that time as giving me fresh courage. The "I am" words of the Gospel created something in me that radiated from a centre, raising me above the temporal. And the image of the woman taken in adultery, who had remained alone with Christ — He, the Lord of Destiny, however, wrote with His finger into the earth the consequences of her deeds for destiny. This picture exercised a healing effect on me and gave me a feeling of the sovereign independence of human beings, and courage and trust in the future.

On the way from St Petersburg to Paris, Max made a detour to Hamburg to visit me and attended several lectures. In a question and answer session, he put a question which very much occupied him just then as a paradox: Whether it was not Judas, who, in taking upon himself the sin of betrayal, made Christ's sacrifice possible in the first place and was thus the actual world redeemer? Rudolf Steiner rejected this idea, regarding it as unhealthy. Judas had not understood the nature of what Christ brought to the world, and expected that Christ would win the victory over His enemies by means of magic. Through his betrayal he had wanted to bring about an earthly triumph of Christ. Our materialistic culture stood under the sign of Judas. Just as Judas went and hanged himself, so would our culture destroy itself.

I have never seen so many roses as when we arrived in Nuremberg in June to hear Rudolf Steiner's lectures on the Apocalypse. We had obtained rooms on the edge of the city. The scent of blossoming lindens and warm bread filled the air. The gables of the houses, gilded by the setting sun, were reflected in the water. Geraniums flamed bright red against the background of the dark stone walls.

On entering the large, old-fashioned hall of the guesthouse Zum Adler, everyone received a long-stemmed rose as a greeting. The chairman of the Nuremberg Branch, a tall man with large, deep-set, shining eyes, held a brief address. I have scarcely ever seen anyone of more noble appearance: a broad forehead, a fine Roman nose and a beard surrounding a well-formed mouth. His stooped posture, as well as a hollow yet pleasant voice, indicated lung disease. His Frankish dialect, his humour and sincerity at once won my heart; indeed, this man was altogether a disciple of the spirit as I would have imagined one to be. It was Michael Bauer, with whom I was later to become very good friends. He came from a family of farmers; hence his connection to the soil, his matter-of-factness and love of clarity, which, combined with spiritual experiences, constituted his unique persona. His friend Christian Morgenstern wrote of him at that time:

> You are the gentlest of the gentle,
> Since within your being
> The citizens of two worlds are united.
> *(Epigrammes)*

An astonishing health of soul, despite the illness that became ever more serious with the years, stood as an example of how the spirit can achieve independence from the body. As he is known to wider circles through his book on Christian Morgenstern, through Friedrich Rittelmeyer's recollections of him and Margareta Morgenstern's biography, I shall only mention here that his effect on people came especially from his warm way of speaking from personal experience, both in lectures and in intimate conversations. By means of his advice, as well as by his example, he helped many young people especially on their path. By reason of his capacity to enter into the different soul-constitution of another human being, his undogmatic free manner, and many-sided interests, he could be a good friend to Russians first coming into connection with anthroposophy.

Those days spent in Nuremberg, the city of Dürer's *Apocalypse*, were overwhelming. In the mysterious pictorial script of the Revelation which Jesus Christ gave His disciples, the destiny of humanity was unveiled for us in its inexorable tragedy. After almost every lecture, Rudolf Steiner shook my hand and said a few words.

When he spoke of Tolstoy as being the representative of the idea of brotherhood, which would only be incorporated in the future Slavic culture, we Russians asked him — my brother and an acquaintance from St Petersburg — whether Dostoyevsky did not stand for this idea still more? Steiner replied:

> Tolstoy has more carrying power; the impulse that works through him is of the future. His thoughts are limited, he is often foolish, but precisely his mistakes and weaknesses show that we have to see in him something that has come too soon

> into this world and is therefore still immature. With such personalities we have to regard deficiencies as the shadow of their greatness. Some sentences of Tolstoy have more weight than whole libraries.

Concerning Dostoyevsky he once said something like the following, "He stands in penitent's garb before Christ on behalf of all humanity."

At the beginning of July, Steiner was to speak in Norway in Ljan, a residential area of villas not far from Kristiania (today Oslo), concerning the Gospel of St John.[26] For the first time in my life I travelled alone to a foreign country and felt quite lost when getting out at a little station in the evening before the lectures began. Nobody understood my request for directions. The blue-eyed station employees and the workers on the road seemed deaf and dumb, as they did not respond to my attempts at being heard and understood. At last I met a German, who took my little suitcase from my hand and led me to the settlement. This was situated high up between two fjords in the forest. It was as bright as day in spite of the late evening hour. I found a room in the hospitable vicarage there.

The next day I hiked through the vast, ancient forest. Dog rose bushes, densely covered with pale pink blossoms, stood alongside grey birch trees overgrown with moss and austere pines. The air was light and transparent as in the high mountains. In the evening I went to the schoolhouse to hear the lecture. The wooden walls of the room, in which sat silent blue-eyed Norwegians, were decorated with fir branches and little red flags. Though it was nine-thirty in the evening, the sun shone brightly through the large windows, illuminating a bunch of bellflowers standing on the lectern. Outside, the silvery waters of the fjord could be seen with their many forested islands. A little bird mingled its song with the words of the lecture.

In the nights as bright as day, I was unable to sleep. I wandered through the countryside. Every flower was clearly visible in full colour. The sky was a delicate silver-blue. The clouds, in which the moonlight and at the same time the sunset and sunrise shimmered, appeared ghostly; the solemn-looking trees brooding. Everything was light and transparent. One hardly felt the weight of one's own body, and strolled about like a spirit among spirits. I felt continuously as though a god strode with me through these woods, whose strength streamed through me. The eyes of people, even of the children, I met on forest paths at night, were translucent and awake. Below lay the fjord in the light of the moon, its surface like pale rose petals, silvery, tinged reddish at the edges. Soundlessly, the fishing boats glided between the black islands. The day came imperceptibly. "You should not wander about at night, but rather sleep," Dr Steiner said, when I met him in the woods with Fräulein von Sivers.

Once, the lecture was to take place on an island. Thus it came about that I crossed over the fjord in a boat with Rudolf Steiner and Fräulein von Sivers. A child sat at the helm. It struck me that the face of Rudolf Steiner in the bright light was quite different from the surrounding nature. I had to think of the contrast of coal and diamond. On the other hand, the face of Fräulein von Sivers with its heavenly bloom was woven of the purest elements of the surrounding nature. The gold of the sun, the blue of the sky and the water, the delicacy of the northern rose she held in her hand were to be found, joined together in feminine beauty. Whenever I saw these two human beings next to each other, I had the feeling that there, quite different worlds met each other in harmonious accord.

When they were invited to people's homes, I was often able to join them. Questions were put to Rudolf Steiner. In answer to a question concerning the task of the Jewish people that had always occupied me, he replied somewhat as follows:

> It is difficult to speak on a theme that evokes a great deal of emotion. Spiritual scientific truths do not countenance sympathy and antipathy, if they are to be rightly taken up. The Jews developed intellectual, deductive thinking. This enabled the human being to become an independent personality. This same people prepared, through generations, a body that could become the bearer of Jesus. In becoming human, Christ brought redemption from humanity's death-bringing isolation from the divine. However, since the Jewish people did not take up this new impulse, the attributes it had developed became retarding forces. What persists in continuing in the old ways — the blood-bond on the one hand, the hardened intellectualism on the other — works to inhibit progress. But in certain circumstances the Jewish people can also have the effect of a leaven, a ferment. That

> does not concern the individual, however, since a particular individual soul goes on developing, and only makes use of incarnation in a particular people as a necessary stage.

I felt the need, once again, to have a conversation with Rudolf Steiner. Various questions preoccupied me. Mainly I anticipated further instructions for meditation from him. But first I wanted to wait and see what he would say.

At twelve o'clock I arrived in the house in which Steiner was staying. He led me onto the veranda, from which the sunny fjord could be seen through the pine trees. "Perhaps you would find it pleasant to sit here?" he asked. "How do you like it here?"

I told him how enthusiastic I was about the natural surroundings, to which he said, "In this region it is still possible to see the figures of the old gods, particularly toward evening; materialistic human thoughts and technology have not driven them away!"

In the course of the conversation he said, "You will not have it easy with spiritual science, because you do not take things superficially. You must now decide either to stay away, or to enter into it fully, in order — wherever it leads — to be able to take something along with you."

I replied that I could not stay away at all, as it was my actual life.

He asked me, among other things, whether I drew from nature here. But I did not have any desire to draw and described to him the kind of painting I had in mind, with its transparent, crystalline, mutually interpenetrating surfaces. The colours would have to be freed from objects, not in an indifferent chaos, however, as often occurs in modern painting.

Steiner said, "I understand, what you say is right." He advised me to work in mosaics. From the old art of mosaics, the conversation turned to Russian icons, concerning which, like most people at that time, I knew very little. One lived with the picture of a saint, darkened by varnish and covered with a metal shield made of gold or silver, as with a cult object, without having any notion of the work of art lying hidden behind it. Only a few connoisseurs and collectors of icons — and Old Believers — knew of their artistic value. A few years later, particularly during the Revolution, this was discovered by artists when the miracle-working holy pictures worshipped in the churches were transferred to exhibitions, their golden metal coverings having been removed.

Restorers freed the paintings from their dark varnish and later overpainting.

Steiner said, "If one were to study the *podlennik*" — he pronounced the word with a certain difficulty — "one would arrive at true imaginations, for these compositions and colours are founded on clairvoyantly perceived realities." (The *podlennik* refers to the preliminary basis for the composition of single icons, with indications of the colours.) I had my doubts at that time, concerned that clairvoyance might do harm to art.

"Does one not have the urge to create artistically," I said, "because of an unconscious presentiment of a reality one would like to create and make visible? Besides, what arises from consciousness is no longer artistic."

Rudolf Steiner attempted to make comprehensible to me, that as long as spiritual science takes hold only of the superficial layer of consciousness, the intellect, one obviously cannot create artistically. But things ought not to remain at that. In order to create, one would first have to immerse oneself in a particular mood.

"I too," he said, "if I am to give a lecture, do not determine in advance what I shall say, but immerse myself in a particular mood, out of which I then speak."

I had not given expression to all of my questions, yet when I looked at the piece of paper at home on which he had indicated a few things, I discovered that each of the questions I had still wanted to put were answered *in a single stroke*, as though he had reached to their source in me.

My brother and Lyubimov were expecting me in the Black Forest. I found Alyosha, who had meanwhile completed his doctorate, inwardly consolidated and cheerful. He was about to return to Moscow, to become a private instructor at the university.

The equilibrium that I believed I had found in Norway was to a certain extent put to the test by news from Moscow. Vyatsheslav, who wanted to spend the summer with his children and Miss Minslova in the Crimea, not far from Koktebel, had a discussion with my mother in passing through Moscow, which she had arranged. She demanded a promise from him to dissolve his relationship with me, which however, he did not give. She required that I now come to Moscow, in order to speak with him for the last time.

This interference in my life, this conversation with him about me at a time in which he was completely given over to the pain of the loss of his wife, filled me with outrage and hurt my feelings profoundly. At the same time, Max wrote to me that he was of the opinion that I should be somewhere near Vyatsheslav, so as to be able to gradually clarify the relationship. It was touching how Max was continually concerned only about me. "Without having to ask anybody, you can after all come and stay in your own house in Koktebel. If you think it would be better, I can go away for a period of time." I was unable to accept the offer and remained in Germany.

Meanwhile, in the Crimea, Vyatsheslav received my painting of Lydia. Miss Minslova wrote to me that, on seeing it, he was able to weep for the first time. Through her he let me know that he "bows before the artist who created such a work." The exaggerated and official nature of this response pained me beyond words.

In September, after one of the lectures in Leipzig in the series, *Egyptian Myths and Mysteries,* Marie von Sivers handed me a letter. I held a fountain pen in my hand, the cap not yet screwed on, with which I had just been writing my notes. I recognized the handwriting of Vyatsheslav, opened the envelope and read a letter employing the formal "you" as a form of address; his first since Lydia's death. These lines were so unnatural and peculiar, that I stood there numbed with pain, not noticing that the ink from the fountain pen was dripping onto my hand. However, I felt someone take hold of both my hands firmly in his own — in spite of the ink — consoling me. It was Rudolf Steiner.

From Leipzig I visited Weimar. Goethe's house and park remained unforgettable as *the* house and *the* park; the place from which to contemplate life ever and again.

In the pure-red autumn forests of the Harz Mountains, the cries of fighting and wounded stags could be heard. Their mysterious antler-crowned heads could be seen peeking out from a nearby copse. Among the ancient oaks and stones with runes etched on them, I encountered a mighty Germanic elemental world, quite new to me, yet somehow kindred. This was so different from the light-filled, fluid one known to me from my homeland.

I stayed in Berlin over the winter, in order to hear further lectures of Rudolf Steiner. In the circle gathered around him, however, I did not really feel I belonged. However, when my brother came in January and we went to Munich together, where Rudolf Steiner admitted us into the restricted esoteric circle, a source of strength opened up for me that re-enlivened my soul.[27] In these lessons spiritual truths were mediated in a ritual-symbolic form. Rudolf Steiner had to link on to an existing historical tradition, in order to have the formal authority to conduct such a ritual. However, this ritual in pictorial-ceremonial form had no content other than what he had drawn from his own spiritual research, to be taken up with complete circumspection, as corresponds to our time.

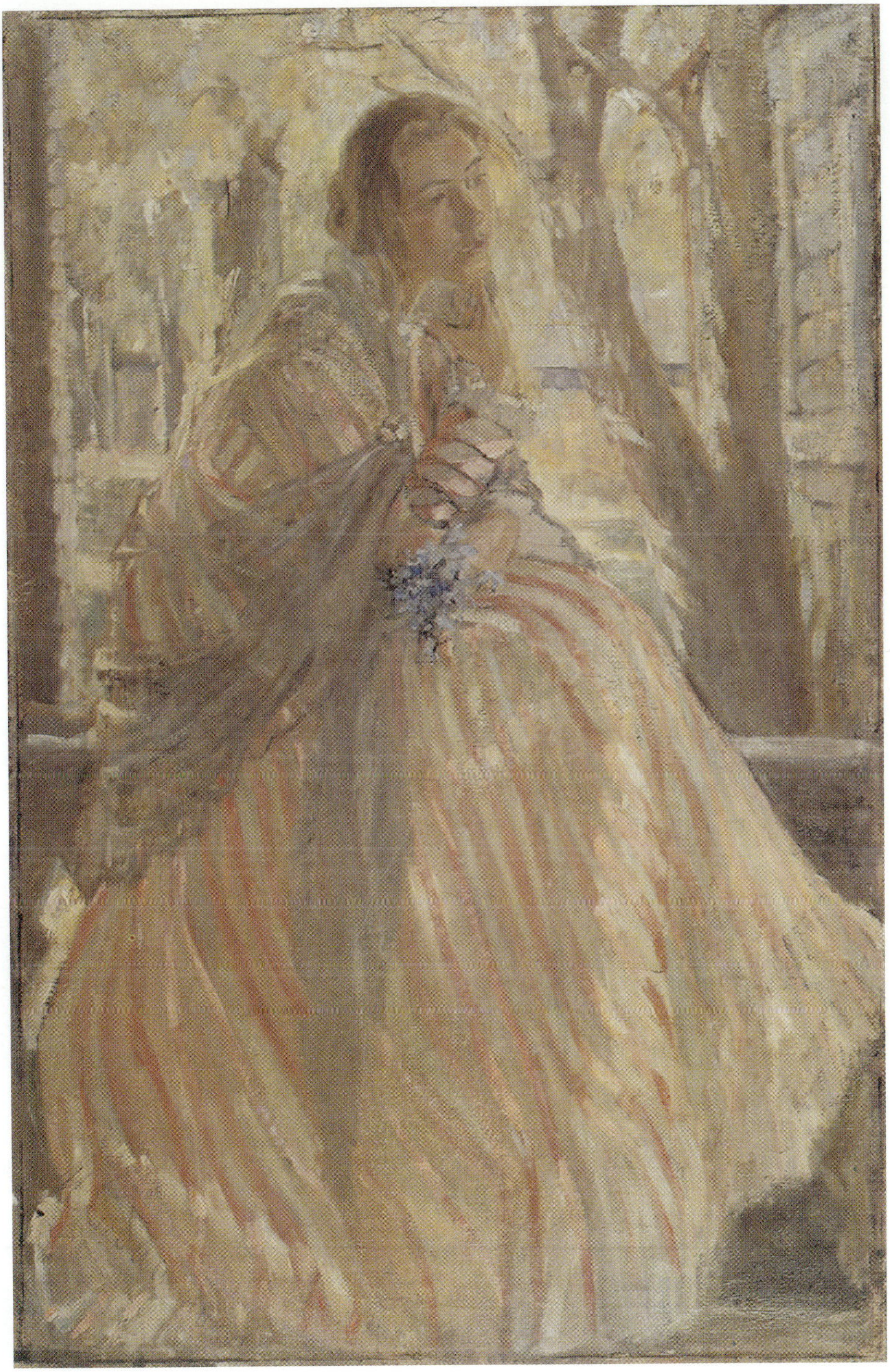

Portrait of Nyusha Ivanova, 1903. State Kustodiev Gallerg, Astrakhan

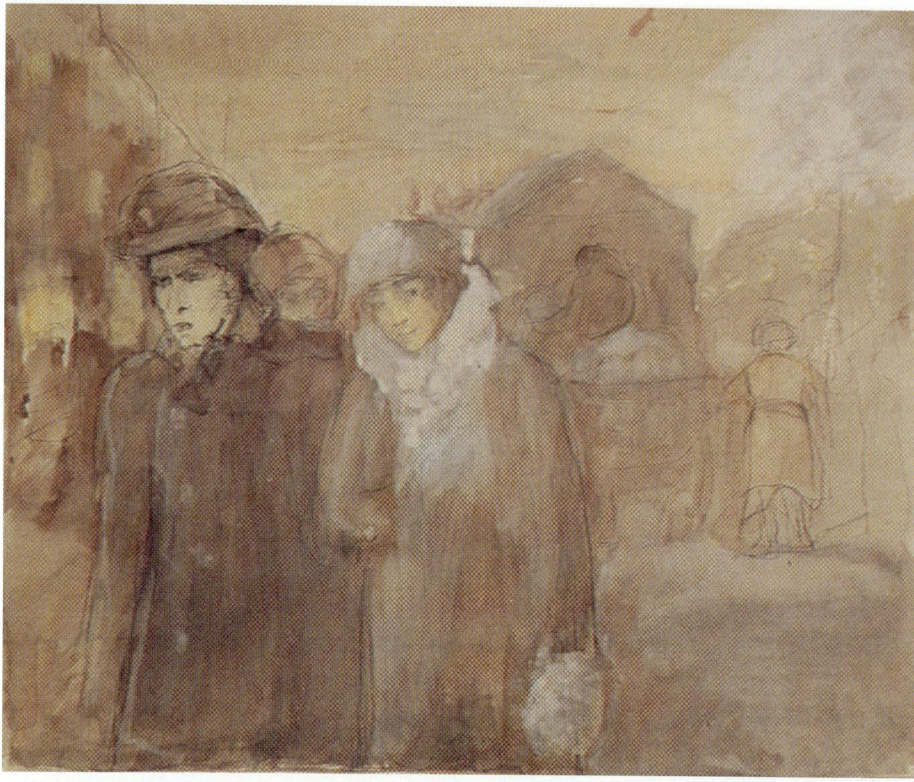

Winter in Moscow (undated). Voloschin House Museum, Koktebel

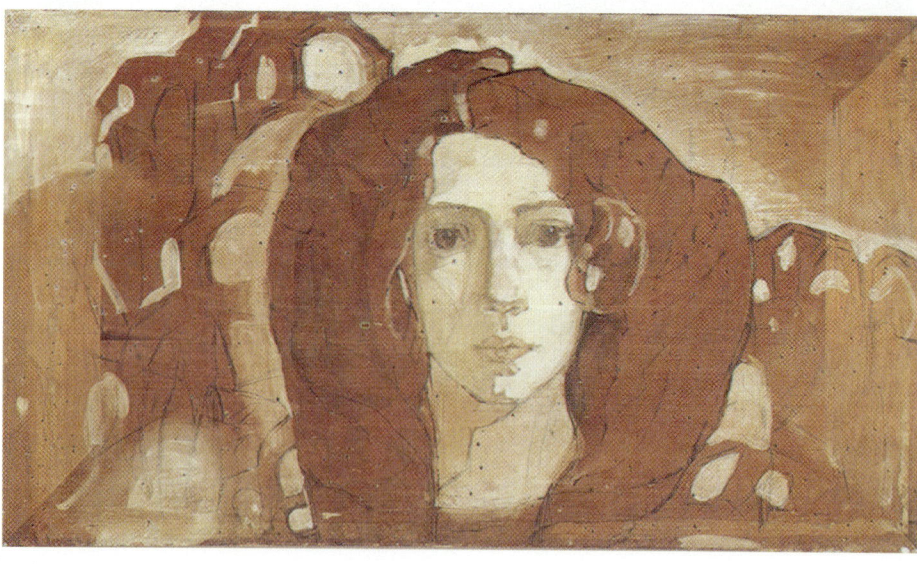

Self portrait (undated). Coloured wood. Voloshin House Museum, Koktebel

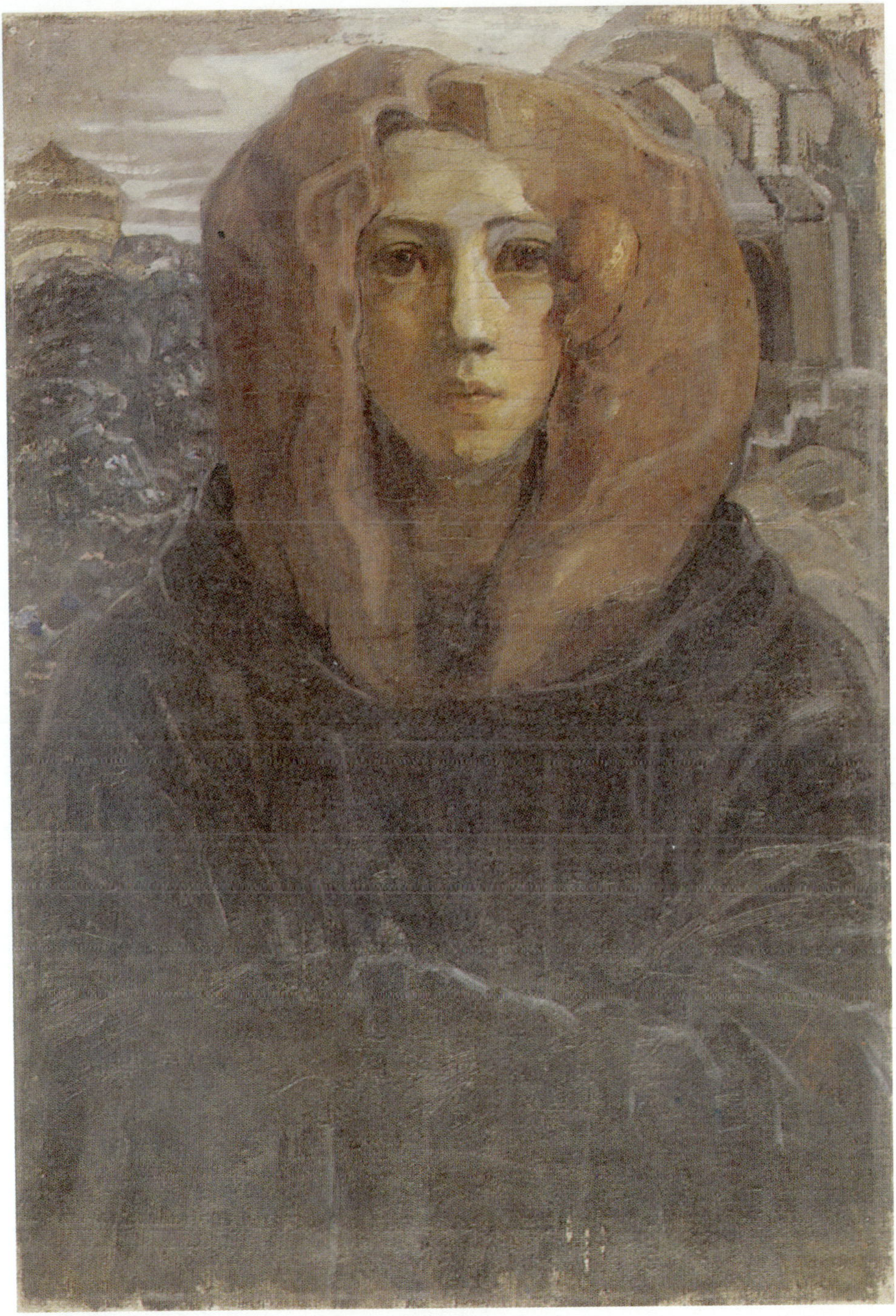

Self portrait, 1905. State Savitki Art Museum, Pensa

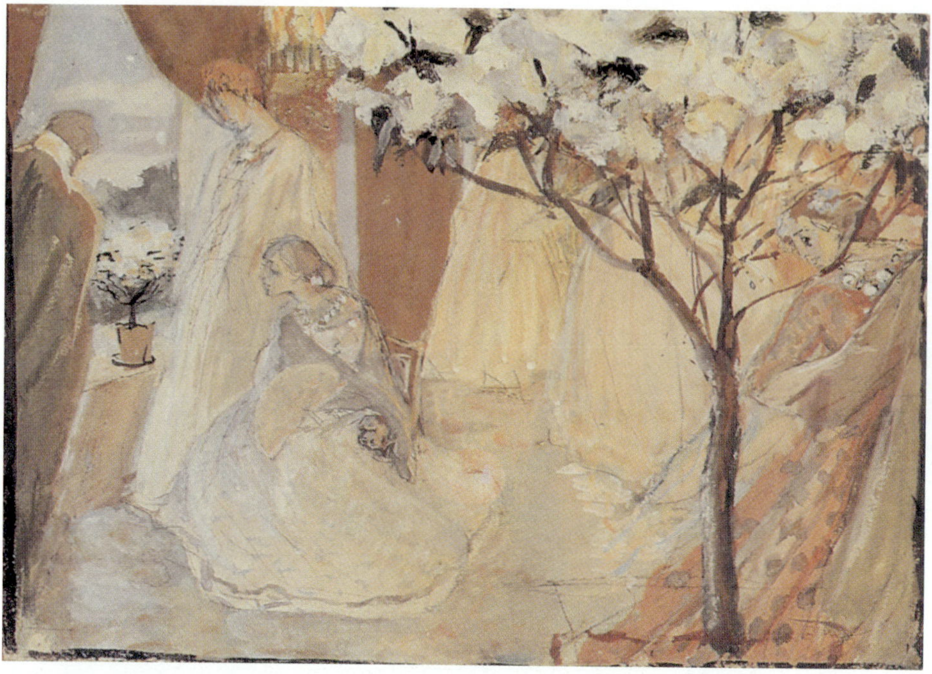

Flowering Trees and Women (undated). Voloshin House Museum, Koktebel

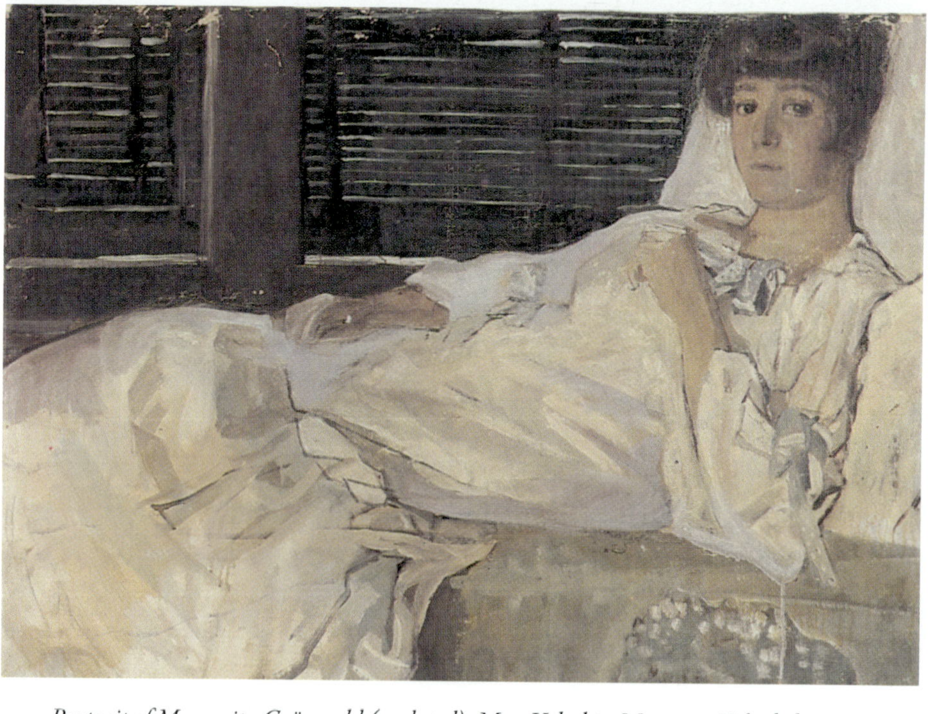

Portrait of Margarita Grünwald (undated). Max Voloshin Museum, Koktebel

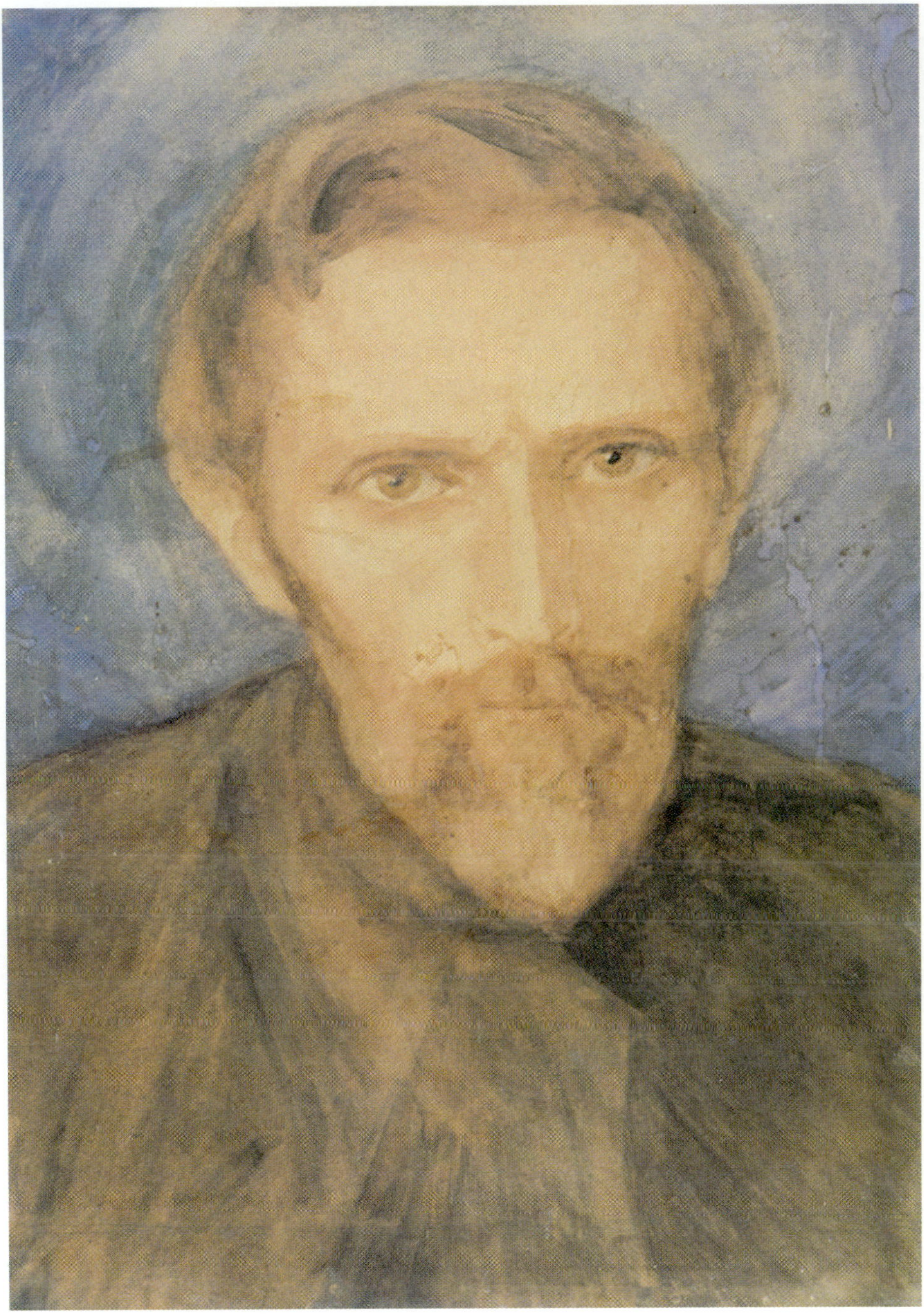

Michael Bauer, second portrait, ca. *1926. Michael Bauer School, Stuttgart*

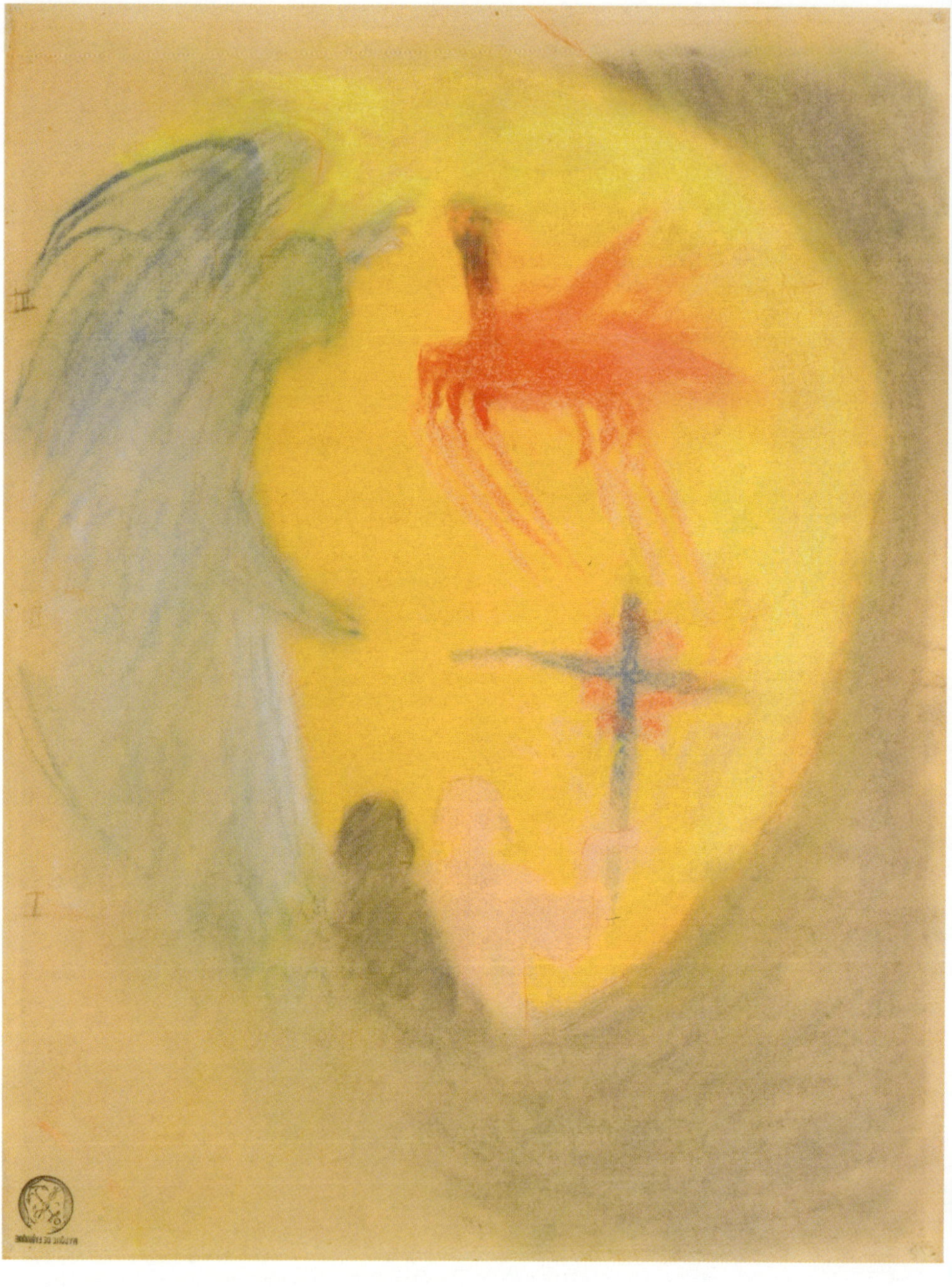

Margarita Woloschin/ Rudolf Steiner, soloured sketch for Stavic Man

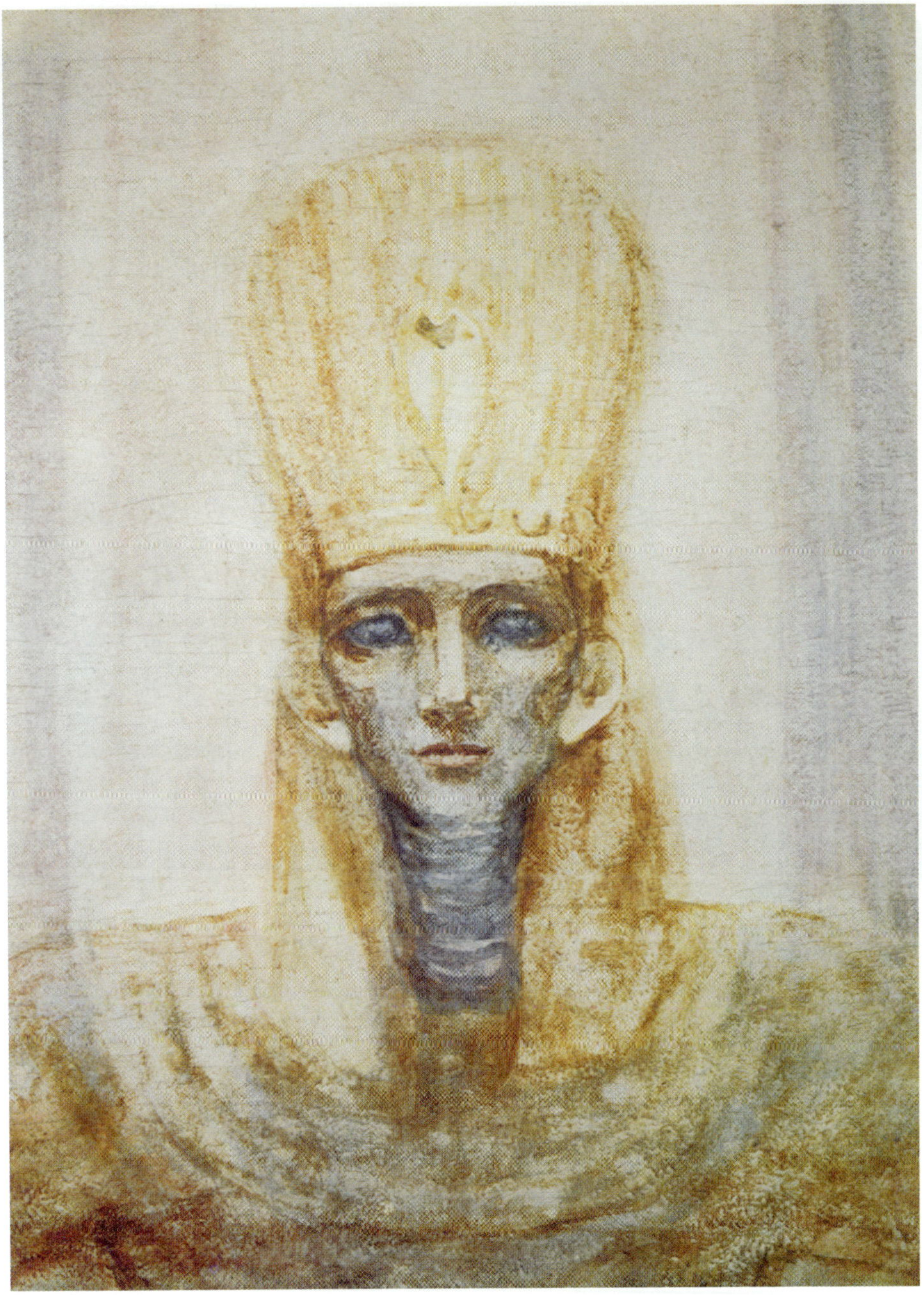

Egyptian. *Study after the Goetheanum Cupola 1916/17 by Margarita Woloschin*

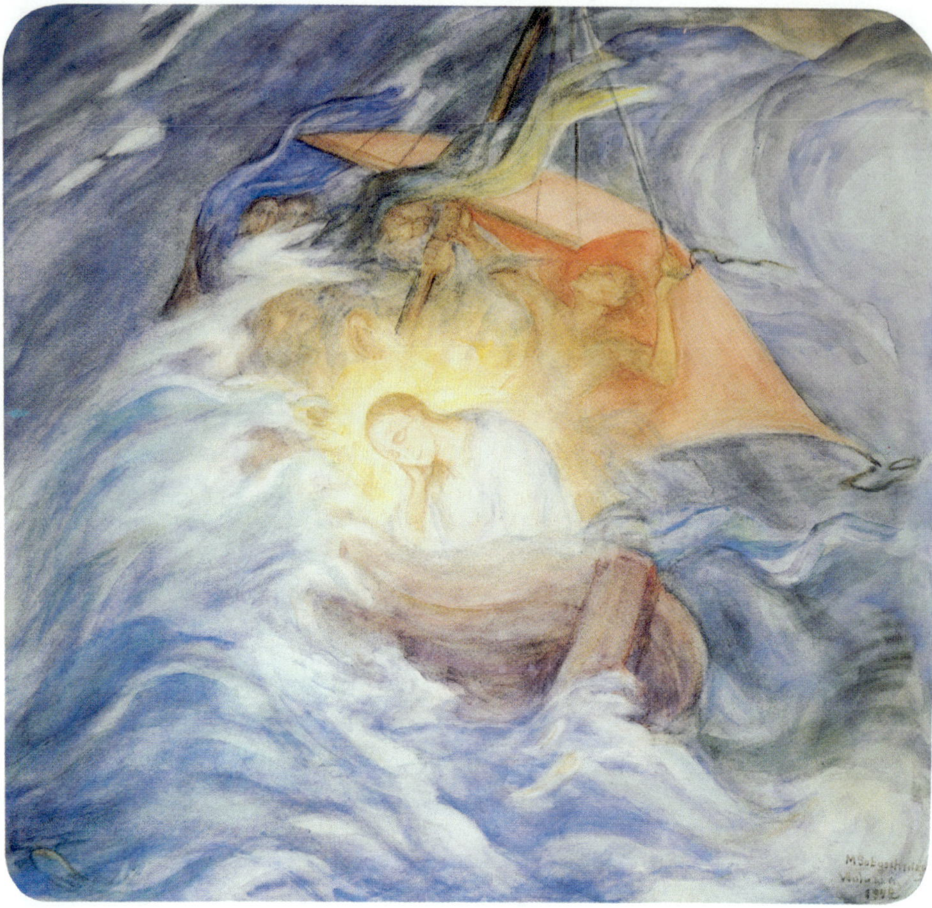

Sleep during storm II*, 1942. Private collection*

Digressions

In the spring of 1909 Miss Minslova arrived in Berlin directly from the Tower. She spoke exclusively of Vyatsheslav. "He thinks only of you, he speaks only of you. Now you'll have to meet with him." I took fright and did not let her words reach me inwardly.

At Easter I was in Cologne, where over a period of several days Rudolf Steiner gave instruction in the context of the religous-symbolic ritual. The soul mood into which one was transposed through this work, allowed me to experience the Cologne of the time of Albertus Magnus and his pupils with unusual intensity. At that time I first got to know Meister Eckehart, whose complete works I translated a few years later from Middle-High German into Russian.

I also followed Rudolf Steiner to Düsseldorf for his lecture series, *The Working of Spiritual Hierarchies in the Heavenly Bodies.*

At the end of the conference Nyusha appeared to take me to Paris for a few weeks, where she lived with the Balmonts. The prospect of staying once again for a while with these close friends in the beloved city was too tempting for me to resist the invitation. With regard to anthroposophy, or rather the Anthroposophical Society, Nyusha reacted disapprovingly, to the extent that her phlegmatic personality permitted. "They want to explain everything," she said in her slow drawl. The intellectuality paired with sentimentality, which struck foreigners with regard to Germans at that time, especially within the Society, went against the grain with her. In any case, she was completely under the spell of Konstantin Balmont, whom she loved devotedly. This love was so selfless that Katharina Balmont, with whom she was close friends, felt her presence in the house to be a great help. On staying with them in Paris, I came to recognize just how difficult Katharina's life was.

In the evening, when Nyusha and I had arrived there and were approaching the neighbourhood of the Balmonts' house in Passy in a carriage my cousin became restless. Her eyes scanned every café where guests sat outside on warm days, to see whether she could catch sight of the poet somewhere. She had a premonition that he had disappeared from home again that evening. Each time he completed a poetic work he was in an overwrought state from inner exertion and resorted to alcohol, everyday life being unsatisfying to him. It usually began with his thinking the lamplight too weak. In all the rooms he would screw the wick higher on the petroleum lamps, then in common use in Paris, not noticing that the lamps began emitting smoke. If no attention was paid to this, there would soon be a layer of soot on every object in the room. In his state of inner disquiet he would head out to a café. There even just the smell of alcohol put him into a state of inebriation. Though he did not drink much, he at once made himself conspicuous and started quarrelling. If Katharina or Nyusha did not succeed in bringing him home, he would be thrown out of one café after the other, ending up in a nightspot for carriage drivers or some dark dive. The next day it would be necessary to look for him in every police station in Paris.

His wife had succeeded to a certain extent in managing the unfortunate situation until Helena came into his life.

I had already seen this moonish creature, Helena, in the company of Balmont earlier. She accompanied the poet like a shadow. Unprepossessing, always in a black dress with a train — not fashionable at that time — a green veil wafting around her, she spoke like him, in an affected poetic manner. She also appropriated his handwriting so completely, that it could not be distinguished from his own. From a painterly standpoint, I found the greenish colour of her face quite interesting against her dark blue eyes. The expression of her dry lips resembled those of a fish gasping for water. When we ate together in the restaurants of Paris, she never ordered anything other than black coffee and sardines. At home she always lived behind lowered Venetian blinds. This woman was possessed of megalomania, in the same way as Balmont himself.

Far from curbing his illness, for nights on end she wandered with him from one restaurant or saloon to another, assuring him that he was divine, no matter in what condition. He divided his life between the apartment of his wife in Passy, in whose orderly atmosphere he could work, and Helena, who had a child by him. That was the situation I encountered. Katharina Balmont suffered beyond words, but called this suffering "egoistic," and never complained. She wanted her daughter, then eight years old, to retain her father, and for him to have the possibility of working.

Balmont naively thought his wife had so much vitality and so many good friends that the situation was easy for her to bear, whereas Helena could not exist a day without him and in the event of a separation would immediately take her own life. Katharina Balmont was then forty-one years old. Her regal beauty became still more radiant in consequence of all this and she veiled the situation with humour.

Nyusha's premonition was confirmed; Balmont did indeed not come home that evening. They lived in a little house with a garden. I enjoyed sleeping "at home" once again, in the brightly wallpapered little room where all objects were so familiar, under the same roof with people close to me.

In the morning I was awoken by my door opening. But no one walked in; instead someone crept alongside my bed, slid up to me and suddenly, close in front of me, I saw an elongated childlike face, shining cat-like eyes and a laughing, beautiful large mouth. "What's with you? What's with you, little Margarita? You have orange coloured eyebrows and walnut eyes! You'll have to be put in a museum. Such pinkish-golden hair, too, has never been seen. Into the museum with you!" It was Nina.

We were soon close friends and I made a portrait of her. She was a child full of fantasy and mischievous charm. Her mother raised her strictly and sensibly, and her education bore fruit. I met Nina later during the Revolution as a twenty-year-old young woman and mother, and was able to follow the development of this very talented, strong and warm personality still further.

Balmont returned home the next evening. The day after that he lay with one eye covered, in his darkened study, where I was permitted to sit with him. He asked me various things about Rudolf Steiner, about his teaching concerning Christ, and then suddenly said "Why did Christ dismiss Judas from his presence? Why did He send him away?" And he wept. Through what hell his soul had to go ...

If I adjusted myself to his subjective world, I could speak with him quite well. It was a strange dream world, like a decadent reminiscence of a sun cult from ancient times.

Why were so many women able to love him devotedly all their lives? Even such an independent, healthy human being as Katharina? And such a sensitive person as Nyusha? Was it the childlike honesty and innocence with which he entered into every situation in life?

In his library I found many rare and valuable books dealing with Russian folk customs and traditions, which I studied particularly on this visit to Paris. I was now able to understand this world on the basis of my newfound knowledge, and it presented itself in a new light. Actually, there is no Russian mythology in the sense, for instance, of the Greek or Germanic. The Russian folk are acquainted with a rich and differentiated world of nature spirits, of forest, field, house and stable goblins and mermaids. The spiritual principle, however, is represented by the God of the heavens and of the sun. Mother Earth is identical, in popular belief, with Mary the Mother of God, with Sophia. The church service before the sowing that I experienced on our estate, when the boy carried the icon of the Mother of God in front of the priest, was the expression of this belief. It was the custom in old Russia, in taking an oath, for the one swearing to lay a piece of turf on his head. Later, this piece of earth was replaced by an icon of the Mother of God. The earth was conceived as a living being, and is probably still regarded as such today in country districts. "In the Earth lives the Holy Spirit," says an old Russian proverb, or "You shall not lie, for the Earth hears it," "Nourish as the Earth nourishes, teach as the Earth teaches, love as the Earth loves." Those expelled by the Church may make their confession to the earth. That accords with the scene of the woman confessing in the Gospel, in which Christ writes her destiny into the earth. I could now also understand why the earth was once called "widow" and how she becomes, after the Mystery of Golgotha, the Bride of Christ.

In this connection I envisioned the possibility of a new art of landscape painting, with a healing effect, such as had existed with the image of Isis with Horus, and in Russia with the virginal Mother with the Child. These were now no longer only mystical pictures for me, they corresponded to a cosmic reality.

Artists and emigrants from various countries frequented the Balmonts, such as the Polish writher Stanislav Przybyszevski, the author of the novel *Homo Sapiens.* Among others, I got to know a Jew there, who had been condemned to death in Russia as a terrorist, and who had succeeded in fleeing abroad. One could see in his gentle and sad glance all the hardship he had been through. He lived in poverty, working in a factory in Charanton and sharing the life of the proletariat there, among whom, I was told, he had a lot of standing. Like many others, he also asked me about spiritual science and described to me the uninhibited attitude of the simple workers in regard to spiritual matters. "They are open, without prejudice and are seeking."

I visited him in Charanton in the workers' settlement, where I found him surrounded by many children. I did not tire of telling him all that I knew and gave him various books. Already I saw not only him, but the entire labour force of Charanton taking the path of spiritual science!

Ten years later, during the Russian Revolution, I read his name in a Soviet newspaper. Comrade R. had returned home to Russia. He was received honourably and celebrated, and was assigned an important position.

Finale

If I think back to my stay in Paris, I have to smile at the creature I then was. On the one hand, I was filled with the magnitude of the truths I had taken in, considering myself in all naivety as their herald. On the other hand, I enjoyed in full measure the magic of Paris. It was spring and everything was in bloom. I was passionately interested in fashion, which at that time evoked the Empire style, craning my neck to look at the elegant ladies as they drove by. I still see the hat and the transparent scarf interwoven with pearls I wore then. The dammed-up zest for life of a young person burst through. I actually lived in the expectation of a reunion with Vyatsheslav. ("He thinks only of you, he speaks only of you ... In the summer he wants to come and see you ..." Had I not heard these words from Miss Minslova?)

"What's this? You have 'Greuzeified' yourself," Marie von Sivers teased me, deriving the word from the French painter Jean-Baptiste Greuze, when I appeared in Kassel for coffee at her place and she observed my new attire. Rudolf Steiner, who joined us, made no teasing remark, contrary to his usual habit. I had the feeling this time that he came to us from an enormous distance. The black pupils of his eyes seemed to take up the whole space of the iris. His voice, too, sounded unfamiliar as he thanked Marie von Sivers for the cup she handed him. I have never experienced him like that — either before or later. He soon left, without having asked or said anything, which was not his way. Otherwise, in everyday life his attention was turned completely to the life around him.

I had come to Kassel to hear Steiner's lectures, *The Gospel of St John in Relation to the Other Gospels.* Between the stay in Kassel and a summer conference in Munich, I wanted to participate in a course on various painting techniques, grounding, colour preparation and the like, with a painter who had been recommended to me. Before that I had another conversation with Rudolf Steiner. Today I am ashamed of the impudence of my questions.

"I can't understand why you speak about the great secrets, for example, about the hierarchies, in front of people who afterwards make them into coffee *klatsch*. Is something not thereby lost to the spiritual world?" In the Russian Church the names of the hierarchies were only pronounced once a year in a quite special divine service, at which everyone knelt with heads bowed. Rudolf Steiner answered with great earnestness, somewhat as follows:

> Only in another cultural epoch will it become evident what the truths now absorbed will have brought about in human souls. The occultist has to create as nature does. Nature is lavish. Out of millions of herring eggs only a few become fish — all the others are destroyed; that is a mystery. And if only half a human being will have taken up what I have to give, I shall regard my mission as fulfilled.

And he repeated, "Only *half* a human being."

I was devastated by the expression of pain with which he spoke these words. I then asked why he had the play by Edouard Schuré performed in Munich. "I think it inartistic, like a poor oleograph."

"I'm glad you find it inartistic; I do too. But I can't after all have the naturalistic dramas of Gerhart Hauptmann put on!"

He considered Hauptmann a very talented dramatist, "but it is not what people need in the present circumstances."

"Couldn't one perform Aeschylus or Sophocles?" I suggested to Rudolf Steiner reprovingly.

"With those actors? Oh no! I have too much respect for those great spirits to risk that with the people I have available. You see," he continued, "yours is a contemplative nature, but I must be active. And I have to work with the means I have at my disposal." He looked at me, "Is it disagreeable to you?"

"Yes," I admitted, and thought, horrified: Perhaps in other fields as well, he only gives us what we human beings need, and not the absolute!

It was raining when I walked through the streets, and the rain mixed with my tears. Why was I so disconcerted? Had Rudolf Steiner ever demanded belief in authority? Were the truths he gave us not convincing and fruitful in themselves?

Most of us are inclined to accept only one judgment about something as being true. We at once accuse someone of a contradiction who represents, in certain situations and from different points of view, an apparently conflicting standpoint on the same subject. "A thing has to be considered from twelve points of view at least, if one is to come to a judgment founded on reality," Rudolf Steiner once said to me. How he must have suffered when his utterances were pinned down and made into dogma, a fixed scheme, instead of being made use of as a help in coming to one's own independent experience of reality. The effect could be particularly ruinous when words he had spoken decades ago about some occurrence or personality, were used in the battle of opinions. In my own case, hearing contradictory things, as it seemed to me at the time, about Edouard Schuré, whom he had praised so much only a short time ago, the ground under my feet trembled.

My need for firm dogmas made me insecure. I wanted to have the "final truth" right away.

I judged mainly from an aesthetic point of view; a "pedagogical moment" was unknown to me.

In the hotel a telegram awaited me: "Are you coming? Vyatsheslav." And at the same time, by chance, there was a money order from Nyusha. All plans were thrown overboard.

On the night train from Kassel to Berlin I met Steiner with Marie von Sivers again. They invited me to spend the day with them on the Motzstrasse in Berlin before the departure of the train to Russia.

I had brought revolutionary literature with me from Paris, which I had not yet read, and made use of the day in Berlin for this. Obviously, I would not be permitted to take this with me over the border. Included were the last letters of the condemned terrorists, for example, Ivan Kalyayev, the murderer of Grand Duke Sergei. Among the books there was a portrait of the well-known provocateur and terrorist Evno Asef. Rudolf Steiner looked at it with great interest during the shared evening meal; in fact he asked me for permission to keep it.

"What do you make of this person?" he asked.

"I can't understand him," I admitted, "he poses a riddle for everybody. The revolutionaries idolized him on account of his boundless courage. He prepared assassinations with great expertise and afterwards denounced the conspirators to the police. But when his friends were hanged, he wept. In other cases he allowed the assassination to take place. For a long time no one had any notion of his double role."

"Look at this face, this forehead," said Rudolf Steiner, "he cannot think. Look at the lower part of the face, it shows an uncontrollable bull-like drive, without will. That's why he appeared so courageous. But he only carried out what the police demanded, or what the revolutionaries wanted. And he was sincere when he wept at the execution of the revolutionaries."

After a few moments, Rudolf Steiner asked me across the table, "Could you love a human being, behind whom another will always stands? To everybody he would appear strong, but behind him another's volition would stand the whole time?"

I was shaken, but I stammered, "Yes, I believe I could."

What did he want to say with that? Who did he mean by that?

"Just come back healthy," he said to me on parting.

At the station in St Petersburg I was met by Miss Minslova, with a letter from Vyatsheslav. How contrived and unnatural were the lines he wrote! I drove directly to the Tower. It was noon, but I had to wait until Vyatsheslav got up. In the rooms I had previously appreciated for their simplicity, a lot of superfluous furniture now stood, which had arrived with the children from Geneva. There was dust everywhere and the air was musty. Like a grey mouse, the woman friend from Geneva who was responsible for bringing up the children, scurried about among the furniture. She did not seem well-disposed toward me. Wherever one looked, there was an enlarged photograph of Lydia. Only, I did not sense her free spirit here.

Summoned by a telegram, Lydia's daughter, Vera, arrived from the country, where she had lingered with friends. "I experience Lydia through Vera," Vyatsheslav said to me.

Hour by hour, I remember those three days in St Petersburg. In thinking back now, to my surprise, it is as though nothing had passed! Fortune and misfortune arose with the same intensity as before. The difference consisted only in that one could quickly close the door on part of one's memory, if the pain was too much.

Vyatsheslav's relation to me had not altered. He told me as much, as we stood alone in front of the picture of Lydia. On a blackboard he drew a tree with chalk, half of which was withered, the other half covered with blossoms. "That is my soul," he said.

Just at that moment, Vera went past the door. He called her and asked, "Vera, I love Margarita. What should I do?"

The answer was, "Be true to Lydia."

I myself was no longer the awkward, insecure child I had been previously. With my whole being I felt the portentous nature of this relationship and now had the courage to take it upon myself as destiny. I also saw clearly that the sultry, mystical atmosphere, in which Vyatsheslav lived, was unhealthy and potentially disastrous for him. His "garland" of sonnets for Lydia, which he read to me, appeared to me a mummification of the living. I did not find Lydia's spirit in them. The whole life in the Tower was as though displaced into an otherworldly sphere in which natural life could only wither. The beyond, on the other hand, was dragged down into a personal, wish-filled region. So as to remain near Vyatsheslav, I decided to move to St Petersburg. My friend Boris Leman found living quarters for me and Miss Minslova with a studio on Vasilyevsky Island.

I spent the last weeks of summer on our estate. Never did the power of this earth, the splendour of the shimmering trees, the cornfields humming with bees, appear so festive, so grand; the forests so imbued with reverence, so full of expectation in reaching to the sky.

On returning to St Petersburg, I found Vyatsheslav inaccessible. He was as though under an alien spell. I withdrew. Miss Minslova, who lived with me, but spent every day in the Tower until late in the evening, came back more and more in a state of despair. "He is not himself, he is no longer himself," was her constant refrain. She herself appeared to me to be no longer quite herself. After a time, Vyatsheslav married his step-daughter Vera.

[

IV

Between Two Answers

The Bells of the Invisible City of Kitesh

I lived a secluded life in my studio, through whose large windows I saw the masts of the ships on the Neva passing by. But I was unable to paint.

My work on Meister Eckehart, whose writings I translated into Russian, was a help to me at this time. I studied Novalis and wrote a few poems.

I then seized the opportunity to embark on an apprenticeship with the famous icon painter Tyulin. The Tyulins had been known for centuries as masters of icon painting. They belonged to the "Old Believers," as those Orthodox believers were called in Russia who did not recognize the reforms of Patriarch Nikon in the seventeenth century and who upheld, in their beliefs as well as in their customs, the strict forms of Old Russia. They preserved the Old Russian traditions and were connoisseurs and collectors of icons.

When I entered Tyulin's residence, he showed me a few of the most beautiful panels of this high art. He himself was not yet old. The regular features of his face, the almond-shaped eyes, the narrow nose, every curve of the locks on his forehead and beard, the wrinkles around his eyes, everything appeared to be modelled on the pattern of old icons, as though the handicraft of his forebears had impressed itself into his life-forces and formed his body accordingly.

His workshop consisted of two clean, sunny rooms. The pupils were mostly simple peasants, who came from various remote regions — from Kiev, from the White and the Black Sea, from the Urals and from Smolensk. A devout, concentrated mood predominated in this workshop. From six in the morning till evening, the men sat there stooped over their work.

Tyulin had a very beautiful wife, who never turned up, however. I saw her only once, when he went with her to watch the first flights of the pilot Sergei Utotshkin.

This combination of the Middle Ages and technology brought to mind the workshop of Leonardo.

When I was permitted to choose an example to copy from among his icons, in my cluelessness I at once selected three. He smiled and had me order three panels of corresponding size from a master carpenter known to him. They had to be made from ancient alder wood, with a raised outer rim and an inlay at the back, so that the wood would not warp. I had to purchase the materials from various dealers as prescribed by Tyulin. Eight varnished spoons of lime wood, from which the handles had been cut off, served as painting dishes. Such a dish was held in one's left hand and the pigment rubbed together with egg yolk using the thumb of the right hand. Egg yolk was used as a binder, mixed with equal parts of *kvas*, a Russian drink made from fermented rusks. There was always a smell of rotten eggs in the workshop.

Every phase of the work was begun ceremoniously with the sign of the cross. Whether the chalk ground was prepared — applied four times onto the wooden board covered with gauze and scraped repeatedly with a knife, so that it finally resembled a mirror — whether gold was rubbed on, mixed with gum Arabic, or whether gold-leaf was applied to the grounding with a peacock feather. Before each of these procedures the master announced solemnly, "And now we shall begin this," at which master and pupil crossed themselves.

It was a sacred handicraft; and in his uprightness and assured competence, the master really was a master. When he showed me how to hatch the rose-red wings of the angel with a fine-pointed brush, (these fine brushes could only be bought from him), a very difficult art, he carried it out with consummate skill. One did not see the individual strokes; the wing feathers shimmered in an unearthly rose-gold. Afterwards, the broken lines were polished with a cow's tooth.

The reader, having come to know me a little by now, will hardly need to be told that I did not sit in the workshop from six in the morning until evening. The work was extraordinarily arduous and I did not even finish one icon the whole winter.

The icon I painted was called *The Saviour of Merciful Silence*, to which there was a pendant, *The Saviour of Good Advice*. In both pictures Christ was portrayed as a winged angel; the first in reddish robes, with rose-red wings and hands crossed over the breast; the second in blue robes, with white wings and the gesture of proclamation. The "silent" one in red conserves its activity, life and warmth, within. The "speaking" one rays it out, giving out warmth from within, relinquishing itself in selfless blue. Later, when I took account of the "visual-moral effect of colour" in the sense of Goethe's indications — and this became my path in painting — I had to think of these archetypal pictures, of the old imaginations, as shown in the icons.

I lived entirely on my own; only Boris Leman visited me regularly in order to introduce me to the significance of numbers as taught in the Kabbala. That was his spiritual path. Or the writer Prishvin, who took me to a few churches of the Old Believers, where, for the first time, I saw quite large icons with a "cosmic" feeling to them. He also accompanied me to a gathering of followers of Little Brother Ivan.

This Little Brother, a quite simple man who could hardly read and write, had the gift of freeing people, through the power of prayer, from the alcoholism so prevalent in Russia. For thousands, this signified an indescribable release, and thus a large community of cured men and their wives had formed around him, who venerated him in their profound gratitude. They sat closely packed in a huge factory building, the wives wearing white headscarves. Little Brother Ivan, in a white Russian smock, read the Gospel; he read haltingly and very indistinctly. From time to time he interrupted his reading and asked a question, to which a multi-voiced, spontaneous answer came. For example, at the place in the story of the Three Kings where it says, "The star stood still," he suddenly asked, "Does the star still stand?"

And everyone said, "Yes, the Star still stands."

Or, "Christ went through a heathen country ... Is our country a Christian or a heathen one?"

"A heathen one," the crowd answered. The Gospel was brought into the present. There was a living, non-sectarian, and not at all fanatical atmosphere.

Soon afterwards, these meetings were forbidden and Ivan put in prison.

I asked Vladimir Dzhunkovsky, the Governor General, with whom we were friends, "Why does he sit in prison? After all, he does so much good."

"But he is a sectarian; he diverts the people from the Church!"

"But what if the Church does not give people anything?"

"If we were to give the sectarians a free rein, where would we get to?"

he said in his self-assured, naïve manner. It could be seen clearly enough where we in fact got to in Russia ...

While staying in Moscow over Christmas, I visited a teahouse with my brother, in which peasants and workers of quite different worldviews got together every Sunday after the mass. Curious faces, apostle heads could be seen there. A large Bible in which things were looked up, went from hand to hand. A fat, healthy-looking farmer asserted that a person, who really believed in God, would not need to die. He understood that in physical terms. The martyrs were killed otherwise they would not have died. We, however, did not believe firmly enough in Him, therefore we died. He hoped, so it seemed, to live forever on the earth in his vigorous body.

"And what would be the use of that?" said a peasant in felt shoes with holes in them, "always living in the same body?"

"No, we must lay it aside from time to time, in order to come onto the earth again and again, and continue learning."

The possibility of reincarnation was suddenly broached. Among the speakers there was a red-haired peasant, who looked astonishingly like Socrates. We were told that entering into a discussion with him was forbidden to Orthodox missionaries, since he defeated everyone with his logic. He had an extraordinarily clever, whimsical face. I remember little of what he said, only that he remarked, "I can only believe in what I find within me. Outside of me I find no God, if I have not found Him in me. If I did not have the sun within myself, I would not be able to see it. Like can only be grasped with like; just as I can only grasp a firm object with my firm hand." Freedom and the Fall of Man were spoken of.

"The Fall of Man had to come," someone said. "If the human being were only a creature of God and had no freedom, he could not love God as God wants to be loved. You see, suppose your hand loves you. Is that enough for you? No, you want to be loved by a creature like yourself. That is how it is with God. He wants to be loved by a being that is god-like, that stands freely beside Him, therefore he lets the human being take these paths, erring and recognizing his error. The prodigal son is preferable to Him than the other son who always remained with Him."

The proprietor whispered something into the ears of several of them. The Bible disappeared. Each peasant drank his tea as though he had nothing to do with the others. I learned later that on that particular day these conversations had been forbidden by the police.

On the way home I spoke with the little peasant in the tattered felt shoes. I had him give me his address, because I was interested in his ideas concerning repeated lives on earth.

"Write to me about it," I said.

He answered, "If you put a stamp for the reply inside your letter."

But his letters were so illiterate that I could hardly read them; I only understood that he referred to the Apocalypse.

It was still the time when at each Whitsun festival, people from all over Russia gathered in the north at the invisible city of Kitesh, on the shore of the Bright Lake, in order to speak about spiritual matters. According to legend, this city was saved from the Tartars in being made invisible by means of a virgin's prayer. In its place, there is now the lake. Those well informed, however, know where the churches of Kitesh are located, and candles were sent floating on pieces of wood to the images of various saints, so that the whole lake was filled with floating lights. Whoever was pure of heart heard the bells of the invisible city. For whole nights, murmured conversations took place around the lake concerning matters of faith, by the Orthodox, Old-Believers, followers of sects, Tolstoyans and other seekers, as well as circles of intellectuals who had found their way there.

The Native City

One day in early spring, three guests appeared, wanting to visit Miss Minslova — Nikolai Medtner, the well-known composer, who had come to St Petersburg in order to give a concert of his own works, accompanied by his brother Emil, the publisher of the publishing house Musagetes, and his wife. I met them for the first time. Even by their external appearance, the two brothers made a considerable impression. Nikolai looked astonishingly like Paracelsus. His head was somewhat too heavy for his overall figure. The brow predominated between two tufts of hair at the temples. The Medtners had German and Spanish blood, which lent them an unusual mixture of restrained passion, seriousness and thoroughness.

The music of Nikolai Medtner could be compared with Schumann, only it was more elemental and, to some extent, even demonic. Something magical could be sensed in his *Fairy Tale*. It was as if he invoked earth spirits, delighting in them, only to banish them, unredeemed, to their caves once again. Like the artists of past ages, he was almost possessed by his music. Thus he was capable of having a droshky coachman stop in the middle of the street and tearing off a scrap of poster from a wall so as to note down a theme that had just occurred to him. In taking a respite from music, he occupied himself with astronomy and botany, and contemplated Madonna pictures. He owned a collection of reproductions.

His brother Emil was taller and slimmer than him, with dark hair and a southern complexion, and shining deep blue eyes, that combined in a strange harmony. He too had wanted to take up music as a profession, intending to become a conductor, but had studied law instead and accepted a municipal position, in order that Nikolai could live a life of music unhindered. He now wrote essays on music and philosophy under the pseudonym Wölfing. Still, a certain dissatisfaction remained. I have never met a person who entered with such subjective ardour into

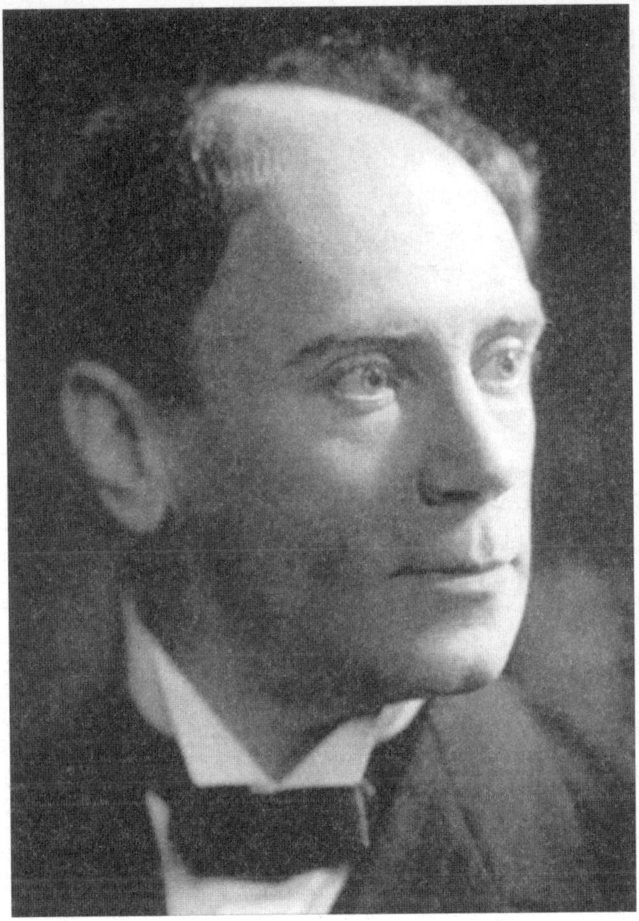

Emil Medtner, 1915

the history of culture, despite having a philosophical training. He could pace back and forth in the room raging, as though full of hatred for some historical personality who had lived two thousand years ago. In showing enthusiasm, his blue-violet eyes acquired a still warmer lustre, even filling with tears. Touching in this masculine and so talented human being was the devotion with which he held tribute to the genius of another. Just at that time, German friends had granted him the means to found his own publishing house, which he called Musagetes, after Apollo's designation as leader of the Muses.

The poet Andrei Belyi (the pseudonym of Boris Nikolaevich Bugyaev) had also come from Moscow to hear Medtner's concert. They spent the evening of the next day with us. When Belyi developed an idea in his characteristically imaginative and ingenious manner, Emil Medtner turned to me smiling and, indicating the poet with a glance, said quietly, "They want a motto from me for my publishing house; the genius of Belyi is my motto, my banner. I do not want a programme."

I asked Emil Medtner on parting, whether I might paint him and he stayed on a few days longer in St Petersburg for that purpose, while his wife returned to Moscow with his brother, who could not do without her care and support even for a day. Otherwise, the three of them were inseparable. The tragic element uniting the three began to dawn on me and this premonition surfaced in the portrait. A peculiar rose-red cloud loomed in the grey sky behind his head. I painted Medtner in his characteristic pose — with his left hand he took hold of his right elbow, his skunk coat thrown over his shoulder. The pale southern complexion together with his black hair resulted in a tension of light and dark. I do not know where this picture, later bought by the museum commission, is located.

Having told him something wordlessly, concerning his destiny, it seemed that an inner cramp resolved itself which had affected him throughout years of silence. He discovered he could express himself and we became very good friends.

My translation of Meister Eckehart's works, which I had worked on without thinking initially of publication, was now to appear under the Musagetes imprint, which also published Jakob Böhme's *Aurora*. This stood in contrast to the publisher of the Scales, which represented the French Symbolists and the slavophile, religious group around the periodical *Puty* (the Path), supported by Margarita Morosova. Musagetes was oriented more towards Germany, in keeping with the editor's love of Goethe, Kant, Nietzsche and Wagner. But he had no predetermined programme for the publishing house. Everything came about as though of itself, out of the circle of friends and the creativity of single contributors.

Miss Minslova also left St Petersburg. However, she did not say where she was going. I transferred my flat in St Petersburg to an acquaintance and went for the time being to my parents in Moscow. In the summer, Medtner wanted to go with me to Norway, where Rudolf Steiner was to speak about the mission of individual folk-souls in connection with Germanic mythology, but I was kept from going by the serious illness of my grandmother, who lay in a villa near Moscow.

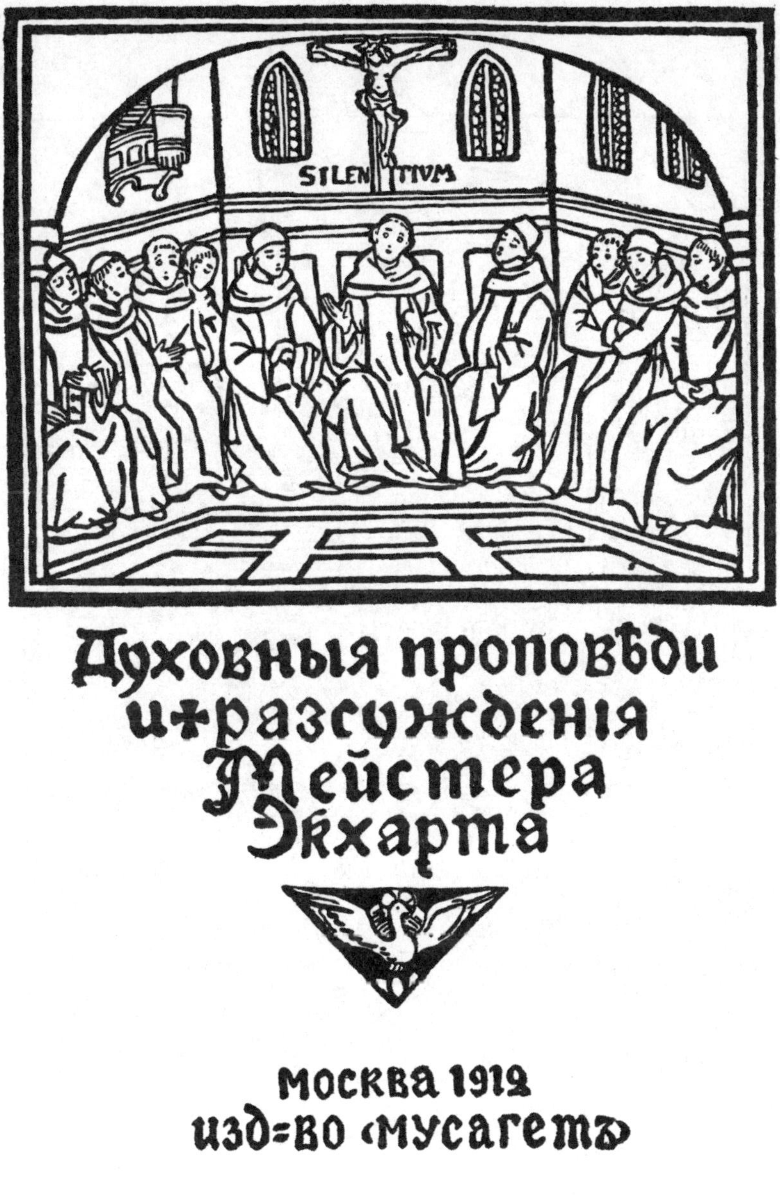

This and next two pages: cover, frontispiece and title page of Margarita Woloschin's translation of Meister Eckehart's works

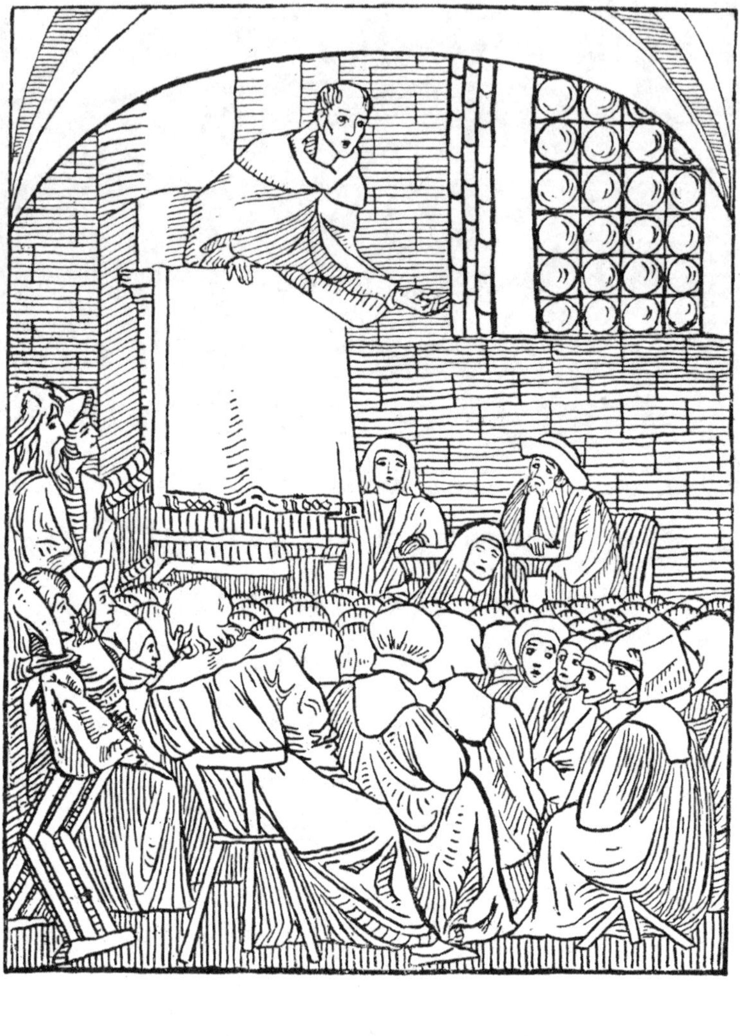

МЕЙСТЕРЪ ЭКХАРТЪ

Проповѣди и разсужденія

Переводъ со средне-верхне-нѣмецкаго
и вступительная статья
М. В. Сабашниковой.

Издательство «Мусагетъ».
МОСКВА, MCMXII.

The intimate, tender bond which had existed earlier between her and me, had weakened after my marriage. My formless way of life was something she could not understand. She never again asked me about my life and I felt inhibited in her company. A mutual estrangement had set in. Alexandra surrounded her with the greatest imaginable care and looked after her until her death in August 1910. My grandmother had arranged her funeral in advance, stipulating the priests who were to hold her requiem mass, the shop from which the palm fronds were to be ordered for the decoration of the church, the menu for the funeral banquet in a Moscow hotel etc. The funeral procession stretched for kilometres, from the city gate through the streets to the church. In front of all the houses with which my grandmother had had a business relationship, people stood, lining the curb side. An intercession was spoken for the dead. Representatives of various institutions that had received endowments from her were present. Only now did I learn that she had built one of the buildings of the public university, a mental asylum, a school and renovated many churches.

"Who are you, and who are you burying with such pomp?" a passer-by asked my uncle, the diplomat, with whom I sat in the carriage.

He answered promptly, "The one we are burying is a shoemaker." My grandmother had inherited a large shoe business from her parents. "And we are her children."

Having lived much of the time abroad, attending this ceremony, which was almost a state funeral, was a strange experience for me. Eight priests celebrated the church service. The coffin was interred in the family mausoleum. At the meal, numerous guests were present, and Aunt Alexandra appeared to me youthful and beautiful during those days. She said, without any sentimentality, "I believe my little mother would be satisfied; everything went according to her wish."

After the funeral, I stayed with her in her rooms in the villa. "Yes," she said reflectively, plaiting her hair, "that was a strong, clever and affectionate woman."

In a sense, only the two of us knew of this woman's affection. Toward everyone else my grandmother had been stern, particularly with her own children, apart from Aunt Alexandra. There was something of an Old Testament streak in her personality. She prayed a lot in her room at home in front of the icons and at church services, to which she had herself driven regularly. In my childhood I found the manner in which she prayed off-putting. With passionate fervour she would repeat the words of the priest, while tears flowed incessantly down her cheeks. Was it provocation, legitimizing oneself before God, or contrition? Her raised head was tense. Having combined them into a cross, she pressed her fingers firmly to her forehead, to her breast and both shoulders. Her greatest worry was the failure of her sons. All-powerful, she was incapable of doing anything to redeem their inferiority. But she locked this up in her heart.

In the room in the villa where she died, two nuns read psalms and prayers for forty days and nights, standing alternately at a lectern. These monotone rhythms sounded continuously in our ears.

"My little mother," Aunt Alexandra said to me after a few days, "left me a few million. The other sisters received their share upon marrying, so I am now the main heir. As I do not want my nephews and nieces to wait for their inheritance until I am dead, I shall give them a certain amount every month." I had never had so much personally. My father's businesses continued to suffer. I had been living on what I earned from time to time and on what Nyusha, with whom I stood in a quite sisterly relation, gave me. I did not know how to deal with money.

To begin with, my life now became still more unstable, as a result of this new-found freedom of movement. I decided, for example, having just rented a studio in Paris, to spend the winter in Rome, transferring all my possessions there, but remaining nonetheless in Munich. Another time, I interrupted my return journey to Paris from Prague (where the lectures, Occult Physiology, had been held) in Stuttgart, in order to read a particular book about various mystics in the regional library that I needed for writing the foreword to my Eckehart translation. The poetic royal seat, as it then still was, appealed so much to me that I stayed on, living in solitude for weeks in the Silber Hotel, where I could do my work. In the evenings I frequently went to the opera at the Interim Theatre. Was this liking for the city a presentiment that it was to become my second home one day?

My restless external way of life was, however, only a picture of my inner state. Already twenty-eight years old, I was recognized as a poet and painter, and yet still did not know my path. Spiritual science remained a theory for me, though I would have denied this at the time. I took up the new findings with enthusiasm, but they remained in the sphere of the soul without becoming a conscious path.

An Outline of Esoteric Science had just appeared, but I was unable to make much of it at the time. I did not understand how one could speak in such a matter-of-fact way about these things. I did not realize that Steiner strove precisely to hold back his own feeling in his books. A great renunciation was involved in seeking to express truths in factual sentences deriving from profoundest experience. Those receiving such truths had to imbue them with warmth and life out of their own soul-forces. In this way, the reader was left free in the highest sense. Such truths were seeds. Without thus entering into the thoughts for oneself (only brought to life by means of concentration and meditation) they remained dead. I actually still felt them to be dead at that time. Oppressed by such ideas, I looked to enliven my soul with sources originating from earlier periods.

Makary, the Shepherd

I found myself in this state in the summer of 1910 in Paris, when on the Boulevard St Michel, Alexei Remizov told me about a shepherd in the Urals near Verkhoturye:

> If this shepherd, so it is said, prays at dawn, kneeling, his face turned toward the sunrise, or in the evening toward the setting sun, then the whole herd stands closely packed, cows, sheep and goats, immobile in the same direction.

I should like to see this picture for myself, I thought. When I arrived in Moscow three days later, my father, wanting to have a rest from work, proposed a trip by boat on the Volga and Kama. He was a Siberian and travelling was his element. I requested that he extend the planned journey as far as Verkhoturye, and the next day we set off. We needed one night of travelling in order to reach Nishni-Novgorod, where the ship was boarded, and another five days on the Volga and Kama. On this trip one did not really see much of the landscape: a broad river, a lofty sky with chaotic cloud formations, a few god-forsaken villages on the shore. Everything lay there as if in a dream, looking back at you as though awaiting redemption. This feeling renewed itself for me on every journey through Russia. After the final berth on the Kama, we had to travel another whole day by train over the Ural Mountains. Through the window, tall, slender pines could be seen, whose tops bent like cypresses in the wind; the forest meadows were red with willow herbs; the mountain air clear and bracing. The train did not go as far as the city, so we drove by carriage for quite a few hours in the night through the forest and came to Verkhoturye just before sunrise. The stars still blazed in the cold green sky when we caught sight, between the black pine trees, of the white cathedrals of the city, which otherwise consisted only of wooden houses. The coachman drove into the courtyard of a white cloister, built like a fortress. A monk accompanied us along a corridor of colossal breadth into a white cell. The walls of the cloister were possibly one metre thick. My father lay down on a bed; I stretched out on a hard bench under the window and fell asleep, with memories of ancient times wafting through my mind. In the morning I went to mass in the cloister church. The monks were tall and robust, with a strong head of hair, and did not appear at all suited to their black monk's habit. The brutal force and passion of their choral singing alienated me as well. Unable to endure it, I left. Only much later, in Germany, did I learn that the cloister in Verkhoturye was a place of exile, where monks and sectarians, who had sinned against the Church, were sent to do penance. But they secretly continued in the same ways there. Rasputin came into connection here with the orgiastic sect, Chlysty (flagellants). When I asked about the shepherd, nobody knew anything about him. I telegraphed immediately to Paris: "What is the name of the shepherd?" and received the answer: "Makary."

Makary! He had not been a shepherd for a long time and lived a life of solitude in a hermitage eight miles away. We rented a carriage and drove on through the forest. The peasant farmer who drove us asked me, "Is this Makary supposed to be the man who built himself a nest in a tree and lives like a bird? Or is it the other one, who wears heavy chains on his body and swears at people so terribly?"

In Russia Fools for Christ are a widespread phenomenon; I have known some. True Fools for Christ one seldom sees among the many who merely claim to be. Under the term Fools for Christ there are charlatans, adventurers and people of a pathological disposition. Thus I continued on, without expecting anything from the meeting with Makary. The hermit's habitation was located in the woods in a paradisaical meadow, on the shore of a transparent, clear lake. A monk showed me a cabin, "He lives there with the chickens." My father sat on a felled tree trunk and I went hesitantly into the cabin. The door stood open, but was barricaded with a few blocks of wood. In an empty room with small, closed windows, in the midst of clucking, fluttering hens, stood a man of tall build and somewhat stooped posture. He held his arms raised up, the palms of his hands open, as though listening with his hands to invisible currents. His face was timeless. Deep furrows spoke of a care, a care not his own. His eyes seemed to know no sleep. He was dressed like a peasant, only he wore a monk's cap on his head.

From time to time he turned in various directions and looked to the side and above, as though having to see into something quite exactly. He was serious and stern. There was in fact something altogether very stirring about him. He had a certain presence, and one sensed a capacity for face-to-face seeing. It must be a *starets* [a holy man], I thought, and kneeled down at the door, since I knew that a *starets* is greeted kneeling.

But he looked at me over his shoulder and said quietly.

"One should not kneel." Then he shouted at two squabbling chickens and came over to me, still holding his hands above him. "What do you want of me?" he asked.

"I ask for blessing," I replied in my embarrassment, since I had not prepared myself at all for a conversation.

"We are no clerics or monks who pronounce blessings." And he looked over the walls as though into the distance. Then he asked me again, "Perhaps you want to ask me something?"

"I actually only wanted to see you." And suddenly I uttered what had tormented me for some time, "Why ask?" I said, "It has been permitted me to learn much about spiritual things ... but my heart has been dead for some time, I love nothing anymore ..."

He asked me with whom I had come and other things about my family. Then, suddenly addressed me in the familiar form, "What do you do?"

"Painting."

At that his face was aglow with indescribable joy.

"How wonderful, oh, how beautiful that is!" he said. "God has stamped His image on all things. I understand little, and find few words, but the words which God lays into my heart, these I shall say." He began to speak, always looking as though into a far distance, as though he were endeavouring to see something above my head. From time to time he folded his hands in front of him, otherwise he held them raised up. Speaking appeared to be an effort for him. His words were indistinct, sometimes too quiet. More than half of what he said I could not understand. I grasped only fragments.

> Christ wishes to give His Image, He came in order to give His Image and not to take. Only for the Turks and Tartars is it forgivable not to know this. But we Christians must know that since He lived on earth, everything — a stone, a cloud,

> a flower — is His Image. And when Luke the Evangelist painted the Child with the Mother, the Child wanted it done; wanted to give His Image. Yes, and the woman ... she only held out a handkerchief after all, a simple piece of canvas ...[28]

Makary made this gesture of reaching out with his hands.

> But He gave His Image. So must you extend your soul ... one has to have a thirst. Work, and have patience. Get up in the night and pray that God recognizes His Image in your pictures: that your work may be counted among His works, that through your works His work is done; for He also yearns for His Image. Pray for grace. Jonah, the prophet, he was a saint and yet was trapped in darkness for three days. How then should we sinners be without darknesses? Even in the time when Christ lived on the earth, the Angel only descended once a year, in order to enliven the water. Have you read about it? Can you read and write? And we, what do we want? We have built churches everywhere, but God is not in them. We have healers as well, without a Saviour ... That's how far our learning has got us ... Yes!

After a silence he said, "What a great gift has been given to you, what love do you want beyond that? With that you can also attain knowledge. Now I have said everything I have to say."

He now accompanied me outside and advised me to drink tea in the hermitage.

While waiting for me outside, my father had remembered that in a few days a banking deadline would expire for him in Moscow. My poor father! He had continual money worries, as though pursued by Furies. So we only had time to drink our tea in the hermitage and catch the evening train to Moscow from Verkhoturye.

The monk who prepared the samovar for us asked whether Makary had looked up or down in the conversation with me.

"If he looks downwards, it is not a good sign." He told of having been a wealthy farmer. "But, you know, in the world generally, farmers curse and complain too much. I don't like that. One day, I dropped everything and went away. Even now my wife does not know what happened to me. I did not say goodbye to her."

"Did you then not love your wife?"

"On the contrary, we got on very well together. But you see, out there ... the complaining ... Here there is peace and quiet, and spiritual well-being, I prefer it that way."

In the railway carriage that evening we got into conversation with a merchant from Verkhoturye. He asked where we had come from, and the purpose of our journey. I answered, somewhat embarrassed, that we had come from Moscow to see Makary. I was afraid that would seem rather fantastic to him. But he was not at all surprised:

> Yes, Makary is a famous man. Last year the Tsar himself had him come to him in Zarskoye Selo. When he summoned him the next morning and asked how he had slept that night, Makary said, "I slept badly."
>
> "Why did you sleep badly?"
>
> "Your concerns weighed on my heart."
>
> "How do things stand with me, in that case?"
>
> "Well, things look bad for you." The Tsar was so grateful to him, that he donated vestments of silver brocade to our cloister church and had a large piece of land allocated to the cloister as a gift.

Seven years later the Tsar was murdered with his family.

A few weeks after that, in a conversation with Rudolf Steiner, I became aware that he knew about this visit.

"When you asked the monk whether you should occupy yourself with painting ..."

"I did not ask him, whether I should occupy myself with painting," I protested.

"But the question lay in your heart; and when he spoke to you of Saint Veronica, he answered you from the heart." Dr Steiner drew arrows raying out from a point. "I, however, answer you out of the cosmos." He drew arrows directed from the periphery to the point. "And you stand in between, and cannot as yet unite the two answers." And he instructed me to practise my meditations more energetically.

Philadelphia

Roaming in the garden at the end of summer, one may occasionally hear the sound of an apple falling to the ground. There can then be a peculiar feeling of time fulfilling itself, a sense of a mysterious natural order by which things ripen and at a certain moment comes to pass, seemingly quite suddenly. In the falling of an apple from the branch, a "sun-world" comes in touch with the ground, entrusting itself to the earth.

It happens like that in human life as well. Something ripens in the soul over a period of years. Just why it comes to light at a particular moment, we cannot immediately comprehend. Thus I am unable to say why I suddenly knew, single-mindedly, in the year 1911, after hearing the series of lectures, From Jesus to Christ, that I was to connect my life with the spirit-deed of Rudolf Steiner. Personal considerations, the wish to live with like-minded people in Russia, for instance, had then to take second place.

I chose Munich as my place of residence, the artists' city, where Rudolf Steiner, in cultivating the artistic element in the Anthroposophical Society, put on his Mystery Plays every year at summer conferences. This was made possible by the understanding and devoted commitment with which Sophie Stinde and her friend Countess Pauline von Kalckreuth entered into his intentions.

Sophie Stinde guided the Munich work with great seriousness. The idea of a building to provide the plays with a worthy setting arose there first of all. Thus Rudolf Steiner often lingered in Munich, giving lectures and holding consultations.

I took my meals at Frau von Vacano's, who ran the vegetarian restaurant Fruchtkorb (Fruit Basket), and the little guest house belonging to it. She later became known for her excellent translations of the works of Vladimir Soloviev, under the pseudonym Harry Köhler. A strong personality with a lot of drive and enthusiasm, she had been raised in Russia. However, in her these qualities were combined with a tendency towards an imagination run wild. Thus in the "Fruit Basket," certain fruits of pseudo-mysticism ripened. I asked myself, does Rudolf Steiner not see that? Why does he not intervene? Only after a few years, when things had continued *ad absurdum* and were easily recognizable, did he say how embarrassing it was for him, to be surrounded continuously on lecture tours and in lecture halls by ladies in lilac. This colour was worn because he had once said that violet had a visual-moral effect that was spiritual. These were only trifling matters, but in serious matters also, Rudolf Steiner allowed people their freedom. It is a law of genuine modern esotericism that the teacher does not influence the pupil in their will-life. He provides knowledge based on trust in the pupil's higher being and in the guidance of destiny, which is to show him the true path.

In the Fruchtkorb I got to know Count von Lerchenfeld. He lived with his family on his main estate, Köfering, and came to all the anthroposophical events in Munich. His elegance and charm were seemingly inborn. He was strongly connected to family traditions, loved hunting with a passion and could tell jokes well. The significant thing about him, not recognizable from his way of living or his thoughts, lay rather in his destiny. Destiny is integral to the personality. And it was Otto von Lerchenfeld's destiny not only to want to help his teacher Rudolf Steiner, to whom he was unconditionally loyal, but actually to be able to do so at decisive moments. Thus he gave a large amount for the building initially to be built in Munich. In 1916, in view of the catastrophic situation of Germany, he put the question to Rudolf Steiner, "What needs to be done? Things cannot go on like this," whereupon, over a period of several weeks, Rudolf Steiner developed for him the idea of the threefold social order.

"Tell me what your objections are," he said to the Count, "so nothing remains unsolved." Making use of his connections with influential statesman, Otto von Lerchenfeld attempted to get them to understand these ideas. However, some of them had no time, while others could not reconcile these ideas with the existing imperial regime. Or they were not sufficiently unbiased, not awake enough to take up the ideas for a social structure which the times demanded, capable of saving the world from further catastrophes. Later, when Rudolf Steiner gave the new methods for biodynamic agriculture, Otto von Lerchenfeld made his large estates available for the application of this method. He had the warmest interest in everything evolving in the Anthroposophical Society, and helped single initiatives wherever he could.

Close bonds of friendship connected me with a Frenchwoman, Lotus Peralté, a painter, and with a Polish sculptress, Luna Drexler. The Frenchwoman, then already in her sixties, was a small, slim figure with short curly black hair, and a half-lion, half- eagle-like face. She always wore a simple, close-fitting dress of a desert-sand colour. On her talon-like fingers shone large emeralds and topazes she had brought with her from India. In winter, she wrapped herself in a broad fur scarf, also the colour of the desert. She was authentic in everything, and she went her solitary artistic and esoteric way, misunderstood by most people. She seemed predestined for a hermit's existence.

In her bearing and gestures the twenty-five-year old Polish woman resembled a knightly squire. She was all soul and filled with fiery enthusiasm. Her voice vibrated with emotion. Like most of her people, she was a passionate patriot. Later, after the First World War, she was able to serve her country as a member of the Polish Sejm (parliament) and as head of the anthroposophical movement. But she died young. Through her, and her friends, I got to know the mystical movements around Joseph Wronski and Adam Mickiewicz.

Christian Morgenstern was already known to us as the excellent translator of the works of Ibsen. His shining eyes had impressed me when, without knowing who he was, I had met him at anthroposophical events. He lingered for months at that time in the sanatorium of our friend Dr Peipers, though I was unaware of this. I also did not know that the young Swiss man, who regularly attended the study evenings held by Fräulein Sophie Stinde, was the poet Albert Steffen. At that time, I was struck by his Dantesque profile and the unusual earnestness of his eyes. There was a transparent look of mildness on his face, whose sharply drawn features recalled his rocky homeland. I only got to know him in Dornach ten years later.

The people I got to know in Moscow, in the spring of 1910, belonged to circles that had a connection to Vladimir Soloviev. The philosopher himself had been dead for ten years, but his spirit made itself felt among various groups of people in Moscow. In these new friends of mine, there lived a certain apocalyptic mood, a presentiment that a new revelation was possible and a concrete esoteric Christian path. It was interesting that, with a few of them, Soloviev's mysticism united itself with Goetheanism. It was their opinion that natural science ought to be permeated with Christian impulses, while spiritual science should achieve the exactness of natural science. Most in this circle were academics of varied educational backgrounds. Soon afterwards, many of them came to anthroposophy, and a circle was formed to which the friends of my earliest youth belonged, with whom I had once discussed spiritual problems while skiing. This circle signified, for me personally, a home within a home, since an exchange of ideas was now possible. In continuing to receive the spiritual truths in Germany, I not only took them up for myself alone, but could now pass them on to friends through letters, notes and newly published books. In personal conversations with Rudolf Steiner as well, I mediated between individual friends and him. Once, an acquaintance wrote to me who did not as yet accept the path of anthroposophy, saying he had confidence that the "Virgin of the Rainbow Door" — an image of Soloviev — would protect Russia from everything alien to it. He meant anthroposophy in this case. When I translated the letter for Rudolf Steiner, he looked straight ahead. I shall never forget the deeply moving earnestness of that gaze, or the sound of his voice, when he said, "May this Virgin protect Russia from the terrible future approaching it. For terrible things are building up over Russia." That was at the end of the year 1911.

Here I should like to give an account of an individual I met in the circle of the Musagetes publishing house. His destiny seems to me symptomatic of a certain kind of person.

His actual name was Lev Kobylinsky, but his little book of poems called *Stigmata*, along with a few essays appeared under the pseudonym Ellis, and that was what he was called in the circle of his friends. He had first become a Marxist and seemed almost prepared to kill anyone who did not share his conviction. Then he became a glowing admirer of Dante and the spirituality of the Middle Ages. He lived in a run-down hotel, the Don, on the squalid Smolensky Market Square, and his dream was to erect a Gothic cathedral on this square. His friend Nilender, who shared a room with him, dreamt a different dream. He lived in the world of Orphic Greece and was at that time translating the fragments of Heraclitus. Neither of them had any money and they led a chaotic life. Ellis had an uncanny ability to imitate people, but this always went in the direction of caricature, of the grotesque. His sudden conversion to anthroposophy, the nature of which he had not grasped at all, gave us all something of a fright, since his crusading began immediately. When, on the day I arrived, I saw him standing in his galoshes in front of the main post office in Karlsruhe, in the pouring rain, I foresaw what was in store for me. And it turned out I was right; he requested sponsorship, so as to be accepted as a member of the Anthroposophical Society. Only members could participate in the lecture cycle for which he had come. I knew he had spent all his money on this journey. But how was I to sponsor him? After all, I knew his tendencies only too well. I went earlier to the location of the lecture and explained the situation to Rudolf Steiner.

"You can by all means sign the recommendation," he said, "I shall assume the responsibility for it myself."

Ellis did not as yet understand German. I reported the content of the first lecture to him, in which Rudolf Steiner spoke of the spiritual path, of the inviolability of the will of another, which may only be addressed via thinking and not by means of direct influence on the will. Thus the human being is left free, the only appropriate way for our time. Ellis did not want to believe me; to such an extent did this thought contradict his own orientation. He checked up on me with other Russian participants, who confirmed my words, and was baffled. "Humanity sits in a mess: it cannot be helped at all by being left free," he thought.

Having returned to Moscow, Ellis began making propaganda for anthroposophy in which, however, he saw only a new dogma. Friends there wrote to me in Munich, that I should request Rudolf Steiner to restrain him from his proselytizing activities, with which he was raising a cloud of dust. Rudolf Steiner only smiled and said, "Ellis has to speak. If one were to lock him up in prison, or, like Papageno, put a little padlock on his lips, he would still find a way to speak." Soon, Ellis came to Berlin and Rudolf Steiner put in an endless amount of time and effort, attempting to restore the equilibrium of this agitated individual. But we received abusive letters from Ellis, in which he reproached us all with being tepid in regard to Rudolf Steiner. That was the first phase. Then came the second. Ellis began to hate the whole Anthroposophical Society, and levelled the reproach at Rudolf Steiner that he left people free, demanding no obedience from them. Once, I heard Rudolf Steiner saying to him jokingly after a lecture, "And you, Mr Ellis, are a rebel."

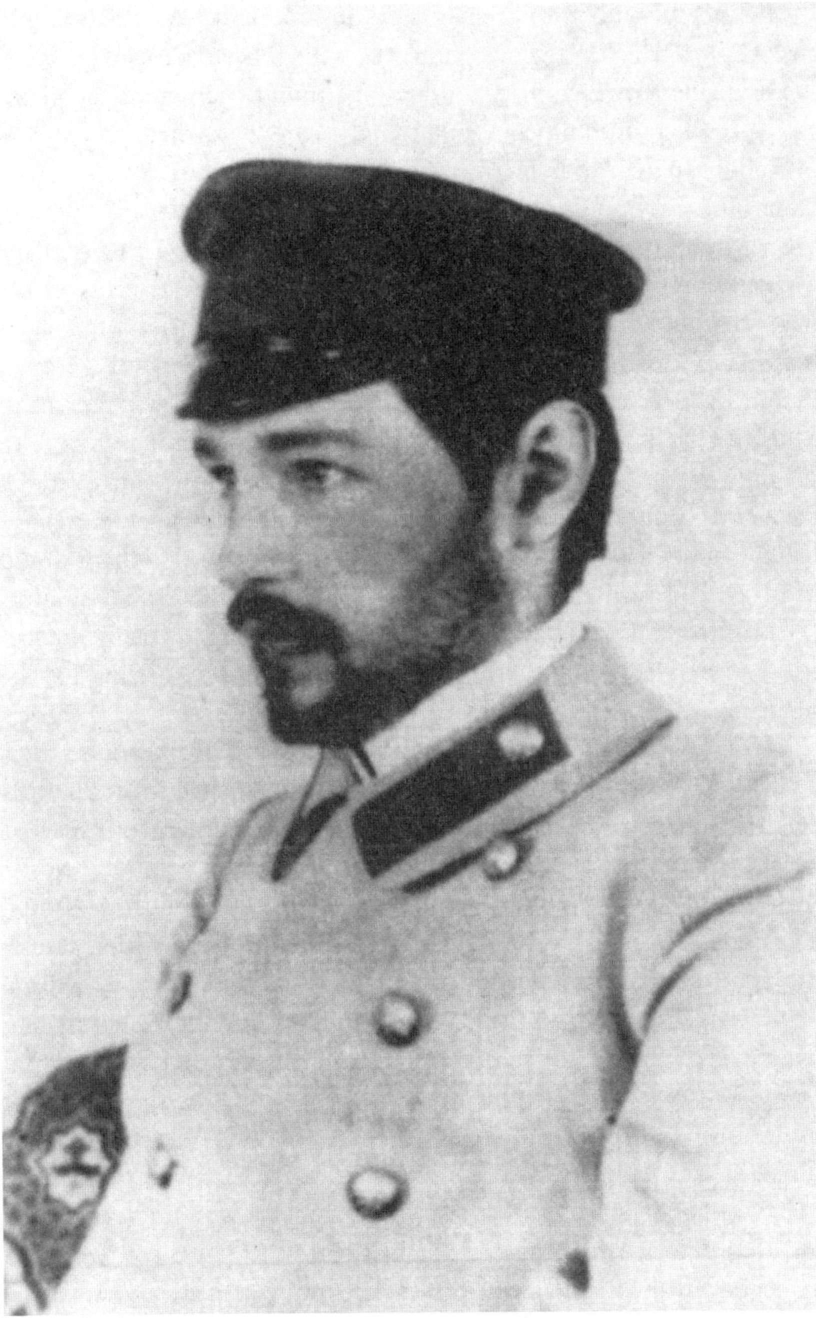

Ellis (Lev Lvovich Kobylinsky) around 1900

"Oh no, *Herr Doktor*, I remain your loyal knight." And pointing to the people in the hall, "These, however, will all have to burn."

Gradually, however, he transferred his indignation from the pupils to the teacher, becoming an embittered enemy of anthroposophy and of Rudolf Steiner. In his writings he fought in the ranks of those who grant humanity no spiritual freedom.

In March of the year 1912, after much hesitation, I finally made a start on my large triptych *Three Sacrifices*. While painting on the narrow right-hand wing, which portrayed the sacrifice of Abel, I received a telegram from my father saying my mother was seriously ill and I should come to Moscow immediately. Steiner was present in Munich just then, and was leaving for Berlin that evening. I drove to the railway station, to take leave of him and to tell him I had to travel. He heard the news of my mother's illness with great sympathy, saying a few encouraging words to me. It had become doubtful, whether I would be able to participate in the lectures he was to hold in Helsingfors (Helsinki) at Easter. That was particularly distressing, since my Russian friends intended going there, in order to meet Rudolf Steiner for the first time.

My father met me on the platform in Moscow and, from his face, I saw right away that my mother's condition was serious. She had been taken to the private clinic of a well-known surgeon, since it was thought that a surgical intervention might become necessary. At home I encountered Polya and Masha with eyes red from crying. They told me in what churches and chapels, before which saints, they had lit candles and petitioned short services for the healing of the sick. Seeing my mother, I got quite a shock. Her pupils had widened from fever and her large eyes, otherwise grey, now appeared completely black. Her expression was stern, almost hard. After a few days, however, the immediate danger receded. The operation proved superfluous.

It was the beginning of Holy Week. On Tuesday my friends left for Helsingfors; there were twelve of them. On Thursday I received a telegram from them: "Your presence is indispensable." With that, I knew they wanted to make my decision easier. I showed the telegram to my mother. She looked at me reproachfully with her big eyes, but did not say anything. Toward evening I drove through Moscow to the station with very mixed feelings, just at the hour when in all the churches each person stands holding a candle and hears the twelve chapters spoken of the sufferings of Christ.

The next morning my friend Boris Leman fetched me from the railway station in St Petersburg and brought me to his uncle's house, where he lived. Boris had meanwhile lost his bride. He looked even thinner than before; his face was now almost corpse-like. At the lunch table he jested, pulling his cousin's leg, but I noticed that he hardly ate anything. I asked his cousin about it and learned that he had hardly eaten for months. She was worried about him. But in this peculiarly passive family, they all lived alongside each other without interfering in the least in each other's affairs, despite being fond of each other. Parents, daughters and nephews lived in this house next to each other as though in a hotel. Alone with Boris, I asked him what his fasting was supposed to mean.

"I cannot eat anything."

"What does the doctor think about that?"

"I haven't asked him, I have already known for quite some time that I am to die this August of a stomach ulcer. Previously, I had only one anxiety ... having to abandon my bride. She would not have been able to endure life without me. Now she has gone ahead, and I can die with relative ease."

I asked, "But is it right to depart from life like that without a fight? After all, life on earth is of value, since only on the earth are we free, and able to develop further. Is the time of death in any case preordained with absolute inevitability?"

He replied, "For a long time already I have known my hour, and am so prepared that it would be impossible for me to remain."

I asked him about his attitude to Steiner. Three years ago he had still been opposed to him. He answered that his standpoint was now quite different. In the meantime he had studied many of Steiner's works and had undergone inner experiences, allowing him to recognize Steiner as the greatest initiate on the earth.

"Why then are you not in Helsingfors, where you could after all so easily meet him? That I cannot understand."

"Yes, that you can't understand. But, you see, though it would be the greatest stroke of good fortune for me to see and hear him, I have no right to good fortune. It would only mean taking. On the basis of what one is permitted to receive, one has the obligation to do something for others. Putting it in trivial terms, it would be a luxury for me. Just imagine if the question were to come up as to who should take over the work in St Petersburg. I know I am the only one who comes in question. Even so I still could not take it on. Understand me correctly, I have at most a few months to live. But let us not talk about it anymore, it is very painful."

Early the next morning, on the Helsingfors platform, I saw all my Moscow friends, as well as a few German friends from Munich and Berlin. While we were having coffee together in the station restaurant, seeing people united, who till now had belonged for me in two quite separate worlds, seemed like a dream. The most improbable person there was a Russian, Gorodovoi, a Tsar-policeman, in a foreign city in which Russian was being spoken.

The first two lectures of the cycle, the Working of the Heavenly Hierarchies in the Kingdoms of Nature, had already taken place. They were summarized for me and I was told about the events of the last few days. Ellis had also come from Berlin. For years he had worshipped Marya [Sisova] as his Beatrice, and was now almost out of his mind, because she had come to the lecture course together with Vikentyev, as his bride. He spoke with Steiner about his grief; she was after all "providentially predestined" for him. Steiner answered, if she had been destined for him, it would have come about, so that was not the case after all. He consoled Ellis, even putting his arm around him and kissing him, whereupon Ellis imagined himself to be Steiner's favourite pupil.

After the lecture on Easter Saturday, Rudolf Steiner was to go with us Russians and a few Germans to the Russian Orthodox Church, for the Easter night mass and stay afterwards for the traditional Easter meal. The church we attended was unfortunately a garrison church; the congregation consisted only of soldiers with dour faces. The choruses were sung, boringly and rather pitifully, by sleepy boys. Rudolf Steiner joined us in standing throughout this service, and also at the mass which followed, which was very tiring for the remaining Germans, not used to standing for so long. We did not arrive at the hotel till around three o'clock in the morning. There the good Kleopatra Christoforova, the hotel owner, had ordered the Easter meal for us. We arrived in the joyful mood which animates every Russian on Easter night, especially glad to have Rudolf Steiner celebrate with us. He stood at the door of the dining hall and shook hands with each of us. The rapturous enthusiasm with which we were filled encountered his very earnest, stringent, questioning look. When we had taken our seats at the table, he cut the Easter bread into a hexagram, shared it out among us, stood up and held an address, the meaning of which was as follows:

> The whole history of mankind is the Entombment of the Godhead. We, with our consciousness, are only capable of celebrating the Entombment on Good Friday. We do not have the ability to comprehend Easter with our intellect. We can only celebrate Easter in vowing to follow the path to the spirit.

I now understood the austere, questioning look which had met our illusionistic joy. Only much later did I begin to grasp the full meaning of his words. I write this in the year 1942, after it has become clear just where the history of mankind has led and where it will continue, if a sufficient number of human beings do not freely resolve to seek the path to the spirit.

One day Rudolf Steiner announced to us that he would hold a special lecture for Russians about Russia.[29] Our small circle gathered in one of the guest rooms of the hotel. Never have I heard Steiner speak in such a heartfelt manner, indeed so personally, as then. It was as though he wanted to imbue the soul of each one of us with every word, spoken with infinite warmth. He spoke of the young folk-soul of the Russian people, concerning which he was able to learn in the spiritual world that it could not yet fully manifest itself. In what the West has come to know of Russia, in the great impulses of Tolstoy, in the arresting nature of Dostoyevsky's psychological insight, in Soloviev, there is too much of what has been adopted from the West, even if the Russian folk-soul is clearly to be felt in it. But this soul has more to say. He showed us the path to this folk-soul of ours. It poses the profoundest questions to the spirit, questions which will have to be put one day and without the answer to which humanity will not be able to live in the future. He spoke of genuine human love and kindness, of empathy, of a refined, intimate power of observation, of an intense personal bond with the powers of existence. And of questions only capable of arising out of the European East, which had been put to him by those connected with the Russian folk-soul.

The Russians have the task of imbuing the spirit with soul, of finding the soul belonging to the spirit. But the danger with Russians is that the soul often remains stuck in what is personal. The fire, the warmth of enthusiasm can be a hindrance in taking up the spirit objectively. By reason of its geographical position, Russia is placed before two temptations. One of these temptations is the influence of the materialistic West, materialistic ideas having nothing to do with the Russian folk-soul. The second temptation is the one coming from the East, once a spiritual culture arises. There is the obligation to know that with all the greatness of this spiritual culture of the East, the human being of the present has to tell himself: it is not the past that we have to carry into the future, but new impulses. We may not simply take up the spiritual impulses of the East. Russia has to cultivate what the West can itself bring forth out of its own spiritual sources. Then the time will come, in which Europe will begin to understand what the Christ impulse actually is in the spiritual development of humanity. A great responsibility rests upon us. We must convert the impulses we derive from spiritual knowledge into will impulses and into deeds. These two great temptations can only be overcome if we find the path to the folk-soul, which has taken this responsibility upon itself for the sake of humanity.

My friends all wanted to have personal conversations with Rudolf Steiner, at which I often had to act as interpreter. The bright, wide corridor of the hotel, in which we often waited a long time, pacing up and down, has certainly remained unforgettable for all of us. Inwardly we were filled with love for Rudolf Steiner, as well as for each other. It was like a weak premonition of the community of Philadelphia in the Revelation to St John, which is said to be the archetype of the future Slavic culture, whose mission will be that of brotherhood. It was still childlike, rapturous and personal with us, but there was a substance there that I found again later among these friends in Russia.

In order to understand what united us so closely, it has to be borne in mind that in the course of these days we were becoming acquainted with the spiritual realities at work behind external nature, in the heavenly bodies, in colours, in times of year, in the growth of plants etc. The dualism of religion and science was not overcome by means of a vague pantheism, but by exact spiritual scientific research. What we received was neither dogma nor superstition. The path of knowledge was always set forth at the same time, and this could be understood and tested. It was a schooling in moral deepening. The Finns, as well as the Russians, have a strong spiritual relationship with nature. These exalted and magnificent spiritual findings called forth in us — I can say this of the circle of my Russian friends — the feeling of rediscovering the "fatherland," by which I mean our own divine origins. In each one of us, this feeling lived in the form of awe and gratitude. We knew that the same feeling was shared by the others. On meeting others one knew, even without knowing them personally — the Finns are very reserved — that we are all one in this most important, most central spiritual concern. And what is love other than the deepest feeling of such common ground.

My friend Boris [Leman] had suddenly decided to come to Helsingfors, in order to hear Rudolf Steiner and speak with him. Since I had to act as interpreter, I was present at the conversation. Rudolf Steiner adopted what seemed a strangely aloof manner, such as I was otherwise not used to with him. He listened silently to what Boris had to say about his situation. Then he only said, "By all means just wait for your death. That is a possible attitude one can have."

I had eliminated myself from the conversation; I only translated. Nonetheless, Steiner's last sentence seemed depressing to me. Boris told Rudolf Steiner that two young ladies had come with him, with whom he had done spiritual scientific work, and since he would be "leaving," he asked him to receive them. Rudolf Steiner lowered his head then he turned to me and said, "I have spoken to the gentleman only because you wanted to help him."

And he dismissed us. Boris teased me at once in the corridor outside, "You see ... he is the only sensible person. You and everyone else only wanted things to be different from what destiny determines."

Boris stayed on for several more days. He was endlessly kind to everybody. We bought traditional Finnish objects made of birch bark and Karelian wood, and he gave everyone little presents. He also heard the lecture on the Finnish epic *Kalevala*, which had a special significance for him.

When the cycle of twelve lectures was completed, I travelled to St Petersburg, where I stayed for two days with Boris. I discussed the impending work in St Petersburg with him and Trapesnikov. Boris wanted to take this work upon himself "provisionally." A solar eclipse took place during these days and the ghostly city of St Petersburg appeared still more ghostly in this wan light.

Boris did not die as he had expected, but regained his health. Rudolf Steiner said later, the possibility of death had definitely existed for him at that time. However, if a human being makes the decision to serve the spirit, his destiny can take a different turn. Boris had received the necessary strong impulse in Helsingfors. Steiner did not want to influence him personally. This explains his reserved attitude.

V

The Open Secret

The Mystery of Remaining Silent

In the year 1912, a group of Russian Old Believers turned to the Moscow publishing house Spiritual Knowledge with the request for a book about the *starets* Seraphim of Sarov, which, however, was not to be written in the usual unctuous manner of the Orthodox synodal publications, and the publisher assigned this task to me.[30] In my next conversation with Rudolf Steiner I asked him about this figure, so significant for Russia and still present in the consciousness of the people. St Seraphim had died in 1833 and it was still possible then to meet people who had known him. The reports concerning his words and deeds, particularly his healing powers, still effective after his death up until our own time, were no mere legends. It can be said that this figure overshadowed the Russia of my time.

Rudolf Steiner evidently knew about him and said to me, "As an individuality the holy Seraphim is one of the greatest, but in this incarnation he did not work by means of thinking. One has to look at his deeds. Go to the place where he lived. You will then certainly know how to write about him."

Thus I travelled by train with my father to Sarov, to the cloister in the great forests in the province of Tambov, east of the Volga. When we stepped out at the station, it was the eve of the saint's birthday, celebrated on July 19. From there one still had to travel by horse-drawn carriage for several hours. Thousands upon thousands of pilgrims came to this celebration, in spite of it being harvest time. Again and again we overtook larger and smaller groups of them. Burdened with sacks full of chunks of dried black bread, their provisions while hiking for weeks, they resembled a caravan in the desert. They strode in a cloud of dust, each with a large staff in the right hand, most of them barefoot or in shoes woven of birch bark, the women with their dresses gathered up. In spite of the many miles that already lay behind them, they proceeded lightly and rhythmically. They seemed to walk on air, as though at one with the landscape. Forests were left behind, clouds following them. Fields spread out around them like wafting sheets. We overtook creaking peasants' carts pulled slowly by straggly little horses. These were loaded with old men, cripples and sick people lying on hay or on red cushions. In a dusty village with houses that stood far apart, our horses had to rest. The coachman stopped in front of a large shed where a samovar was offered us within a roofed-over forecourt, and we partook of tea and pastries in the midst of obtrusive chickens that flew overhead. A few of the peasant's carts also rested here. Only now was I able to observe the sick people more closely. And what faces they had! With most of them, their dark skin seemed stuck to their bones. Their eyes, with dark rings around them, appeared all the lighter and bigger. At that time in Russia, in the country the sick mostly went without medical help. Hospitals and ambulances were miles away, often run-down and neglected, lacking medicines, and the doctors frequently became drunkards out of despair. Along with their relatives, sick people simply bore their fate, willed by God, with patience and resignation. On seeing these paralyzed, consumptive human beings consumed by suffering, yet not distorted by it, one could sense an important secret in their suffering without bitterness. Here a path was left open for the spirit, which shone as through a window into our world.

The sun had begun to set when we arrived in Sarov, and the bells of the cloister rang at the close of the evening service. Every lodging was filled to overflowing. Only with difficulty did we find a room for the two of us, I then hurried to the cloister and positioned myself at the arched Paradise Gate. Amid the pealing of bells, thousands of people strode past me shoulder to shoulder in the direction of the setting sun, which lit up their faces and reflected itself in their eyes. Under the deep measured chiming of the bells, the stream moved slowly on. And this stream on whose banks I stood was *Russia*, for they had in fact come from all over this vast country. I saw tanned faces deeply furrowed with wrinkles, shining deep-set eyes with an uncommon gaze directed as though at some far-off goal: old men with hair as "white as the moon"; curly, thick blonde, red or coal-black heads and beards; old and young women with their headscarves, along with older and younger children. Sorrow, humility and a withdrawn expression could be read on almost every face. The historical life of this people had to be taken into account, if one was to understand what the holy places meant for

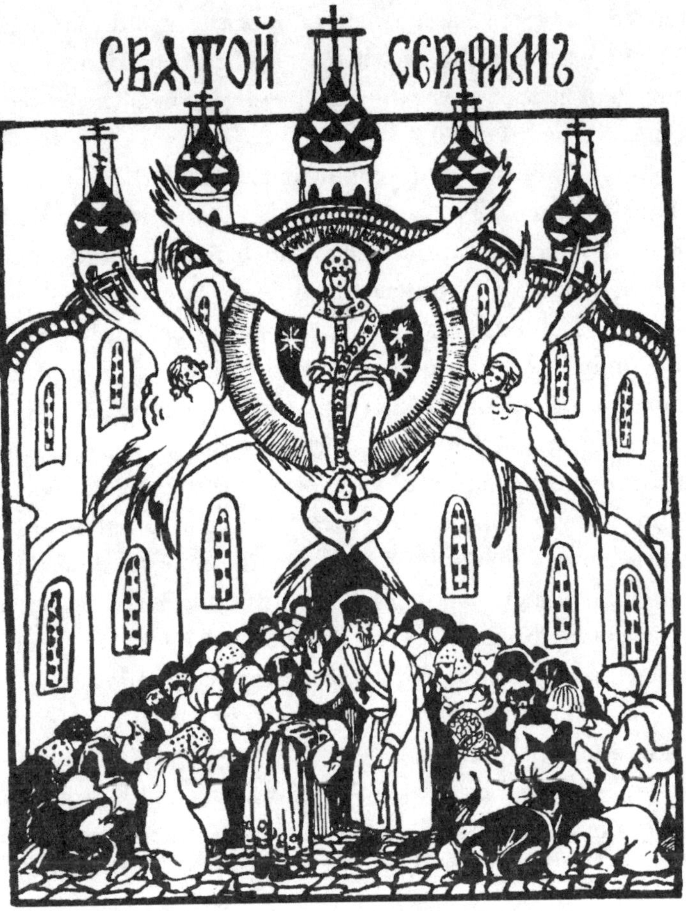

St Seraphim. Illustration by Woloschin for her book published by Spiritual Knowledge

those making such pilgrimages. The centuries of the Tartar yoke had to be borne in mind, the three hundred years of serfdom, the perpetual dominion of the lash. From the White Sea to the Black, from Siberia to Kiev, the Russian people went on pilgrimages, their gaze turned toward a distant aim.

The stars already gleamed above as I returned to the cloister. As far as the eye could see in the dimness, small wood fires burned on the field alongside the cloister wall, where people huddled or lay asleep, while others conversed quietly. These quiet sounds made by thousands of people rose up like a strange murmur from the earth. The camp seemed without end. Here and there the Seraphim's name was spoken, his deeds were related, his prophecies, his appearances. It is said that he appears now here, now there in Russia, wherever his help is needed. However, he was to be experienced especially here in Sarov where the whole region was permeated by his deeds.

Seraphim may be pictured stepping out of the dark pine forest in his white smock, so deeply hunched over that he has to support himself on an axe. He wears a monk's cap, has long white hair and a large copper cross on his chest beneath his trimmed beard; in the bag over his shoulder he carries the Gospel. His slender, relatively short nose confers something dove-like on his face. His almond-shaped blue eyes have a penetrating look, and the power of those eyes is considerable. They express the whole inexorable, consuming knowledge of the sins of the world and at the same time, the joyful, irrevocable certainty of redemption. Fused into a single look, these contrasts make it comprehensible how this human being came to be given the name Seraphim, meaning "the flaming one." A mere report of his words and deeds cannot impart what is essential about him. One has a presentiment that, had it not poured itself out as healing love over the earth, sanctifying both water and air, this same gaze might have reduced one to ashes. "God is fire, God is love," he would say.

Prochor, as the world first knew him, was born in Kursk, where his father was a builder and had erected the cathedral in that city, among other buildings. When Prochor was three years old his father died. At seven years of age, he fell from the scaffolding of the clock tower and yet remained unscathed. Repeatedly thereafter in his life, Prochor experienced a similar immediate intervention of supersensible powers. As a ten-year-old boy he was healed of a serious illness, in having a vision of the Mother of God by means of her icon which was brought to him. Again, as a novice of twenty-four, following an illness of three years duration, having received the last anointing, she appeared to him in an inexpressible light, between St Paul and St John, and he regained his health. This same phenomenon reoccurred when Seraphim was once attacked in his hermitage by three robbers, who beat him almost to death.

Prochor received an education customary for the sons of merchants at that time. With the aid of a Bible, he learned reading and writing from a sexton. He helped his brother in the shop, but the business profession was unsuited to him. After his miraculous recovery in childhood, his mother saw that he would become a monk, and this corresponded to his own wish. As a young man he made a pilgrimage to Kiev with other young people, visiting a monk who possessed second sight and directed him to go to Sarov. This monk gave him a brief and simple prayer as his main exercise, "Lord Jesus Christ, be merciful unto me." He was to say this prayer at all times, even when working, speaking it softly and later only in his mind. Finally it was to become one with his pulse beat. By this means, he was told, he could attain the purity enabling him to receive the Holy Spirit.

After a long journey, the nineteen-year-old Prochor arrived, in November 1778, at the little church belonging to the forest hermitage at Sarov, on the eve of the traditional celebration of Mary's first visit to the Temple. Throughout the eight years of his novitiate he read the Gospels in his cell, as well as the Epistles of the Apostles, and the mystical writings of the Eastern Church. He worked in the cloister bakery, as a carpenter, and as a forester, together with other monks. His free hours were spent in the forest in prayer.

At thirty-five, Seraphim withdrew to a forest cell. Other hermits saw that he sometimes stood absorbed in contemplation while working. He would go every Sunday to Sarov to attend the mass, bringing back the dried bread that served him as nourishment for the week. He shared this with birds and wild animals. Snakes would creep peacefully up to him, and a large bear visited him occasionally, returning into the forest at his bidding.

"In the cloister," Seraphim once said, "the hostile powers with which the monks fight are like pigeons. Here in the solitude, they are like tigers and leopards."

When evil powers stormed the soul of Seraphim, he would kneel night after night on a block of granite in the forest, speaking the prayer of the publican. He did the same in his cell by day, continuing this for a thousand days and a thousand nights. He made this known not long before his death, so that the granite block in the forest would be sought out, since it had received a healing power from the prayer.

In every human being, Seraphim saw the divine archetypal image, merely clouded over by the dust of earthly life; just as the sun "sees" in the seed the future plant, calling it into existence. He awakened in people their hidden and forgotten higher being, strengthened the forces of love in them and helped them to order their destiny. Out of the superabundance of his healing powers achieved through sacrifice, he was able to shorten the path of suffering for others. When brought a sick person who had been paralyzed for many years, Seraphim asked him, "Do you believe in Christ?"

"Yes," was the answer.

"Then you are healed."

And the one paralyzed was able to make full use of his hands and legs. Yet when he wanted to thank the old man, Seraphim said, "What! The wretched cripple Seraphim made you well? Only Christ is capable of healing. You must thank Him."

In the chronicles of the neighbouring Diveyevo Convent, which had been under Seraphim's spiritual guidance, I read the following. An aristocratic estate owner, Nikolai Motovilov, whom Seraphim had healed of a severe illness of many years standing, came to see the old man in his hermitage. It was November and snow was falling. The old man had him sit on a tree stump, and squatted on the ground in front of him.

"It has become known to me," he began the conversation with his guest, "that from your youth on, you have asked after the meaning of life. No one could give you an answer."

"Indeed, that is so," said Motovilov. "I was continually seeking the meaning of life, but no answer could satisfy me."

"The meaning of life," said Seraphim, "consists in apprehending the spirit of God, the Divine." The questioner admitted to being unable to understand that. Seraphim likened the Holy Spirit to a breath of life, through which the human being stands higher than other creatures and is similar to God. He attempted to make the meaning of his words clear to his guest in pictures, speaking of the manifestation of the Holy Spirit as an inexpressible light.

On another occasion, Motovilov asked him whether the devil really has the horns and claws he is generally portrayed with. The old man smiled.

"Sir, having studied at university, can you still believe that demons have horns and claws? Being of a spiritual nature, how can they? And yet this image does correspond to them. An image is necessary, hence they are represented as dark and ugly."

The morning following our arrival, my father and I went to the festive mass. The cathedral accommodated only a fraction of the crowd.

Even the cloister courtyard was unable to contain the large numbers of those attending. Most stood outside during the long service, of which not a word could be heard in the courtyard; yet absolute quiet prevailed in this crowd of people. When the sarcophagus with relics of the saint was carried around the church and the church choir sang, a commotion arose. Frightful, inhuman cries could be heard coming from possessed people, from epileptics, from the "cryers," as those women are called in Russia who suffer fits of madness; there being more possessed women than men in Russia. The attempt was made to drag them to the coffin. They convulsed and resisted strongly, so that four men could barely hold one woman. When they succeeded in bringing her through the crowd to the coffin, and she touched it, after a loud shriek (in which a sub-human world announced itself) she became absolutely quiet. The constriction had eased and she followed the procession of her own free will, supported by a relative. Over the heads of the crowd, hand-woven linen rolls were thrown from all sides in the direction of the coffin, sometimes caught and flung further, they surged like waves toward the coffin. This was the offering of the women to the saint. In cabins scattered across the whole of Russia this linen had been spun and woven on long winter evenings by the weak light of wood fires.

At midday, we ate on a peculiar, high scaffold which appeared rather fantastic. Sitting at long tables were entire families from the social strata of the semi-educated merchants and estate owners, from the farthest provinces. However, there were hardly any from the military, few members of the clergy and almost no intellectuals. Having meanwhile become used to Western features, I saw no happy medium here; all seemed slightly grotesque. Several individuals were so corpulent that the chairs broke beneath them. But then there were also those who were excessively gaunt. All kinds of psychological tendencies came openly to expression: arrogance, timorousness, subservience, gloominess, humour, kindness. Clothes and hats, worn ineptly and in an idiosyncratic manner, were equally odd. When not dressed quite plainly, the women wore modern clothing, except that Parisian fashion took on Russian characteristics, becoming absurdly exaggerated. Among all these faces there was not a single indifferent one, and in all of them I saw a certain piousness.

In the afternoon we rented a horse and carriage in order to visit the saint's forest hermitage. The forest consisted of majestic ancient pine trees, linden and maple trees. The midday sun shimmered through the foliage. In this otherwise silent forest there was now a good deal of commotion, since the sick people came to the healing spring, which had been purified and bordered with stones by the old man, as well as to the granite block on which he had prayed for a thousand days and nights. In an obtrusive manner, the monks in the saint's hut wanted to sell small crosses and pictures to the pilgrims, disturbing the mood which still reigned here in nature. And yet something of the very deepest quiet could be felt, communicating itself directly to the heart and streaming from the heart into the limbs.

An invisible blossoming, an inaudible ringing could be sensed within. The air and the water preserved what remained of the saint, so that a life-engendering force worked even now in these surroundings. And here the truth of a strange story took on meaning for me that I had read in the chronicle of the Diveyevo Convent:

> Once, in deep winter, when there was a severe frost and the snow lay particularly deep, two young nuns of the convent were working in the forest not far from Seraphim's hut. The old man stepped out and signalled them to come. He held in his hand a branch with strange blossoms and fruits they had never seen, inviting the nuns to partake of them.

The next day I drove alone to the Diveyevo Cloister, whose spiritual guidance had been taken on by Seraphim at the request of the dying abbess. The nuns came to him to ask for advice; he never actually went there himself.

From the pages of the chronicle I learned of little Marya [Melyukova], a country girl who came to Sarov at age thirteen with her sister. After the two had received the old man's blessing, he said, "But Marya is not to go home, she should remain in Diveyevo Cloister."

The chronicle relates that Marya was very beautiful, had long, golden plaits, an oval face with blue eyes of angelic purity. She was gentle and spoke little. The saint entrusted her with important secrets concerning the future. However, at eighteen, having overexerted herself carrying stones for the building of a new church at Diveyevo, she died. For her burial, Seraphim arranged for vestments of the highest clerical rank to be sent to her, as well as his own velvet cap for her head. On this occasion he is said to have wept. "Others always carried one stone," he said, "she carried two or three at once; overstraining herself." Marya had belonged to an order of twelve virgin sisters, millers who worked in the Diveyevo mill and had a special task, deriving directly from the Queen of Heaven. "Nothing takes place in the mill," Seraphim said, "that does not take place at the behest of the holy Mother of God."

In the manner in which this mill came about, there was something ceremonious and mysterious though it was also to serve the practical needs of the cloister. One day the old man sent for Michail Manturov, a property owner previously healed by him who supported the cloister. He presented him with a wedge and asked him to drive it into the ground in Diveyevo. He designated the exact place. Manturov returned, reporting to him that his instructions had been carried out. After a few weeks he gave him a second wedge, again with precise indications as to where he was to drive it into the ground. This repeated itself with the remaining wedges, determining the plan of the mill.

I drove alone to Diveyevo on a hot summer's day, and the grass smelled of thyme. Visiting the sister of the museum director, Alexei Petrovsky, who was a nun, I found a somewhat embittered and fanatically Orthodox intellectual, who administered the cloister pharmacy. As she tended to complain about her surroundings, her presence was little help in becoming aware of the mood of the place. She showed me the mill and also the "little grave" the saint had requested be dug. On this site, he said, the Mother of God had herself set foot. "This place," he prophesied, "will one day become a rampart up to heaven. When the Antichrist rules on earth, he will not step over it."

I asked Miss Petrovskaya, "Is the simple-minded Pelageya, who lived in the cloister at the time of the holy Seraphim, still alive?"

"Certainly, she is now a hundred and fifteen years old. But, go to her alone; I shall not go to her because she always insults me."These simpletons, Fools for Christ, found to my knowledge only in Russia, are sometimes referred to as the Blessed, or God's People. In the West they would have been confined to mental asylums. In Russia they often made their way, wandering from place to place over the entire country, and were received with great respect by the people; or they lived in cloisters. Gifted with second sight, they remained childlike, speaking as though in pictures. Within monastic or convent life, which can easily degenerate into inflexibility, hypocrisy and over-ambitiousness,

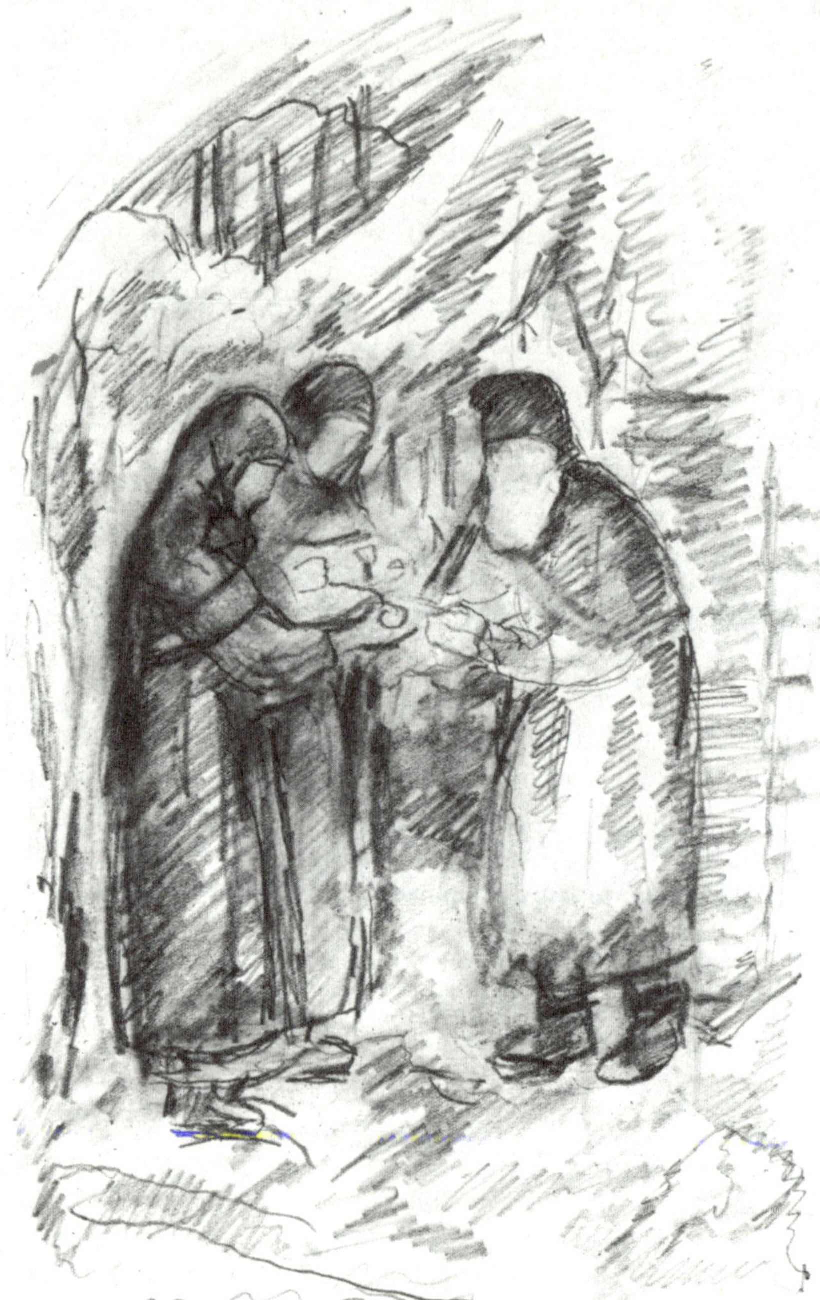

St Seraphim and the millers. Pencil sketch by Woloschin

these human beings had a salutary effect, acting outside the limits of normal reason and social behaviour. External authority could make no impression on them. History knows of instances in which they scolded a tsar, or drove an archbishop out of the Church.

In the Diveyevo Cloister there had previously been a simpleton called Seraphim of the Seraphim. I saw her portrait: an angelic but suffering face. While she was still alive, another simpleton came to the cloister, the Christ-Fool Pelageya.

"It is too early," the first one told her, "wait until I am dead, then you will replace me."

And Pelageya went back into the forest where she had come from. For years, she continued to live alone in this forest, without a roof over her head, summer and winter. It was not known what she ate or why she did not freeze to death. After a few years she came and stood at the edge of the forest once again, looking at the window of Seraphim of Seraphim's cell. However, she was waved away with a motion of the hand, meaning, "It is still too early," and Pelageya left.

The third time, she appeared on the first simpleton's death day, and remained from then on in the cloister. Sister Petrovskaya told me, the old woman played with dolls. In this way she would prophesy one person's death, that another would go on a journey, or she lectured the person.

"Go there alone, if you really want to," she said, and showed me the entrance to Pelageya's cell.

Between two enraptured nuns sat an old woman wearing only a coarse, loose chemise open at the neck. Her white, unkempt hair was left untied and hung from beneath a child's hood. The most peculiar thing about her was her skin, consisting of folds and wrinkles almost like an elephant's hide. Robust and stout, Pelageya moved brusquely and abruptly. As I entered, she greeted me and ordered the nun respectfully helping her, to give me a cup. She then poured tea from a teapot herself, to the point where the saucer was inundated.

The nun whispered to me mysteriously, "Be pleased, it is very good if Pelageyushka pours so much tea. It is a sign that she likes you."

The old woman said something which was unclear, and the nun translated for me. I stayed only a short time in the cell, as it was unbearably muggy there. Also, the sultry, superstitious atmosphere around this somnambulist, who "dreamt" with her actions, did not appeal to me. I had, in any case, seen the phenomenon of a human being who, by reason of an abnormal interaction of her physical and spiritual organization, was not subject to the normal effects of temperature on the body.

I was now glad of the opportunity to wander alone to the graves of little Marya and the other disciples of Seraphim. They lay near the church, beside the cloister's first abbess. A great silence surrounded these graves overgrown with grass. In this silence, I attempted to gain a sense of the destinies of these women, and of other people who had had a connection with Seraphim. A secret, seeming to point to the future, surrounds these humble souls.

"Words are tools of our time," Seraphim had said, "but keeping silence is the mystery of future ages."

A renunciation on the earth is transformed in the spiritual world into a force. What is no more than a little grave on the earth will reach to heaven and, when the Antichrist comes onto the earth, will form a rampart against him. One has a sense of this secret in this silence.

Russia too is silent. What speaks in Russia now, indeed shouts, are its demons. Its true being must be sought in parables. Does not the mill with the twelve women millers appear as an image to be deciphered? In the language of Christian esotericism, the soul that has undergone purification, that is prepared to receive the spirit, is called "the pure, wise virgin." The Mother of God on earth was the embodiment of that pure, divine being called the Virgin Sophia, the Wisdom of God. Through Seraphim she became the Abbess of the order of the twelve millers. They surrounded her like twelve apostles, each mirroring a ray of the Christ-Sun. Likewise, one who knows the stars, sees in the sky not just a soul-less mechanism, but the traces left by spiritual beings that ray out twelve forces from the twelve constellations of the zodiac. Does the soul that is to become pure and wise not live as an ideal of the future already in the rich, passionate soul of the Russian people? The image of the mill, set in motion by the power of the elements, either air or water, and grinding the seeds from which bread is to arise, is a picture. Bread is after all the symbol of the human body. But the Greek word *symbolou* refers to the "coinciding" of spiritual and physical reality. The mill of Diveyevo was to be administered by the wisdom of God. Thus, Seraphim placed this mill in the forests beyond the Volga as an image of the future mission of the Slavic people. And in this regard, the initiate of our time indicated that it would determine the arising of future generations according to divine, cosmic laws. This image may be said to work into the future like a seed placed into the earth.

The fiery will of Seraphim was such that his own life-forces became one with the holy and healing forces that are effective in nature. The rock on which he prayed, the spring which he blessed, were part of his own essential being. His spirit united itself with the earth, which since the Mystery of Golgotha is Christ's body.

Witnessing the procession around the church, when the white strips of linen drifted in waves over the heads of the crowd from all sides toward the coffin of the saint, I thought of the hands that had woven them as an offering to the saint on dark evenings in cabins across Russia. This seemed to me a picture of the soul of Russia weaving a sheath for the spirit.

The Mysteries of the Word

In August, I returned to Munich to attend the Mystery Drama performances, with which the anthroposophical summer events began. I was now to see the Mystery Plays for the first time on the stage.[31] On reading the first drama, it had initially meant so little to me that I could have repeated the words of Estella in the Prologue as corresponding to my own impression. She terms this style "didactic-allegorical," saying it "looks at cardboard cut-outs, instead of living people, and admires a symbolic course of events." And when Rudolf Steiner asked me at that time about my impression, I had to admit ashamedly, that I could not as yet find a relation to it.

"If people were to take it up in the right way, I would not need to write any more books or give any more lectures," he said to me.

And when, straight afterwards, he himself read Scene 7 of this drama, the scene in the Spirit Land, my inner response to the rhythms and sounds of these words was so strong and immediate that their effect on me was conclusive, in fact blissful, in spite of all my opinions and prejudices. As Rudolf Steiner told us, this work matured in him for twenty-one years. It is the metamorphosis of Goethe's *Fairy Tale of the Green Snake and the Beautiful Lily* Like a seed, like a depiction in miniature of the new mystery character of our age, this *Fairy Tale* pervaded the inspired soul of Goethe, to enter the general culture. Now, in the year 1912, as the mighty scenes passed before me on the stage, I could experience the words of Sophia in replying to Estella:

> You believe it only possible to have thoughts about a character; while it would have to take shape of itself. You do not wish to recognize that thought immerses itself in the creative spirit, touching the primal source of existence, revealing itself as the creative germ. As little as the forces of the seed first teach the plant how to grow, but show

themselves to be the living essence within it, so our ideas do not teach; they pour themselves into our being, giving rise to and bestowing life within us.

In seeing the events unfold on stage, I now no longer experienced these figures as bloodless or abstract. I recognized living archetypes in them, at work in my own soul, in other human beings, as well as in the great events taking place in the world.

As though mysteriously among them stood
the full archetype of Man;
it shows itself sub-divided in many
souls, just as the one light
reveals itself in the rainbow
in many different colours.

In this way it was possible to experience oneself within the diversity of these figures, through which there shone the true picture of Man. *"Know thyself,"* was the pronouncement of the divinity, directed to the neophyte in the Eleusinian mysteries. And what emerged as an answer from the soul of the mystic following such knowledge were the word, *"You are."*

When I once asked Rudolf Steiner whether the Bible stories were historical fact, he answered in the affirmative, and when I was astonished that it was possible for all these personalities and events to be at the same time symbols and embody ideas, he said, smiling, "God is a great dramaturge — He rehearses until it is finally right." When I questioned him further, concerning the Virgin Mary, who is at the same time the Virgin Sophia, he explained to me, "Mary was a pure woman; through living next to Christ Jesus, she became so refined that only pure wisdom itself could live in her." He said that St John, who is the bearer of love, could not have been effective on the earth without this form-giving wisdom. Therefore, He united them both under the Cross.

Here is not the place to say more about the content of the dramas. One has to experience them in the order of their "architectural" composition, in their dramatic action, in their form of speech and colour-mood. To "explain" or "interpret" them would be to misconstrue them. Here it is not a matter of rational comprehension, but of the soul's transformation.

The following summer, I was also able to participate in the preparations for the Mystery Dramas. Over a period of six to eight weeks, the new fourth drama, *The Souls' Awakening*, together with the third, *The Guardian of the Threshold*, were rehearsed. Sets and costumes were produced in this short period of time according to Rudolf Steiner's indications. Later, in his course on dramatic art, he went into the use of colours on the stage. Each scene of the plays was written down and given over to the printer directly before the rehearsals.

As I entered the hall for the first rehearsal, where all the participants of the play were gathered, the chorus of gnomes was just then being gone through. Steiner took a short, round wooden dowel in each hand, and while hopping in a crouching position, he demonstrated how the gnomes would have to move and how they were to do eurythmy with the wooden dowels. On this occasion I saw the young girl for the first time through whom he had introduced this new art, Lory Smits. She was eighteen years old, a slim girl with chestnut-brown hair and shining blue eyes, framed by dark eyebrows. She resembled a Greek *Kore*, her arms especially recalling those of a Greek sculpture. I heard Rudolf Steiner say to her, "Fräulein Smits, you know the principles and can now develop the eurythmy forms for the gnomes and the sylphs." He chose the cast himself for these spirit choruses. I belonged to the sylphs and, as a matter of course, to the Luciferic beings. During the midday break, Lory Smits practiced with the "sylphs," and we had to appear right afterwards before Rudolf Steiner at the rehearsal. None of us had had any notion of eurythmy before that!

Seeing Lory Smits demonstrate the individual sounds, you had to hold your breath. In her movements there was what can be experienced with a flower bud; something held back physically, but radiating ethereally into space. In his address before the first eurythmy performance, Rudolf Steiner said that eurythmy had become possible due to the personal attributes of Fräulein Smits. And on a later occasion, with her this art had really passed over into flesh and blood. If her personal destiny had not later prevented her from developing eurythmy further, I believe she would have imbued it with a particular cosmic and sacred character. She resembled a little priestess; there was something Apollonian and radiant in her manner.

How rich was this time in which we were together with Rudolf Steiner from morning till evening, experiencing him also as a producer and actor. Most of the parts were allocated by him, according to the nature of each player. And the effect was unique, since no one imagined their achievement to be anything exceptional. All served the whole with humility.

In the role of Maria, one experienced Marie von Sivers as she was in life; fiery and serving the spirit unconditionally. And it was a fine thing to experience, along with her earnestness, her childlike directness, her humour and her laughter, which she often did not master, so that during the rehearsal she was unable to begin her monologue. It was through human qualities of this kind that the Mystery Drama performances came alive at that time.

Understandably, the wish arose with those who had recognized the significance of the Mystery Dramas, to free them from the atmosphere of the operetta house, where they were performed, and to create a worthy setting for them in Munich. They wanted to erect a building, the architecture of which corresponded to the spirit of the mysteries of our time. Thus several Munich friends went to Rudolf Steiner to request a design for a building, to be constructed under his supervision. Large sums had already been made available for this. Probably no one was as yet fully clear about the wider cultural implications of this request. After some reflection, Rudolf Steiner accepted this plan in principle, and a building site was purchased. A building association, the *Johannesbauverein* — named after the main character in the Mystery Dramas — was founded. This drew many small, as well as large contributions. The building was to stand surrounded by residential housing for friends. When I was asked whether I wanted a studio in one of the houses, I replied, somewhat cluelessly, that in terms of destiny, I probably belonged in Russia, and would have to work there later on. Disconcerted by much I had seen that was inartistic in visual art in the Society — occult seals, dramas by Edouard Schuré, various pictures hanging in the living rooms of anthroposophical friends — I was sceptical about what arose from our midst in this way. I had long since recognized the significance of Rudolf Steiner's work for our entire culture. It was, therefore, both inconsistent and superficial of me to regard these pedagogical expedients as though they realized his artistic intentions. I harboured an unconscious anxiety, a fear that what was to enter culture by means of anthroposophy would initially have a paralyzing, deadening effect on those intimate soul experiences, those delicate moods of the soul which cannot be comprehended in concepts, from which artistic fantasy emerges. A world of such moods lived in me, which I wanted to give shape to and protect. I was in the situation of the wealthy youth, not wanting to hand over what I possessed. From a certain point of view, my anxiety was justified. I lost this world for many long years, and counted in Russia as a frightful example of the detrimental effect of anthroposophy: "Look," it was said, "this girl showed genius; what became of her?"

The reason for my lack of productivity was not anthroposophy itself, however, but the manner in which I had taken it up: theoretically, without sufficient energy in penetrating to the sources of my own spiritual experience. I have already referred to the inner dichotomy in which I found myself then. In addition, at that time it was hardly possible to assess the extent, the sheer scale of the crisis of civilization. I was still unaware that it is less a matter of whether individuals achieve something of greater or lesser significance out of forces they have brought with them, than of laying new seeds for the future. Very few knew then that humanity stood before an imminent catastrophe, and that everyone, along with our whole culture, would have to go through nothingness, in order to find something new beyond this nothingness. History had reached the point where a curve leading from the periphery to the middle ends and another begins next to it, leading to the periphery, as in the zodiacal sign of Cancer. Whoever does not willingly take the risk of plunging into the void, stands to be hurled into the void by world events.

The plan to erect the building in Munich fell through. The aesthetic building committee of the city of Munich rejected the design by Rudolf Steiner.

Destiny spoke through a minor architect who sat on this committee, and believed the effect of a church he had built in the neighbourhood would be undermined. Swiss friends offered a site for the building on a hill in Dornach near Basle. *Bluthügelweg* (Blood Hill Road) was the name given the road leading onto this hill (after a historic battle fought there in 1499). Now the building was to stand in the open, exposed to the eyes of the world, arousing not only interest, but also hostility. Since the building was now not in Germany but in a neutral country, the representatives of eighteen different countries were able to work together on it during the First World War, though they fought each other outside. During the Second World War also, the continuity of the anthroposophical work at the Goetheanum was not interrupted.

The Visible Word

From my earliest childhood, when I still did not know the conceptual meaning of many words, I responded inwardly in such a lively manner to their tones, that their sounds not only formed a mental image, but had to be expressed with the whole body. When our maids sang the popular song, "Tyrant, tyrant, oh, why do you love me!" I felt the "t" as something descending onto me from above, the "y," pronounced as an "i," went through me from head to foot, the "r" set me in motion; "an" had me push myself off from the springy sofa with splayed legs. This jumping on the sofa was for me "Tyrant, tyrant"! They also sang a sad folk song, "and the peahen flew away, over the wide, blue sea..." Peahen is *pavà* in Russian. With "p" I had first instinctively to draw my "wings" together to my head, then spread them out, in a "v" move as though carried by the waves of the air, in "a" spread my wings again. Sea, *moryà*: through the "m" it was deep, through the "o" encompassing. In the "r" this water rolled, in the "a" it extended itself, and so on.

I also remember how my brother and I, when we were still not yet able to pronounce the words properly, made philological observations, even conducting debates about what an object really ought to be called, before going to sleep in our little beds. When at four years of age I had to begin speaking French with the governess, I found the words not at all similar. In the Russian word *voda* (water) there was water, the waves in "v," the encompassing roundness in "o," and in "d" the soft falling. And *eau!* How naked and impoverished. Or the word *épi* (ear of corn) instead of *kólos.* In *kólos* one heard after all by means of the "k" at the same time how it had something that stood; the "o" is warm and oval, in the "l" life unfolds, and it rustles and shines with its awns in the "s;" *épi* was dead and fixed. I refused to start; and for a long time did not want to repeat the French words. Later, as every child remembers, in learning poems it was first of all the sound which meant something. The actual meaning often only occurred to one years later. In my early youth I liked a poem by Balmont in which he reproduces the mood of spring in words with "l" running over many lines. In this way the watery, budding aspect of spring was conveyed. In my first poems I made use of alliteration and Vyatsheslav Ivanov, who worked quite consciously with certain sounds and rhythms — he possessed knowledge in this art — encouraged me in this. There is a sonnet by him in which my name, Margarita, is unsealed in accordance with its sounds.[32]

The legend makes sense to me according to which, after the Creation, Adam gave every creature its name. He alone could do this, because all attributes that each creature possesses combined in him, just as individual sounds are contained in a word. That the creative word, concealed in the human being, can also reveal itself through its gesture is something I experienced in eurythmy. Now I grasped what Rudolf Steiner had meant in asking me after the lecture on the prologue to the Gospel of St John, "Could you dance that?"

A pupil of Steiner, Clara Smits, had the thought that, by means of certain movements corresponding to the life organism, one could harmonize it, strengthen it, and in this way have a healing effect on the entire human being. After the sudden death of her husband, her eighteen-year-old daughter had to take up a profession, and the girl wanted to learn an art of movement of some kind. The mother asked Rudolf Steiner's advice. He sent for her and gave her the rudiments of eurythmy.

"Now the little one has to learn many things which she will afterwards have to forget," he said.

When I got to know Lory Smits at the Mystery Play rehearsals, she was already permitted to give courses, and I took part in them. I remember being moved to the point of tears on seeing Rudolf Steiner's poem, *Der Wolkendurchleuchter,* performed in eurythmy for the first time:

> The cloud illuminator
> May he illuminate
> May he irradiate
> May he shine through
> May he warm through
> Even us.

Three figures moved in a circle, their faces turned toward the centre. In raising their hands, spreading them out or crossing them, taking a step out from the centre or toward the centre again, they formed a living architecture, a visible prayer. I experienced the same thing with the representation of *Hallelujah* or *Evoe*. The movement for every sound corresponded completely to my own feelings.

The poet Andrei Belyi came to Munich at this time with his young wife.[33] In my studio he got to know Lory Smits and eurythmy. For him too, it was a matter of recognizing what he had always known. In Moscow he had a kind of poet's academy where he studied the rhythmical and phonetic laws of poetry with young people. Lory Smits showed him the arm movements for the sounds of speech and the figures which the feet followed, so as to correspond to the character of the poem in terms of thinking, feeling and willing. In this way the inner order of the poem was made visible, its true worth was revealed.

In comparing single words in different languages, which she demonstrated, we were able to recognize the special character of each folk soul.

At the conclusion of the conference there was a semi-public eurythmy performance in which I participated. When Lory Smits presented Goethe's poem *Charon*, dressed in yellow and with the Tao in her hand, she made the impression of being very tall in her hieratic movements.

It was agreed that I would go to Düsseldorf and stay with the Smits for a few months, in order to work with Lory. However, it was not a matter of being untrue to painting, which I did not know how to continue. Naturalism no longer satisfied me, Expressionism in the form in which it had appeared seemed arbitrary to me. Cubism struck me as an expression of the atomizing forces of our time. A realistic rendering of visions such as was sometimes to be seen in occult circles, I viewed as the worst kind of non-art. From eurythmy I hoped for a fructification of my art.

Lory Smits often told me how Rudolf Steiner had introduced her to this new art. Nothing dogmatic was taught her, everything derived from experience. She learned to experience the vowels as an expression of specific moments of inner life, the consonants on the other hand, as a response to the external world. He would describe a landscape in a peaceful mood, and as an answer to this a gesture arose; when the mood of nature changed, becoming turbulent, the gesture altered correspondingly.

What Rudolf Steiner indicated was always a "point from which much could be developed," to use Goethe's expression. A series of exercises with copper rods required considerable dexterity, and Steiner valued dexterity.

When he came to Cologne for the Christmas conference, we showed him what we had worked out, and we were asked to perform our programme, not only at this conference in Cologne but also in Berlin soon afterwards.[34] The scene of the "penitents" from *Faust* was adopted, just as we had done it then, in the *Faust* performances in Dornach, for as long as this scene was presented in eurythmy.

The work in eurythmy had a significant impact on my life. I now felt different in my body, stood with greater certainty on the ground and at the same time more lightly. And how much more intimate and direct did my relation to nature become, in experiencing the gesture of the plants and the mountains, the nature of the air and water around me as "belonging" to me. More aware, more in control, I felt myself become more open at the same time, more transparent for the life of the world, as though invisible feelers extended from me, reaching to the stars, scanning the invisible.

At that time I saw eurythmy mainly as a new art which, in spiritualizing the whole human being, was able to have a stimulating effect on all other arts. Its far-reaching significance became ever more manifest, to the extent that the tendencies of our civilization unmasked themselves. As yet, one could have no notion, just how rapidly the deadening tendencies would march onwards, gradually making human beings into robots. These mechanizing, and at the same time animalizing, forces threatened to destroy the image of Man. Rudolf Steiner worked to counter these powers by means of his indications in every field of culture.

Having returned to Munich, I heard with keen anticipation reports of the progress of the building in Dornach, on which a number of friends were already actively engaged, and I intended going there myself after Easter.

Between the Mystery Plays in Munich and my stay in Düsseldorf, I visited Max in Koktebel together with Nyusha, and was pleasantly surprised that I was received without inhibition and with great warmth by his friends in Theodosia. His mother, as attached to me as ever, approached me in an especially touching manner. He himself could not hear enough about eurythmy and the future building. In his art he had acquired great mastery. His poems were then mainly dedicated to his country and its past. Today, I still think back with gratitude to those autumn weeks.

I went to Moscow for the official opening of the Russian Anthroposophical Society.[35] As I drove through the streets brightly lit by the moon on that cold September evening between Pretshistenka and Arbat, wax candles burned in every church and chapel for the festive service; it was the eve of the birth of the Virgin Mary. I was glad the dedication took place just on that evening, and that all of Russia celebrated with us. On this occasion we commemorated Soloviev as the first to experience the meeting with the Virgin Sophia after Dante. Our celebration took place in a basement room next to the small church of the Ascension of Mary over the Graves. Candles were lit, and all the women wore white. For the first part, which was to have an official character, we had invited the district police chief, for political reasons. He sat there, awkward and embarrassed, quickly excusing himself as soon as there was a pause. Then our chairman spoke to us on the theme of responsibility, a word that often crossed his lips on other occasions as well. He did not stand out as having special talent, was perhaps somewhat stiff, but reliable, thorough, and imbued with deep seriousness. I read the poem by Soloviev, *The Three Meetings*, in which the Virgin Sophia herself is addressed, which bestows something magical and heartfelt on the poem. Then I attempted to characterize the task before us in Russia, and the particular dangers connected with Russia's future mission.

We asked Rudolf Steiner for a name for the study group in Moscow, expecting that it would be named after Vladimir Soloviev or another great mystic. We were astonished, even taken aback, when we heard the name, Mikhail Lomonosov. Whoever gave a thought to Mikhail Lomonosov anymore? In school we had learned the odes of this eighteenth-century poet by heart. They had seemed pompous to me, and yet at sixteen I was carried away involuntarily by the majestic and vivid descriptions of nature, linked to the deepest religious thoughts. His was a curiously stirring destiny. Born in the year 1711, the son of a simple fisherman on the White Sea in the province of Archangel,

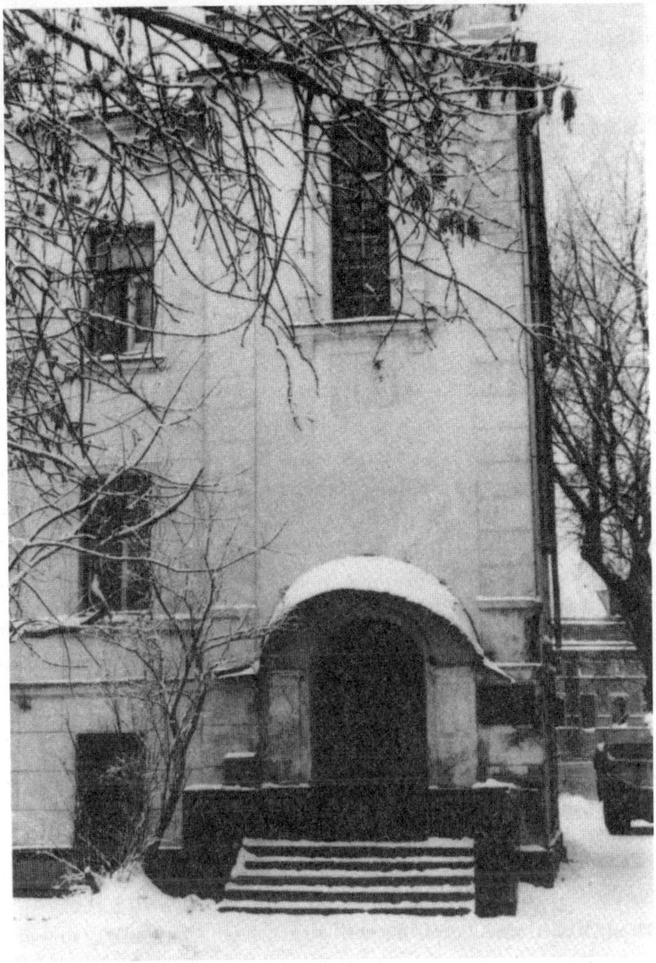

The house in which the Anthroposophical Society in Moscow was situated in the winter of 1917/18. Then called Poleuktow Street, now No.5 Sechonow Street

he was named after the country's patron saint, the archangel Michael. One finds impressions in his poems of the northern lights, the starry sky, of sunrises, which can be experienced only in this region close to the Arctic Circle, where cosmic effects take precedence over earthly ones. As a boy, he secretly left his family and went on foot all the way to Moscow, in order to gain an education. The city (it was right after the death of Peter the Great) still consisted, apart from the Kremlin with its white churches and the many golden cupolas, entirely of wooden houses with painted carvings. This fisherman's son was to become the founder of Russian culture, the first to establish the laws of the

Russian language, its grammar. A great mathematician — recognized as a genius by the Swiss mathematician, Leonhard Euler — he was a physicist, chemist and astronomer, and anticipated spectral analysis. He made discoveries in various areas of science and invented a kind of glass-mosaic, with which he executed a number of murals himself. Yet he lacked self-control and was an intemperate drinker. He stood for the idea that science and religion are two sisters, daughters of one creator. To see a contradiction in them meant slandering their "father." The scientific researches of Mikhail Lomonosov were little understood in Russia; he had no successors. Peter the Great saw the technology in Europe and brought it to Russia, being possessed of a spirit that denies the spirit. Mikhail Lomonosov was the first Russian not to think in an outdated, medieval manner, but to be inspired by the spirit of modern times, and to direct his vision freely into the universe. With that, he led Russian culture out of its eastern, dream-like mysticism, caught up in what is emotional, and united it with European spirituality. And yet he sought, in keeping with the true nature of Russia and its patron saint, the Creator in the creation. He sought the Word that underlies the creation of the world, and that became flesh in the Son of Man.

Only gradually did I come to understand that this is our task also. The mission of Michael in our time.

In a remarkable coincidence of destiny, at the same hour in which we were gathered in Moscow to celebrate the founding of our Anthroposophical Society, the laying of the foundation stone of the Goetheanum took place on the Dornach hill. It took place amid a thunderstorm and rain in the evening, by torchlight, in the presence of a small group of friends who happened to be in Dornach by reason of destiny. Later, when the building was sacrificed to the flames in the transition of 1922 to 1923, once again, at precisely the same time, the Russian Anthroposophical Society was banned by the Bolshevik regime.

The House of the Word

The day's work was over when I climbed the Dornach hill for the first time. From below, I already saw the two cupolas of the building between the blossoming cherry trees. At that time they were not yet covered with the silvery, shining Norwegian slate, but only decked over with fresh wood, and they shone like two golden orbs in the light of the setting sun. Up on the path between the canteen, then still a small wooden shed, and the building site, I encountered a crowd of artists in light-coloured work clothes coming down from the building. I knew most of them from Munich. The evening sun was mirrored in their shining eyes. The blue eyes of Max Wolffhügel remain as an incidental impression in my memory, and the sunburnt face, as though carved of wood, of his friend Strauss. They greeted me as blessed spirits might greet a newly arrived soul in Paradise.

I entered the building site alone. The building was still full of scaffolding, both inside and outside. Behind it could be seen the large shed of the carpentry workshop and a few smaller sheds. I went in through the south entrance into a rounded concrete hallway, where parts of the huge architrave stood: masses of wood three metres high, consisting of laminated boards, which indicated in rough outline the intended sculptural form. They had the effect of rock formations belonging to primeval ages.

A few had already been worked on and carved by artists in accordance with the wax model by Rudolf Steiner. The surfaces of this sculpture were crystalline and plant-like at the same time. One form flowed out of another, led to the next, completing and perfecting it. Nothing was separate in itself in this space; it was as if a being were revealing its love in manifold transformations. I was relieved of my anxiety that the new forms would remain alien to me. For the soul these forms were of kindred origin.

The next morning I heard from a distance the tapping of hundreds of hammers and mallets. "It is coming into being," was the exhilarating feeling. Can there be a greater good fortune than to participate in a work of whose necessity one is convinced? It would seem that the cathedrals of the Middle Ages must have been erected with the same enthusiasm. It was touching to see old people, able only to sharpen our gouges or grind the colours, doing this faithfully over a period of years. I believe the friends who collaborated in those months in Dornach will agree with me when I say that we were filled at that time with the purest enthusiasm. If, later on, our mood sometimes clouded over, it was because each of us brought along with us dead thoughts from the world; doubt, illusory feelings, lack of courage, or an overestimation of our own personality. And when the fury of the World War was unleashed, the work in Dornach had to be continued under this tragic sign.

On entering the building on that first morning, I received a gouge and a mallet like all the other artists. I was directed to a capital in the concrete hallway and shown how I was to carve. In a room over in the carpentry workshop stood the model of the building that Rudolf Steiner had modelled himself in wax. One saw in cross-section two circular spaces with their intersecting cupolas, a larger one conceived as the auditorium, and a smaller one as the stage area. Based on this model and the plaster model of the architrave, the group leaders indicated to the carvers the surfaces they had to free from the superfluous mass of wood. Layer by layer the wood was taken away with a gouge. The direction of the grooves had to follow the direction of the surface, so that they constituted a kind of hatching, on which the light played. Even though a large amount of this wood was to be removed, one had to work in a conscious and alert manner, so that the foundation out of which the forms grew did not suddenly become too thin, potentially creating a hole.

Around midday the hammering gradually subsided. Rudolf Steiner entered the hall. He appeared to me younger and fresher than during the lecture cycles. In Dornach, on account of the muddy grounds, he wore high boots, which together with his customary frock coat, recalled the time of Goethe. I was told that he had begun to carve himself the day before. We followed him into a shed where sections of the architrave were set up. He climbed lightly onto a few crates and began to work. We stood behind him, and I could see his profile and his hands. For a long time he carved silently, his features concentrated and jubilant, as though he were inwardly listening in on something beautiful; it was like a

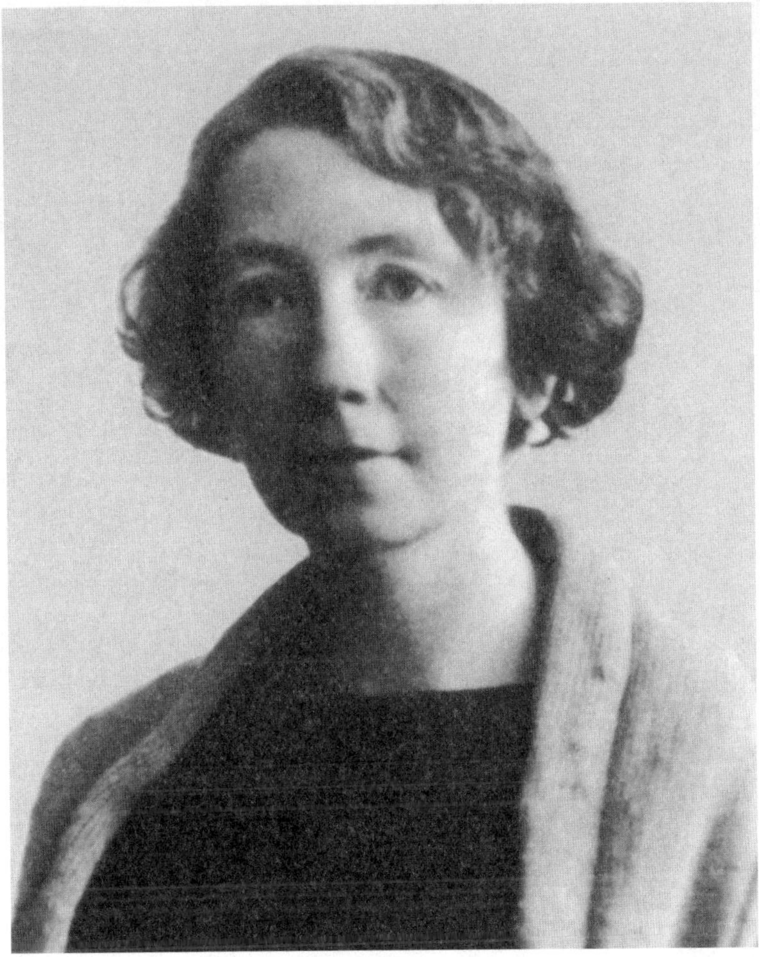

Margarita Woloschin around 1914

dialogue with the wood. Cautiously and unfalteringly he took away the wood in layers, as though seeing exactly the limits of the form hidden within it and as though only wanting to free it from the superfluous material. Then he said something like the following, "In sculpture one has to feel the planes, one must be mindful of the planes in space. The edges in sculpture must arise as an outcome, as the boundary between two surfaces; they may not be determined beforehand. One has to be curious about the edges, that helps a lot."

He turned to a little black-haired Austrian woman and said to her, "You must put off working for a few days; you have over-exerted yourself." She did this only reluctantly.

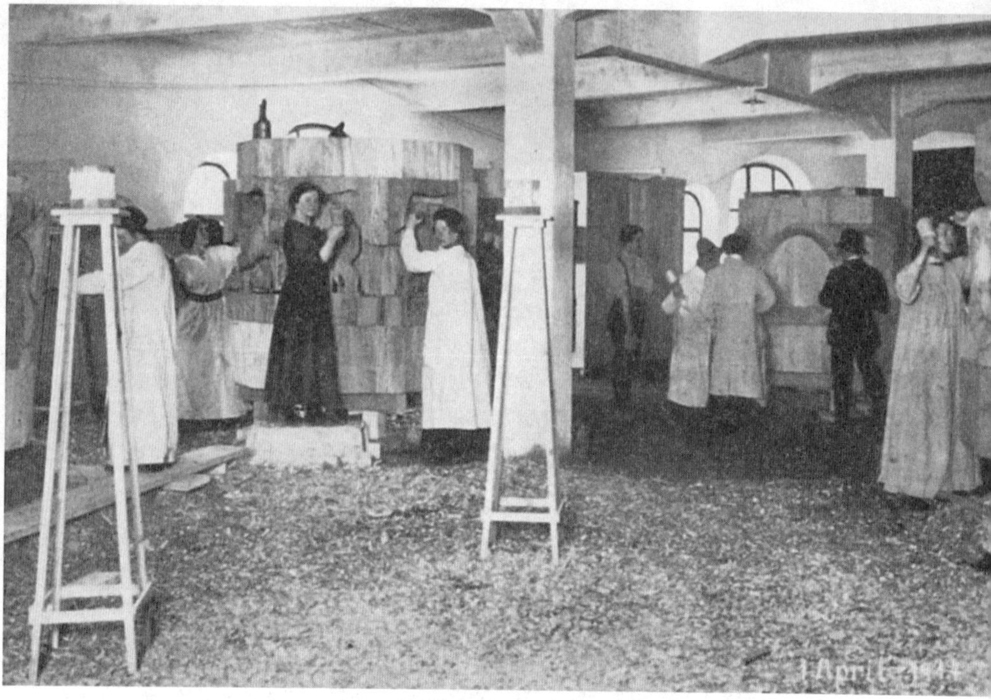

Carving the capitals of the first Goetheanum, April 1, 1914

When I greeted Rudolf Steiner soon after that, he asked me how these forms pleased me. Each time he greeted one, and one met his affirmative glance, it was as though this moment were anticipated out of the future. One had the feeling that the one he was greeting and who was permitted to greet him was, in fact, not really fully present. Inwardly, one answered with a solemn promise to be fully present some day. His gaze, in which lived the highest victory, spoke at the same time of the whole gravity of a world tragedy, indeed a world catastrophe. The love which one met in this gaze was akin to death; it gave direction and at the same time renewed courage. On each occasion one was almost torn out of time, and for this reason had to be strong and matter-of-fact in order to be able to answer objectively. And on this occasion I could not do that. Thus my reply was inept and much too reserved, so that he could not possibly infer from it how much I loved these forms already. He said, "You will take to them. I would like you to learn to understand this building with its single axis of symmetry. Here for the first time a building with a single axis of symmetry has been attempted."

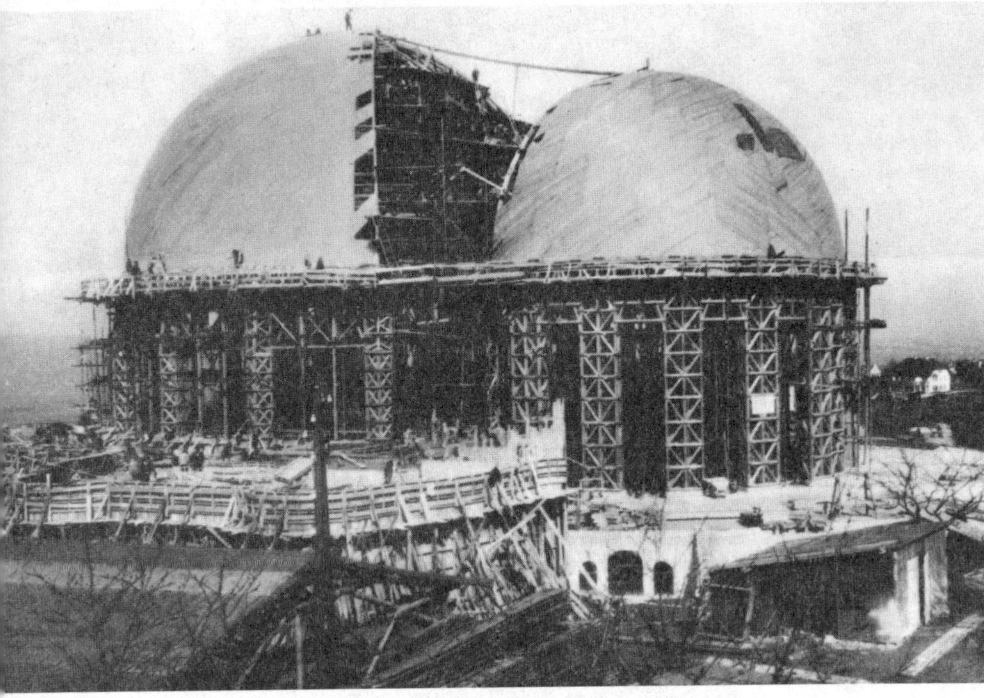

Building the two intersecting cupolas of the first Goetheanum

At midday we all went to the canteen. At well-scoured tables sat cheerful people. At the table of the "strong men" (painters and sculptors), most of whom I knew from earlier on, I noticed a mature, bearded individual of Roman appearance in a blue smock. I was struck by the healthy freshness of his complexion. He had long fingers and wore a signet ring. It was the leading engineer, Joseph Englert, director of a Basle construction company, a native of the Alpine region of Grisons, who advised Rudolf Steiner in technical matters. On the way back to the building after lunch, I made his acquaintance, and asked him what Rudolf Steiner had meant, in speaking of a single axis of symmetry with this building. He invited me into his construction hut, showed me the ground plan and explained the numerical relationships underlying the building.

It was a matter of two intersecting circles. Seven columns on each side carried the mighty architrave of the larger space, which was to be the auditorium. The smaller architrave of the stage area was supported by twelve columns. The amphitheatre-like incline of the auditorium required the seven columns to become increasingly higher toward

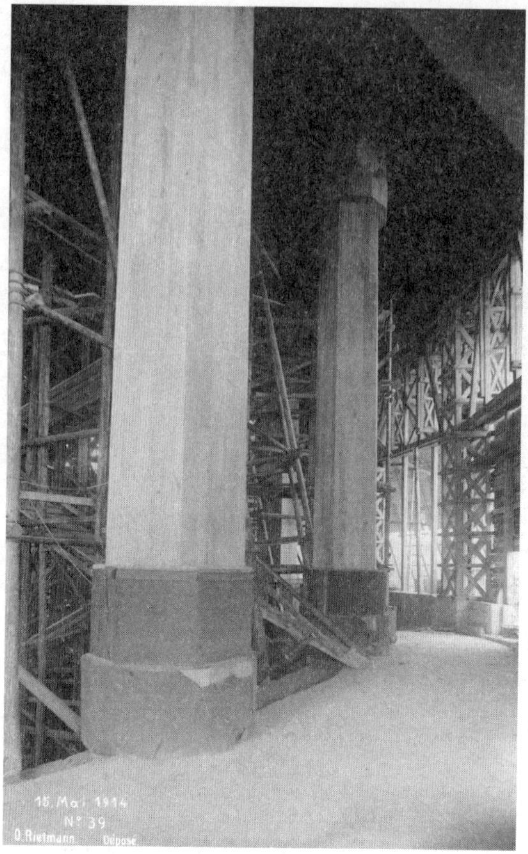

The pillars of the first Goetheanum, May 1914

the proscenium and correspondingly thicker. The sculpture of the capitals, of the bases and of the architrave underwent a development, so that in this building only the right (south side) and the left (north side) mirrored each other, overcoming the static nature of the closed form and bringing about an experience of movement, of ongoing development.

In the course of the next few days, the engineer guided me over the scaffolding, and showed me the construction of the small cupola. Both cupolas were double-shelled, on the principle of the violin sounding board. It was a remarkable experience to stand in the space between the half-spheres arching one over the other of the inner and outer roofing of the small cupola, where all normal spatial relationships were as though annulled.

Since I lived rather far away from the building, I often spent the midday break in the construction hut, and my new friend told me about the conversations he had had in the mornings with Rudolf Steiner.

"Today I told him," he recounted, "that the gentlemen of the construction company, who are against anthroposophy, wanted to delegate the construction of a city slaughterhouse to me at the same time, to annoy me, which of course I rejected."

But Rudolf Steiner had said in reply, "As long as meat is eaten, slaughterhouses have to be built, and it is after all an interesting task to build a slaughterhouse on a really practical basis."

At that, I thought of Tolstoy, who believed he had to flee civilization as something evil, while Rudolf Steiner united himself with it, in order to gradually transform it. From what the engineer told me, I was able to infer with what attentiveness Rudolf Steiner treated his co-workers. One day he noticed that something was troubling the engineer. Asking after the cause, he learned that his optician had ascertained a cataract in one eye that threatened to pass over to the other eye. In answer to the question as to whether he had had a difficult youth, the engineer had to answer in the affirmative.

"This illness is a consequence of it," said Rudolf Steiner, "but we shall try to halt the process. On no account will it pass over to the other eye." He prescribed a tea, which the patient was to take at certain intervals, and gave him at the same time a meditation. The engineer did not complain anymore later about his eyes. As far as I know, he retained his power of sight into old age.

Once on coming to work, we learned that Rudolf Steiner would be holding a lecture that morning for the co-workers. We gathered in the carpentry workshop and looked for places to sit on wooden boards, crates and machines. When Rudolf Steiner entered, he seemed pleased at the motley impression made by his audience.

This lecture was the first of a whole series which he at first held only for the co-workers on the building, then for an ever larger circle of friends from outside. He began by indicating the increasing responsibility, the more assets friends place at the disposal of the building. What was intended with this building, he said, could only be a small beginning in a new direction. We would have to assume responsibility for this on our own account, since the critique of experts was always derisive when something new was placed into the world. Then he related how, during his period of study in Vienna, he had become acquainted with the ideas of the architects active there, whose materialistic conception of art drove one to despair despite their brilliance. Ornamentation, the whole style of building was derived only from technical and utilitarian considerations. He spoke of our building, in which the interior architecture was an expression of the word spoken within it. This building was an organic whole.

Every morning Steiner went over the building site with Marie von Sivers and leading co-workers. The groups which then formed around him reminded one of Raphael's *School of Athens*. One of them would unroll architectural drawings in front of him, of window frames or doors; others showed him plywood panels with painting grounds. Yet others came to him with plaster models of the capitals, seeking a solution to sculptural problems. Conscious of their limitations, each wanted only to learn and to serve the great work. And Rudolf Steiner, who had taken upon himself the greatest difficulties and concerns with this task, with what warm gratitude did he receive the smallest collaboration!

In correcting an architrave he once said, "This form here is too bombastic, it has too much of a potbelly." What he meant with that, I understood only gradually. Only with time was I able to grasp the nature of the sculptural forms of the Goetheanum, of sculpture in general. The art of sculpture arises when the human being has the need to project those forces which enliven and shape his body into space, bringing them to a state of rest. This "rest," however, has nothing static about it; it is the equilibrium of polar forces, a state of dynamic tension, of rhythm in a living form metamorphosis. In accordance with the law of the living, a hollow has to follow an elevation; a contraction must follow an expansion. What happens sequentially in time, here becomes spatial. Sculpture has to hold the living centre between fixed mineral form and unformed "bombast." Thus the double-bent plane is neither rigid nor formless. I remember how Rudolf Steiner demonstrated this principle, in twisting and bending the border of his felt-hat.

"The forms of our building," he said, "are not taken from nature, even if some people will look for similarities to nature. The artist can learn from nature how she creates her forms; but he may not stop short at the stage of an apprentice, but must create out of the same sources out of which she herself creates." And suddenly, turning to me, "Do you not believe that, Miss Sabashnikova?"

He always called me — intentionally, as he said himself — by my maiden name. In answer to his question, I replied, "Oh yes, I do."

Afterwards, however, I asked myself, whether as a matter of fact I was as finished with naturalism as I thought I was. Naturalism certainly did not satisfy me, still less theosophical-symbolic pictures, head-oriented or visionary creations. Cubism, which treated what is living like something dead, seemed to me demonic, and what I had experienced till then of Futurism, arbitrary. I loved the ancient mosaics and the Russian icons, but did not know what language the spirit active in the present required.

One morning, while I was carving, the engineer whispered to me that I should come with him. In the large auditorium space, the scaffolding had been dismantled. The capitals were already mounted on the columns. A crane lifted the giant blocks of the architraves, to be inserted in between the columns and the cupola. This cyclopean work appeared child's play for modern technology, so easily and rapidly did everything proceed. The engineer, who directed the assembly, seemed to me like a magician.

After the evening meal, I went into the building again. It was the time of year when the days are longest, and the setting sun threw a warm light through the open west facade of the building onto the variously toned wooden sculpture. Then dusk began to fall. Suddenly I heard footsteps, and someone switched on the light in the large cupola, which cast a glaring light on the architrave. It was Rudolf Steiner, who had come to look at the sculptural forms. I wanted to withdraw so as not to disturb him, but he began the conversation himself.

"It will have to become quite different," he said, "it has not yet come to life." Rudolf Steiner looked at the forms for a long time and said once again, "Everything will have to be reworked still."

There was a great sadness in his gaze. How lonely he must be! None of us at that time could create these forms out of our own experience. When the scaffold was put up again, the carvers continued working on the architraves for several years afterwards. And yet in these few days in which the hall could be seen as a whole, it made an inexpressibly festive, solemn impression.

The sculptural forms of the architrave in the larger space were different in character from those of the smaller space. As the first wave, carved in simple surfaces from the almost minerally hard white beech-wood, the architrave arched over the main entrance in the west, evolving further toward the east in the so-called "snake motif." However, from the east powerful forces came to meet it. This dialogue of forces determined the forms and their movement. The relief-sculpture proceeded through various woods (ash, cherry, oak, elm and birch), rather as the bow of a violin brushes against different strings. And each wood responded out of its own nature. Later, when Rudolf Steiner elaborated on the nature of single folk-souls from the forms of the capitals of the large hall, he said that he had discovered this correspondence only afterwards. Thus archetypal laws spoke through these forms which could be recognized in various phenomena and in diverse fields. When an artist admitted to Rudolf Steiner, that he could make nothing of these forms, he replied, "And yet, my dear fellow, you experience these forms every night!" This meant that every night the spirit, in freeing itself from the body, was in that realm of consciousness where these creative archetypal images were at work, and where there was no longer any "inside" and "outside," valid only for our day consciousness. These archetypal pictures and forces, always present in our subconsciousness, were here raised into consciousness through art.

In the small cupola space one experienced the direction above-below as, so to speak; a "breathing." I felt the sculptural forms of this space as having a "crystalline" sound. Between the two last columns in the east, under a carved vault, the so-called "baldachin," the large wooden sculpture was to stand, in which the entire building resonated harmoniously. Uniting above and below, right and left, it was the starting point and at the same time the culmination of the whole space; a human figure standing on a small projection of rock. The *Representative of Humanity*, as Rudolf Steiner called it, avoiding a dogmatic designation. From the right, lowered hand a force seemed to go into the ground, to a being that writhed in a deep cave beneath the rocky outcrop. This figure had a human head, bat wings and quite contorted, root-like, gnarled limbs. The left arm of the central figure was raised to another being, which plummeted head-first from the heights, itself breaking its wings, unable to bear the proximity of the Christ. With this being the countenance had mobile forms;

wings connect the ears and larynx, and appeared to resonate with the harmony of the spheres. Everything about the upper and lower figures was opposite.

With the figure below, the lower half of the countenance predominated, pointing to a strong connection with matter. The forms of this figure were as if carved from without, concave, the slit-eyes set at an angle, and everything was as if knotted and contracted from the cold. On the other hand, the brow of the upper being was over-large, the forms seemingly inflated from within in headstrong obstinacy. The features approximated the Greek ideal with regard to the protruding bridge of the nose and the almond-shaped eyes. The central figure was a balancing out of these contrasts, an affirmation of what was tragic, in which suffering was transformed into strength and love. This impression renewed itself for me every time in contemplating the statue. And I had to think of the words of a simple Russian woman, "Christ needs nothing, He shines also in darkness."

The number of co-workers on the building grew. People came from many countries. From Moscow — one after the other — our friends appeared. The colourful society wandering the paths of Dornach and Arlesheim was different from what the conventional local population was used to. It was colourful in a literal sense. I saw the nice, innocent Polish woman from Paris in an immeasurably large hat, in glaring orange or red clothes, walking along with an elegant Dutch musician. I saw the Frenchwoman with her ancient, half-eagle, half-leonine face, short black hair, close-fitting shirt-like dresses without sleeves, wrapped on cool days in her broad fur shawl. The Russians, intentionally or not, looked mostly rather odd. All these various figures, from Schwabing (Munich's bohemian quarter), the *Quartier Latin*, or Moscow, aroused offence among the conservative village people. Already the fact that lights were burning with us till late in the evening, counted as disreputable waste. Soon the Catholic priest began preaching in the church against anthroposophy as an unchristian teaching.

The Walls Dissolve

Soon after my arrival, Rudolf Steiner applied sweeping surfaces of colour to the large cupola of the wax model. Several painters had already received their sketches for the large cupola from him and were working in studio-like rooms in the building. It was foreseen that I should paint in the small cupola.

"You must be patient," Rudolf Steiner said to me, "and carve a while longer; I also must wait until it comes to me."

To put questions to the spiritual world and wait reverently for the answer, as though waiting for grace, does not mean being passive. We could daily observe with what energy Rudolf Steiner sought for new technical and artistic procedures, trying things out again and again, overcoming the greatest obstacles.

Once, in the early days, when I visited the studio of an older painter, Hermann Linde, who was working on his studies for the painting in the large cupola, Rudolf Steiner came to him and they spoke about various things in connection with the plant colours, with which the painting was to be carried out and which were produced according to his indications. The grounding and the painting medium were spoken of. The gesso primer had to be very white, so that the light shone through the transparent layers of colour. It consisted of chalk, casein and various resins. Wax, cellulose and the resins of the second transparent layer were to protect the fine plant pigment and keep it vivid, as in the blossoms. On these transparent layers, the colours remained as though suspended in space and shone through. I stood to one side, without taking part in the conversation, and thought of the historical moment we were experiencing, when an initiate was fructifying with his knowledge the various realms of life, even into the technical details.

"Why are you standing apart so piously, saying nothing?" Rudolf Steiner asked me wryly.

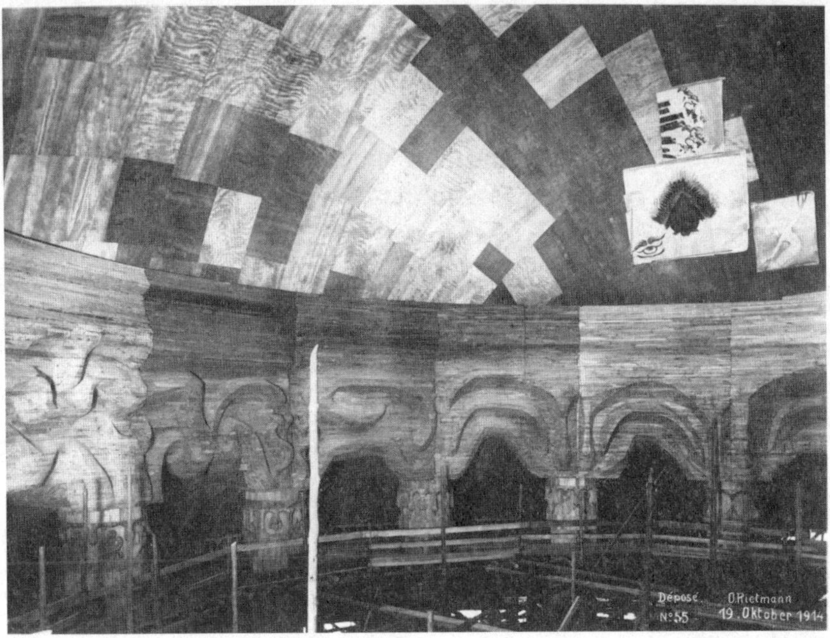

Looking into the larger cupola, October 1914

"I understand too little of organic chemistry," I said in embarrassment.

If I had at that time only understood the hint: take an interest, set to work, study, seek! An attitude of passive piety was of no use to him.

Climbing onto the scaffolding under the large cupola from time to time, I saw huge images rising on the domed ceiling. In the east, where the two cupolas intersected, a large violet surface was laid on. It opened like a chalice toward the east and found its conclusion in the small cupola. From the east a red wave surged, diverging to north and south. It sent out an orange and a yellow curve and poured itself out into the green and blue space of the western half of the dome. Out of the dynamic of the colours, the warmth surging from the front and the coolness surrounding it and merging into the depths, there arose on both sides of the dome a kind of whorl. Pictures of the creation of the world emerged from this movement of colours. Nothing in this building was an after-image of the physical world, but was like a new creation out of the primal Word. And here in the world of colour the Word had become life in the lustre of red, and shone in yellow as the light of the spirit into the blue-green darkness.

These images were such that only a child in their naturalness and naivety, or a great master could have created them.

At that time, astonished like a child, I saw the details arising one after the other, without asking much as to their meaning. Later, having contemplated the single motifs in their relationship to each other over a period of years, I came to experience the dramatic colour interaction as a whole.

The large cupola corresponded to the head of the human being. Humanity's past from primeval times up to the Greek period was presented in it. However, with a work of art, the essential thing is not the content which can be put into words. With this art of painting the incredible drama of the colours was the essential thing, each undergoing its "destiny." The red first surged from the east as the lustre of divine life, was bestowed upon creatures in the form of red rays by blue or blue-violet beings (selflessly stepping back in their blueness), till in the middle of the cupola — in the motif of the Fall of Man — a being appropriated this red to itself, appearing as Lucifer amid the cultural epochs: In the large cupola, the "fall" of the red; in the small cupola, the "redemption" of the red.

Just as the sculptural forms of the two spaces were quite different in character, so too were the painted cupolas. In the large cupola the colour curves predominated, out of which single motifs emerged. In the small cupola, it was the figures that predominated. The red, which in the large cupola proceeded from the divine, undivided lustre of life, went as though through a Fall. It was redeemed and hallowed in the small cupola, in the roses over the *Slavic Human Being* and in the Christianized Lucifer of the central composition. The red blood, bearer of the egoistic "I" became pure, like the sap of the rose, through the Cross, through the sacrifice of redeeming Passion it became the bearer of Christianized individuality. Here the mystery of the Grail was consummated in the world of colour. Golden yellow, the lustre of the spirit, which appeared in the landscapes of the large cupola paintings as "sky," now became the garment of the Redeemer.

Over the dark hill of Golgotha, in light-filled yellow, one saw Him, the same figure as appeared below in the wooden statue, with the same gesture between two world powers, the left hand raised as though victoriously. From the heart of Christ, Lucifer rose amid red flames into the greenish easterly heavens. At the request of the painters,

Rudolf Steiner painted in the small cupola himself. What movement, what glowing life swept like a storm through the streams of colour, veiled one over the other, weaving through everything and creating un-spatial spaces! Out of this becoming, out of these flooding waves, the countenances of the various entelechies looked out. They were characterized with reddish lines, the features mostly asymmetrical and far removed from the classical beauty of the Greeks, yet beautiful through the earnest appearance of truth. A chiaroscuro arose which did not serve sculptural form, but expressed the conflict between the beings of light and the beings of darkness. Cosmic spaces opened up through colour perspective. One believed one heard the converse of the hierarchies, and yet in this thunder there was peace. The small cupola was warm, festive and harmonious in its effect.

Representatives of each cultural epoch formed a circle in the small cupola paintings. I had been given the representative of the Egyptian culture to paint. Rudolf Steiner brought me a small sheet of paper in my studio; the composition was drawn in coloured crayons, and a second time in pencil.[36] The Egyptian initiate, in blue and yellow tones, sat hieratically on a throne, the arms resting on two transparent supports, passing over from sapphire blue into dull green. Behind him there were two triangular shapes, one bluish-violet, with the point directed upwards, interpenetrated by the second in cool rose, with the point below. These painted thrones corresponded to the variously carved seats at the base of each of the twelve columns. Over the Egyptian, an angel towered in cool rose tones, above which was an archangel in fiery red.

Other painters also received their sketches at this time. On measuring the surface I was to paint in the cupola, I noticed that the wings of my angel and the arms of my archangel projected far into the region of my two neighbours. Disconcerted by the lack of space, I communicated my predicament to Rudolf Steiner.

He said, "That does not matter at all. In the spiritual world things do not stand side by side, they interpenetrate."

The next composition I had to paint was the *Slavic Human Being*. In peach-blossom tones, the figure of the Russian stood looking up to the vision of a rose-cross. A dark *doppelgänger* split off from him. A blue angel, blessing the Russian with one hand, pointed with the other to a strange being approaching him from heavenly distances: a winged horse in red with a human face and eight legs. This being gave us a lot of trouble. Rudolf Steiner drew it again much larger, so we could grasp it, but this second image was in every respect like the first. When I asked him how the face of the Russian was to be shown, he said, "You should not represent him as anguished and sentimental, but optimistic about the future and strong."

In the small cupola we worked together peacefully. Our figures likewise stood next to each other peacefully. They were "well-behaved," expressionless, neither disturbing nor furthering each other, until — as already mentioned — as though by storm, Rudolf Steiner altered everything with his own painting.

Things did not proceed as peacefully in the large cupola. There my French friend, Lotus Peralté, by means of the strong, glowing colours with which she carried out the monumental head of the *Ancient Indian*, drove her neighbour, the good old gentleman from Prague, Richard Pollack, into the ground. In his view, the paler the colours were, the more spiritual they would be. And he painted them so "supersensibly" that they were hardly perceptible from down below. Since he was deaf, his wife developed a strong voice. She sided forcefully with him, and under the echoing dome there sounded a frightful "war in heaven."

If one of the painters complained to Rudolf Steiner about his own, or about someone else's "inability," he said the point of working on the building consisted also in people learning from it. What was our "ability" or "inability" in any case with regard to this absolutely new task?

"One is never up to a task, one evolves with the task."

In the summer, the Glass House built for engraving the windows was dedicated with a lecture by Rudolf Steiner.[37] We had decorated the room with garlands of roses and set up long rows of benches in front of the lectern, which stood under one of the two cupolas. I saw that Rudolf Steiner was himself moved by the beauty of the domed space. It was evening and diagonal rays of sunlight fell onto the warm wood of the walls. He stood in front of the tripartite, still unglazed windows. A storm brewed. With urgency, with warmth, indeed with awe, Rudolf Steiner spoke about the task before us, which extended far beyond anything of a personal nature and demanded of us the best forces of heart and mind. The building was to be the educational means of transcending what is personal. In the future, such buildings would be as though legislative, opening the way to conditions worthy of the human being. Meanwhile, a powerful thunderstorm broke and the lecturer had to raise his voice, in order to drown out the thunderclaps. When we stepped outside, the storm had passed. To the west the evening star shone solemnly in the pure blue-green sky.

In the Glass House the artists worked on etching the panes of coloured glass for the tripartite windows of the building. These panes were mounted, for the time being, in the windows of the workshop. The technical apparatus for this work was similar to an electrical dentist's drill. Light places were etched out with a carborundum stone in the transparent coloured material of the glass, which had to be prevented from overheating by continually trickling water over it; also to eliminate glass dust. Thus the image arose through lightening the shadowy depths. The artists sat on high stools in waterproof coats. In this work, as one of them told me, a real conflict took place between the darkness, signifying at the same time the weight and density of the material, and the light, brightness and translucency of the material. With activity, light arises; with inertia it remains dark. Thus the artist experiences the spiritual reality of light and darkness in the very process of working. The sketches of Rudolf Steiner, often barely indicated in pencil, bore a quite different character from the sketches for the cupola painting. More unassuming, yet more mysterious, they were filled with a ceremonial peace, as can be experienced on the face of one who has died. How powerfully effective they were in the building, when the sunlight itself conjured these drawings onto the tripartite windows, which shone like precious stones beneath the dim carved vault separating the architrave and the wall! — The first triptych was green, the second blue, then violet and peach-blossom, arrayed symmetrically in the south and north. These windows neither merely opened a view on to the external landscape, nor did they only transmit the sober white daylight. They pointed paths into another world.

Coloured light flooded through the building, transforming the three-dimensional space into a qualitative, living, differentiated one, calling forth coloured shadows on the surfaces of the columns and the sculpture. The rows of wooden seats with their rounded backrests shimmered like flakes of mother-of-pearl, and each person moving about within this living space took on an ever-changing appearance. The "reverse perspective" of the architecture, brought about through the fact of the columns increasing in size toward the east, completed this new experience of space.

On leaving the large hall through the door in the west, the visitor's gaze fell upon the large red window triptych in the vestibule, on which the so-called initiation motif was portrayed; an enormous countenance, surrounded by cosmic forces. To the immediate left and right of this human being a lion and bull in priestly garb "murmured cosmic secrets to him, on the waves of the tone ether," as Rudolf Steiner expressed it.

In the ancient mysteries, the godhead greeted the mystic with the words, "Know thyself!" And in accordance with this knowledge, which was at the same time a creative act, the one so greeted found in himself his divine origin, and his answer was "You are!" In like manner, the spirit of this building greeted the one entering by means of its forms and colours, challenging them to self-knowledge, and what then arose out of the depths of their being as an answer, came to meet them in this countenance, revealing their divine nature within the cosmos.

Beneath the large countenance a light, winged figure conquered a dragon. This archangel, free of all earthly weight, looked straight ahead into the distance.

"If Michael were to look at the dragon, he would have to affirm it," said Rudolf Steiner.

In these enigmatic words, does the key not lie to the art of the Goetheanum as a whole? In fact, to Rudolf Steiner's battle against the power that would regard what is externally perceptible alone as reality?

When the architrave was brought into the building, space was gained in the carpentry workshop, and Rudolf Steiner had a stage built there for eurythmy and the performance of scenes from *Faust*. For the first time, humoresques by Christian Morgenstern were then presented in eurythmy. Through eurythmy, the purely poetic element in these humoresques emerged to full effect. Performances of these humoresques certainly also had a pedagogical effect. In a spiritually oriented society, an unhealthy sentimentality, a mystical eccentricity can assert itself, with certain kinds of people, and humour is a salutary antidote to this.

From the *Faust* performances, it is unforgettable to me how Rudolf Steiner demonstrated the part of Mephisto for the actor playing this role. He was hollow, smug as a decadent dandy, listless as a drunkard, cynical, full of mockery and at the same time unspeakably sad and hopeless, in voice and expression. A shudder ran down our spines. The choruses of the women and youths on Easter eve were presented in eurythmy.

Once, while Rudolf Steiner and Fräulein von Sivers were away, Jan Stuten composed the music for the choruses, and we vocalized in eurythmy the words of the singing, with enthusiasm. How we were scolded by Fräulein von Sivers on her return for this complete lack of style; vocalization to music! She then had the singing of the words and the vocalization of the speech choruses presented separately, one after the other. Sensitive souls would certainly have had opportunity to feel offended at this. But whoever possessed an organ for the greatness of her personality and saw how impersonally it was meant — like a thunderstorm breaking out, not applying to people, but justified in objective terms — could not take it amiss. For she was just as inexorable with herself as with others. One had, on the one hand, not to regard oneself as too important, and on the other, be free and independent. Along with this seeming severity, one could experience in her a great, altogether unsentimental motherly kindness.

When Marie von Sivers took over the direction of eurythmy, Rudolf Steiner was able to give the existing group further indications in this art; various new "forms," preludes and the magnificent *Twelve Moods,* in which zodiac, planets and the motion of the sun are depicted. When he read us the verses for the first time himself, one had the feeling, "The word surges through the world, and the world-formation takes hold of it."

But at once, as a companion piece, he had us do a different version of the *Twelve Moods,* a satire on twelve different gaffes, resulting from sham occultism. Whoever was amenable, could practise self-knowledge here.

Life in Dornach so arranged itself that one always found oneself working together with others. The day took its course with carving, painting, practising and rehearsing for eurythmy and scenes for *Faust.* Eurythmy, as the expression of all supersensible events, incorporated itself in such a self-evident manner, that one could no longer imagine *Faust* without eurythmy. Rudolf Steiner gave lectures four times a week — also on *Faust.* In addition, a fifth lecture was planned just for the workmen on the building.

It was agreed among the members that, as long as Rudolf Steiner carried the burden of the work on the building, individuals were not to trouble him with personal questions, and that rule was adhered to. But often he enquired about one's personal concerns himself! One sensed that he kept everyone in mind.

When I once had to miss a *Faust* rehearsal on account of illness — I was to appear in the "Chorus of Insects" that were shaken out of a fur coat — Rudolf Steiner teased me the next time around, "I know why you weren't there yesterday: you did not want to portray a louse!"

At this opportunity, I asked him, "Why do people have various idiosyncracies, so that, for example, strong men pass out at the sight of a spider?"

He answered, "These animals have a beautiful group soul in the objective soul world, whereas the human being in that world is a horrible worm."

It seemed to me that he spoke the words "a horrible worm" with great revulsion. I stood before him just then in a white eurythmy dress — almost an angel (only with the passage of years does one discover that one is no angel).

"In seeing it, a meeting takes place unconsciously with the group soul of this animal, and the human being experiences the sight of it as a reproach; he gets a shock. The shock mirrors itself here as aversion."

The Ark

In mid July, Rudolf Steiner went to Sweden to hold lectures in Norrköping. My friends, the Bugayevs, and I travelled with him, and from Russia friends went there as well. The weather was extraordinarily hot, so that the meadows, which in Sweden are otherwise green, had acquired a brownish tone. During those days, the newspapers brought news of the assassination attempt on Rasputin in Siberia. We had no idea at that time what significance this event had for world history. If Rasputin, who was decidedly against the War, had not been hindered by his injury during these critical days from being with the Tsar, the declaration of war would certainly not have followed and Europe would have looked different today. At that time we saw in this peasant only a rake and a charlatan. That the Russian folk-soul spoke through him in spite of everything was something we had no notion of.

The lectures which Rudolf Steiner held between July 12 and 16, had a particular impact, due perhaps to their being held directly before the catastrophe of the First World War. They brought us to an awareness that the twin goals of human evolution are the development of free will and the comprehension of the divine. For this reason Rudolf Steiner referred to the Fall of Man, through which the human being became able to distinguish good and evil, and the event of Golgotha as two religious "gifts." Without these momentous events the human soul, which had become darkened in the course of earthly evolution, would never have been able to find its essential being. I remember the stupendous impression made on me by Rudolf Steiner's description of the mass of people at the condemnation of Jesus; how they shouted furiously, expressing thereby their disavowal of the Being through whom they could alone recover their humanity. With that they said in effect, "We no longer want to be human." Humanity had arrived at the point where it had lost itself.

Of central importance for me during these days was the clarification of the question of the relationship of personal responsibility, in terms of destiny, to the forgiveness of sin through Christ. Through atonement, we can balance out the consequence of sin for ourselves. Indeed we want to regain what we have lost in worth through guilt. However, what our guilt has brought about in the world, Christ is able to take upon Himself and extinguish, because He comes from another world. It becomes a question, not of "I and self-redemption," but of "Christ and world-redemption." Having united Himself with the forces of death, He was also able to overcome the forces of death.

The friends who gathered for this cycle were shown slides by Rudolf Steiner of the building still in progress, and from this distance it became still clearer to us "Dornachers," just what it meant to be granted the opportunity to work on it.

The Bugayevs and I decided to visit Arkona on the island of Rügen on the return journey from Norrköping, the site of the old Slavic mysteries of the god Svantevit. The white rocks rose from the sea, which on that day was dark violet and foaming. A wind went through the thin grasses on the heath. Only a few traces are left of the sanctuary itself. This region had an extraordinary appeal for me, and I would gladly have stayed overnight so as to have the possibility of entering more fully into the mood, of which I experienced only a vague presentiment. We were lying on the high, steep incline over the sea when I made this suggestion to my friends.

"No," said Assya [Turgenieva] resolutely, "what can old mystery sites give us now that we are working in Dornach? I want to go back and not miss another day."

This impatience and exclusivity seemed to me then rather fanatical. What does one day matter? But I soon understood what difference one day can make. Bugayev, with his literary name of Andrei Belyi, sought a connection to what had once been on this island and said, "I feel how the whole ground shakes from battles; here wars must have been fought between Slavs and ancient Germanic peoples." He was in a peculiarly nervous frame of mind, bordering on persecution mania, as it seemed to me.

After a nocturnal journey, we arrived in Berlin early in the morning. The air had not cooled during the night and remained motionless. From the station restaurant where we had breakfast, we saw endless crowds of day trippers filing past.

Horrified, Bugayev said, "Just look at these young people. It is dreadful. They do not yet know how matters really stand, or just what they bear within them. They resemble animals that carry larvae of other animals within them, from which they will die."

When we arrived in Dornach, the sultriness there was equally unbearable. One thunderstorm broke after another without bringing relief. But what a "thunderstorm" was gathering on Europe's political horizon!

On the day of the declaration of war, Steiner had gone with Fräulein von Sivers to the *Parsifal* performance in Bayreuth. Only with difficulty did they succeed in getting back over the border.

The next morning, I met him in Dornach on the way to the building. He looked very serious, in fact, deeply concerned. I expressed regret that the building had not been finished by August, as he had wanted. Now it would certainly be difficult to bring it to completion. But he answered that in relation to what this catastrophe meant for humanity, it was no longer so important.

"It is now a question of more serious things, of terrible things. But," he added, "we want to bear whatever may come with composure and strength."

Several Russians left Dornach immediately and were only able to reach the German-Russian border after contending with many difficulties and much abuse. Unexpectedly, Max arrived during those days from Russia. He told of having travelled everywhere on the last train.

"All doors closed behind me, and I managed to save myself, as the last animal on Noah's Ark."

In July, Rudolf Steiner had made acoustic experiments in the building and had been satisfied with the results. The first sounds we heard echoing in the building, however, were those of the cannon barrages. The windows in the carpentry building shook from this thunder, and Rudolf Steiner had to raise his voice in order to be heard. At that time he gave us a course in first aid, since the possibility existed that Switzerland would become a theatre of war also. He showed us how to bind wounds and carry the wounded. In doing so, he explained to us how in the blood that pours from the wound something lives that works to heal it, and gave us a meditative saying to help us unite our hearts with this nursing care. He then gave us a second verse and said, with this we could test whether we were strong enough to feel the pain of the other as our own.

One has to imagine that eighteen different nationalities were working on our building! During the midday break in the canteen everyone sat immersed in their newspaper. Differences of opinion could arise; the Francophone Swiss, in particular, were filled with French chauvinism.

Right at the beginning of the War, Rudolf Steiner began speaking about the spiritual background of current events in his lectures, which continued to take place regularly every Saturday and Sunday in the carpentry building. However, feelings were then generally too aroused for people to take up these truths objectively, free of national emotions. Thus he had to break off these reflections and deal with other spiritual scientific matters. But a year later, when his listeners had worked their own way through to a degree of objectivity regarding nationality, he was able to take up the subject again, and spoke about it from then on throughout the subsequent war years.

These perspectives signified a path of knowledge, in which listeners were to develop an organ for an unprejudiced view of the present, and a clear look at the future. Rarely did Rudolf Steiner predict anything unreservedly, since in history, besides what is determined from the past, individualities can also act freely on intuition. Unfortunately, the worst possibilities he had foreseen were fulfilled one after the other. Rudolf Steiner did not want to make things comfortable for us. Thus I recollect how on a Christmas evening, when we came to the carpentry building in expectation of a particularly festive lecture, he read us a political speech by Gabriele d'Annunzio, and showed the lie as being a method in politics. During this period when lies, like a mist, made humanity blind, we were not permitted only to float in lofty regions, without fully confronting these things.

In the autumn I received a letter from my mother that arrived via Sweden, which she had written me in the first days of the War. This letter was full of patriotic enthusiasm:

> Do not believe the lying German propaganda, this war is a holy war. In fighting against Germany, our people, which is a Christ-bearing people, fights against the Antichrist. We, all Russians, from the

> upper classes to the lowest social strata, stand
> united as one for our holy cause.

When I told Rudolf Steiner about the content of this letter, he asked whether my mother spoke German and knew German culture. I had to tell him that she spoke German perfectly and had grown up with German literature. This letter was really an illustration of what Rudolf Steiner had said about the various peoples and their relationship to the War.

"For the Italians," he said, "the 'other' is an alien; for a Frenchman a barbarian; for a German an enemy; for an Englishman a competitor; for a Russian the enemy is a heretic. War is something that contradicts the nature of the Russian, and if one wants to force a Russian into war for political reasons, one has to make it a religious war."

Rudolf Steiner made a sketch for the curtain separating the auditorium from the stage: In the middle, a river, on the right bank a pilgrim, who can be thought of as Brother Markus from the *Geheimnisse* (Mysteries) by Goethe. The many paths he has travelled are to be seen in the background, losing themselves in the forest. On a high rock at a distance, our building with its two cupolas could be recognized. Above it in the clouds was the vision of the Cross encircled with roses. And from the other bank, still half covered by a rock ledge, a boat came towards the Brother.

This work was to be carried out by a lady, Camilla Wandrey, who was more "mystically" than artistically inclined. Max — poor Max — was assigned to help her. She painted a bluish-rose mist; he painted strongly contoured geological mountain formations such as he knew from the Crimea, and light refractions in the clouds. Both had to paint in a small room lit only by electric light, and in these surroundings Max became quite melancholic. The rest of Dornach society oppressed him as well: people who lived in dogmas, too often placing a fixed schema between themselves and life — without really having experienced anything — and arrogantly dismissing whatever they heard from someone else. Max was drawn to his beloved Paris and I could not hold it against him. As money from Russia came through more and more sparsely, and Max could earn money in Paris as a journalist, he decided to travel there. We had no notion that it was to be our last parting.

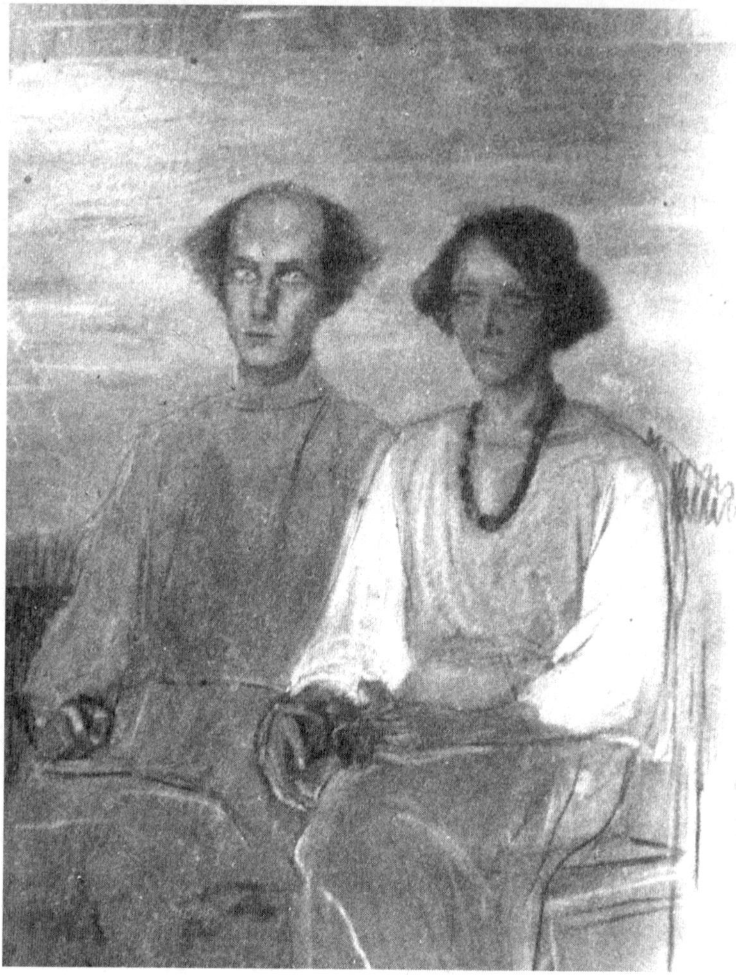

Andrei Belyi and his wife Assya Turgenieva. Portrait by Woloschin 1915/16

Max took from anthroposophy first of all what spoke to him directly. This included, for example, the six exercises which are the precondition for the anthroposophical schooling. These he really carried out in life. He gave his full attention to every human being, left people free, condemned no one. When he was called up, he travelled to Russia, but with the firm decision to refuse military service. He would have preferred being shot than to kill another person. He was found unfit for military service on account of his asthma, however, and escaped that destiny. When I arrived in Moscow in 1917, he was in the Crimea. Russia was torn by civil war and the chaotic conditions of that time made travelling virtually impossible. The Crimea changed hands many times between the Whites and the Reds, till the Reds finally retained power. Max described the desecration in poems. He was, of course, ostracized by those in authority and it was amazing that he survived. How this was actually possible, given his political outlook, I found out only later. When power changed hands, Max saved the Whites from the Reds, the Reds from the Whites. Each was for him a human being in the first place. One of the Reds, who owed him his life, became the Crimean head of the Cheka [the ruthless Soviet state security organization]. The house in Koktebel was made a "retreat" for writers. Max was permitted to continue living there, but he went hungry. In order to feed himself, in one way or another, he collected the beautiful semi-precious stones in the bay of Koktebel and sold them. His poems were copied and circulated clandestinely and he was proud of the renown thus achieved. By way of thanks for having saved the *Chekist*, he was granted a frightful privilege. Out of every group of prisoners condemned to death, he was permitted to gain the reprieve for one of them. In consequence of this, he was hated by the relatives of all the others. In his last letter, he wrote to me about this hatred, from which he suffered continually, without being able to go into the reasons for it. He found a woman who helped him to bear his difficulties. Max died in 1932.

I was able to observe with what intensity Rudolf Steiner followed the news concerning the War. The outcome of the Battle of the Marne filled him with consternation. When I asked whether it could not turn out, as often before in history, that a conquered people "inoculates" the victor, and that Germany, if defeated, would nonetheless emerge spiritually victorious, he said:

> Now, matters stand differently; it would signify a great misfortune for humanity if Germany were vanquished. In particular, if occupied by the Russians and if German culture were destroyed by them, this would be disastrous for both parties, because for Eastern Europe to fulfil its task some day, it must be fructified by the spiritual culture of Germany. Without that the East will not be able to complete its mission, just as a woman cannot have a child without a man.

In looking down from time to time from the hill above the Goetheanum building, it appeared to me like a ship, floating in the middle of the Flood. One heard the rumble of cannons, one saw air battles overhead; forces of destruction raged in the world. In this building, I thought to myself, the culture of the middle, the seed of the future will be preserved.

Meanwhile, more and more co-workers were called away. The table of the "strong men" shrank. Those of different nationalities took leave of each other fraternally, in order to fight at the front; and each took the "building of humanity" with them in their hearts. The mothers, the women, the girlfriends remained, in order to continue the work. News of death arrived. In the carpentry building, hung with black and decorated with pine branches, Rudolf Steiner held funeral services. Gradually, those working on the building became a community of mourners. There was, nonetheless, the sense that whatever happened here, what was worked on and elaborated here, had significance for both worlds.

In 1916, Andrei Belyi was conscripted. Before his departure, I made a double portrait of him and his wife, hand in hand, as they often sat listening to a lecture; like two figures in an Egyptian tomb. A few days after his departure, Rudolf Steiner caught sight of the picture in my studio and said, "What a pity he has gone; he was just on the way to attaining a degree of equilibrium."

"But," I contradicted him, "he is so connected to Russia; doesn't he have to experience this critical time together with his people? He will be able to work there in the sense of anthroposophy."

"In Russia it will not be possible to work, in Russia one will only be able to experience chaos and purgatory. Engineers, perhaps, will still be needed there."

The War, which seemed as though it would never end, pursued one even at night. I found myself in an altogether dejected mood; also because the results of our work did not please me at all. Though I believed I understood the artistic ideals striven for with the building, I considered our ability inadequate to the task. Rudolf Steiner's view, that the building was there for the purpose of enabling people to learn from working on it, was alien to me. At that time, what counted for me was the finished work, not the activity itself. The end result was more important to me than its coming into being. That the path belonged to the goal, I discovered only much later. From this knowledge alone could courage and faith be drawn in creating out of new impulses. No age has demanded courage in greater measure in this sense than our own. Earlier ages supported themselves on tradition. We stood at an absolute zero point and needed to seize the initiative ourselves. An initiate showed us the path both to Inspiration, and to Intuition of our own.

In thinking back to my mood at that time, I see a complete failure on the path I had chosen for myself. It is not easy to relinquish one's own limited feeling of self. In the presence of one who "knows," however, even if he did not require it, one was led to the point where adhering to egoism had to come to an end.

Rudolf Steiner travelled frequently to Germany to prepare the movement for the threefolding of the social organism. Life in Dornach, closed off from the world, I felt to be sectarian and out of touch. Who, apart from Michael Bauer, still took an interest in the cultural phenomena of the modern world? Who else was there who wanted to come to terms on their own with the phenomena of our civilization? We knew everything already, before having experienced it. A quote from Rudolf Steiner stood continually between us and reality. Did Rudolf Steiner not have in mind the very opposite? Did I not need to gather my own experiences?

This question occupied me in coming to the decision to travel to Russia, "for a few months," as I supposed. I talked myself into believing I would have to tell various acquaintances in Russia (who had begun at that time to play a certain political role) the truth about this War. I had not seen Russia in four years. I convinced myself, that it would not be permissible to ask Rudolf Steiner for advice at all, because this journey via England and Norway would be dangerous, also on account of the naval war. I would have to take the responsibility upon myself alone.

In January 1917, Dr Trapesnikov was conscripted and I saw this as an opportunity not to have to travel by myself. When I went to Rudolf Steiner to take leave of him, he asked me whether I was finished with my work in the cupola.

"I have completed my own composition, and by the time the others have reached the point where we can coordinate the whole, I hope to be back." Then I added, rather uncertainly, "Although one cannot know, what will come." And I said that to one who was a "knower"!

"Yes," he said with a smile, "one does not know what will come. Therefore, there is no reason to remain nailed down in one place." I took this sentence as confirmation of my plan. In parting he said to me, "Whatever happens, we shall remain united in the spirit!"

VI

The Giant's Shadow

Turbulent Homeland

The idea was that we would reach Russia via Paris, England and Scandinavia. Dr Trapesnikov, who felt his involuntary parting from Dornach as a misfortune and dreaded returning to Russia, regarded my step as foolishness. Having otherwise been so well disposed toward me, he was now irritable and uncomfortable.

Through the frosty morning mist, I saw the familiar outlines of Paris, but it appeared ghostly. It was like the shadow of Paris in Hades. The clocks all showed different times. Hardly any cars were to be seen on the streets, only a few old-fashioned carriages with limping horses. Almost all the ladies wore long mourning veils. The few men were soldiers on leave, or wounded. Instead, I saw many black people. Unusual for the lively French was the silence in the trams and restaurants. In the look on people's faces, I encountered hardness and earnestness, their mouths expressed dogged will. In that especially cold winter, Paris remained without coal due to a deficiency of organization. The women performing the unaccustomed men's work of street cleaning, railway and postal duties, did so with patience and humility; qualities otherwise not typical of French women of their social standing. In the general affliction, the nobility of an old heroic nation showed itself.

On the day of our arrival, the Germans had declared a major blockade. On account of the danger of sea travel, women were not granted visas for England and Dr Trapesnikov travelled there alone. It took weeks before I received permission to return to Switzerland. On finally obtaining it, I did not travel to Dornach, since Rudolf Steiner was not there, but to the Engadine. I saw this countryside I loved so much for the first time in wintertime. Almost threateningly, the abyss of the sky yawned a dark blue above the snow, which was dazzling for the eye. The waterfalls, petrified to ice, formed upright folds as on the garments of archaic Greek statues. In my childhood, I had known St Moritz as a small village with a modest guest house. Now I saw a deserted city. The huge hotels were closed because of the War and resembled Assyrian mausoleums. It seemed to me as though 2,300 years not twenty-three years had gone by since then. It was as if I were witness to the rising and passing away of a culture. I felt myself torn out of life's connections and brought here to the boundaries of existence, within the silence of eternity. Amid this frozen world, the newspapers brought an incredible piece of news: Revolution had broken out in Russia; the kingdom of the Tsars was at an end. I did not trust the first news and awaited a disclaimer. But the newspapers continued to report unprecedented events. For Russia itself, it also appeared to have come unexpectedly and almost unintentionally. The limits of popular patience had been overstepped and the "ice" of the rigid regime on the great river of Russia burst. In the course of a hunger strike at a factory in St Petersburg, a soldier, ordered to shoot at the strikers, had struck his own wife. Suddenly he no longer shot at those striking but at the police. Now, the whole regiment disobeyed the order to shoot at the workers. I read about the decisions of the Duma and the abdication of the Tsar. "I shall cultivate flowers in Livadia; after all, I love flowers so much," he said. A Provisional Government with Prince Lvov as president had been constituted. I hoped peace would now follow.

In the little guest house in Silvaplana where I stayed, lived the family of a German officer who was at the front. The ladies inquired only whether the events would bring about peace, and did not interest themselves further in the matter. I found the silent "eternity" of the mountains around me unbearable, given the storm the news had provoked in me. I went frequently to the inn where the stagecoach drivers ate. There I encountered a quite different level of interest in current events. There was discussion, and they wanted to hear many things about Russia.

In the spring, a letter from my father reached me via Sweden:

> We are experiencing miracles! The Russian people have given up alcohol from one day to the next. From one day to the next, the despotism disappeared. Russia is free! Everybody on the street feels fraternally related, embracing and kissing each other as at Easter. People congratulate each other mutually on the "great, bloodless Russian Revolution!"

And I was completely cut off from Russia! A friend wrote to me from Dornach, saying an extraterritorial train for everyone who was against the war would soon travel from Zurich, through Germany and Sweden, to St Petersburg. Two such trains with emigrants had already left. I went to the address indicated, to inquire about it.

"Have you rendered service to the Revolution?"

"Not that I know of."

"Then you may not join us."

Grieved, I went away, but soon turned back and said, "I recall having done a service for the Revolution, if you can see it as such, in being able to free several 'politicals' from prison, through my relationship to Governor General Dzhunkovsky."

The connection to governor general Dzhunkovsky was hardly a recommendation in this case. But it was important to them that a few private persons came along, who did not belong to the Party and could bear the costs of the journey themselves. Thus my "services" were recognized.

On the platform there was a large crowd of people departing, together with those escorting them. The Swiss socialist, Robert Grimm, travelled with the train as a neutral mediator. At the border, eight German soldiers came aboard as sentries. How pleased I was to see them! Deeply moved, I looked out at what had now become, in a certain way, a sacred country for me, and that in those summer days appeared like a miraculous garden. In the fields I saw Russian prisoners of war making hay. But the stations we passed through were almost deserted, since they were not to be entered, as stipulated by a strict military regulation. At mealtimes the soldiers brought us, free of charge, a good meat soup with bread, probably so that we would report in Russia that people were not going hungry in Germany. I had no notion then of the world historical significance of this train on which I travelled, nor the reason why Ludendorff had arranged it. I did not know that Lenin and other leading communists had travelled to Russia with the first of these trains. Stragglers and their families travelled on our train, mostly rather dirty, nervous and arrogant people. It was in a manner of speaking, a prologue to the experiences which were to come.

From the Swedish border on, where Grimm and the German soldiers left us, the privation began. At none of the little stations at which we halted on sidings was there anything to eat. Thus hungry days and sleepless nights went by. In only two large cities were we honourably received as socialists returning to their homeland, with a wonderful meal served on the platform and ceremonial speeches by fine-looking, blue-eyed Swedish socialists. Our company of hungry, unwashed, unshaven, unkempt people flung themselves like wild animals on the food. There was no speech of thanks in response to this welcome. Ashamed beyond words, I had to content myself with thanking the gentlemen personally.

This journey in fourth-class carriages hitched to goods trains, lasted several days and nights. In Stockholm, the news came from the Russian Consulate, that we would not be granted permission to enter Russia. The political wind had reversed direction: Alexander Kerensky was preparing his offensive. Swedish acquaintances I visited advised me either to travel back, or to remain there, since they had heard there was a famine in Russia. But no, I did not want to do that! In the end an entry permit came through after all. And the same unbearable ordeal began all over again! Before we arrived at the Finnish border, my travel companions formed a choir to rehearse the *Internationale*, since a festive reception was anticipated.

Haparanda, the Russian border![38] The night as bright as day. On the platform there was a company of tall, bearded soldiers from Siberia. Sadly and gloomily they looked into the distance. All of them, as they told me, were homesick.

"What kind of a country is it! There isn't even a proper night here!"

A nervous, fanatic comrade from our company began talking against the War from the carriage window and shouted out propaganda slogans he had learnt. However, he came up against a decidedly dismissive mood, and this gradually grew to become a threatening cloud, which suddenly broke through, "Those are the devils that subvert our front! We spill our blood for holy Russia and they betray us! Strike the cursed agitator dead!"

There would certainly have been a pogrom if the train had not started at that moment. The curses followed us for quite some time. I sat down in the dining car so as to be free of my travel companions. Three tall, elegant gentlemen of distinguished appearance were sitting at a nearby table, discussing the incident. From the way they spoke, I became aware that they were travelling on behalf of the Provisional Government.

"We shall not let them into St Petersburg at all, but arrange (Kerensky's name was mentioned) for them to be arrested in Beloostrov (the border between Finland and Russia) and transported to the Petropavlovsk fortress. They'll only bring us harm, these rogues!"

One can perhaps imagine the feelings with which I spent the last night of this journey. Though we were not arrested in Beloostrov, in St Petersburg there was no festive reception either. I discovered that my entire luggage had been stolen from the baggage car. Changing money, I received postage stamps instead of cash.

At the house of Boris Leman and Klavdya Vassilyeva, with whom I stayed while awaiting news from Moscow, I heard about the events of the last few months. Finally an answer came. It was not easy to get into one of the trains. Soldiers streaming back from the front clung to them like grapes. Through the open windows I heard conversations conducted that summer night on the roof of the carriage. These were joyful, energetic, young voices, such as one had never heard earlier in Russia.

"We want to build up our country, so that all human beings can live like brothers. All who want it, will get an education, on and on, with no limit!"

Then I heard, "Police? Why police? If everyone has enough, there will be no stealing and no murder. Just think: no envy, no hatred anymore!"

"But the bourgeois aren't going to hand over everything voluntarily," one of them objected.

"Oh, who knows, perhaps they will after all; or it will simply be the law ... What a wonderful new life we shall have, with no prisons, with no force ...!"

Again and again I heard these young voices, brimming over with joy, "How splendidly we shall build up the new Russia!"

And so it went on happily through the bright, warm night till day came and I arrived in Moscow.

The people, standing in queues in front of the shops in ragged clothes, looked pale and miserable. There were embittered faces, filled with hatred. Never had I seen such angry faces in Russia. It was as though everything that had crouched, humiliated, in the cellar previously, now found its way into the light of day.

Entering our house, I first embraced Polya.

"What can we give you to eat?" she said, and could not really be glad to see me on that account. Masha, who had become very thin, wept with emotion. When my mother heard that I had come through Germany, her joy was diminished.

"For God's sake, that is betrayal of the fatherland! No one must find out about it!" My elderly parents seemed lost to me.

"To think," my father said, "the peasants are simply cutting down our forests! In many dispatches to Interior Minister Shtshepkin I have requested protection for our estates. All to no avail."

Later, I became friends with Shtshepkin. He said to me, "My desk was piled high with such dispatches. What was I to do? We had no power. Complete anarchy prevailed."

"Two railway carriages full of wood for the winter were also stolen from us; we shall freeze." My mother told me that she had been dismissed, with no explanation, from her position as director of libraries. She was not to appear there anymore, and her pupils would not defend her. At that moment, I was looking through the window into the courtyard. A horse drawing a wooden carriage fell over and died. At once, women raced out with knives from every basement room and kitchen, in order — squabbling and bickering — to cut off pieces of meat. Now I knew how things stood with us. Visiting our relatives and friends, still scattered in country houses near Moscow, the lying propaganda I heard about Germany appalled me. But I myself was of course not unbiased, and made the mistake of confusing the spiritual mission of Germany and the deeper reasons for the war, with judgments about the current political representatives of Germany.

Moscow at that time presented a strange picture. Soldiers in grey were everywhere. They went about the streets, sat and lay in every public garden; soldiers hung like grapes around tram carriages, travelling on their roofs. Every train arrived draped with soldiers. In every shop, at every kiosk there was a crowd of soldiers. Kerensky held his speeches at the front, to inspire the army for the offensive. Yet demobilization took place in effect at the same time, with elemental force, as a result of the magic words of the communists, "Peace and country." Soldiers first plundered the bases, and then went home to plunder the estate owners in their home villages. Every wall and fence of the city was plastered with posters; but hardly had someone put up a poster, an appeal with programme points, than the next person tore

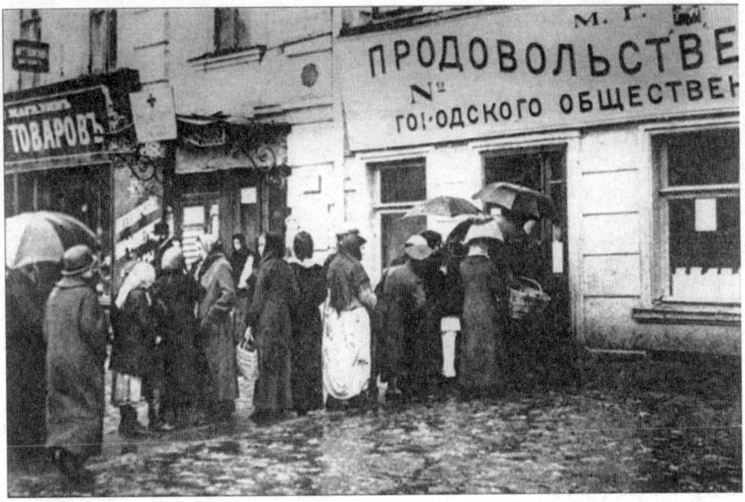

Queue at a shop in Moscow in 1917

it off and stuck up his own. At every main entrance, groups of people stood cracking sunflower seeds. The Russian peasant is a virtuoso at separating the kernels from the shells in his mouth. Earlier, this had been done more to pass the time, but now it was prompted by hunger. Embittered and despairing, passers-by had the shells spat in their faces. Whole heaps of shells lay in front of every doorway. The streets were not swept anymore, freedom having been proclaimed. Gusts of wind lifted the dust, the shells and the scraps of various proclamations, swirling them through the air.

A friend told me one day, she had to give her nanny several days off so that she could plunder the estate owners in her village community, "Otherwise I'll come too late, and everything will be shared out among our peasants," she had said.

My father, whose health was not good, needed to spend a few weeks in the country. It was still possible to obtain rooms in a private guest house near Moscow. I went with him. We now wandered as we once had on our estate, through fields and forests. The Revolution freed my father from the oppressive responsibility, the entanglement in money matters. In fact, he heaved a sigh of relief and his childlike, innocent soul began to blossom again. I am thankful to destiny that we were able to work through some of the basic writings of anthroposophy together at that time, to which he was very open. Before that, he had not had sufficient peace of mind for this. It was to be his last period of happiness. Later came the time of dire need.

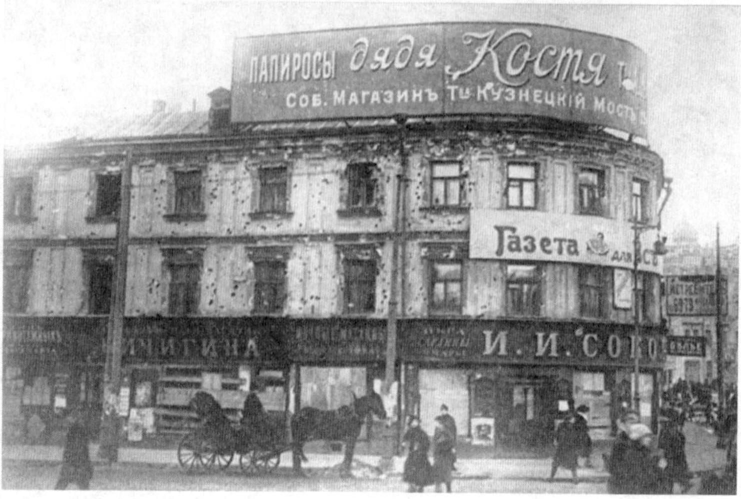

Building with bullet holes and the corner of Great and Small Nikitskaya Street

His illness worsened and he was no longer able to work. Kittie, who was spending the summer not far from us, came to visit me. This was during the tragic days following the so-called "Moscow consultation," which took place in the middle of August in the large theatre. At that time, the political division between the left and the right became an abyss; and between Kerensky and General Kornilov a mistrust arose that was soon to lead Russia to catastrophe.

"What will happen to Russia, what will happen to Russia?" Kittie repeated in despair. That was the last time we saw each other. She died the following winter of exhaustion, after having been evicted forcibly from her apartment, with no vehicle and no help with moving.

Alexandra Alexeievna, the writer, had sold her parents' house several years before and now rented two rooms in the old Empire-style house of a general who had passed away. She gave the smaller one over to me. The lady of the house, her son, a young nobleman and two old former ladies-in-waiting lived there in a reactionary, embittered mood. On the other hand, Alexandra followed events with positive interest, which she retained until her death in 1925, though she had by then not only lost her entire fortune, but also often found herself in mortal danger as a former millionairess. She was surrounded by young people whose university studies she had made possible. For as long as she was rich, she had loaned them the money, so that they would not feel dependent on her. Later they gradually paid it back. With her substantial library

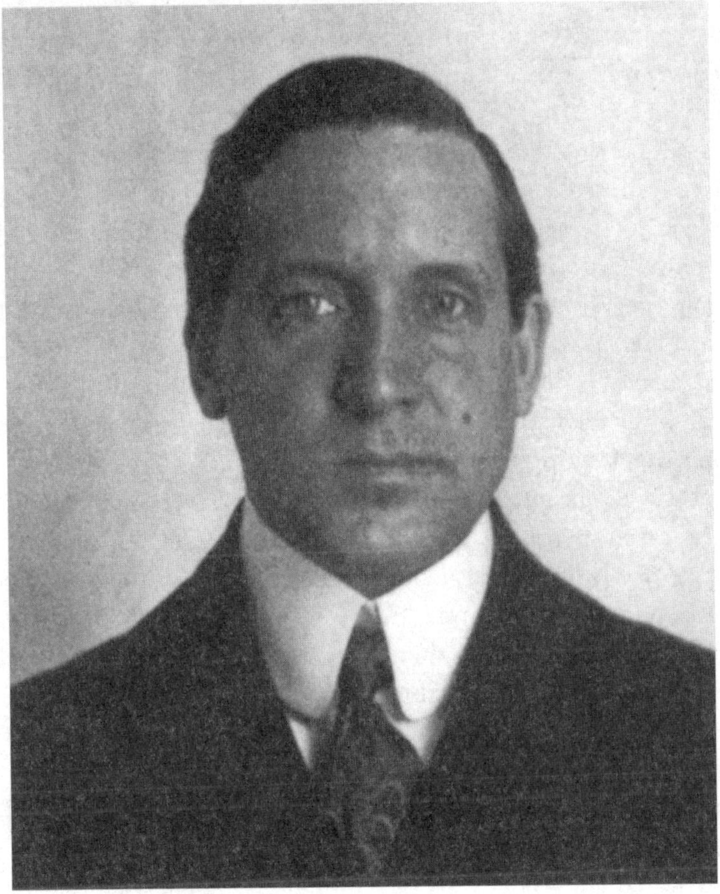

Trifon Trapesnikov around 1915

and her great erudition she was able to contribute to the spiritual development of these young people.

At that time I devoted myself above all to the anthroposophical work. Dr Trapesnikov, from whom I had been separated in Paris, had spent several months in London, and we arrived almost at the same time in Moscow. Whenever our circle gathered, a wonderful cheerfulness came over us. It remained that way throughout the difficult years I spent there with my friends. We were pleased to see each other, recognizing in the other person a helper in the general cause. Everyone felt stimulated and enhanced in their own capacities through what the others achieved. Various groups came together in the large hall of the Society every evening. Fourteen people applied themselves to eurythmy, which I was able to mediate, as far as it had been developed at that point in Dornach.[39] After a year, we performed the Easter Scene from *Faust*, as it had been practised in Dornach, and as it is still presented today on the Goetheanum stage. This shared work helped us through the darkest years. In the time of total anarchy, when streetlamps were smashed and there was shooting and shouting in the pitch-dark night, we still met, evening after evening.

From the February revolution on, and for some time after the Bolshevik seizure of power in October — for as long as the Communist Government was diverted by other things — there was relative freedom of thought in Russia; freedom of speech. Poor Russia; the fatherland of a people that requires freedom for its very existence, for which freedom is no abstract concept, no ideal, but the breath of life. In these few free months, anthroposophy could be presented in public lectures. Andrei Belyi, especially, imparted it in a uniquely creative way, gathering an enthusiastic audience around him.

In the chaos that arose at that time in Russia, when rigid forms were loosened, it was not only brutality and darkness that came to the surface with elemental force, as might now be supposed. The great questions of life welled up out of the depths, such as perhaps only the Russian folk soul can ask in just this way; and "without the answer to which, humanity will not come further." One can understand what it was that so intoxicated Alexander Blok or Andrei Belyi, about the revolution at that time. The "inner breadth" of Russians has its shadow side, as with all attributes of the soul. The Dionysian-Luciferic, which abhors the constricting forms of life, positively jubilates when these forms are set fire to. Many poets paid heavily for their illusions later on. Through Andrei Belyi, I met Sergei Yesenin, the young poet of the people. I had the impression that this delicate poet-soul was both torn and injured as a result of the intensity of its experiences, and the conflicting nature of current events. It is known that he took his own life a few years later.

In the house that had once belonged to the slavophile, Chomyakov, in which the stylish furniture of the early nineteenth century had been preserved, futuristic poets and painters gathered around a married couple who had returned from emigration abroad. There I got to know a number of them, including Vladimir Mayakovsky. These artists distinguished themselves in that they destroyed form and, on the other hand, through an exaggerated self-esteem, formed a counterbalance and substitute for true human dignity. Their talent and originality were undeniable. When Mayakovsky declaimed, "That's what I am — Vladimir Mayakovsky, whose eye veils the circus in cloud," it sounded rhetorically magnificent.[40] By means of a peculiar sentence build-up, his language became tremendously dynamic. He appeared to swim in this as in a living element that he fully mastered. Nothing conventional or abstract could be found in all these poets. Here, a battle was waged against the ideals of the past, merely borrowed from antiquity and felt to be untrue. The arrogance of an "unbound" Prometheus did not shock me. It could be regarded as a sort of childhood illness. It was only alarming that along with this wealth of soul, one had the feeling, that here demons were at play. It is known that this proved disastrous for Mayakovsky himself, in that he also took his own life. There were such destroyers of the old forms, even before the First World War. Artists who justifiably negated naturalism, but found no path to higher spiritual realities, got caught in the subnatural and demonic, the realm from which modern destructive technology was derived. The spirituality of earlier times had drawn its substance from direct perception and experience of the divine, enabling it to combat the demonic. The humanity of our time stood between the subjective soul element and the "iron necessity" of an external godless world. In the Russia of the revolution I saw this duality in all its tragedy. Politically as well, it was a sign that the middle was lacking. There was only the youthful Russian folk, as yet without their own culture, abandoned to alien influences and the decrepit culture of the entente. The gap, which Germany had to fill, if it comprehended itself and its task, I felt at that time most profoundly.

The members of the Provisional Government were human beings of a certain culture. They wanted nothing for themselves personally and endeavoured to satisfy everyone, to grant freedom to all parties, not to act prematurely and not to impose anything on the people. By means of a "general, equal, secret, direct vote" in the Assembly to determine the constitution, which they had prepared, the people were to make their will known. But why had they wanted to force the people, against their obvious will, to continue the War, which meant only "senseless murder"? They even saw the need to reintroduce the death penalty, which had already been abolished. Yet the death penalty was so repugnant to the Russian people, that under the tsarist regime, groups of peasants again and again had sent petitions to the Tsar, requesting him to annul the death penalty in Russia, putting their freedom and their lives at risk in doing so. Since the Bolsheviks demanded peace, in order to get the people on their side, the adherents of the Provisional Government were for the continuation of the War. I could not understand this logic. With their splendid speeches, these people seemed to me like the will-o-the-wisps in Goethe's *Fairy Tale*, whom he called the "gentlemen of the vertical," and who were only able to give out abstract wisdom in minted coins and no "fruits of the earth." The elemental force of the Russian people was affronted, as the great river was affronted in this *Fairy Tale* when gold fell into it. It had also to be borne in mind that these men of the Provisional Government — I later got to know several of them personally — were not at all prepared for their task. Whereas the communists had worked out their revolutionary plans in detail while in exile, the events came quite unexpectedly for the Provisional Government, and none of them was resolute in taking the cross of power upon themself. True to the old ideals, which had nothing to do with the present situation anymore, they deserted their positions one after the other, so as not to have to compromise their conscience, handing Russia over to the Bolsheviks. Instead of the constitutional assembly, we got the Bolshevik coup of October.

We sat at home for four days while the battles raged in Moscow and our walls were riddled with bullet holes. In contrast to the fearful mood of her surroundings, Alexandra Alexeievna was calm and collected. When a wine warehouse was plundered nextdoor to us, all manner of atrocities were expected of the drunken perpetrators and we were advised not to undress at night. She, nonetheless, went to bed in complete composure. From the clock tower of the Strastnoy Cloister, the Bolsheviks shot with cannons. When the shelling of heavy artillery began, becoming more and more intense, it was feared that our wooden house could catch fire, so we went to the cellar, in which a tailor lived. He appeared to take me for a communist and whispered in my ear, "I sent my apprentice out scouting. Our people will carry the day!"

In these days I was able to read *Faust* for the first time from beginning to end. Things went similarly for me later on, during the counter-revolutionary uprising of sailors in Kronstadt in 1921, when I was locked in my room in the Commissariat for External Affairs in St Petersburg.[41] There was danger of the house being stormed. I was able to read all three parts of the *Divine Comedy*. In such situations one is seemingly lifted out of time and place.

When the fighting died down and the communists had won, I hurried to my parents. The battles had been heaviest between the Pretshistenka, where they lived (and where the general staff was located) and the Kremlin. The streets looked eerie; pools of blood everywhere and ravaged government buildings. Groups of ordinary people stood around gloating. Then came the first snow, mercifully covering and purifying the traces of the disaster. I found my parents in good health, but despairing.

That same day, we anthroposophists gathered in our hall, though we had made no actual appointment to do so, and read the essay on the principles of true socialism by Rudolf Steiner.

After a few days, all banks, all safes, everything stored in warehouses, was confiscated; obviously all landed property as well. In every house, silver, gold and fur coats were requisitioned. From one day to the next, we had nothing anymore. But we were not unhappy about it, feeling it as a liberation from the consciousness of guilt that everyone experienced in one way or another, by belonging to a privileged class.

Typically, conversations among people contained a confused mixture of folk superstition and the latest slogans of communism. Soldiers coming from the front "deepened" the revolution. First, the chauffeurs were the heroes of the day, since no one could catch up with them if they had "socialized" something. The tempo with which they could disappear from the scene of their crimes gave them a new sense of freedom. Then sailors appeared to be even bigger heroes. A lock of hair fixed with brilliantine hung out at an angle over one eye from under their caps. They had so much money that with bundles of "Kerenskys" — the forty-ruble banknotes printed in the Kerensky period — they more or less threw them around.

"Why stint with your brilliantine, comrade? Pour a whole bottle on it right now, I'll pay!" That was their style. Dance places were set up everywhere. Sailors and soldiers danced the one-step and foxtrot with "Jacobin" women. Even the revolutionary sentries danced the foxtrot at their posts.

"No," I heard a peasant sigh, "first they should have given us education, then the Revolution. They gave us dim, uneducated people the Revolution too soon. It cannot work."

Another said, "How can we live without the Tsar? Like this, there will be no order; he'll have to be brought back."

"Why? After all, he has been dethroned, because with his war he set Russia on the path to ruin."

"But perhaps he has meanwhile become level-headed again ... after all, we cannot really do without the Tsar ..." When peasant women sang the *Marseillaise*, they sounded infinitely wistful and tearful.

Soon after the coup, the painter Igor Grabar, our friend Dr Trapesnikov and Nikolai Mashkovzev went to the government with the proposal that they be given authority to preserve valuable art and cultural monuments from destruction by the uneducated masses. From this arose the great organization "For the Protection of Monuments of Art and Antiquity." Trotzky's wife headed this organization, though she understood nothing about art, and Dr Trapesnikov became her right hand. In this way much good could be done for art as well as for individuals. Not only castles and art collections, but also their owners were saved. More often than not such a house was made into a museum, and its owner was permitted to live there as a custodian. That is what happened with the houses of the art patron Sergei Shtshukin, the icon collector Ilya Ostrouchov, and Ivan Morosov, among others. Tolstoy's Yasnaya Polyana also became a museum. Trapesnikov gained general respect and recognition for his conscientiousness and thoroughness in this regard.

Chimeras

Entering the canteen of the painters for the first time on the Pretshistenka, I found them all in an elevated mood. I saw nearly every painter of note, including Petya Kontshalovsky, now a celebrated master of the school of Cézanne, whom I had not met since my childhood. All were full of plans. There was talk of a state-subsidized edition of artists' monographs. At last, I thought, there will be a monograph of Alexander Ivanov, about whom I have already reported, and I proposed him; but everyone only wanted to publish themselves. A communist painter asked me whether I wanted to work as secretary of the painting division in Prolet-Cult (Proletarian Culture). With this institution just then being set up, a workers' education centre for art and science was to be created for painting, poetry, music, dramatic art, history and political economy. The Moscow Prolet-Cult was to become a centre for Prolet-Cults in the whole of Russia. But the yardstick was to be not just all-Russian, but all-European. "Soviet Russia will open up new paths in all fields and lead the way for all countries," it was said. For that reason, a secretary able to conduct foreign correspondence was being sought. It was also to be my task to organize studios for painting and art lectures in various districts of Moscow. Did I want to do that? Of course! Was it not the fulfilment of the deepest longing of my soul, to open the way to art for our people? I had come from Dornach, from the source of the new artistic impulses, and was to work at a centre that was to be a criterion for the proletariat throughout Russia. I was so happy that hunger, cold, and the fact that I had no roof over my head, and slept somewhere else every night, did not matter to me.

The Prolet-Cult was located in our area in the Moorish palace of Morosov, a merchant and art collector, that had been requisitioned for the purpose.[42] It was one of the fantastic, ornate houses such as these not all-too educated millionaires had built earlier, and whose gaudiness actually fitted in quite well with the oriental character of Moscow. The

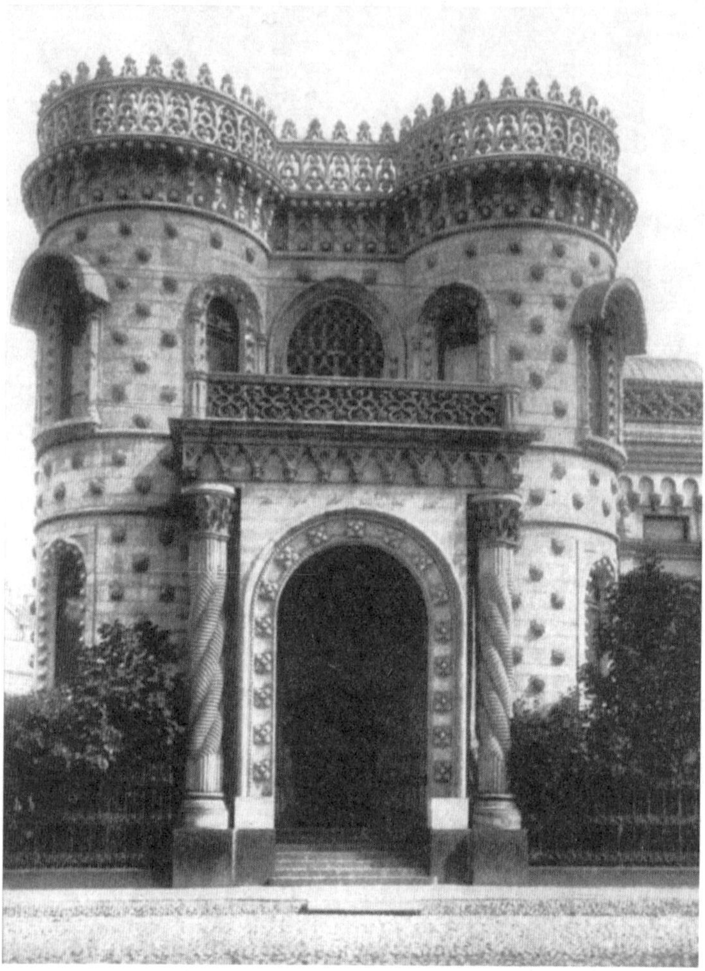

The house of Morosov, the art patron

doorman, a former servant of the owner, regarded the intruders with silent indignation, viewing them as mean people making themselves at home in the manorial rooms. As someone "of standing," he hoped to find in me similar feelings to his own.

I was eager to find out who my co-workers would be. The communist cell consisted of three dyed-in-the-wool Marxists. But this cell did not at once step strongly to the forefront. At the first meeting I recognized the director of the musical department, an acquaintance who had participated in my introductory course in anthroposophy. The graphic designer was a very likeable and competent artist who addressed me at once on the subject of anthroposophy. Soon Andrei Belyi and Vyatsheslav Ivanov came as instructors in the department of poetic art. Prince Sergei Volkonski, the former director of the Imperial Theatre, taught dramatic art. He was a follower of the interesting method of François Alexandre Delsarte, which is based on the threefold nature of the human being, and taught in accordance with this method in the Prolet-Cult as well. A pupil of Kusma Petrov-Vodkin gave painting instruction.

The pupils who came were, for the most part, factory workers, people interested and open to what they received. And already the first charcoal drawings I saw after a few days surprised me as something quite new. The lines, the shapes were no mere passive imitation of nature, though stimulated by nature, they recorded what was reborn in the soul. Here at the outset was what modern artists were seeking. Not a contrived, thought-out expressionism, but a self-evident attitude to the world. Those belonging to this social strata brought a new dynamism, capable of breaking through the boundaries of static, three-dimensional form: that is, what had to be conquered in the Renaissance so that the spirit could fully incarnate, but had now become static and passive, leading to naturalism in art. These human beings, I thought, will be capable of breaking through this! They do not live only in their heads, mirroring what has already come into existence. They live in the heart and limbs, in which the will and the future are active. Their attitude to the results of their work was also refreshing. They regarded their work with a certain humour; for them, actually doing it was the important thing. What actually arose was but the trace left behind by this activity, and for them of no special significance in itself. They lived rather in the actual process of becoming something new and in keeping with the times. And how happy these people were to have the opportunity of being creative, which actually meant "being human"!

The house of the Prolet-Cult was near the military school, where, every night, people were shot. In the lodgings where I stayed for the most part, the shots could be heard all night through the wall. But during the day I saw the pupils of the Prolet-Cult, who longed for the true meaning of life and had the deepest questions concerning existence.

With what trust and what gratitude did they receive what they were given! At that time I lived in this state of dichotomy. When various acquaintances reproached me for not sabotaging communism, but working in Prolet-Cult, I replied, "What we have to give workers has nothing to do with political parties."

I was convinced that Bolshevism, so alien to the Russian people, would only last a short span of time, as a transition phase. On the other hand, what the workers received by way of a share in culture — the generally human element — would remain after Bolshevism had disappeared completely. It was moving to see these people, greenish-looking and puffed from hunger, listening to lecturers in the icy cold of the auditorium. Where else were such faces to be found; souls full of devoted attention? And we were privileged to give them, finally, what was of real value in life not only for them, but for us as well.

Together with various friends who were art historians, I worked out a programme and we held art lectures in the districts of Moscow in which Prolet-Cult had rooms. Showing slides proved difficult with the inadequate lighting, but it worked out even so. This was mainly because the lecturers were filled with the same degree of enthusiasm as the listeners. In one lecture with a large audience of workers, Andrei Belyi took issue with the counter-revolution. The counter-revolution, so he said, actually wanted, as the remnant of a bourgeois outlook, to reassert materialistic views after the great changeover had already occurred. And he spoke of the deeds of Rudolf Steiner, who had broken through the boundaries of knowledge and pointed out new paths to the spirit. With that, he called forth such enthusiasm from his audience that he was lifted up and carried through the hall. It was astonishing to see how a way of speaking that was in fact not at all easy, nonetheless went over so well with the workers. These souls were quite evidently enquiring after the higher meaning of life. That is what they wanted to know about. Those studying poetic art in Prolet-Cult valued Belyi as well; an interesting poetry group grew out of it. But in the course of the winter, the communist cell began to notice that Marxism came off badly. Thus I had to submit the general concept of the lectures on art history to the "cell" for review. What they were unable to understand, they laughed at.

> Your lectures are bourgeois; they don't comprehend our ideas at all. They would actually have to develop the emergence of art out of the class struggle. Comrade X can do that. He

> will hold a lecture in basic Marxism before every art history period, and put everything squarely on the foundation of economic materialism. Your lecturers will only have to supply the illustrative material. You should guard against adding ideas of your own. Here is the programme which you must adhere to.

Thus the work was gradually made impossible for us. Andrei Belyi and Vyatsheslav Ivanov had the same experience. The director of the musical department was best able to work without being thus "enlightened." With his orchestra organization extending throughout Russia he was able to exert an influence for the good.

One evening a woman came to me, to enrol in a painting course. She mentioned her name as Marya Bshestok.

"Have you perhaps come from the front?" I asked. Quite a lot had been heard concerning a woman of this name, who was supposed to have had no equal in bloodlust.

"Yes, I am Commissar Bshestok and I have come directly from the front in order to deepen the revolution in the country." She had a very tired voice and infinitely sad eyes, such as I had seen with many *Chekists*. Soon she appeared at meetings as a representative of the students, with all manner of complaints. The teachers were unjust, some say too much, others too little, the lighting was bad, people were freezing cold. As if the whole of Russia were not freezing! But she did not yet know this. The quiet work became impossible; the mood in the studio changed completely.

In the cell of the Prolet-Cult a startling idea was born. The trains travelling in every direction in Russia were to be painted with propaganda images. Painters as well as the pupils were to apply to do this work. Each would receive the daily ration of a soldier of the Red Army and pocket money in addition. The carriages to be painted stood on sidings at various train stations. It was bitterly cold. I had to write down the names of those who applied and assign painters to various places. The artists waited in trepidation to see whether they would be accepted. Humiliated by need, they were an excruciating sight. Among them were a number of acquaintances of mine.

In the Prolet-Cult it became more and more difficult for us to conduct our work according to what we ourselves had in mind. The cell drew in the reins tightly. Sometimes, in lectures given by Bolsheviks for the workers, I would hear them sneer at Tolstoy or at Dostoyevsky. These Marxist lectures were referred to by the workers as "religion lessons," since they were obligatory, in the same way that religious instruction had been earlier. A dead hand was laid on everything, destroying any germinating seeds. I saw disappointed, cheated human beings. The feeling of brotherhood inherent in the Russian soul was transformed by devilish propaganda into hatred of the bourgeoisie. Observing this was worse than cold, hunger and terror. "Fear not those who kill the flesh, but rather those who would kill the spirit."

Gradually altogether different people came to the evening courses, having quite other aims in mind. There were unpleasant scenes. The composition of the teachers also changed. I stayed on for a while as a "consultant" at meetings of the Prolet-Cult.

On the day of the anniversary of the October revolution, Andrei Belyi fetched me and we wandered through the streets brimming with people. On that glorious October day, Moscow resembled an old Russian fairy tale. Not only were the houses decorated with red material — though the population went about in rags — one could admire huge posters by well-known painters in a futuristic style, and the houses themselves were colourfully painted the length of whole streets. Red Square was teeming with people, as it had previously been only on Palm Sunday. One did not see the dull hopelessness on faces as under the tsarist regime. In spite of the famine, people remained trustful and optimistic about the future, believing in freedom and seeing themselves as masters of their country. Like children, or the population in some fairy tale, people marvelled at the festive decorations. Two gleaming silver aeroplanes appeared above, circling in the deep blue sky over the square. Such a blue sky occurs in Russia only at the beginning of autumn. Everyone looked up expectantly. Clouds of silvery doves appeared to float down from the sky. Against the background of the white churches and golden onion domes of the Kremlin, this seemed like a prophetic image for Russia. The Russian people were always waiting for manna from heaven. However, these were no doves, nor a Dove Book that once fell from heaven, but white pieces of paper. People grasped them in the air, picked them up from the ground. The words on them spelled out an appeal for bloody revenge against the bourgeoisie.

Now the second chimera was to enter my life. I became a co-worker in the Department of Theatrical Performances in the People's Commissariat for Education and received an assignment in the Children's Theatre Department. But just what this task consisted of, I was never able to find out. I question whether the director of the Department, Mrs Olga Kameneva, the sister of Trotsky, a midwife by profession, knew this herself. We sat in expectation of something that would, of course, happen someday in accordance with the "all-Russian standard of measure." A great many meetings took place with well-known theatre directors, poets, variety artists and circus people. I got to know, among others, the clown Vladimir Durov, world famous for his animal tricks. His eyes seemed to have something in common with animal eyes. He was a convinced communist.

"I have solved the social problem," he said to me, "with me, the wolf lives peacefully next to a goat."

Later I saw this "community." The wolf trembled in front of the goat.

At one meeting, when the Commissar for Public Education, Anatoly Lunatsharsky, was present, I was to present a plan for the development of the children's theatre. Since nothing could actually be carried out, the emphasis was on projects instead. The theatre director, Vsevolod Meyerhold, was enthusiastic about my proposals and considered them the starting point for a theatre of the future. Lunatsharsky was also of this opinion. It was very easy at that time to drum up enthusiasm in Russia. With his pointed beard and slanted eyes, Lunatsharsky's face had something that corresponded to Lenin, Trotsky and the other leading communists, making them similar to each other despite the dissimilarity of their features otherwise, something goat like, Mephistophelian.

One evening, Comrade Kameneva invited me to Lunatsharsky's reading of a drama by Ivan Rukavishnikov. We met under the gate of the Kremlin, that fortress of Bolshevism, which no mortal could otherwise enter. Let through, we ascended the great staircase of the old Boyar Palace. A painter, who had also been invited, was unable to contain himself for sheer happiness and obsequious deference. "How unexpected! What good fortune!" The subservience revealed itself for which certain people seem born.

Apart from the poet Rukavishnikov and his wife, among the guests was the taciturn poet Yurgis Baltrushaytis, then the Lithuanian ambassador in Moscow, and the director Meyerhold, along with party members whom I did not know. Comrade Lev Kamenev, who appeared to me quite conventional, received us amiably. It gave one a peculiar feeling to be under the vaulted ceilings of these old Russian halls in this company! In a corner on a sofa sat Lunatsharsky with the very beautiful Mrs Rukavishnikova, who was evidently his mistress. She had black hair and wore a silk dress with a broad, pleated skirt, like the Jacobin women of the French Revolution. He was reading from a book in his hand; she giggled.

Then he came up to me and said very patronizingly, "I have heard that you are now to take over the direction of the painting department in the People's Palace of Art. You may rest assured that this work will always find sympathetic interest from me."

Then he inquired whether I was "the direct pupil of Steiner."

I confirmed it, and had to think of the cry of the native Americans on seeing the ships of Columbus, "Woe betide us, we have been discovered!" As one of his friends told me, Lunatsharsky had "swallowed" *Esoteric Science* by Rudolf Steiner in one go during his exile in Geneva, and had compared it with a Bach fugue. However, he now no longer believed "in the astral adventures of Herr Steiner."

Lunatsharsky was the bard, so to speak, among his comrades, the nightingale. But whether or not they took him seriously, I do not know. Later he was relieved of his position, not being considered sufficiently thorough in his communism. In an attempt to prove his loyalty, his last deed was to ban the Gospels. Everyone had to give up their Bible, house searches were conducted, and grievous was the fate of anyone in whose house the book was found!

His recital of the one act play by Rukavishnikov was really excellent. This dramatic scene was based on Pushkin's work, *The Mermaid*. Seduced by the Prince, the miller's daughter drowned herself in the Dnieper and became a mermaid. All manner of fiendish spirits gathered around her father, who had gone mad, and decided to lure the Prince into the Dnieper, in which they succeeded. This piece was incredibly forceful as well as poetic, but unbearable in its eeriness on account of the subhuman element haunting it.

"An actual human being, an ego would have to appear here as a counterweight," I said, when the work was being discussed afterwards. I looked around. It seemed that here I was likewise among goblins, among masks, all plotting disaster. After midnight everyone was served a cup of weak tea without sugar and a small slice of black bread. The intention it seemed, was to say: You see, we have no more than you! Then again, the cups and teaspoons were decorated with the crown of the tsars.

The moon was dazzlingly bright and the snow crunched under my feet as, in a strange mood, I stepped out through the Kremlin gate at two o'clock that night. At my parents' house, I knocked on the front door in vain. The old folks heard nothing. On this frosty night, I had to walk for a long time through the streets empty of people before finally finding shelter for the night. The doors were barricaded everywhere and no doorbells functioned. Yet, strangely, at that time I was never afraid. During that whole time in Russia, I felt as though "under golden rain."

My connection with the People's Palace of Art, which Lunatsharsky had referred to that evening in the Kremlin, had come about as follows. Prior to the evening described, I had gone to Sologub House, famous for its architecture and décor, and described by Tolstoy in *War and Peace* as the house of Count Rostov. In this house the office of the Painters' Association was located. I wanted to inquire about something and landed by chance in a meeting of painters. In a semicircular wing of this house, a kind of free Academy of Painting was to be set up. I took part in the meeting with the result that after half an hour I was chosen to be the director of this Academy. I asked the poet Rukavishnikov, the head of the Palace of Art, whether there was enough money; whether we had enough fuel to heat the rooms in question, whether paints, brushes and canvas would be allocated to us. He thought these things would all be available, since the People's Commissar Lunatsharsky was very interested in the matter and would make everything available. I myself received a charming, poetic room upstairs in the house, with antique furniture and a blue-tiled stove from the seventeenth century, and was to take my meals in the kitchen of the Palace of Art. Considering the cold and hunger I had had to bear that year, but especially the impossibility of working productively, it can be imagined how happy I was at this fairytale transformation in my destiny. "You can move in right away," said Rukavishnikov. His beautiful, sphinx-like wife smiled in a friendly manner. They also lived in this house. A plan of work already took shape in my mind: courses in Goethe's colour theory, exercises in the visual-moral experience of colours, as well as sketching from nature for those who wanted it.

When I visited my parents and told them about it, my mother said, "Oh, with you everything is always so fantastic!"

I had to admit the truth of that. I packed my little suitcase and went to the Palace, where for the first time in quite a while, I slept in a well-heated room. The canteen turned out to be less appealing. I was given a soup-plate of hot water with a few small slices of unpeeled potatoes. A codfish tail floated in it. Responding to a notice in the newspaper, masses of people came to enrol for the courses. I rented easels, and prepared an introductory talk. When the easels were brought and I submitted the bill to Rukavishnikov, he became evasive.

"The suppliers will have to wait: I have no money."

He expressed himself in a peculiarly vague manner. I noticed that he was intoxicated. On the second day, the stove in my room was no longer heated. I asked the doorman the reason for this.

"For today, I can bring some more wood," he said, "but for tomorrow we have no more." Rukavishnikov was in a still more problematic mood.

"Yes, yes," he said, "we can't heat the house at all anymore."

I turned to his beautiful, ever-smiling wife, "How can we get fuel?"

"We shall now have to incorporate our Palace of Art into the Military Department."

"Why?"

"Well, so that X," she named a Bolshevik general, "will help us!"

I looked at her, baffled. She smiled in her sphinx-like manner. Soon I learned that she had just then been unfaithful to Lunatsharsky and had become the mistress of an important member of the military.

Again, I wandered without a roof over my head, sleeping somewhere else every night. I had no work and went hungry. The theatre authorities ordered me to an institution, the name of which was composed of initial letters and quite unpronounceable. I was to direct a Children's Club every evening, which was to be a model club for the whole of Russia. I told the children fairy tales which we dramatized on the spur of the moment. I painted, sang and did eurythmy with them. We were peaceful and happy together. From time to time educators appeared from other places, to learn from me just how such a children's club should be conducted, since I was, of course, working in accordance with an "all-Russian standard." Pedagogically, I was an absolute lay person.

My advice was based on my own healthy feeling and on the lecture by Rudolf Steiner, *The Education of the Child.* The educators assumed this was the new direction desired by the state. I had to copy a diagram in which the all-Russian bureaucratic machine, partly non-existent, was portrayed in circles and lines. The abbreviated names of the offices, composed of initial letters, appeared to me like the names of little devils. Can there be a name that does not connect with an entity? I was permitted to do this work at home. In the office sat the philosopher Nikolai Berdyayev in a fur coat and a boyar hat, warming his hands on a glass of hot water. When he saw my work, he said, "I envy you for being so 'productive.' I myself still do not know what I have been hired for."

After fourteen days of sick leave I went to the administrative office to collect my salary and rations, but at every desk there was an unknown face.

"I do not find your name on the list," the cashier said.

"Why? After all, I am the director of the Children's Club."

"Citizen, you are at the wrong place. We are ..." and she gave an unfamiliar designation. "We moved in here several days ago."

No one had any idea what authority had been here previously. I searched for it in vain. It had dissolved without a trace.

Artistic Pause

The year 1919 was perhaps the bleakest year following the Revolution. In view of the particularly cold winter, the impossibility of heating the houses was devastating. By then all the wooden fences of the city had already been used up for firewood, making it possible to pass through wonderful gardens and parks. The nightly delivery of wood on the basis of false papers had not yet been organized. All water pipes and drains froze up, so that when there was a thaw, the pipes having burst, people got the effluence on their heads. It was strictly forbidden to transport bread from the country into the city. At railway stations it nearly came to pitched battles fought between soldiers and so-called "sack carriers." The bread shared out from time to time in "house committees," depending on what category one belonged to, an eighth, a quarter, or at most half a pound per day, was a compound mixed with straw, which crumbled immediately. To buy flour or grain, one had to go to black marketeers in dark cellars, with both sides fearful of being denounced. Black marketeering was subject to the death penalty.

Typhus became an epidemic. It was spread by lice, and how were they to be combatted? They did not perish in boiling water, nor did frost destroy them. There was no soap of any kind. On the street, figures wrapped in cloth were often to be seen drawn on sleighs: sick or dead people. There were no longer any coffins in which to bury people. A plan of compulsory service was instituted, to cremate corpses in large factory furnaces.

In November, Polya's nephew came from the front and spent the night with us. The next morning, seriously ill, he had to be taken to the military hospital. After a few days, Polya became sick with typhus fever. I scoured the apothecaries for camphor and other medicines, encountering embittered pharmacists in the empty, cold rooms filled with vapours, who only shook their heads in answer to every question. They had nothing to sell. I looked after Polya until I could do no more, due to her worsening condition. The delirium of those sick with typhus fever is frequently like a state of insanity. Patients often have to be bound. We brought Polya to the hospital, to the famous specialist Dr Marzinovsky. Two farmhands carried her out of the house. At that time both my parents had the flu. I now looked after them, until one evening I could no longer move on account of back pain. The next morning I had a high fever — it was typhus! Two workers carried me out and I was brought to the same hospital in which Polya lay. She died on the day of my arrival, but I learned this only much later. While all the sick were being admitted to the hospital, we lay on stretchers in the snow in front of the majestic baroque building from the time of Tsar Paul I. With his tall, noble bearing, Dr Marzinovsky appeared to me like a knight. On account of the danger of infection, he wore very high, close-fitting boots and close-fitting overalls. In spite of my high fever — over 41 C (106 F) — I was able to provide exact answers to everything he wanted to know. Throughout the illness I retained consciousness, and was in fact sharper and more awake than otherwise. I was able, for example, to call to mind whole scenes from *Faust*, which I could never have done while in a normal state of health. Also, I only needed to think of someone and that person stood clearly before me. Once, when I thought of Michael Bauer, he appeared to me so immediately and palpably, that I feared he might meanwhile have died, and I was now meeting his departed soul. In Russia we were indeed cut off from the whole world. Just at that time, as he later told me, Michael Bauer saw me lying there in torn sheets and thought I must have become seriously ill. In the hospital there was no disinfectant, no soap, no fuel, and often no light. And there was only a watery soup to eat, with frozen, unpeeled, rotten potatoes.

For the first few hours, I lay in a hall with sixty raving women. It was harrowing. When I gave my name in answer to a question by the head nurse, she asked me, whether I was related to Dr Ivan Sabashnikov, who was at that time also in the hospital as a typhus patient. It was my uncle, the psychiatrist, of whom I have already given a brief account. He now lived in Moscow. We had not known that he had become ill in the meantime. This relationship brought it about that I was transported to a smaller room; I lay there with two women doctors, who were, however, unconscious for the time being. The next day Dr Marzinovsky hauled my uncle, who was already learning to walk again, up to my bed.

Despite all external misery, the months of my illness belonged, in a sense, to the happiest of my life. On being able to lift my head again, through the large window next to my bed, I saw the snow-covered park with ancient linden trees. At night, especially during the Christmas period, the stars stood out vividly between the branches and seemed very large. Gratefully, I felt myself as if supported and carried by these stars. "The stars are the home of spiritual beings, and light is only their outer manifestation." I had the feeling that whatever may happen, even falling into the abyss, one falls into their arms.

Relatives and friends did not visit me. I knew they simply had no strength to cross the city on foot. I received no food parcels as other sick people did and yet had to praise my good fortune in being able to lie here. Once, Nyusha came. She spoke so quietly that I thought I had gone deaf — deafness can be a consequence of typhus — but her voice was weak from exhaustion. My joyful mood communicated itself to the others, and our room became the dayroom for the nurses when free. I barely had time to recover from my illness, being called upon to relate stories, recite and to sing in front of people. At night also, when others slept, or were raving in delirium, I received visits from nurses on night duty. Once, at Christmas, a doctor introduced himself to me, there as a stand-in, and I recognized him as a friend from childhood who had joined us in taking dance lessons with a French ballet master in our large hall on Nikitskaya Street. His name was Pestel, the grandson of the famous Pestel. He told me about his life and his experiences on the front. He could comprehend neither the unscrupulousness of the tsarist generals and officers, nor the unscrupulousness of the present dictators. In this doctor, who may have been thirty-three years old, I got to know a serious and honest human being. Though he did not have a drop of Russian blood in him, he was an earnest Russian patriot not easily found among Russians themselves. But he was in despair.

"How can one continue living?" he said, "if serious about one's duty, about truth and honesty?"

I tried in vain to awaken in him a measure of trust in the powers of existence. He would have liked to pursue the conversation further. But as a doctor, he felt he should allow me time to sleep.

"Tomorrow we shall have to continue our conversation," I said.

"I have replacement duty only tonight."

"Then we shall have to see each other when I am well again."

I learned later that he took his own life a few days after this meeting. To this day I have a sense of having failed him.

At midnight on New Year's Eve the senior consultant, Dr Marzinovsky, came to me with two tumblers of champagne. His wife lay unconscious, dangerously ill with typhus in a single room nextdoor. Sick people either slept or raved all around us. If he did not willingly depart this world, it was because the will to heal held him back. Dr Marzinovsky had discovered various serums, all of which he had tried out on himself, despite mortal danger. Later, when I was again able to walk, I watched him bind wounds every day. In consequence of the lack of disinfectant, many patients got blood poisoning from injections, so that limbs had to be amputated. When this upright, tall figure kneeled over a patient, I had to think of Julian the Compassionate; his movements expressed so much devotion.

The earnest conversation we had on that New Year's night was our first and last. However, the beautiful thing about times of catastrophe is that human beings are seemingly torn out of the temporal and meet each other as is otherwise only possible after death.

"Now I certainly ought to go," I said to him, once able to walk again after a paralysis of the legs lasting a week.

"And what awaits you outside?"

"A room without heat, no care or help."

"With your heart dilation you should not move about. Stay here with us a while longer."

God knows, I would gladly have done so, but the typhus epidemic had not passed. There were sick people in the corridors, lying on the floor, and it would have been irresponsible to continue taking up another bed. Thus he had to discharge me. But it was no easy matter for me to leave, and the paramedic who accompanied me and carried my small suitcase through Moscow, seemed like the last angel out of Paradise.

When I appeared as a tottering figure at my parents' residence, the place looked like a night shelter. Laundry hung this way and that in the damp air on clothes lines strung throughout the living room. My brother lay unconscious on the sofa with pneumonia. The doctor had not come for several days, and his condition was getting worse. Since my parents were too weak from exhaustion, I had to go out and fetch the doctor at once myself. When I rang, a distraught girl opened the door, "Our master, the doctor, died yesterday of typhus," she said.

Not far from us there was a Red Cross hospital. I went there. The distinguished-looking head nurse informed me that they were on the point of closing down her hospital.

"Do you have a connection to the Red Cross?" she asked nevertheless.

I said, "Would it be appropriate under the Bolshevik regime to refer to Governor General Dzhunkovsky, who was chairman of the Red Cross? We are very good friends of Vladimir Dzhunkovsky." At that, the faces around me all beamed.

"Our doctor will visit your brother today, and tomorrow morning you can bring him to us." The next day, two servants carried Alyosha, all muffled up, out of our apartment. He was placed next to me in a small droshky sleigh; it took all my strength to hold him. The horse shied easily, and when a car came towards us — fortunately there were few cars then in Moscow — the horse veered onto the high snow bank. This was not cleared away during that very cold winter, which had a lot of snow. With every jolt, the patient groaned, and the small sleigh was in danger of tipping over at any moment. At the door of the hospital, I had to lean the patient against the back of the coachman holding the horse until I had fetched the nurse. If the two of us eventually regained our health despite everything, it was certainly meant to be.

Chimeras Once Again

After this "artistic pause" I had once more to look for work. I did in fact receive an offer that turned out to be the fourth chimera. One would indeed have to have a leaning toward illusionism, as I did at that time, to still believe in the possibility of finding a reasonable job in this chaotic period, in which old traditions were being thrown overboard. Ideas that recognized the laws of human life, capable of leading to practical applications, were altogether lacking. Instead, golden rules were violated on the basis of theories that were fundamentally one-sided, flawed and untrue.

In the famous castle of Prince Galizyn, two hours from Moscow, the Commissar for Public Education, Lunatsharsky, had founded a training centre for child prodigies in painting. Out of a hundred orphans from the factory centres around Moscow, a commission chose the most ingenious ones, and an elite forty children were assembled in this castle. The director of the school was a businessman with a large family, having no connection to art or pedagogy. He had applied for this position to keep himself and his family afloat. Noted painters and other teachers involved had the same aim. Each family lodged in a different corner of the castle, which had countless rooms, and led their own private lives there, without bothering much about the forty orphans. The "educators" were, in principle, in favour of freedom in education. The children could do what they wanted. I slept below, next to the children's dormitories. Though I had been invited only for artistic instruction in this school, I tried to bring some kind of order into this chaos. The plumbing did not work in the castle; we had to fetch the water ourselves in a barrel, with the help of a limping horse. When it became cold, it turned out that there was also no heat, and we collected bundles of twigs so as to keep ourselves warm to some extent with open fires. For months, food consisted of lentils and worm-eaten herrings, served partly in dog dishes, partly in wonderful Sèvres porcelain belonging to the castle.

There was no timetable. No rhythm was introduced at all. When I requested the support of the director of the school in getting the children to bed on time, not letting them run wild till two o'clock in the morning, as they often did, he answered, "Why? I like to see my children fall asleep in the midst of their boisterousness."

During the day I would try to keep the throng in check by drawing one of them. The other children then stood and watched with interest. They didn't want to do anything themselves. Why not indeed? In education it is a well-known fact that pronounced talents appear with some children, only to disappear completely after puberty. Such capacities flare up like reminiscences from earlier lives, later to metamorphose into something entirely different. Among our "child prodigies" there was a boy who rendered Roman buildings and figures with a surprising degree of graphic perfection. A girl painted and modelled the same motif again and again: a human being bound to a tree and pierced through with arrows. This portrayal of St Sebastian does not occur in Russian iconography. In the factory milieu from which these children came, there could have been no models for such an image. Very soon the older children did not want to paint at all anymore, and the younger ones imitated their behaviour. It is plainly erroneous to want to determine a child's future on the basis of faculties and tendencies appearing prior to puberty. Developing a talent one-sidedly in order to cultivate geniuses, as was the intention in our castle, serves only to hinder the proper development of the whole human being, and in effect raises cripples. The absurdity of this endeavour soon showed itself.

There was no illumination in the castle, and I sat with the children during the long evenings at a huge marble fireplace where we burnt twigs. By the flickering light I told them fairy tales, sagas and what I knew of foreign countries and peoples. For a while things went well, but then two groups began to form among the children and one group drove the other away from the fireplace. The situation grew worse every day and the children ran wild. They held it against the teachers that they had to go hungry, even though things were no better for us. They could not abide the lentil soup anymore. They ran across the tables and threw things onto the parquet floor, the Sèvres porcelain as well as the dog dishes. Children, who could otherwise be charming, started behaving as though possessed. The much touted freedom they were to be given — whether based on theory or merely for convenience — led to perversity. A child needs guidance.

"It is actually quite nice here," a visiting inspector said, consoling me. "In other houses the children are harassed. As punishment for a misdemeanour, a child is woken up during the night and prevented from sleeping, for instance."

I explained to the head of the school, as well as to my colleagues, that I considered it dangerous nonsense for none of them to bother about the children; also that I could no longer accept responsibility for this. Nothing happened, so I left. Things did not get any better for the children, and for me a period of acute starvation began. After a few weeks, I caught sight of a throng of grey gnome-like figures on the snow-covered street in front of the Rumyanzev Museum. They ran across the street to me, surrounding and embracing me; the children from the Galizyno Castle. They had been brought to Moscow to be shown the museums. Unfortunately, on just that day the museums were closed.

"Instead, we have seen you!" they cried.

But my heart ached in sympathy for them and in the consciousness of my powerlessness. After a few months I learned that the school had been disbanded and the children transferred to various homes for young criminals. That is the point to which this experiment in education finally led.

There were further similar experiences I have no wish to report. No matter where I went, there was the same impossibility of working. I decided to break this chain, if possible, and wrote to four acquaintances in other cities, asking whether they knew of any job possibilities for me. The first reply came from St Petersburg, from Konstantin Ligsky. The son of a Russian village priest, Ligsky had joined the Social Revolutionary Party in early youth and was sentenced to forced labour in Siberia. From there he succeeded in fleeing abroad. I got to know him in Dornach, where he earned his living working with concrete. He knew little of anthroposophy, but the building impressed him. Being artistically talented, he was able to help later with the engraving of the glass windows. From time to time I had helped him out, when he was in financial straits. He went back to Russia almost at the same time as I did, and wrote to me from St Petersburg asking whether I could find work for him, since he was in serious difficulties. His party was persecuted by the communists. However, at that time I had been unable to do anything for him. Now I turned to him with the same question and received an immediate answer. I should just come; he would have a suitable position for me in the Commissariat for Foreign Affairs, where I could be employed in the library for foreign literature. I would also get an apartment in the same Commissariat and meals from the Hotel International, should I be willing to paint a portrait of Lenin for this same authority. A train ticket was included with his letter as well as a travel permit. Mrs Balmont's daughter, my young cousin Nina, wrote to me at the same time, also encouraging me to come to St Petersburg. There was little reason to deliberate, and I left, to my parents' dismay, since travelling between cities was then practically impossible for private individuals, so that we were to be completely cut off from each other.

The Other City

When I appeared with my little suitcase at Ligsky's, I was surprised to find him living in a palace.[43] His young wife, a German noblewoman, whom he had got to know in Dornach, had had the courage to go to him through both fronts during the first days of the cease-fire. "Why did you not telegraph me?" he asked. "I would have fetched you from the station by car." I knew there were only three cars in St Petersburg. What had Ligsky become, that he could have fetched me in a car?

My apartment, consisting of two rooms and a kitchen, was charming, and warm from central heating. Only the gilded furniture horrified me. Ligsky smiled, "Those were selected by a co-worker, Comrade X, but he was kicked out when the party was purged." Thus I inherited his golden furniture. Then Ligsky led me through the rooms of the Commissariat to the Library and introduced me to the director. She was a radical communist. The young ladies, her co-workers, looked at me distrustfully. They were former ladies-in-waiting who took me for a communist because Ligsky introduced me. I asked him whether he had reconciled himself with the Communist Party. "One has to overlook small differences and help constructively wherever something is being done for the social order." It gradually dawned on me that my concrete-worker was no less than the Chief of the St Petersburg Commissariat of Foreign Affairs. I found him altered, which struck me particularly in his sombre look. The Library, for which I wrote card indexes in printed lettering, had been assembled from works stolen from every foreign consulate.

For the portrait of Lenin I was to create, I received a midday and evening meal delivered to me from the Hotel International as advance payment. Only leading communists stayed in this hotel, and prominent foreigners who were to be shown that people were well off in Russia. Every day, one received chicken with rice and that was during the great famine which Russia was then experiencing. At midday, more and more starving friends began to present themselves at my place.

The two cities of Moscow and St Petersburg (I have been unable to get used to the name Petrograd or Leningrad) had always been two quite different worlds. The difference was strongly in evidence now as well. Moscow, the oriental city, the city of the boyars, of the patriarchal nobility, the old merchant guild and the peasants, retained its colourful, chaotic, noisy character in these years of the revolution. Having become the centre and seat of the Bolshevik government, it was filled with the feverish activity of the Bolsheviks. The few passenger vehicles and lorries that existed belonged to those in power and were driven at breakneck speed by men dressed from head to foot in leather. In St Petersburg, sparsely populated in consequence of the famine having struck there earlier, a deathly stillness prevailed. It was astonishing to see how few footprints and sleigh tracks there were in the snow on the endless, straight avenues seeming to lead on forever, as in the desert, the closed shops and display windows boarded up. In summer, grass grew everywhere, on the grandiose Nevsky Prospect, on the square at the Mariinsky Theatre. And this seat of the tsars, with its austere palaces and state buildings, its broadly laid out squares over which, as it seemed, more sky could be seen than in other cities, now showed itself in its whole majesty. I was moved again and again by this unique beauty, whenever I crossed the boundless Neva with its shining granite embankments — in winter on the iced-over river, in summer by bridge — in order to reach the Academy of Fine Arts. My young cousin Nina Balmont, whom I had first come to know as an eight-year-old girl in Paris, now lived with her husband, a gifted futuristic painter, Lev Bruni, and their small son in the Academy building. She was now twenty years old. Tall and beautiful like her mother Katherina Balmont, she possessed the same warmth of heart as well. Full of life, a joyful mischievousness, brilliant notions, she had creative ability in thought, word and deed. The *starets* Nektari of the Optina Monastery, near which the Brunis had lived for a time, had her come to see him every day, and once said to her, "The gift of joyfulness has been given you, which you must share with others."

Lev Bruni, not much older than his wife, concerned himself with art and piety. He was a spiritual son of the *starets* Nektari, and occupied himself little with the intellect, even despising it. His words, chosen with effort, were full of originality and resourcefulness. His bold, fine sketches were always a new creation. At that time he sought to portray, for instance, "the tracks of things in space," or a hand raised in blessing, distilled to a dynamic sign. In this I saw something essentially modern, the striving to include time in our field of vision.

With Bruni's friend Vladimir Tatlin, who also lived in the Academy and who was then already viewed as a celebrated master, this tendency underwent a kind of materialistic distortion. In his workshop I saw the model he had made for a communist monument. It was a building in three parts, in which each piece turned on its axis by means of a mechanical device. The lower storey had a rhythm of one year, the second of one month, while the third turned on itself in one day. Here the information service and the press were to be housed. In this way, those working there were to be made aware of time. Tatlin was also the inventor of that peculiar "art," known as Constructivism, which assembles all manner of objects — glass bottles and building blocks, scraps of paper, rods and wire — are assembled in order to achieve a harmonious synthesis of different materials. Tatlin's project was accepted. I have not heard whether it was ever executed.

As I wanted to come to terms with various directions in modern art, I became Tatlin's pupil. The master made an object especially for me: a wooden board painted yellow ochre, partly lacquered, a matt-black piece of paper with a white border stuck diagonally across it, on which a triangular brass plate was attached. I painted it at home impressionistically, without understanding what he actually wanted. He was in no way satisfied. I had to paint it again, and reproduce the local colour everywhere independent of light effects, for example, the colour of the metal, without reflections. I had to pass a "comb" cut from cardboard, with umber on it, across the surface of painted wood, thus applying a wood-grain pattern to it, and so on. I had to lacquer what was lacquered, leave matt what was matt. It was almost direct imitation. He called this "objective painting."

Among my first impressions in St Petersburg was a memorial meeting at the writers union in celebration of Pushkin's death-day. It was a January evening. The hall, weakly-lit, was unheated and stuffy, and people dozed off. On the podium, I recognized, among other well-known academics and literary stars, now no more than a shadow of their former selves, the journalist Anatoly Koni, who had done much to uphold the law during the liberation of the peasants from serfdom, the critic Akim Volynsky, and the poet Alexander Blok. None of these three speakers could resist quoting Pushkin, in *Eugene Onegin*, "The time has come for the pen to rest." It was as though these words expressed their most ardent feeling.

I saw Alexander Blok for the last time that evening. In the spring he died of exhaustion. Those in power had not allowed him to go to Finland, where he might have been able to recover. At his funeral, attended by everyone to whom Russian literature meant something, thousands of people came. No speeches were held. Not a word was spoken; a profound silence sanctified this tragic death.

There was no longer an anthroposophical group in St Petersburg when I arrived there. The branch leaders and others had fled the famine and gone south. I met only a few members. A degree of spiritual freedom still prevalent at that time tolerated the existence of the Free Philosophical Academy, founded immediately after the Revolution with the collaboration of Andrei Belyi. In 1920–21 he was in Moscow. Receiving a request in the spring, to hold a public lecture there, I agreed with a certain hesitation, having never spoken publicly before. My subject was to be Goethe's *Fairy Tale of the Green Snake and the Beautiful Lily*, with regard to which new truths had occurred to me from the most varied points of view. I only did not know what to wear for the lecture. The weather was warm, and I had neither a summer dress, nor shoes. I only possessed a pair of peasants' felt shoes worn in winter. Chance came to my aid. The Commissariat handed out fine white linen to the library employees, for aprons. However, we all made use of this to sew new clothes, and I even made shoes from it as well. On the splendid Sunday afternoon on which I was to speak, I went with a beating heart through the streets of St Petersburg, painfully feeling every little pebble through my cloth soles. The auditorium had glass walls on opposite sides, through which the newly sprouting trees could be seen. With the audience sitting not on chairs but on large oriental carpets (no chairs could be obtained for the Free Academy), I lost all diffidence and was able to speak freely. My footwear turned out to be quite appropriate on the soft carpet. Following a discussion after the lecture, a group of about twenty people stayed on and expressed the wish to work systematically on matters of spiritual science. In this small circle of people, who had not previously known each other, and who then gathered regularly at my place, there were some who accomplished significant work in various fields.

Among others, there was the senior consultant of a large hospital, two orientalists, a philosopher and a noted painter, as well as a farmer from Novgorod. As a result of the diversity of the problems brought forward and the concrete nature of their knowledge, our study evenings acquired a rigorous character, which was a good schooling for me. And the catastrophe in which we were all caught up, had the effect of bringing us closer together in human terms.

From spring onward, as the days grew longer, I was again able to paint, and made a beginning on the promised picture of Lenin.

Ligsky put a number of his own photos at my disposal, and Bruni, who knew him, described the fresh, warm colour of his complexion and the somewhat reddish tone of his hair. One cannot actually paint a good portrait without making a living connection with the spirit of the person. It is a matter of giving oneself up to and "awakening" to their persona. It was painful in this case to experience the features in question: the massive, protruding forehead in which one sensed a heavy brain-mass that determined thoughts deriving from matter; the Mongolian eyes, the relatively short nose, a strong lower lip. Abstract intellect, combined with a strong force of will, predominated in this face. Feeling, the middle region, came up short. Some, who had known Lenin well earlier, related to me, that although he concerned himself with the Marxist system, he never wanted to inspect a factory. Life did not interest him. He wanted to realize an abstract ideal. The Terror was also something abstract for him. In private life he was considerate and modest.

The portrait was accepted by the directors of the Commissariat and hung.

Now I could at last start on a picture that I had wanted to paint since my youth, having once seen it on the inside of a mother-of-pearl shell: the coming into being of a human figure out of a whorl, the figure itself half-kneeling in quiet solemnity. I thought of the picture as the *Birth of Venus*. I now painted it in large surfaces and it acquired certain stylistic qualities as a result of a restriction in the colours; I only had white, ochre, vermilion, umber and just a little cobalt at my disposal. It was not yet finished when the favourable working conditions I then enjoyed were suddenly interrupted. Ligsky was ordered to Poland, as the first communist representative there. In order to save on personnel, massive dismissals took place. Those in power did not consider how the population was to survive. It was characteristic of this government of the people that it did not feel responsible for the people. Those in authority were as though strangers to this country.

"It is not important," a communist told me, "whether a few million die. There will soon be paradise on earth." In the summer of that year there was a time when travelling by tram did not cost anything. But the trams were so over-full that it was a dangerous undertaking to travel on them. Solely on the basis of a doctor's prescription, people were to receive free medicines at apothecaries. However, most medicines were unavailable. After a few weeks the famous NEP, the New Economic Policy, was instituted which meant that private trade was again permitted within certain limits.

After Ligsky's departure, the new Chief of the Commissariat of Foreign Affairs having dismissed a large part of the staff from one day to the next, I no longer received food from the hotel and had to clear out my room. I carried my picture, the *Birth of Venus*, one and a half square metres in size, on my back all over the city, since I had no permanent place to stay. Completing this picture now appeared to me the most important thing in my life.

A German I had become acquainted with in the Commissariat of Foreign Affairs left me his canned food on his departure; thus I did not die of hunger. But I acquired a pulmonary disease. I wandered from one medical check-up to another, queueing up to the point of fainting, and witnessed frightful scenes of human misery. Finally it came to the point where I was permitted to travel to a lung sanatorium in the province of Novgorod, where for half a year I went hungry and froze.

My return to St Petersburg took place on a winter's night spent in an ambulance with broken windows in the company of a madwoman and her attendant. Arriving at the apartment of friends with whom I had rented a room, it turned out that there was no possibility of heating the place at all.

In the circle of friends who had impatiently awaited my return, we once again began the mutual work in studying spiritual science. They tried to find work for me so that I could remain in St Petersburg, but it proved hopeless, and to my great regret I had to leave the fine work with these dear friends and return to Moscow. Under the New Economic Policy, my parents had the possibility of selling their crystalware, which had by chance remained stored in the cellar. In this way they enabled me to undertake the return journey.

Revolutionary Jurisdiction

By way of further characterizing the political situation in Russia, during those years, I should like to report on two trials involving close friends of mine, at which I was present. One of them took place soon after the Bolsheviks seized power, when the new government was still seeking to gain the sympathy of the peasants, and concerned a clash with a high-ranking monarchist. The other, three years later, was a court case against twenty-nine liberal intellectuals, among whom were many academics, at a time when communist power had been consolidated.

Our friend Vladimir Dzhunkovsky, the former governor of Moscow, later adjutant of the Tsar and finally chief of police, was not shot like other high tsarist dignitaries immediately after the Bolshevik putsch, but remained confined to Butyrki Prison. One day we learned that his trial by the Revolutionary Tribunal would take place publicly. Everyone could testify for or against him. During this first period of the regime, the Communist Government still had to take the mood of the people into account. It was known that Dzhunkovsky was very popular with the peasants and with intellectuals. A farming development near Moscow had even been named after him by the peasants. As a matter of course we went to this trial, held in the hall of the former mercantile union. As it happened, we met our friend right on the steps. He embraced and kissed us, unnoticed by the guard accompanying him. His appearance was gripping. He had a large beard, which he had not worn before, and his eyes, which seemed to have become still bigger and brighter, transformed his face so that it resembled an icon. He radiated great calm.

Hearings still proceeded at that time without rigid formalities. Hardly had Dzhunkovsky stepped into the hall than the peasants crowded round him and he embraced them. They gave him a bottle of milk, bread and eggs. On the podium stood a bust of Karl Marx, stylized like a sphinx, next to the judge's long table.

The chairman of the tribunal was the deputy head of the Cheka, Lette Peters, infamous for his cruelty. Under the tsarist regime he had had to endure much, and now exercised revenge on the victims of the Terror. Something fascinating about his face caught attention, so that I was hardly able to turn my eyes away from him. Oddly, in appearance, he had a certain similarity to Beethoven, but was very blonde, without eyebrows and with white eyelashes. His face spoke of endless grief and weariness. His voice sounded equally austere, tired and somewhat ironical. He spoke in very broken Russian, and one had the feeling that he was altogether a stranger here. He did not know the names of people familiar to all Russians, nor those of large industrial centres, nor important dates. As though he were the unconscious tool of a demonic power, he had to sign ever more death sentences and could not stop, despite having grown tired of it. I came to recognize the Cheka everywhere by this sad, "extinguished" look. The two other judges were ordinary workers.

Vladimir Dzhunkovsky stood to attention before the tribunal, yet as an inwardly quite free and independent person stands before his legal superiors. At first this surprised me, but then I understood that for this religious human being, the words of the Apostle Paul, "Where there is authority, it is prescribed by God," had validity even under these altered circumstances. He answered every question very precisely and frankly. Explanations were crudely forbidden him at first. One could almost envy this person his unified, unproblematic, orthodox-monarchical worldview.

"How many people were condemned to death in Moscow during your tenure as governor?"

"I do not know, it did not concern me, since I had nothing to do with it," he said.

"And that did not interest you?" Peters asked sadly and wryly in his broken Russian. Among other things, the defendant was now asked, whether he had really been opposed to Rasputin, as follows from certain letters of the Tsarina. Passages were read from these letters in which the Tsarina called Rasputin "our friend."

"Yes, that is true."

"Why were you against him?"

"Because his role damaged the prestige of my Tsar."

"So you wanted to support the power of the Tsar?"

"But of course! After all, I would otherwise have been a despicable human being, a cad, if I served him and had not wanted to help him!"

"Did you voluntarily accept the post of chief of police?"

"Yes."

"Why?"

"Because it seemed important to me that the police force was reformed and better organized."

"So you were altogether in agreement with establishing a police force?"

"Of course! Things are not possible without the police. Now they are called the militia, but it is essentially the same thing."

"The prisons in Moscow were under your jurisdiction when you were governor; you are responsible for what happened in them."

"Absolutely. For that reason I also tried as far as possible to have order and humanity prevail. You can compare the earlier regulations, now fluttering around everywhere on the floor of the Butyrki Prison, with the new ones. How much milder the earlier ones were!" And Dzhunkovsky quoted the old ones by heart, paragraph for paragraph.

He was then asked why a village near Moscow carried his name.

"Because I helped the peasants to acquire ownership of their land."

The peasants of this settlement were then requested to report on the matter. Their speaker was an old man. I still remember his words quite well. He began, "It was like this. We had too little land! The land given us after the liberation of the serfs had to be divided up further and further among the members of the growing village community. Finally, everyone had only very little, and each of us after all possesses a wife and children, pigs, chickens and the like. Life was made more and more impossible for us. We tried this and that, drafting petitions saying we needed more land, all in vain! No official paid any attention to our predicament. So we decided to turn to the highest authority, and went ..." (at this point the speaker's voice took on a highly respectful tone) "to the Governor General himself. And lo and behold, he received us without anger, in fact rather like a father. He listened to us attentively, understood our complaint, and sent someone to us to check up on everything, promising to present our concerns to the Tsar. Soon he returned with a deed signed by the Tsar, and we were granted what we had wished for. We emerged from our state of poverty, seeing light at last. Then out of gratitude, we named the settlement after our interceder, Dzhunkovsky."

Peters inquired about the number of peasants and the acres in this community and then asked whether there had previously been any revolutionary uprisings in this village.

"God forbid! Never has anything of the kind occurred. Sometimes, why should sins not be admitted, our lads drink rather too much, play the harmonica and sing, but rebellions have never happened with us, thank God!" The effect of this loyal declaration was touching in this setting.

Other witnesses came forward. A waiter had known Dzhunkovsky from an organization for combating alcoholism, the same one in which my mother had been responsible for the libraries. This old waiter related how, at a popular festival which was to take place in the riding arena, the Governor General had advised him that the food would have to be both inexpensive and good. The old man wept, "Yes, yes, that's what he said; it would have to be inexpensive and good." Another described how Dzhunkovsky had intervened on behalf of the students who had been imprisoned. The actors of the Artistic Theatre described how, when the censors had banned further performances of *Julius Caesar* by Shakespeare after the first performance, he had lifted the ban. A soldier had experienced Dzhunkovsky at the front, and spoke of him as of a "sun-hero." Only one witness was against him, which then proved, however, to have been based on a misunderstanding.

Finally, there was the prosecutor's address. He argued that, as a servant of the tsarist regime, Dzhunkovsky deserved the death penalty. Throughout this whole speech, I looked at our friend. He was quite calm, sharpened his pencil and made notes. Then he was permitted a concluding word. After correcting several statements, he said, "I came before the revolutionary tribunal with a clear conscience. I leave with a clear conscience and shall calmly accept any verdict, however severe it may be."

Then he was led away, and the judges reappeared. There was complete silence. Peters read out the verdict, "The defendant Dzhunkovsky is sentenced to death by firing squad. In view of some services to the people, this is commuted to life imprisonment."

After the final words, the tension dissolved into applause and cheering.

"This is not a theatre for your amusement," said Peters morosely, in a tired tone of voice.

Dzhunkovsky spent several years in prison, and was then suddenly released. His sister, Eudoxie, had been a lady-in-waiting and was just as Orthodox as her brother. She once told us that in a dream, during the time of his imprisonment, she had heard an intercession sung, addressed to three saints whose names she had never heard before. She searched in the church calendar and found that these were the names of three patron saints of prisoners. She sent the prayer to her brother in prison, so that he would be able to say it himself. On the holiday of these three saints, she requested that a priest celebrate the church service in her house. During this service Vladimir Dzhunkovsky came into the room. He had suddenly been ordered to pack his things, and was declared free.

The coachman who drove him by sleigh, after both higher and lower ranking personnel had accompanied him to the gate, asked him en route, "Who are you, to be escorted out so honourably by the entire prison personnel?"

"I am Dzhunkovsky"

"Are you related to our governor?"

"I am the same person."

"What!?" The coachman pulled the horse up and climbed down from the box seat. "Let me take a look at you! God, how you have changed! You have become so lean! With that beard, I would never have recognized you. But today I'm going to drive by every teahouse and announce to all other coachmen that our governor has been freed!"

That was about four years after the outbreak of the Revolution. Dzhunkovsky subsequently lived from private language lessons. He told us that during his first period in prison before the trial, he had frequently been taken out at night to be shot and then returned to his cell. This procedure was the worst experience of all. "That's something no one's nerves can stand," he said. And yet he had appeared quite calm in court. Later — after my departure — he was rearrested and, before the outbreak of the Second World War, he was shot.

In the spring of 1921, a trial of the Revolutionary Tribunal took place in Moscow involving twenty-nine people, largely professors. The only woman among them was Tolstoy's youngest daughter, Alexandra, who shared his ideas.

Only the closest relatives and friends of the accused were admitted to the hearings, which lasted several days. I was permitted to be present because the husbands of two of my friends were co-defendants. I was living with one of them, Mrs N. Shtshepkina. During the time of the Provisional Government, her husband had been the Interior Minister.

The expectation in Moscow, in 1919, was that the White Army of Admiral Alexander Koltshak from the east, and that of General Anton Denikin from the south — having reconquered the country from the Reds — would also liberate the capital from the Bolsheviks. This would probably have come about if the Allies had not betrayed them to the Communist Government. At that time, a group of academics had joined together with the aim of forming a Provisional Government, so as to prevent chaos in the transition period, and a tsarist reaction. This organization remained absolutely secret. The transcripts of meetings were retained by a good friend of mine in his head, possessing as he did, a phenomenal memory, which could be depended upon absolutely. When the communist regime triumphed, no documents of any kind existed concerning the work of this group, and some of its members decided, each on his own, to serve the fatherland as far as was still possible in the new circumstances.

The young, outstandingly talented Valeryan Muravyov, the son of an old tsarist minister, belonged to this group. During the Provisional Government he was Minister of Justice. After the dissolution of the committee mentioned above, he wrote a letter to Leon Trotsky, in which he sharply criticized the organization of the militia. Although, as a precaution, he had sent the letter under a pseudonym, Trotsky of course succeeded in tracing the author, and he had to appear before the feared dictator. Contrary to his expectations, the Commissar expressed the greatest interest in his exposition, requesting positive suggestions from him, which Muravyov went into. At that point, Trotsky offered him leading positions in two commissariats. The enemy of the Communist Government, Muravyov, arrived home fascinated by Trotsky's cleverness and far-sightedness. I experienced something similar, incidentally, with the owner of a well-known art publishing house. The old gentleman, who thoroughly hated the communists, was once called upon by Lenin to discuss the publication of a work. Having returned home, he repeated with a sheepish smile, "I have to say it, he has a captivating personality; an absolutely captivating personality!"

In these legal proceedings Muravyov's situation was now very critical. It was not accepted that the conspiratorial group, of which he was in fact a member, had not existed for a whole year. For him, as for Shtshepkin and Leontiev, who were found to have had a connection with the White Army, the death penalty had to be expected.

The matter had come into the open only as a result of the statements of a few participants themselves, arrested on quite different grounds. Out of nervousness and a "literary" urge, in their reports to the Cheka, they characterized their comrades as politically important figures, arousing suspicion that political activity was involved. Since no documents existed, however, nothing could be ascertained. Thus the participants, after months of enduring hunger, cold, vermin and interrogation, would probably have been released, if what they had discussed very quietly in their cells among themselves had not been passed on by one of their own to the judges. That was an appalling discovery, seeing as they were connected by bonds of friendship and trust.

Gradually, it emerged who the traitor was. None of us could comprehend it. Among the wives of the accused, my friend was a key figure. People came to her for advice when steps were to be taken on behalf of those arrested. These were very complex situations, since if nothing were done for a defendant, he could be forgotten for years in prison and come to a miserable end. But an intercession could have the consequence that, brought to the attention of those in power, he would suddenly be shot. One had to weigh the political configurations, the psychology of the *Chekists* in question at the particular moment. Shtshepkin heard again and again from his friends, just what his wife's support meant for the others. This gave him strength to bear his fate.

On the evening prior to the trial it suddenly became known that the defendants had been granted a defence counsel, an old, well-known lawyer. But as he still had no documents, the reports of the defendants had to be written down for him overnight, so that he could gain an overview before the hearing. So as to help out, I went to the apartment indicated to me, where a number of friends, mostly wives of defendants, were already at work. I received a report that someone had started already. In my haste, I did not look at the signature underneath, but continued writing. I wrote more or less the following:

> The monk Philotheus regarded Moscow as the "third Rome," and the unique calling of the Russian people — according to his view — was the formation of a state in which brotherhood was to become a reality. [The writer also saw the solution of the social problem based on brotherly love as being Russia's mission, and viewed communism as the false anticipation of this, on the erroneous foundation of materialism, which views the human kingdom as the continuation of the animal kingdom, and proclaims class struggle as a social principle.] Here lies the tragedy of our time and the blame which attaches to communism. It does not correspond to the true ideals that live in the Russian soul, but gives it only a kind of surrogate, a deception.

Only after having written these thoughts down, which I felt as entirely my own, did I read the signature, "Muravyov." I was amazed: these statements, as it seemed, were intended for the Revolutionary Tribunal after all!

Towards morning, the completed copies were brought to the lawyer, who had to prepare himself for the hearing in the few remaining hours.

After we had taken our seats in the large amphitheatre of the auditorium — in which I had heard the most beautiful lectures and concerts from childhood on — the three judges of the revolutionary tribunal, three plumbers, sat down at the judges' table. The lawyer, Nikolai Krylenko, an intellectual, known for his brilliant speeches, functioned as prosecutor. Through a small door the defendants were led in one by one.

I saw the noble figure of Shtshepkin; in the short distance from the door to his place, he cast a searching glance over the audience. I was sitting next to his wife, and saw how their eyes met, smiling at each other. Such a moment can go to make up the worth of a lifetime; over and beyond the certainty of his approaching execution, shone the victorious confidence deriving from their mutual love and esteem.

Suddenly through the rows of listeners I heard whispered, "Judas!" The man was led in who had betrayed his friends. Throughout the trial, the judges listened attentively to the answers of the defendants.

"Please be quiet," one of the plumbers said when a murmur arose during testimony. "We have to be able to hear everything, after all every word counts here." They seemed astonished at what they heard from the accused. A human encounter took place between the workers and the defendants — with these so-called bourgeois people, in whom they now saw, not enemies of the state but human beings who had fought and suffered for the rights of the people in the time of the tsars. Prince Sergei Urusov, a former governor during the regime of the tsars, who had been imprisoned then on account of his widely read book *Notes of a Governor*, answered in reply to the question, as to how long he had been in custody at that time, to general amusement, with a note of humour, "Just as long as now! At that time I sat in prison so-and-so many months, weeks and days ... and now, up until today, I have sat in prison again for exactly the same number of months, weeks and days. It is in fact precisely the same period of time."

If one considers the situation of the defendants and imagines, from what hell they were brought here and what awaited them, one begins to appreciate what is required to still summon up humour in such a situation.

It struck me that men like Shtshepkin and Leontiev, who did not mince words in stating their personal attitude to communism, were treated with respect by the judges, whereas the informer was treated with a hint of condescension.

The trial had gone at first very unfavourably for the accused. Shtshepkin and Leontiev did not attempt in any way to deny their relation to the White Army, since this point affected only them and had no bearing on the others. They knew they were to expect the death penalty for this.

Muravyov's situation was likewise utterly hopeless. While he was being questioned, things suddenly took an unexpected turn at the most critical moment of his interrogation. A message was brought in and handed to the presiding members of the revolutionary tribunal. When the judges and Krylenko had read this letter one after the other and spoken quietly with each other, they notified the crowd that Comrade Trotsky was requesting the Revolutionary Tribunal's permission to be allowed to appear as a witness for the defendant, Muravyov. They found, however, that the matter was clear enough and no further new material was needed. But now the old, experienced defender spoke up: It is impermissible for any court to leave something out of consideration which could clarify a case. If a personality such as Commissar Trotsky, who is overburdened with work, wants to contribute his testimony in the cause of justice, he is not to be refused.

To refuse Trotsky! At that time, Trotsky was the actual dictator of Russia. His request for permission to appear as a witness, the hesitation of the judges, was just a comedy, a ploy to present the Revolutionary Tribunal as being the highest, most impersonal authority in Soviet Russia. The judges withdrew for a consultation. A tense interlude followed, since Trotsky's intervention was capable of giving the whole trial a new direction. When the judges returned, they explained that Trotsky was to be admitted as a witness and that he would appear immediately. Then his bodyguards — soldiers in old Russian helmets — filled every aisle of the auditorium. The small figure of Trotsky appeared in strict military posture before the tribunal, thanking it for granting him permission to appear. In his speech, in which he obviously wanted to exonerate Muravyov, he spoke of the psychology of Russian intellectuals, expressed in typical fashion in Muravyov.

"The will" — as Trotsky thought — "works in the upper layers of human consciousness." (On this point he was unfortunately mistaken!) "This will is swept along by Soviet efficiency. However, the lower regions, the deeper layers of consciousness where thinking lives, are haunted by all manner of mystical views and traditional ideas. What fantastic nonsense he prattled on about to me concerning Russia's mission! He even mentioned some monk or other called Philotheus! (And with that Trotsky pulled a sneering face — the personification of Mephistopheles!) Thus a conflict lives in this person. Muravyov wants to work with us and is capable of it. I value him as a worker."

Then Trotsky pointed out that the conspiracy had existed only at the beginning of the Soviet regime. Now, however, everything had changed, since the Soviet State had been successful and had consolidated itself. He spoke of foreign policy in which one could use such people.

Since, as pronounced nationalists, the accused declared themselves for the unity of Russia, they were sincerely in agreement with Soviet foreign policy and came out themselves for the war against Poland. As this war was a great success, affording the Soviets a sense of security, Trotsky's intervention in the trial was made psychologically possible and gave the proceedings a new direction. In spite of the dazzling speeches of Krylenko, who wanted to condemn four people to death and demanded life imprisonment for the majority — he had the frivolity to quote the Gospel, calling it an "immortal book" — the judges did not pronounce any death sentences, even if the punishments were still harsh enough. The traitor was acquitted "for services to the state."

The last statements of those convicted were almost entirely a profound declaration of belief, a language of the soul, whose ideals no longer had any roots in the present. And like cloud formations striving away from the earth, these could not assert themselves over against the flagrant, cubistic, materialistic world-picture with its schematic consistency.

Countess Alexandra Tolstoy was condemned to a fifteen-year prison term, because the meetings had taken place in her residence, the content of which she had no knowledge of.

"You certainly also prepared the samovar for them," Krylenko said scornfully.

Her approximate final words were, "Human beings can only take my body captive and detain it, my spirit remains free; they have no power over it. They can kill my body, my spirit is immortal."

At this, Krylenko wore an sardonic, bored expression, as though to say: We know these Tolstoyan phrases well enough! Trotsky's bodyguards, however, suddenly awoke from their apathy and craned their necks to hear better. These may have been the only words to have left behind a trace in their souls.

Spiritual Luxury

The first German journalist venturing onto Russian soil after the War was Paul Scheffer.[44] I was happy to meet a German and to be able to show him Moscow. We visited old churches, museums, private art collections and cloisters of the Old Believers, where he was able to see the oldest icons. I introduced him to a few social circles, including that of Nikolai Berdyayev. The renowned Thursday evenings with Berdyayev with their introductory talks and discussions still continued, in spite of famine, cold and terror. People sat in fur coats, breathed out clouds of vapour, and for tea, which was no tea, the famous "flan" was served, which had become smaller and smaller and had by now transformed itself into a creation made of potato peelings. But at least the tradition was upheld!

At that time Berdyayev's wife converted to Roman Catholicism. Father Abrikosov, who was active on behalf of Catholicism in Moscow, did not otherwise permit members of his congregation to attend the gatherings at Berdyayev's, because the liberal ideas could supposedly have harmed them. The hostess herself, however, was sufficiently immune and consolidated, in his opinion, that she could participate. She sat silently at the samovar, her face impassive, and I felt her to be like a definitely contoured, hard rock, on which the ideas of the others simply shattered.

It was admirable that Berdyayev could still preserve his spiritual freedom, given his attachment to his wife. Whereas she had found a concrete inner path, I felt his philosophy to be sterile, when all is said and done. Even though supported by feeling, it remained stuck in the realm of abstract thoughts.

On his Thursday evenings one could meet the most interesting people. The Orthodox priest Pavel Florensky spoke there. Unforgettable to me is a personality from this circle, who had occupied himself all his life with the Apocalypse and held talks on it several times.[45] At first I was the only anthroposophist attending these intimate lectures, but others joined later; in them he met with the most interest and understanding for his work by far, in fact in the end he spoke only within such an anthroposophical circle. After my departure from Russia, he was sent to Siberia, his life-work of thirty years annihilated.

"You do not know in what spiritual luxury you live here in Moscow," Paul Scheffer once said to me. "The universal learning, the many-sidedness and the lively interest to be found here, does not exist in the West anymore."

I also took him to the meetings of proletarian poets, where in a huge, over-filled, unheated hall, by the meagre light of a petroleum lamp, the rising stars presented their works. Scheffer did not understand Russian and I attempted to translate a few poems for him. It annoyed him that I prized the gifts of the proletariat over bourgeois culture. I was indeed enthusiastic about these poems. The directness, freshness, will-imbued quality and quite individual, rhythmical richness and "cosmic" feeling in these works revealed a new dimension, as opposed to the subjective and passive nature of bourgeois culture. I am convinced that what emerged in this way from the souls of workers would gradually have found the right paths, revealing what was truly of our time, if it had not been suppressed and systematically diverted onto other paths by the Marxist doctrine and the system of Terror. Any kind of free spiritual work was gradually made impossible. One could only speak in parables or riddles, so as to hide thoughts not tolerated by those in power. One compromise after another had to be made. The lie became a condition of living, and made life an "unworthy process."

Through Scheffer, who sent his correspondence via a German courier, I succeeded in writing to my foreign friends. In reply, I received an invitation to Holland from an acquaintance! My thought was that my lung sickness might perhaps offer grounds to be released abroad by the authorities for a course of treatment. It was clear to me that if I were to remain in Russia during this famine, I would have to succumb to my illness. But it was just as clear to me that once I was outside, I could not risk coming back and must take leave forever of my parents and all the friends with whom I was deeply united as a result of shared destiny! It was very difficult to come to such a decision. And thus for several months I took no steps to secure the exit permit. My father asked me again and again whether I had undertaken anything to enable me to travel. He loved me above everything, I was the joy of his life and yet the good man insisted that I make the journey in order to save my life, knowing fully that we would not see each other again in this life. But I also postponed my departure because I still wanted to see and experience so much here in Russia. For example, I had wanted for a long time to visit the *starets* Nektari in the Optina Monastery. And I wanted to get to know the old Russian art in Novgorod. An archaeologist had invited me to participate in an educational trip to Novgorod, so as to copy the murals in the church of St Sophia. If I were to obtain the exit permit, I would have no money to travel abroad anyway, I said to myself as a pretext for doing nothing. But the excuse of not having enough money was knocked out of my hands by destiny. A publisher ordered from me a series of portrait drawings of well-known personalities regarded as representative in various fields. Thus I was enabled to have a series of interesting meetings. For example, I got to know Professor Lev Tarasievich, director of the Biological Institute, solely on account of this assignment. I experienced him as an energetic, lively and charming person who, along with his specialist scientific interests, also cultivated religious and philosophical ones. He could only sit for me during his brief midday breaks, and I owed many stimulating ideas to these sessions. Thus I could hardly believe it, when a few years later I heard that this religious human being with a positive attitude to life, full of initiative, had taken his own life. For such personalities, working in Russia had become impossible.

One of my further models was the philosopher Nikolai Berdyayev, and also the art historian Pavel Muratov and the writer Boris Saitzev, whom I had known earlier.

I told my publisher how interesting the conversations with these personalities were for me.

"Write it up," he said, "we shall add these conversations to the drawings and call the portfolio: *Men who had to remain silent.*" He wanted to publish the portfolio after the fall of the Bolsheviks, which he anticipated in a foreseeable future.

Vyatsheslav Ivanov was one of the prominent people my publisher wanted me to make a portrait of. He now lived with his family in Moscow, where I had already encountered him frequently at various gatherings. Ten years had passed since our last meeting. This re-encounter was not really a meeting. I saw a white-haired human

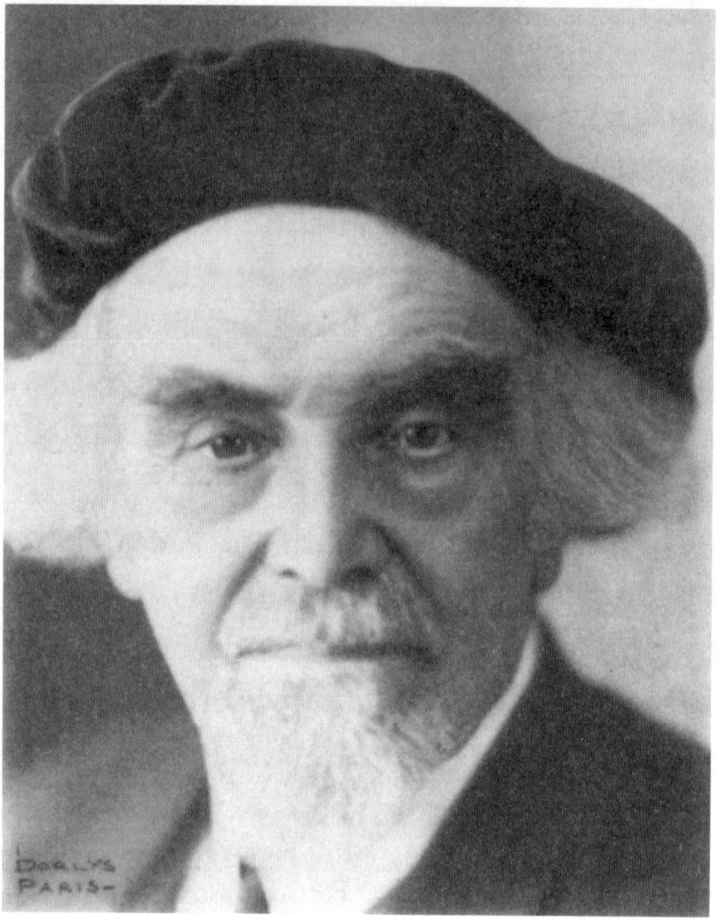

Nikolai Berdyayev. Last photograph

being with a finely chiselled, clean-shaven face. Since he had worn a beard earlier, the smile that crossed his thin lips was unfamiliar to me. The accomplished language, the abundance of myth-creating fantasy, his dialectic, all shone with their old lustre; but they now seemed to me husks behind which I could discern no substance, no real kernel. As little as a heap of ashes resembles a flame, so did this Vyatsheslav Ivanov resemble the earlier one.

Once, in a private circle, when Andrei Belyi read an article about him in his presence, written for a literary encyclopaedia, I was rather taken aback at the mercilessness of his judgment of Ivanov. It seemed to me that Vyatsheslav must have felt annihilated and have wanted

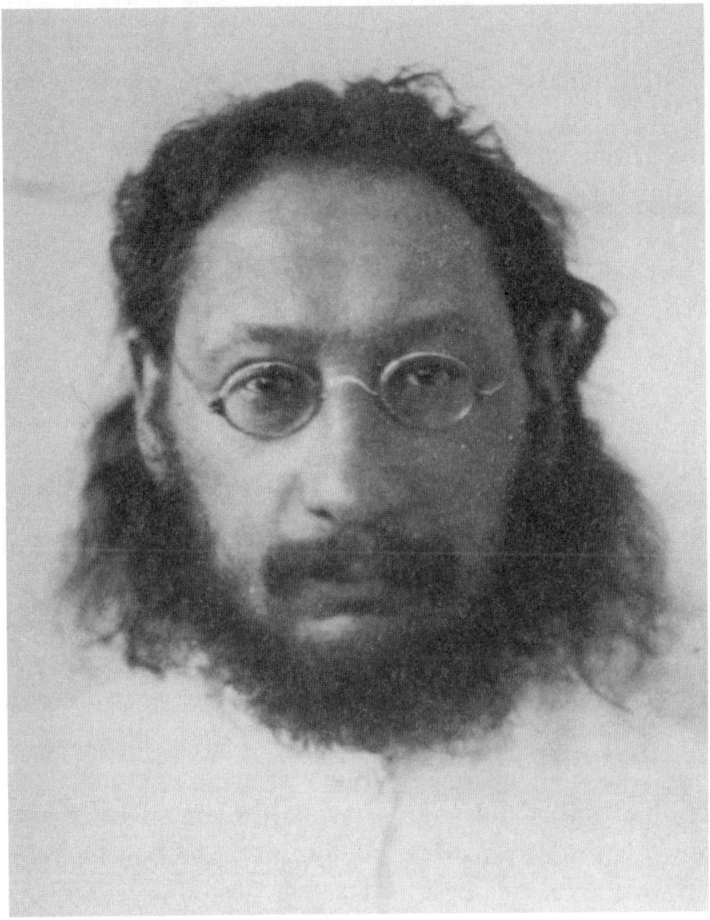

Pavel Florensky around 1928

to protest against it indignantly. The next day he said to me, "Belyi showed me the Guardian of the Threshold. And what did I do? I went past him!" I did not contradict him, but thought to myself, "Now you can defend yourself against your *doppelgänger* with your dialectic and the images always at your disposal. But at the final Threshold none of that will help you!"

I now wanted to draw him just as I thought of him. But it turned out differently.

In making a portrait, one's own thoughts and feelings fall silent. One is given over completely to pure perception and in this space made free, in this "state of selflessness" something else is at work. The further one goes, the more every facial feature and the whole countenance assume the inherent laws of this particular personality, and take on the appearance of truth. An objective love takes over, involving nothing personal, being rather an affirmation of the human being in "becoming." It is the Angelos in me who sees in this way, while the Angelos of the other would reveal himself. I am unable to say it better. But I have experienced it too often to doubt the reality of this mystery. Thus the red-chalk crayon drawing of Vyatsheslav was beautiful in this sense. And I regret the peculiar circumstance whereby the original disappeared during a house search and the already completed matrix vanished at the printers.

My meeting with the actor Michail Chekhov in the context of these assignments was altogether characteristic. At that time I neither knew him personally, nor from the stage. The times were too filled with catastrophes for me to have gone to the theatre.

Apart from the singer Shalyapin, no stage artist was so well loved, even idolized, as Chekhov. For various strata of Russian society, he was a source of spiritual consolation. I was reluctant to ask such a celebrated young artist for a sitting, thus someone else undertook to arrange it for me. When I arrived late as a result of a misunderstanding, he opened the door himself, a non-descript person of medium height, "I was afraid you would not come! I've been standing on the balcony for two hours already, waiting for you," was his greeting. I set to work at once, since his time was limited. He told me how much he loved my book about the holy Seraphim. From a quotation, he had gathered that I knew Rudolf Steiner. On learning from me that I had been Steiner's pupil, he was delighted and wanted to hear a great deal more about him and about anthroposophy. In the course of the work, a very strong coffee was brewed, which signified a great luxury at that time in Russia. I had to come to terms not only with the interesting face of my model, but also with the profoundest questions anyone had asked me. In this nervous face enlivened by humour, the large forehead was extraordinarily well formed, the other features soft and mobile. One knew that this face was capable of unlimited transformation. In his questions there was nothing abstract. They arose rather from the strongest inner experiences that had plumbed the depths of hell. Each one of his words was seemingly newly formed, every sentence idiosyncratically joined together. In answering these questions, I myself was able to experience once more the magnitude of what I had to communicate. Intensity and the greatest elasticity seemed the essential thing with Chekhov. He did not consider problems lightly or let go of them easily. I was later also able to observe how thoroughly he pursued things, how capable he was of real study.

When he mentioned one of our mutual acquaintances, screwing up his eyes or moving his lips slightly, it often sufficed to conjure this person up in his essential being, and at the same time with all his temporal weaknesses. In such portrayal the individual was neither judged nor idealized; his essential nature was brought home to one with love and humour. Such a way of seeing people seemed to me in itself Christian, in the true sense.

I had the feeling, however, that Chekhov's thoughts tended at that time to flee reality. He was visibly startled when, in answer to a question concerning Rudolf Steiner's relation to the theatre, I told him about his activity as director of the Mystery Dramas. There I experienced, as often before, how difficult it is initially for an Eastern mind to accept that the meaning of Christianity is not a flight from the world, but the transformation, the spiritualization and Christianizing of human culture and of the whole earth.

On this occasion, Chekhov accompanied me home in order to see a picture I had just finished painting. This was the *Birth of Venus*, which had come about despite the stresses and strains I had gone through.

"It is," he said, "a continual emerging, a motion within tranquillity. How is that possible?" And suddenly he began to laugh, and laughed and laughed. I looked at him in astonishment. Finally he regained his composure.

"Don't be angry with me, it happens to me when I am moved by something. I had such a fit of laughter when I visited *starets* Nektari in the Optina Monastery. I began to laugh and could not stop. Then he laughed also. We stood in front of each other and laughed, and at last he said to me: 'There are more things in heaven and earth, Horatio, than are dreamt of in your philosophy.' I had to laugh like that as well when invited to see Fyodor Shalyapin for the first time. It is frightfully embarrassing."

The next evening he appeared on stage for the last time before going on a trip abroad, in the drama by the poet Armand called *The Archangel Michael*.[46] He played the leading role, a tyrant and villain,

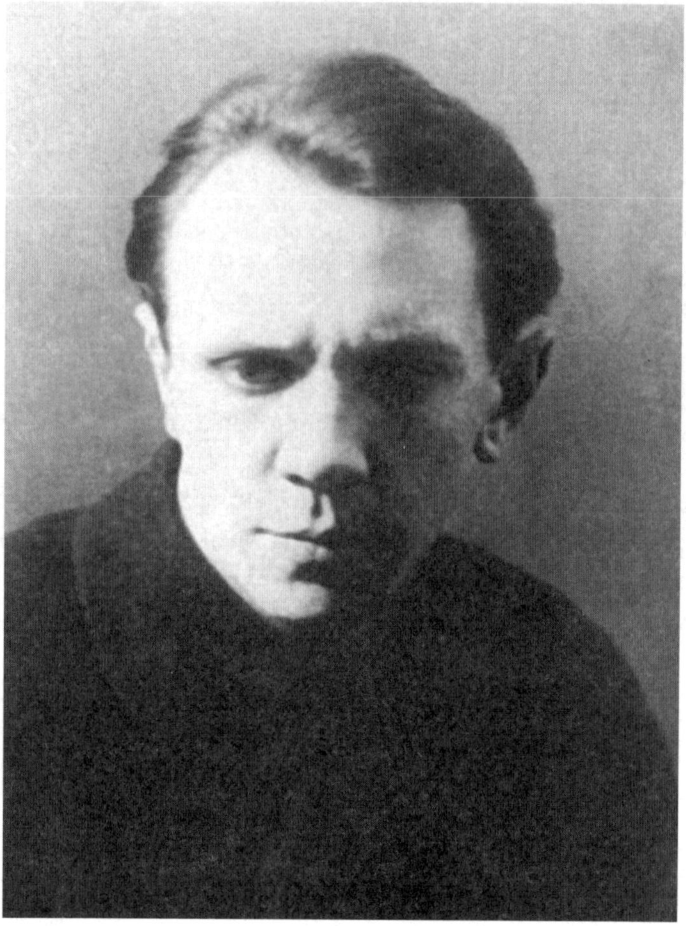

Michail Chekov around 1917

against whom the tormented people prepared an uprising. When I went backstage after the first act and Chekhov spoke with me, I could not recognize him in his make-up, with the best will in the world. This face was like the essence of evil. "I can't play the part anymore," he said, "I feel that I am myself placing something bad into the world and am becoming ill in doing so."

His greatness was revealed in the following act, in which he had no lines, but only stood there silently. In spite of remaining silent, he continued to be the centre of attention, since he gripped the audience by means of a force that radiated from him.

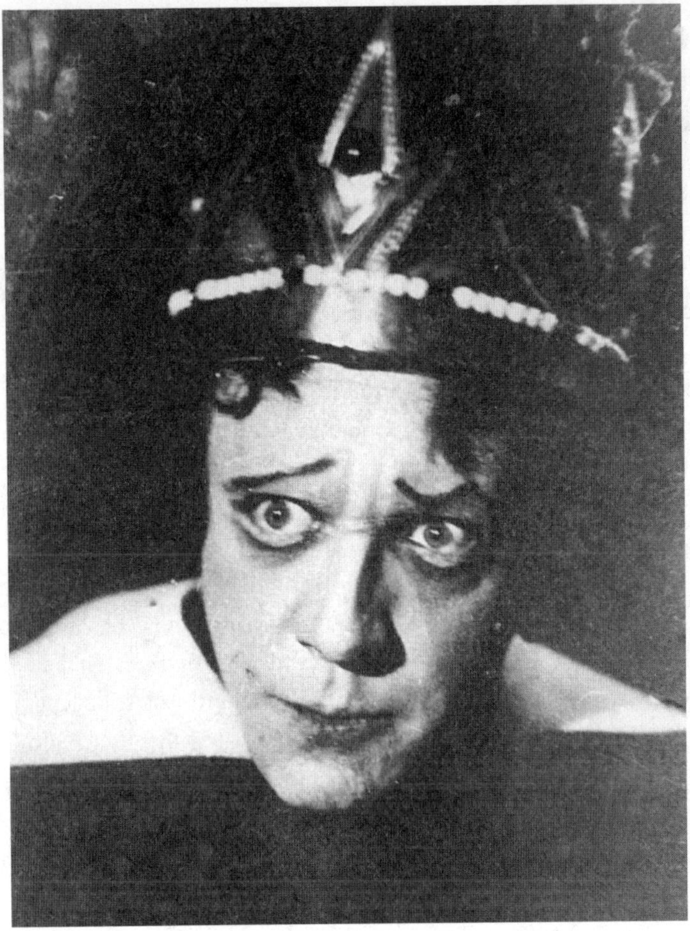

Michail Chekov as Eric XIV in Strindberg;s drama of the same name. Around 1921

Later, after my departure from Moscow, when Chekhov played his Hamlet, I was told that, in spite of the tragic element, in the end he transformed everything into light. Spiritual light rayed out over the darkness and over the people, so that innumerable members of the audience, in their gratitude, ran after his sleigh, accompanying him home. He received stacks of thank you letters from every quarter of the population. People asked him about his world-view, "What do you believe in, to be able to act like that?"

A few weeks after this first meeting with him in Moscow, I met Chekhov by chance on an out-of-the-way street in Berlin. The first thing he said to me was, "I went to the Motzstrasse, and have acquired 'his' picture." (He meant a picture of Rudolf Steiner.) I later met him in Stuttgart; he had participated in a lecture cycle in Holland.

Chekhov could no longer remain in Russia, since freedom of any kind was made impossible on the stage. How he was mourned in Moscow! After Rudolf Steiner's death, I often met him in Breitbrunn at the Ammersee at the house of Michael Bauer and Frau Margareta Morgenstern, with whom he had become close friends. After years of battling for the creation of a school of drama in Paris, England and America, he (the great artist), landed in Hollywood, in films!

Another personality who came my way unexpectedly, I was not only to draw for my publisher, but also to paint: a traditional ethnic folksinger who had come to Moscow from the White Sea, and appeared in schools and at public events of the Commissariat. He had actually come from his village to obtain hemp for fishermen's nets and salt for his village from the authorities in Moscow. However, he only received approval from the Cultural Commissariat, on the basis that he was to sing. Scholars wrote out the texts of his variants of folk legends and they were made into gramophone records, since this music could not be reproduced in the form of notes. He was a fine-looking old man, with large clear eyes, an eagle nose and a grey beard. "A righteous face," a woman said on seeing the picture. He could sing twenty-seven long sagas and knew hundreds of songs.

"How many songs I know, I cannot tell you. My memory is like a wound-up ball. If I am in top form, then things unfold smoothly and I can sing countless songs, maybe around two hundred; but if I am depressed and not in the mood, then I hardly know a quarter of that!"

I painted him over three days in his brown, Nordic coat against a vermilion-red background, as the prophet Elijah is portrayed in icons. On the first day, when he had not yet put his full trust in me, he was cautious and told me only the outer aspects of his biography. He was a fisherman who had built many boats with his own hands and sailed to Norway thirteen times. He had been alternately very wealthy and very poor. He had learnt the heroic epics and songs from his grandfather. That was the custom: transmission from grandfather to grandson. "But with me, it is coming to an end; I am the last ethnic folksinger. My grandson does not want to learn the old ways from me, he only sings hit songs."

On the second day he was more open towards me and related how the Bolsheviks had wreaked havoc in the North; how the fishing nets had been "socialized." No one was permitted to fish, the nets were left to rot and people remained without food, and without money.

Among the farmers of the North the old culture had to some extent been preserved. But what had remained of old folk art — icons, wood carvings, brocade garments, jewellery — was requisitioned, as it was said, for the museums.

"But where were these museums? And who are they, the big men ruling us? They are the former lazybones and good-for-nothings whom we despise. Now they're talking big! Even just thinking about them, it feels as though lice were crawling down my spine!"

On the third day he related still more intimate things about his life; about his first love, an idyll set against the background of the northern landscape, full of infinite purity and drama. He also told me certain traditional magic sayings to counter infatuation, sickness, horse thieving and described instances he had himself experienced where they had proven effective. Unfortunately, I did not make a note of these. I could have listened to his heroic sagas over and over again. It was like a broad river rushing onward. The action took the form of ongoing occurrences which were never concluded. One felt oneself transposed into an elemental stream corresponding to the realm of plant growth.

Now I did not have the excuse anymore that I could not travel for lack of funds and I took the first step. I requested my friend Dr Trapesnikov to ask the director of his office at the Protection of Monuments of Art and Antiquities for approval for my course of treatment abroad, which she gladly did. As already mentioned, she was the wife of Trotsky, the current dictator of Russia. This name had a magical effect and gave me access to government authorities. Even so, I needed six months to get all the necessary papers together. Day after day, I had to go to some authority or other on foot across the city of Moscow, often only to learn that the opening hours or reception days had changed, or that the institution in question had moved or no longer existed. I had to leave eleven photos with the various authorities and receive a stamp eleven times.

Since 1920, Russia had suffered a great famine, affecting many fertile regions in the south and east. The cause was a great drought as well as ruined transport and communications. The fields remained black.

To the east — where people fled in hopes of obtaining something to eat — there were rows of corpses. Some people went mad. Mothers tied their children on one side of the cabin and themselves on the other, so that they could not get to each other. Once, after I had fetched an American aid package at the railway station, I went across a large square where hundreds of starving people sat on the ground. I remember the face of a Tartar, who pointed to his mouth and looked at me with an unspeakable expression.

A year before that, when the Patriarch had seen the famine coming, he made the offer to the Government, to sacrifice all the superfluous gold in the churches to combat the emergency. It was turned down. But now commissars went from church to church, entered the chancel without removing their hats and took away the cross, the covering of the gospel and the chalice. According to old tradition, these religious objects were made of gold derived from countless small offerings from the poorest villages. Other gold objects, lamps and ornamental shields of icons were taken away. Frequently at that time one would see a church surrounded by a crowd of people observing this blasphemy mutely.

As a consequence of the famine, an epidemic of dysentery broke out in Moscow, and the fifteen-year-old son of my cousin Elisabeth lay apparently dying. At the last anointing, for which we gathered, I saw Elisabeth for the last time. Her quiet, reverent attitude remains unforgettable to me. The boy recuperated after the sacrament. But now I became sick and had to postpone my journey again.

By August things were far enough along that I could travel. In the final days I felt only indifference, as though drained of every emotion. I remember sensing my father's heartbeat as he pressed me to his chest in the hallway; I saw the anguished face of my mother, who accompanied me out to the tram stop in front of the house. But my heart was as though made of stone. A near total stranger, a new member of the Anthroposophical Society, brought me to the station and that was fine with me.

First, I travelled to St Petersburg, in order to wait there for the ship which was to take me to Stettin. How beautiful St Petersburg was in the summer! An enchanted city; the great squares, even around the theatre, overgrown with grass; the empty Prospects infinitely vast.

My friends, Boris Leman and Klavdya Vassilyeva, the directors of the Anthroposophical Society in St Petersburg, had just returned from

Rostov, where they had fled the famine in 1918. I was able to introduce them to a circle of people with whom I had worked in anthroposophy, and these were accepted by them as members on the evening before my departure.

Among them was a young girl [Irina Karnauchova], part of whose destiny I should like to relate here. It was my last impression of Russia.

She must have been twenty-two years old at that time and had a wonderful gift for telling fairy tales, of which she knew a countless number from all manner of countries. The Bolsheviks came to Kiev when she was a grammar school pupil there. Together with a friend she helped White officers to flee abroad by preparing passports for them. She had succeeded in appropriating the seal from the commissariat in question in the course of a conversation, and then also in carrying off a stack of new empty passports under the eyes of all the employees, as though she were authorized to do so. She then studied the signatures of the public officials and was soon able to forge them perfectly. The passports were then made up by her, but the seal was kept by her friend. In this way, these children saved the lives of many people. But once, when she came to her friend with the passports in her apron, a house search was underway there.

"Let me go," she said to the Cheka, "I have to prepare for school."

"What sort of booklets are those?"

"English dictionaries." She was allowed to go. But on leaving she saw her friend turn pale — the seal had been discovered. The next day he was shot.

That same night, another friend came to her who was in the Communist Party. "Get into the car and ask no questions, you have to leave town!" he ordered her. She protested but he insisted. He drove her out of the city and said, "Go into the forest and do not show yourself in Kiev!" She knew that he had sworn, on becoming a party member, to make no exception for anybody. "For you I'm breaking my oath. Now run!" he said.

In the forest many others pursued by the Bolsheviks were hiding. From time to time she went home under cover of darkness, to change clothes and fetch food. She was soon joined by her father, whose situation had become precarious as a result of the many interrogations relating to her. They thus lived in the forest in a small hut. The father had a hobby, he played the violin, and despite the danger of being discovered, he also played in their hiding place. One day soldiers came, attracted by the music. The two of them thought all was lost till they discovered that these were White soldiers. There were tears of relief and embraces!

The news that the Whites had reconquered Kiev spread among the fugitives and now thousands moved back into the city from the forest. They could be seen crossing the bridge, skeletal people in rags.

When the Bolsheviks retook Kiev, the family was dispersed. Knowing nothing of her relatives, the young girl remained alone and earned a living as a storyteller. She told fairy tales in children's homes, schools and in the clubs of the Red Army. Once she also did so for the orphaned children of Cossacks who had been shot, an unruly horde no one else dared to deal with. The children locked her in, demanding that she tell stories continuously. They were much more dangerous than the soldiers. She could not hold them in check with fairy tales, but only with more exciting stories such as *The Three Musketeers*. Thus she wandered alone through a Russia in turmoil, until she got to know my friends in Rostov and encountered anthroposophy through them.

Many of my friends, old and new, came onto the quay to see me off. The picture of St Petersburg in its majestic beauty stands indelibly in my mind; between the shining granite banks the broad blue-green, shimmering and sparkling Neva with its white ships rocking to and fro!

Since there was a five-hour delay in leaving, we sat together on crates at the dock and waited. Crossing the Russian border has always been associated with uncertainty, till the last moment one might still end up somewhere other than planned. But the tension that might have arisen as a result of waiting so long was banished by means of the Indian, Japanese, African and Samoan fairy tales we listened to for hours. We were transported into a timeless world. When a friend said to me on parting, "Let us hope that Russia will rise from the ashes, purified by its suffering," the young wife of a painter shot near Archangel said with deep conviction, "Oh yes, from so much innocent blood that has flowed on this soil, only a wonderful crop can grow. This earth is sacred!" What experiences stood behind her words!

The crossing to Stettin was extraordinarily stormy. The futuristic poet Boris Pasternak, the composer Arthur Lurier and I remained the only ones not to become seasick, standing on the bow of the ship that pitched skyward one moment, into the yawning abyss the next.

The Burning Bush

In Russia I had felt the lack of the middle which could establish a balance between two polar opposite directions: one yearning for a return to the lost sources of life and deriving its ideals from what is given by nature, by nationality and by what is transmitted from the past, which however, floats over reality; and the other, which wants to shape the future according to the principle of self-interest. I sought this middle in Central Europe, where Goethe, its great representative, had paved the way to a recognition of the laws of the living. However, I no longer found this way of thinking in Germany and that was one of the profoundest disappointments of my life. Where now was the spirit which, during the War, had spoken in Germany from the letters and diaries of the soldiers at the front? Or had all the bearers of this impulse been snatched away? Were none left behind to continue their spiritual legacy? I came upon resigned people. The great sense of commonality to be experienced in Germany during the War had now been extinguished. Everyone was only concerned for themself, caught up in small egoistic worries and interests. Everyone tended to complain. Cultural traditions had vanished, falling like debris from disintegrating old houses. And it seemed part of the general picture that ladies were to be seen on the streets of Berlin in the middle of the day in glittering evening attire. At night, the countless overfilled cafés with dance floors attracted attention. Everything appeared unreal.

What had happened in Germany? What was the destiny of the movement for the Threefold Social Order, which we had heard about in Moscow and which was supposed to have been the answer of the "middle" to the War?

On arriving in Holland, which at that time had not experienced the War, and where everything went on as before in the same state of cosy complacency, a depression came over me. The maya seemed so hopelessly dense here. I felt myself cut off from the existence I had experienced so strongly in Russia, despite all that was of a terrible nature ... or perhaps just because of it. There one lived within reality. Evil revealed itself crassly, illusions were scattered. What was truly good shone in the darkness, always connected with sacrifice, with martyrdom even. Nowhere had I encountered such frightful faces, but also nowhere such beautiful countenances as in the cities of Russia during the revolution. It was as though the separation of human beings into good and evil ones had already begun. There was room for the clear working of destiny. On the other hand, in Holland, everything congealed, and I would have liked best of all to travel back to Russia immediately. In the house in the Hague, in which I painted children's portraits, the gentleman of the house, very successful in his businesses, gave it as his opinion that everything would get better and better in the world. When I doubted this, he said there was no need to entertain any worries about humanity, since God knew best how to arrange things. Human beings would simply have to leave everything up to God. I had the feeling that these self-assured burghers had long since become divorced from reality, without yet knowing it.

Soon Rudolf Steiner and Marie, now his wife, came with the eurythmy group to the Hague. When I heard the lecture by Rudolf Steiner and felt myself carried on the living waves of his voice, I knew myself to be at home again. After the lecture, he said, turning to me, "Human beings sleep; they are asleep here."

"But in England, as I hear, the conference seems to have gone very well?" I asked.

"Outwardly, yes," he replied, "only outwardly."

I found Rudolf Steiner very changed. He did not appear sick, but I had the sense of a glassy delicateness in his physical substance. This was as though only held together by the spirit, and his movements, still more than previously, seemed initiated by his will working from the periphery. And what struck me especially was his gaze, with which in the interval he seemed from time to time to look for something among the people in the hall. In this questioning look there was such pain, that one shied from meeting him. And yet, the next evening, when I saw him applying red make-up to the necks of the eurythmists, in spite of their protestations — they did not know the effect of the footlights — I could not find anything of that impression anymore.

On the third evening, when Rudolf Steiner held a lecture in a neighbouring city, I was invited by Frau Marie Steiner for a private conversation. She wanted to hear about the destiny of our friends in Russia. But I was eager to learn about everything that had happened around Rudolf Steiner in the five-and-a-half years of my absence. And this was no small matter.

The movement for the threefold social order had meanwhile arisen, which was to fail in the first instance. However, an education and a medical practice drawing their methods from the sources of spiritual science did come about through capable educators and academically trained doctors. From a group of theologians seeking religious and ritual renewal, who asked Rudolf Steiner's advice, the movement arose, now known as the Christian Community.

It will be comprehensible that what interested me above all after my experiences in Russia was the solution to social and educational problems. What I had seen under the Bolshevik regime showed me that a time had begun in which, by virtue of a one-sided materialism, a mechanistic state system was being established, which wanted to destroy the humanity in human beings, turning the individual into a robot.

The threefolding of the social organism — which corresponds to the threefold nature of the human being in spirit, soul and body and reflects a higher trinity — made absolute sense to me. Vladimir Soloviev thought the historical task of Russia, the very idea of Russia was "to realize the complete social trinity." He designated this as "Church, State and Society."

The French Revolution had brought the three concepts, liberty, equality and fraternity, deriving from a spiritual source, and placed them next to each other on the same level, which was a materialistic distortion, leading logically to the chaos in which we find ourselves. Those three ideals belonged to different realms of life: liberty to the spirit; equality to rights; fraternity to the economy.

In his inspired *Fairy Tale* Goethe sets a fourth king (the mixed king) against the three kings (the golden, silver and bronze). This is the regent of our time, allowing the three forces to intermingle chaotically with each other within the human being and in social life, and bring them into an unhealthy state of dependence on each other. In the twentieth century, industry established a kind of unified physical body of humanity by encircling the globe with a technical culture. Egoistic economic strivings of groups, as well as states, leads necessarily to crises. Our time demands of humanity a selfless interest directed to the general well-being — to *brotherhood.*

Later, when I studied Rudolf Steiner's economic course together with those more knowledgeable, I made what was for me a liberating discovery, that the field of banking, as well as ownership or trade, can be imbued with Christian principles and develop in a healthy manner. As a Russian, these fields had appeared to me inherently "evil" from the outset. What spirit-messenger had ever plumbed these depths? "socialism, without human beings educated in brotherhood, is useless," Rudolf Steiner once said.

Equality has its proper place in the rights life. The State only has the task of ensuring that the order generally decided upon is actually carried out. It may neither subjugate the spiritual life nor the economic life, just as little as the economy may determine politics. Indeed, where have we arrived by mixing these things up!

Frau Marie Steiner related this with her fiery objectivity that went directly to the point. She described for me with what success these proposals of Rudolf Steiner, which went into specific detail, had been met. His lectures were received enthusiastically by workers and industrialists in auditoriums and smoke-filled factory meeting places.

"And," I asked, "what caused it to end in failure?"

"After the War the industrialists believed they had found in threefolding a means of protecting themselves against the expropriation that threatened them from the side of communism. When this danger had passed, they were happy to return to the 'good old ways' and abandoned the cause. The proletarians were held back by the unions and by party discipline. In addition, those who were to represent the idea were not mature enough for this. And now," said Marie Steiner, "humanity will have to go through terrible catastrophes, in order to come in the end to a recognition of these truths after all, on the path of suffering."

Rudolf Steiner's art of education takes into account the threefold nature of the human being in terms of body, soul and spirit. Above all, it seeks to support the creative forces residing in every child, not smothering them with an excess of material to be taken up by the intellect, but developing the child's inherent abilities. This art of education wants to help the human being stand in the world and in life with free initiative, not as someone out of touch with life.

Marie Steiner told me with enthusiasm how the children did eurythmy, how both girls and boys sewed, wove, did gardening and carpentry. But then she grew indignant, "They shout and scream in the breaks, and the teachers tolerate it. Why? Do Russian children shout so much?"

I told her about our schools and how two policemen had to stand guard in the school playgrounds to prevent rowdyism. I realized that what I told her about Russia appeared merely exaggerated and implausible in a different milieu. So I did not repeat these things to other people.

Marie Steiner then went into her own special work; the courses in speech formation. Then she asked me about my own plans.

"I have been invited to Dornach by friends, but I doubt whether it is the right thing for me. In the proximity of Rudolf Steiner, one stands as though under a torrent of new truths, but I want to work out what I have already taken up."

I rather expected a spirited rebuke in response to this, but to my astonishment she said, "I can understand you very well. For me, since I am the wife of Rudolf Steiner, there can be no question as to whether I should remain at his side or not. But I often want to work out the indications we have already received in eurythmy or in speech formation. And yet I continue asking questions. One has to ask, as long as he is still here among us. When he is no longer with us we shall have time enough to put his indications into effect."

Why does she talk like that, I wondered? Dr Steiner is in good health and only sixty-one years old. On leaving her, I saw Rudolf Steiner in his fur hat and collar getting out of the car at the hotel entrance. His face appeared to me transparent, and his deep-set eyes very dark.

My Dutch hostess travelled to Dornach for the Christmas Conference. I was unable to go with her because the entry permit had not yet been issued by the Swiss authorities. The consul promised to grant me the visa, if one of my acquaintances in Switzerland could arrange for the authorization to be transmitted telegraphically. But since the friend to whom I turned with this request was preoccupied with the Christmas Plays, my request remained unfulfilled. He thought why should I not wait a few days more after having waited six years to see Dornach again? So my friend travelled alone.

On New Year's Eve the consulate informed me by telephone that I could fetch my passport with the Swiss visa the next day. Hardly had I put down the receiver, than the telephone rang again. Someone who had just received the news by telephone from Dornach, asked me to tell my host that the Goetheanum was burning; but since no one was left in the lecture hall, he did not need to have any worries about his wife.

The Goetheanum on fire? How was that possible? There were night watchmen; there was a fire brigade in Arlesheim. It could not be serious. And we knew how difficult it was for such hardwood to catch fire, in heating our stoves with leftovers from the wood sculpture.

I travelled the next day and, at noon on January 2, I went up the hill from the Dornach train station. It was raining and the fog so dense that one could hardly see more than a few steps ahead. I had been afraid to ask the conductor on the train about the fire. I met no one on the way up, but noticed that the mud on the paths had been trodden to a mush. I went directly to the building. The mist veiled it. I stepped up close to the concrete terrace and saw that the entrance doors, carved of wood, were completely unscathed. So everything was alright! Then I attempted to see through the mist to the second story, but I could not see anything. I went around the building. The wooden buildings nearby were intact, but now — from the east — I saw clearly through the mist: there were no cupolas up there and no walls; there was nothing.

I went down the hill to the canteen and saw pale faces, eyes tired from lack of sleep, coats encrusted with mud. I learned that the building had burned the whole night and the day before as well. Everyone greeted me with, "Too late!"

But these people I no longer experienced as cold, self-assured strangers, as in the Hague. In this destiny we were profoundly united; a community that had lost what was most precious.

A eurythmist related how at five o'clock in the evening of New Year's eve a eurythmy performance was to take place. She had the feeling as if something heavy weighed in the air. In her dressing room, she found the wall mirror lying on the floor, broken in pieces. It had hung on the wall separating her dressing room from the White Room. That made a very peculiar impression on her. It was not comprehensible how this could have happened, and it looked as though the nail had been knocked out from the other side. There was the desire to notify Rudolf Steiner about it, but he could not be found at that moment. Another artist had heard a mysterious noise, like a storm wind between the walls. She was laughed at, since there was no wind at all outside. During the performance, she had the feeling that all her efforts to fight against something she sensed as dark and oppressive were in vain.

The Prologue in Heaven was performed. In the evening there was a lecture in which Rudolf Steiner wrote the words of the "cosmic communion" on the blackboard. After this lecture a group of people remained behind on the Goetheanum terrace; the same ones who had had the initiative to erect a building for the Mystery Plays in Munich. They discussed how it might be possible to get together the money still lacking to complete the building, by means of advance ticket sales for the Mystery Plays in August. Then, they said, the actual requirements of the Goetheanum would finally be met. At this moment, Alexander Pozzo who was a night-watchman in the building (in Moscow he had been a lawyer) came and reported that he had smelled smoke in the Goetheanum, but that he could not find the source. When they followed him into the auditorium, they saw that smoke was coming from all sides and from every crack; thin films of smoke could be seen spreading outside as well. It was discovered that there was, in fact, fire everywhere between the walls. Hence, this must have continued already for quite some time. Rudolf Steiner was notified at once. He came and gave orders, which it was, however, not possible to carry out, since the available means of extinguishing fire were inadequate. The Arlesheim fire brigade was called and then the one in Basle. At midnight, when all the bells were ringing in the New Year, the flames broke through between the two cupolas, illuminating the surrounding landscape; now of such significance for the history of Europe.

All the members participated in the attempt to extinguish the fire; models were salvaged; the central group of the Christ statue, not yet installed in the building and still located in the wooden shed, was brought to safety on an adjoining meadow. Rudolf Steiner was diverted from the fire by people needing help, having been overcome by smoke. Then he went around the hill. In glowing outlines the building revealed its architecture, its sculptural forms. The organ sounded and each of the various metals used lit up in a different colour amid the flames. A tremendous, inexpressible sound arose from this sea of fire, blazing in every colour. The columns burned like torches. The coloured glass of the windows melted. At last, the two columns of the entrance to the auditorium, together with the architrave uniting them, stood out like a fiery gateway.

Rudolf Steiner directed that the carpentry building be prepared for the lecture and the Three Kings Play the next day. Continuity was to be preserved. Reading the sequence of lectures Rudolf Steiner held during these days, there is nothing to indicate that the catastrophic fire had taken place between the lecture of the December 31 and the one given January 1. To the actor who was to play Herod the next day in the Christmas Play he said, this time Herod should appear especially evil.

After the fire, Rudolf Steiner intensified his activity still further. The number of lectures he gave over the next few years seems incredible today. All were fundamental. Their whole orientation may be characterized in quoting the title of one particular lecture series, *Man as Symphony of the Creative Word*. This theme took on a quite definite character according to the field of work of his listeners — the educators, the doctors, economists, farmers, priests, eurythmists, actors and musicians — and went directly into practical questions. Before that, the Word had spoken through the building, now lost, by means of form and colour. It was as though the essence of what had been embodied in it, streamed down again onto the earth, freed by the flames from material substance and raised to a new existence, fructifying every field of culture.

In the summer, Rudolf Steiner already began working on the model for the new building; it was to be no longer in wood, but in concrete. At the meeting at which this new building was resolved upon, Rudolf Steiner drew the attention of the members to the fact that the first Goetheanum was built with money offered freely as a gift, whereas the new building would have to be undertaken with the obligatory insurance pay-out. An enthusiastic American, ready to make sacrifices, asked whether one ought not to forego this, and collect the amount needed once again from means freely given. Rudolf Steiner rejected this: If a heavy weight lies on one side of the scales, it becomes necessary to see that an equally heavy weight is laid on the other.

At every artistic event taking place in the carpentry building, a poster was hung, painted by Henni Geck on the basis of a corresponding sketch by Rudolf Steiner. I had first to get used to this way of painting, which initially I did not understand. In fact, it took me years before I began to comprehend the indications which Rudolf Steiner had given to painters in his colour lectures. In my opinion, they belong to the most mysterious of his lectures, the reality of which is only to be discovered and made use of after years of practice in this new way of experiencing colour.

I took part enthusiastically in a course in speech formation given by Marie Steiner. She had gained practice in the art of speech since her youth and had developed it on new foundations together with Rudolf Steiner. With her, a path is found by which cosmic life is given back to the word, desanctified in the course of cultural development. In speech exercises, I felt how the whole organism was harmonized and healed. One experienced one's whole organism as a musical instrument on which cosmic forces played. In this way spiritual science, in danger of remaining abstract in our intellectual age, was able to penetrate deeper levels of the human being, purifying and enlivening them.

At the end of the summer I had to leave Dornach. Due to political complications between Switzerland and Soviet Russia, Russian nationals did not receive an extension of their residence permits. I found myself in the peculiar situation of not being able to remain in Switzerland, but also of not getting permission to enter any other country. What was I to do? At last, by means of an invitation of the family of Lory Maier-Smits, a permit to enter Germany came through. They had a factory for "claw and horn utilization" near Ulm. Immediately before my departure, Rudolf Steiner returned to Dornach from a long lecture tour and received me in his studio in the carpentry building, where the Christ statue still stood, carried out by him in wood. I now saw it for the first time. I was struck by the expression of pain on this countenance. I asked whether this suffering had also been expressed in the Christ countenance of the small cupola?

"Suffering? I only wished to portray love," he answered, "but they do of course belong together." His last words in this conversation were, "Christ is to be sought in our age in all realms, also in painting."

In Einsingen near Ulm I was now only able to experience the life in Dornach as reflected by others. Some of my friends travelled there every week to hear Rudolf Steiner and to consult him on the results of their work. From time to time Rudolf Steiner came to Stuttgart and

I travelled there to hear him. He spoke about the metamorphoses of destiny of single individualities through various incarnations, out of which the fabric of history was woven. Though weakened by illness, he achieved a tremendous amount.

When the anniversary of the fire approached, Rudolf Steiner re-founded the Anthroposophical Society and took on the presidency himself. Until then he had acted only as a teacher. With this he sought to build a "social structure" to serve as a suitable vessel for the spiritual scientific work. It was as though he were hastening to pass on all he still had to give. In spite of his limited forces, he also undertook journeys to other countries and held conferences there. He achieved a final superhuman feat between September 5 and 23, 1924, which remains a shattering memory for all who experienced it. He held four courses parallel with each other: the pastoral medicine course for priests and doctors, nineteen lectures on the Apocalypse for the priests, a drama course intended in the first place for actors only, but attended by a larger circle. Alongside this he continued the series of lectures on the forming of destiny, held esoteric lessons and also gave the customary weekly talks to the Goetheanum workmen on themes chosen by them.

Following this, he became seriously ill. During the time of his illness, the "Leading Thoughts" appeared in the periodical *Das Goetheanum,* as well as in the "Letters to the Members." These communications took on the conciseness of mathematical formulas. He also wrote *The Course of My Life.*

In the year 1924, I moved to Stuttgart. I followed the news from Dornach with apprehension. Then came the news of his death.

At this time a conference on Waldorf education was taking place in the Gustav Siegle House in Stuttgart. I saw the earnest, pale faces of the teachers, some of whom travelled to Dornach between lectures and sat overnight at the bier. My attempt to travel to Switzerland for the funeral remained unsuccessful. I only saw a photographic image of his face on the deathbed. It spoke of spiritual victory, of courage, united with the deepest humility and ultimate devotion; the devotion of a servant of the Word.

The destiny of every human being who has experienced Rudolf Steiner is like that of Parsifal: what he has met with, he is called upon to seek. The tasks Rudolf Steiner left us, in all fields, are as great as humanity's longing for the spirit.

For myself I can say that the conscious work began only after the death of the teacher. The more mature the human being becomes, the richer the life within and around him. I have come to know myself as part of a wider community. Through all inner and outer hindrances there shine, even if but weakly, those first spirit-seeds which have the potential to rescue the image of Man.

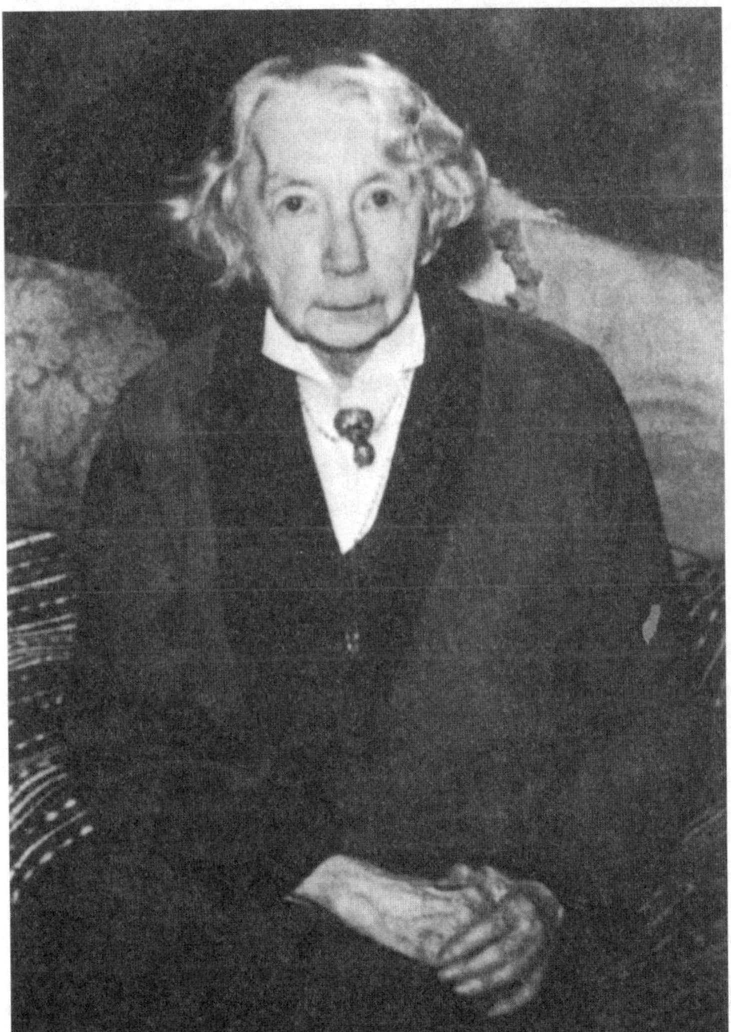

Margarita Woloschin around 1964

Notes

Brief descriptions and dates of persons mentioned in the text are to be found in the Index of Names. For the most part, the following notes are based on the Russian edition of this book, *Seljónaya Smeyá,* Enigma, Moscow 1993.

1 Alexander Ostrovsky was a well-known Russian dramatist in the realistic mode. Of nearly sixty dramas and comedies he wrote, a large number deal with the world of the Russian merchant class.

2 The poem *Summer Rain* by Apollon Nikolayevich Maykov (1821–97).

3 Georg Herwegh was a socialist-revolutionary poet of the period of German history from 1815 to the revolution in March 1848. His widow, Emma Siegmund, was the daughter of a Berlin banker.

4 *Rostam and Sohrab* is an excerpt from the Persian epic *Shahname* by Firdowsi (940–1020); *Nal and Damayanti* a saga from the old Indian epic *Mahabharata* (Book 3). Both had been translated into Russian by the poet Vasily Zhukovsky (1783–1852) at the beginning of the 1840s based on Friedrich Rückert's version. Both works were widely read in Russia in Margarita's youth.

5 The monastery of St Sabbas, situated about 50 km west of Moscow, was founded at the end of the fourteenth century by Sabba Storozhevsky, a pupil of Sergei of Radonezh and father confessor of the Zvenigorod Prince Yuri. Expropriated by the Bolsheviks in 1917 and turned into a museum; returned to the Russian Church at the beginning of the 1990s, ithas been used as a monastery once again since 1995.

6 Interest in the poetry of Charles Baudelaire — the poet from whom French Symbolism took its start — was very great in Russia in those years. The first generation of Russian Symbolists, Balmont and especially Bryusov among them (who translated a great deal from the French), took their point of departure in many ways from French Symbolism and awakened interest in it in many periodicals.

Among the *Petits Poèmes en Prose* there is none that might be translated as "The Gifts of the Moon." Perhaps Woloschin meant No. 20 from *Les Paradis artificiels,* "Les Dons des fees."

7 Woloschin gives the gist in somewhat abbreviated form from Gogol's novel, *Dead Souls,* (Vol. 1, Chapter 11).

8 The publishing house, M. & S. Sabashnikov, existed from 1891 until 1930 and counts as one of the most outstanding literary ventures in Russia. It was continued by Michail on his own after the death of the younger Sergei in 1909.

Fyodor Vassilyevich Sabashnikov spent the last years of his life in Turin. He was named an honorary citizen of the city of Turin for his publication of manuscripts of Leonardo da Vinci.

9 Sadayakko was the female star of a Japanese theatre group who, under her director, the actor and playwright Kavakami Otoyiro, later (in 1901 and 1902) appeared with great success in a number of countries of Middle and Eastern Europe.

10 Dmitri Viktorovich Alexeiev was professor of chemistry at the universities of Perm and Leningrad. He became acquainted with anthroposophy in Germany, where he undertook practical training after completing his studies. After returning to Russia, he travelled on two occasions to Germany again to hear lectures of Rudolf Steiner. In 1911 he joined the first small study group in Moscow, which had formed around B. P. Grigorov and Ellis at the publishing house Musagetes. Also belonging to this circle studying Rudolf Steiner's works were: N.A. Grigorova, B.P. Grigorov, V.A. Achramovich, the Sisov couple, M.I. Sisova, A.S. Petrovsky, the Glier couple, V.M. Vikentyev, Margarita Woloschin, T.G. Trapesnikov, B.N. Bugayev (Andrei Belyi), A.A. Turgenieva and V.O. Nilender. (See V. B. Fedyushin, *Russlands Sehnsucht nach Spiritualität,* Basle 1988, pp. 99f.)

11 The famous lecture of August 14, 1872, *Über die Grenzen der Naturerkenntnis,* was held in Leipzig.

12 The French architect and art historian, Eugène Emmanuel Viollet-le-Duc (1814–1879), famous for his restorations of buildings from the Middle Ages, occupied himself with the art of Russia as well (see, for example, his book *L'Art Russe*, Paris 1877).

13 The following brief report (author unknown) is from files of M.N. Shemtshushnikova. "Tchuyko went to Paris in 1906, and lived there for eight years. He supposedly had pulmonary disease and on that account travelled to Switzerland. However, his illness with which Margarita [Woloschin] commiserated, turned out not to be connected with the lungs, but with the heart. His sketches and pictures are to be found in the depository of the Tretyakov Gallery ... Extraordinarily talented and versatile, he studied science, occupying himself with medicinal herbs and with astronomy. An actor in the satirical theatre, he conducted an elocution studio, and was himself an able speaker.

He was a splendid musician. The pianist Judina valued the experience of playing with him with four hands or on two grand pianos." Margarita Woloschin refers to the decades-long friendship between her and Tchuyko. From a second report from the files of M.N. Shemtshushnikova it follows that, for his part, Tchuyko spoke of her often with his friends. Twice when he was in dire straits, she quite suddenly turned up and was able to save him.

14 The Stanislavski Theatre — the famous Moscow Art Theatre — was founded in 1897 by the actor Konstantin Stanislavski and Vladimir Nemirovich-Danchenko. One of the most important aspects of the method developed by Stanislavsky was "feeling oneself into the role," expounded in several books (such as *An Actor's Work on a Role,* or *An Actor's Work).* Stanislavsky's introduction of a "psychological realism" on the stage was seen as pioneering at that time throughout Europe.

15 *Mir iskustva,* a journal of art and literary criticism, appeared from 1899 to 1904 in Petersburg. *Vesy* appeared from 1904 to 1909 in Moscow. It was an influential organ of the Symbolists connected with the poet Valeri Bryusov.

16 Anna, one of the Andreyev sisters, was married to Yakov Polyakov, who managed his father's textile factory in Krasnogorsk near Moscow and lived on the Banki country estate.

17 Woloschin's picture of Nyusha is in the colour section of this book. This painting was for a time in the private collection of P.M. Dogadin in Astrakhan before being donated to the Art Gallery there in 1918, where it remains to this day.

18 Nyusha's portrait and Woloschin's self-portrait were shown in an exhibition of the Moscow Artists' Union and caught the attention of art critics. In an article on the exhibition, A. Rostislavov (for example) wrote: "Very interesting are the female portraits of Sabashnikova, particularly one showing the figure full-size. How restrained, how finely painted it is, and in what an unusual manner."

19 Oleg Pogibin reports on the circumstances leading up to this cycle of lectures: "In the autumn of 1905 Rudolf Steiner held a cycle of 31 lectures in Berlin at which, apart from his regular listeners, a group of Russians interested in anthroposophy was present. The spiritual abundance received in this way prompted them to invite Rudolf Steiner to Russia, where in a private circle he was to hold his first lecture cycle for a Russian audience in June 1906. On account of the Russian-Japanese war and the subsequent revolution, this did not come about. The same group of Russians now requested that he hold the lecture series, designated to take place in Russia, in France instead. Thus Rudolf Steiner gave the cycle on cosmogony in Paris. This so-called "Russian cycle," held in a

private house for a small circle of Russians and Germans, soon drew other [Theosophical] Congress participants – English, Dutch and French – so that, to allow enough room for all, the venue of the final lectures was transferred to the quarters of the Theosophical Society. Among the Russian members of the audience there were several writers and poets: Balmont, Minsky, Mereshkóvsky and Hippius (the relation the last two had to the published works of Rudolf Steiner remained admittedly superficial, and in fact led to decidedly negative and unfortunate polemics.) The well-known Alsace author Edouard Schuré was present." The publication of the lectures, held from May 25 to June 14, is based on the notes of Schuré and other participants. It is published in English as *An Esoteric Cosmology.*

20 Alexandra Petrova had been friends with Maximilian Voloshin from youth. She was a teacher at the grammar school in Theodosia, and became an anthroposophist. She won the sympathy and high regard of his large circle of friends and acquaintances, entering into a correspondence with such diverse personalities as Anna Minslova, Vyatsheslav Ivanov, and Nikolai Berdyayev. In the Institute of Russian Literature (Pushkin House) there are approximately 40 letters that Woloschin wrote her.

21 The children's story was probably *Oblatshnoye leto* (cloudy summer), which appeared in the April issue of *Tropinka*. In the same year another story by Margarita Woloschin appeared in this periodical, called *Daisy.* She illustrated both herself.

22 Miss Svanseva, a painter, opened an art school in Moscow in 1899 and afterwards in St Petersburg. V. Sérov, K. Koróvin, and Ulyánov taught in this school. Both Woloschin and Michail Tchuyko attended the school.

23 Woloschin's third poem from the series *Lesnáya Svirél* (Forest Flute) appeared in the almanac *Zvetnik Or* (Flower Basket of the Horae), St Petersburg 1907.

24 From the cycle *Solotyé Savésy* (Golden Curtains).

25 The twelve sonnets were all included in the cycle *Solotyé Savésy.*

26 Due to the lack of a stenographic report, the course of fifteen lectures, "Theosophy in Relation to St John's Gospel," given from July 7–21, 1908 are not published in the Collected Works.

27 The restricted esoteric circle referred to was the Esoteric School which Rudolf Steiner inaugurated in 1904 within the German Section of the Theosophical Society.

28 See the legend of St Veronica, who gave Christ a cloth on the way to Golgotha. When He returned it, His features were imprinted on it.

29 The address was held on April 11, 1912. Contained in German Vol. 158. Not published in English.

30 The book was published in 1913 by Duchovnoe Snanye (a translation

into German is in *Der letzte Heilige,* Urachhaus, Stuttgart 1994 (pp. 127–69).

31 In August 1912 the first three Mystery Dramas of Rudolf Steiner were performed in Munich: *The Portal of Initiation, The Soul's Probation* and, for the first time, *The Guardian of the Threshold.*

32 Sonnet 9 of the cycle *Solotye Savesy* (Golden Curtains).

33 Andrei Belyi's wife was Anna Alexeievna Turgenieva, also known as Assya Turgeniev. (As Belyi was a pseudonym, her married name was Bugayeva.) She was a grandniece of the writer Ivan Turgeniev. A graphic artist, eurythmist, anthroposophist, she came to Munich with Belyi in July 1912. From 1914 she lived in Dornach, working for a time as a carver on the first Goetheanum. She carried out the motifs of the coloured glass windows in the form of coloured etchings. Applying a new technique of glass engraving, she carried out the engraving of the windows of the Goetheanum. See her book, *Erinnerungen an Rudolf Steiner.*

34 Steiner held two lectures in Cologne on the Mystery of Golgotha, on December 17 and 18, 1913 (contained in *The Fifth Gospel,* Rudolf Steiner Press 2001).

35 The opening of the Russian Anthroposophical Society took place on September 20, 1913. The celebration took place in a basement room next to the small church of the Ascension of Mary over the Graves *(Zérkov Uspénya Presvyátoy Bogoródicy na Mogilzach).* The church, situated a short distance north of Pretshistenka Street is still standing to this day. The first premises of the Anthroposophical Society in Moscow, where the inauguration took place, was in No. 7 Uspensky Street (now Mogilzevsky Street). The house still stands. The Society was subsequently relocated several times.

The chairman was Boris Pavlovich Grigorov (1893–1945), economist, German teacher. Collaborated in working on the first Goetheanum building; translated Steiners's *Truth and Science* and *The Philosophy of Freedom.* The home of the Grigorovs was also the location of the publisher Spiritual Knowledge.

36 The following is an extract from Woloschin's diary (in Russian): "In November the *Doktor* came to me in the workshop, without knocking, his figure looming up behind me. He held a drawing in his hands. "Can you do that?" It was the *Egyptian Initiate* with the angel and the archangel above him. The same day he drove elsewhere, and upon returning, he brought *Frl.* [Louise] Clason the sketch for Greece [i.e., the *Athene-Apollo* motif] and the sketch for the curtain. – Within a few days, further sketches for the small cupola. They were handed out to [Mieta] Waller, me and Clason. (...) A few days later, in the presence

of [Joseph] Englert, the Doktor said to [Carl] Unger, that up till now, in painting, only I understood what was involved and worked at it earnestly. The course he gave in December (held in Dornach and Basel, 26th and 27th Dec. 1914), opened up a new artistic life for me, or more precisely, it led me back to the source of creativity, virtually to what I had been strong in as a child. And I then became aware of what I owe to the *Doktor,* to art and to our cause." (7th January 1915)

37 The Glass House was dedicated on June 17, 1914. Steiner held the second lecture in the cycle on architecture on the theme of "The Dornach Building: a House of Speech" (published in English as *Architecture as a Synthesis of the Arts,* Rudolf Steiner Press 1999).

38 Haparanda is now on the Swedish-Finnish border, but at that time Finland was part of the Russian Empire, only gaining independence in December 1917.

39 M.N. Shemtshushnikova experienced Margarita Vassilyevna Woloschin as a eurythmist at that time, reporting: "At the Christmas celebration in the Anthroposophical Society a eurythmy group presented itself, led by Margarita Vassilyevna. The words from Luke's Gospel (Chapter 2) were performed: 'And it came to pass in those days, that there went out a decree from Caesar Augustus ...' The eurythmists, who were beginners, only knew the vowels and carried them out with arm movements. Since in every word there are normally more consonants than vowels, a faster tempo is required to carry them out so they are synchronized. The inner rhythm and life of the text being read was brought to expression through movements of the legs, drawing certain forms on the floor. This was something that at the time only Margarita Vassilyevna could do.

"The eurythmists — all in white — stood in a semicircle. In front, at the centre of the ellipse formed by the semicircle of eurythmists and those of the audience completing it, stood Margarita Vassilyevna. Festively and solemnly, the words rang out, the airy movements of the white figures flowing evenly onward, illumined by the warm light of the candles on the Christmas tree. And right in front — No! —was no longer the Margarita Vassilyevna we knew! Tall, slender, surrounded by the flowing, white shimmer of the veil, which fluttered with her movements, she transformed herself into a white flame. Cautiously, her arms sang — in unison with the chorus of eurythmists in the background — the vowels, the whole figure moving and trembling like a candle-flame. Yet this was not the irregular, accidental trembling of a flame in the wind. It was music, a hymn filled with exalted meaning. Her slightly raised head was free of all emotions, transported in prayer or meditation. And the whole body was felt to be in perfect harmony with the garment enveloping it, that moved together with it, to the sound of the mighty words, 'Glory to God in the highest, and on earth peace, good will toward men.' It really was a 'sacred dance,' a living prayer become visible for a moment, that had assumed form in a human body; living music. ... What powers for genuine sacred service showed themselves with this appearance. ... It is very much to be regretted that Margarita Vassilyevna twice failed to hear Rudolf Steiner's call to help bring eurythmy to the world."

40 "That's what I am ..." is from Mayakovsky's poem *War and World.*

41 At that time St Petersburg was called Petrograd (from 1914 to 1924). However, Woloschin did not want to use this name, as she expressly says later. (In fact in the original German she calls the city simply "Petersburg" as it was commonly known in Russian.)

42 The palace was Morosov's private house, built in 1894–98 by V.A. Masyrin. Called House of Friendship it is today a meeting place for foreign delegations.

43 Konstantin Ligsky, nominally a member of the Anthroposophical Society, returned to Russia in 1918 and joined the Communist Party. Toward the end of the 1920s he became ambassador of the Soviet Union in Warsaw, Tokyo and Athens.

44 Paul Scheffer was a journalist and chief editor of the *Berliner Tageblatt.* His books include *Sieben Jahre Sowjetunion* (Seven Years of the Soviet Union), and *Augenzeuge im Staate Lenins* (Eyewitness in Lenin's State).

45 Valentin Alexandrovich Ternavzev, writer and theologist.

46 Armand is not in actual fact the author of the drama, but Nadeshda Nikolayevna Bromlei (1889–1966).

Selected Bibliography

Belyi, Andrei, Assya Turgenieff & Margarita Voloschin, *Reminiscences of Rudolf Steiner.* Adonis Press, USA 1987.

Goethe, Johann Wolfgang von. *Fairy Tale: The Green Snake and the Beautiful Lily,* Steiner Books, USA 2006.

—, *Theory of Colours.* Translated by Charles Lock Eastlake. MIT Press, USA 2000 [1840].

Prokofieff, Sergei, *Maximilian Woloschin. Mensch, Dichter, Anthroposoph.* (Maximilian Voloshin. Human Being, Poet, Anthroposophist.) Verlag am Goetheanum, Switzerland 2007.

Raske, Hilde, *The Language of Color in the First Goetheanum. A Study of Rudolf Steiner's Art,* Walter Keller Verlag, Switzerland 1987.

Stebbing, Peter (Ed.) *Conversations about Painting with Rudolf Steiner: Recollections of Five Pioneers of the New Art Impulse,* Steiner Books, USA 2008.

Steiner, Rudolf, *Colour,* Rudolf Steiner Press, UK 1992.

—, *The Arts and Their Mission,* Anthroposophic Press, USA 1986.

Turgenieff, Assya, *Erinnerungen an Rudolf Steiner und die Arbeit am ersten Goetheanum* (Recollections of Rudolf Steiner and the Work on the First Goetheanum) Verlag Freies Geistesleben, Germany 1993.

Index of Names

Figure numbers in italics refer to illustrations or photographs